MICHEL FOUCAULT AND THEOLOGY

Whilst Foucault's work has become a major strand of postmodern theology, the wider relevance of his work for theology still remains largely unexamined. Foucault both engages the Christian tradition and critically challenges its disciplinary regime.

Michel Foucault and Theology brings together a selection of essays by leading Foucault scholars on a variety of themes within the history, thought and practice of theology. Revealing the diverse ways that the work of Michel Foucault (1926–1984) has been employed to rethink theology in terms of power, discourse, sexuality and the politics of knowledge, the authors examine power and sexuality in the church in late antiquity (Castelli, Clark, Schuld), raise questions about the relationship between theology and politics (Bernauer, Leezenberg, Caputo), consider new challenges to the nature of theological knowledge in terms of Foucault's critical project (Flynn, Cutrofello, Beadoin, Pinto) and rethink theology in terms of Foucault's work on the history of sexuality (Carrette, Jordan, Mahon). This book demonstrates, for the first time, the influence and growing importance of Foucault's work for contemporary theology.

Michel Foucault and Theology

The Politics of Religious Experience

Edited by

JAMES BERNAUER
Boston College, USA

JEREMY CARRETTE
University of Stirling, UK

ASHGATE

Published by
Ashgate Publishing Limited
Gower House
Croft Road
Aldershot
Hampshire GU11 3HR
England

Ashgate Publishing Company
Suite 420
101 Cherry Street
Burlington, VT 05401-4405
USA

Ashgate website: http//www.ashgate.com

British Library Cataloguing in Publication Data
Michel Foucault and theology : the politics of religious
   experience
   1. Foucault, Michel, 1926–1984 – contributions in theology
   I. Bernauer, James W. (James William) II. Carrette, Jeremy R.
   210.9'2

Library of Congress Cataloging-in-Publication Data
Michel Foucault and theology : the politics of religious experience / edited by James Bernauer and Jeremy Carrette.
     p. cm.
   Includes bibliographical references.
   ISBN 0-7546-3353-5 (alk. paper) – ISBN 0-7546-3354-3 (pbk. : alk. paper)
     1. Foucault, Michel–Religion. 2. Religion–Philosophy. 3. Postmodern theology. I. Bernauer, James William. II. Carrette, Jeremy R.

B2430.F724 M495 2002
230'.092–dc21   2002038458

ISBN 0 7546 3353 5 (Hardback)
ISBN 0 7546 3354 3 (Paperback)

Typeset by IML Typographers, Birkenhead, Merseyside and printed in Great Britain by MPG Books Ltd, Bodmin, Cornwall

Contents

Part Four   Foucault, Theology and Sexuality

List of Authors

Thomas Beaudoin is Visiting Assistant Professor at Boston College in Chestnut Hill, MA, USA. He is the author of *Virtual Faith* (Jossey-Bass, 1998) and *Consuming Faith: Integrating Who We Are With What We Buy* (Rowan and Littlefield, 2003). He is working on a book on Foucault and practical theology (forthcoming, Orbis).

James Bernauer is Professor of Philosophy in Boston College. He has an STM in theology from Union Theological Seminary and his PhD in philosophy from the State University of New York at Stony Brook. A student of Foucault for two years, he is the author of *Michel Foucault's Force of Flight: Toward an Ethics for Thought* (Humanity Books, 1990). He is the editor of *Amor Mundi: Explorations in the Faith and Thought of Hannah Arendt* (Nijhoff, 1987) and co-editor of *The Final Foucault* (MIT, 1988). His current project is utilizing Foucauldian approaches in a study of German moral formation on the eve of the Holocaust.

John D. Caputo is the David R. Cook Professor of Philosophy at Villanova University. His most recent books are *On Religion* (Routledge, 2001) and *More Radical Hermeneutics: On Not Knowing Who We Are* (Indiana, 2000). He is also the editor of *Blackwell Readings in Continental Philosophy: The Religious* (2001) and co-editor of *Questioning God* (Indiana, 2001) and *God, the Gift and Postmodernism* (Indiana, 1999), which are collections of studies based upon a series of conferences featuring Derrida in dialogue with Marion and other major postmodern religious thinkers. He is also the author of *Deconstruction in a Nutshell: A Conversation with Jacques Derrida* (New York: Fordham University Press, 1997) and *The Prayers and Tears of Jacques Derrida: Religion without Religion* (Bloomington: Indiana University Press, 1997).

Jeremy R. Carrette is Senior Lecturer in Religious Studies at the University of Stirling, UK. He is the author of *Foucault and Religion: Spiritual Corporality and Political Spirituality* (Routledge, 2000) and the editor of *Religion and Culture by Michel Foucault* (Manchester/Routledge, 1999). He is also the joint editor of the centenary volume of William James's *The Varieties of Religious Experience* (Routledge, 2002) and editor of the papers from the centenary conference on James's Gifford Lectures (forthcoming, Routledge). He is currently working on a book with Richard King entitled *Capitalist Spirituality* (forthcoming, Routledge).

Elizabeth A. Castelli is Associate Professor of Religion at Barnard College in New York City. Her publications include *Imitating Paul: A Discourse of Power* (1991), *The Postmodern Bible* (1995), *Women, Gender, Religion: A Reader* (2001), *Sexuality* *in Late Antiquity* (a special issue of the *Journal of the History of Sexuality*) (2001) and *Martyrdom and Memory: Early Christian Culture-Making* (2004).

Elizabeth A. Clark is John Carlisle Kilgo Professor of Religion at Duke University. She has written widely on issues of women, asceticism, heresy and Biblical interpretation in early Christianity. Among her books are *Reading Renunciation: Asceticism and Scripture in Early Christianity* (1997), *The Origenist Controversy: The Cultural Construction of an Early Christian Debate* (1992) and *Ascetic Piety and Women's Faith: Essays on Late Ancient Christianity* (1986). She has completed a book entitled *History–Theory–Text*. A Fellow of the American Academy of Arts and Sciences, she is co-editor of the *Journal of Early Christian Studies*, and has served as president of the American Academy of Religion, the American Society of Church History and the North American Patristic Society.

Andrew Cutrofello is Associate Professor of Philosophy at Loyola University, Chicago. He is the author of several books, including the forthcoming *Continental Philosophy: A Contemporary Introduction* (Routledge).

Thomas R. Flynn is the Samuel Candler Professor of Philosophy at Emory University in Atlanta, Georgia. He is the author of two studies published by the University of Chicago Press: *Sartre and Marxist Existentialism* and *Sartre, Foucault and Historical Reason: Toward an Existentialist Theory of History, Volume 1*. He is also co-editor of *Dialectic and Narrative* and *The Ethics of History*.

Mark D. Jordan is Asa Griggs Candler Professor of Religion at Emory University. He is the author of numerous works, including *The Invention of Sodomy in Christian Theology* (1997), *The Silence of Sodom: Homosexuality in Modern Catholicism* (2000), *The Ethics of Sex* (2002) and *Telling Truths in Church: Scandals, Flesh and Christian Speech* (2003).

Michiel Leezenberg teaches in the Philosophy Department, Faculty of Humanities, University of Amsterdam. His research interests include the methodology of the social sciences and Islamic philosophy. He has written extensively in these areas, including (with G. de Vries) *Wetenschapsfilosofie voor Geesteswetenschappen* (Amsterdam University Press); *Islamitische filosofie: Een geschiedenis* (Amsterdam: Bulaaq) and *Politischer Islam bei den Kurden* (Kurdische Studien 2).

Michael Mahon is Associate Professor of Humanities at Boston University's College of General Studies. He is the author of *Foucault's Nietzschean Genealogy: Truth, Power, and the Subject* (State University of New York Press, 1992).

Henrique Pinto is the president and coordinator of an association (UNIVERSOS) for an intercultural and religious dialogue. He is also the director of the Portuguese magazine for the homeless (CAIS). He is an invited researcher and a member of the scientific council of a centre of studies (CEPCEP) at the Portuguese Catholic University in Lisbon. He worked, for many years, with the Consolata and Jesuit

Missionaries, in Kenya, Tanzania, East Timor, Portugal, England and Italy. He is the author of *Foucault, Christianity and Interfaith Dialogue* (Routledge, 2003) and is currently working on a study relating religion and immigration.

J. Joyce Schuld received her doctoral degree from Yale University. She has published in the *Journal of Religion* and contributed an essay to 'Considering Religious Traditions' in *Bioethics: Christian and Jewish Voices* (University of Scranton Press, 2001). She has also written *Foucault and Augustine: Reconsidering Power and Love* (University of Notre Dame Press, 2003). She is currently working on two books that relate Foucauldian scholarship and Christian theology: *Michel Foucault: An Introduction for Theologians* for Cambridge University Press and *Missions of Power: A Cultural Analysis of Indian–Christian Relations in the American Southwest* for the University of Notre Dame Press.

Acknowledgements

Some of the papers in this volume were part of a colloquium 'Michel Foucault: Religious Explorations', which was held on April 26, 2000 at Loyola University in Chicago. The colloquium was sponsored by that university's Visiting Jesuit University Professorship, which was held by James Bernauer for the 1999–2000 academic year. James Bernauer wishes to thank Loyola University, its Department of Philosophy and its Jesuit Community for their support during that year.

This book is also the outcome of a continuing dialogue between James Bernauer and Jeremy Carrette on Foucault and religion and they would like to thank all the contributors for agreeing to include their work and for making the project possible. We hope this book reflects the richness of Foucault scholarship within theology today.

Seven articles in this collection were previously published elsewhere:

'Interpretation of Power in 1 Corinthians' by Elizabeth Castelli, *Semeia 54*, Society for Biblical Literature, 1992, pp.199–222.

'Foucault, the Fathers and Sex' by Elizabeth A. Clark, *Journal of the American Academy of Religion*, Oxford University Press, vol.56, no.4, 1998, pp.619–41.

'Augustine, Foucault and the Politics of Imperfection' by J. Joyce Schuld, *Journal of Religion*, The University of Chicago Press, vol.80, no.1, January 2000, pp.1–22.

'Power and Political Spirituality: Michel Foucault and the Islamic Revolution in Iran' by Michiel Leezenberg in *Cultural History After Foucault*, ed. John Neubauer, Aldine De Gruyter, New York, 1999, pp.63–80.

'On Not Knowing Who We Are: Madness, Hermeneutics and the Night of Truth in Foucault' by John D. Caputo in *Foucault and the Critique of Institutions*, ed. John Caputo and Mark Yount, Penn State University Press, University Park, Pennsylvania, 1993, pp.233–62.

'Partially Desacralized Spaces: The Religious Availability of Foucault's Thought' by Thomas Flynn in *Faith and Philosophy*, vol.10, no.4, October 1993, pp.471–85.

Earlier versions of James Bernauer's 'Michel Foucault's Philosophy of Religion: an Introduction to the Non-Fascist Life' apeared in *Budhi* vol.3, 1999, pp.1–28 and *iiichiko* n.66, Spring 2000, pp.6–34.

We would like to thank the publishers for agreeing permission to republish the above articles. We wish to thank Dean Michael Smyer and the Graduate School of Boston College for covering the cost of reprint fees. We are grateful to Sean Ferrier for compiling the index.

Finally, we would like to thank Sarah Lloyd and Ashgate publishers for supporting this project and Magnum for use of the image of Michel Foucault. We also express thanks to Frances Britain for her helpful editorial suggestions.

Introduction: The Enduring Problem: Foucault, Theology and Culture

James Bernauer and Jeremy Carrette

> Critique is the movement by which the subject gives itself the right to question truth on its effects of power and to question power on its discourses of truth … in a word, the politics of truth.   Foucault, 1978, 'What is Critique?', p.32.

> [The church] is a superb instrument of power for itself. Entirely woven through with elements that are imaginary, erotic, effective, corporal, sensual, and so on, it is superb!
>   Foucault, 1978, 'On Religion', p.106.

The dialogue between continental philosophy and theology has been growing in recent years, with new emergent forms of so-called 'postmodern' theology.[1] While the work of Jacques Derrida, with his continuing play with theological themes, has largely dominated much of this discussion, there has been a growing appreciation of other French post-structuralist writers and their engagement with religion. New works and translations are continually revealing important, but as yet unexplored, aspects of a body of literature that reworks traditional theological questions. The work of Michel Foucault (1926–84) is one of the developing fronts of this discussion, with new translations and works examining his contribution to religious, theological and philosophical thought. While Foucault's work has become a major strand of postmodern theology and new forms of body theology, the wider relevance of his work for theology still remains largely unexamined. One striking feature, among many, emerging from theological examinations of Foucault's work is the sense in which his thinking holds a distinctively Catholic dimension, particularly with its visual piety and confessional agenda. This stands in contrast to the predominantly Protestant theological concerns with the 'word' and 'text' of the postmodern gospel. However, what also remains distinctive in Foucault's thinking is his critical analysis of institutional practices, which opens up the wider social and political agenda of theology. Foucault both engages with the Christian tradition and critically challenges its disciplinary regime. He therefore becomes, at once, both guardian and adversary of the Christian faith, a tension which creates the possibility of developing new relationships within Christianity that are more inclusive and less oppressive.

This collection of essays positions itself at the intersection of three important contemporary discussions.[2] First, it breaks new ground in our understanding of Michel Foucault's writings in that it shows the significance of his analysis of culture for consideration of religion in general, and Christian practices in particular. Foucault as investigator of religion is an almost totally unknown Foucault. There are several reasons why that is the case but perhaps the most influential was the decision not to allow posthumous publication of his text on Christianity and sexuality (*Confessions of the Flesh*) which he had almost completed before his death. Fortunately, though, extensive recent research in Foucault's archives as well as Gallimard's decision to publish his lectures at the Collège de France give us a much better understanding of his religious-political interests. This provided the context for a collection of texts from Foucault himself selected and edited by Jeremy Carrette: *Religion and Culture by Michel Foucault* (Manchester University Press and Routledge, 1999). The second discussion is the political functioning of contemporary religion. Foucault's examination of the Iranian revolution in 1978 anticipated forecasts about the need for new tools in the analysis of political–spiritual regimes. More central to his own work, though, is his conviction that a sharp distinction between the secular and religious in modernity cannot be sustained. Foucault engaged in religious analysis because he came to appreciate that the forms of knowledge, power and subjectivity animating western culture are constructed in decisive ways in argument with or acceptance of religious practices and concerns. The third discussion is that of religious historians, educators and theologians about the implications of postmodern thought for grasping the present operation and future possibility of religion. There are indications that we are on the eve of a post-Foucauldian spiritual sensibility, which transforms theological knowledge. In order to map such a landscape it is worth plotting some of the coordinates of Foucault's challenge to theology.

THE CONDITIONS OF THEOLOGICAL KNOWLEDGE

What are the conditions of theological knowledge and what makes the discourse of theology possible at any given point in history? To raise these questions is to take Michel Foucault's archaeological and genealogical projects into the heart of Christian theology; it is to consider seriously the possibility of theology as a form of knowledge taking shape in the historical process. Theological discourse emerges in each period of history according to the epistemic structures that make its statements possible (archaeology). It emerges out of the relations between people and their institutions in order to shape the practices of living (genealogy). This means that revelation and exegesis are shaped according to the regimes of knowledge available at any given moment in time. While this historization of theological understanding may seem obvious, it creates a point of contestation in the relationship between culture and theology. Indeed, the correlation of theology with contemporary culture is a key factor in shaping the nature of the Christian tradition and one which defines much of the present debate in modern and, so-called, 'postmodern' theology. Types of theology, according to Hans Frei, can be differentiated according to the levels of receptivity theologians display towards the existing cultural debates.[3] Such a mapping reflects the 'enduring problem' of the multiple relations between theology and culture that Richard Niebuhr explored in his classic work of modern theology, *Christ and Culture*.[4] The 'enduring problem' continues in the space of 'postmodern' theology, both in the critique of modernity and in the collapsing of the boundaries between theology and culture. Foucault turns much of this debate inside out by raising questions about the nature of tradition, space, authority and power in theology. His work emerges from within the history of Western Christianity – 'as an analysis of the cultural facts' – and brings theology back into history, through a critique of the foundations of theological knowledge.[5]

Foucault's philosophical–historical project, which is neither simply history nor philosophy, refuses to separate theology and culture. Theology is no longer separated out in some binary construction which assumes that the lines where Christian theology ends and the contemporary culture begins are somehow clearly visible. Theology has a history and that history reflects the continual immersion of theology in the cultural environs. Theology evolves through a series of engagements with the contemporary world. It negotiates the changing world and its message through the political, philosophical and social values of the time, even if it refuses to accept fully or acknowledge such values. From its negotiations with neo-Platonic philosophy, through its affirmations of Aquinas, to its excursions with Existentialism, theology has spoken its truth in the conditions of its time. Nonetheless, the past still functions for theologians as an imagined space in which to reconstruct the political present; it exonerates the past as its truth in the present. The struggle of theology is to see tradition as change rather than narrow preservation, which conceals its present politic in terms of continuing an imagined, and constantly reimagined, past.

Theology, in its engagement with Foucault, recognizes the 'history of the present' and acknowledges that all appeals to the past are but, paradoxically, an affirmation of the present political desire for knowledge and power about the nature of truth. If theology is to overcome its archaic preservation of this imagined past it must constantly renegotiate the terms of its tradition in the new spaces of the present world without fear and prejudice. The illusion of theology, as Foucault recognized, was that it held the categories of its thought above the practices of its living community.[6] It competes between the values of preserving the tradition and holding tradition as change. If theology is to avoid becoming simply a library of the past and an elitist model of orthodoxy (radical or not) it must be prepared to explore the conditions of its knowledge and politics of its thinking. Foucault's work provides an opportunity to examine the conditions of theological knowledge and exposes the hidden regimes of power behind the so-called 'virtues' of Christian theology. The naivety of theologians ends with its engagement with Foucault, because Foucault returns theology to its history, to its struggles for authority and power, to its practices of the self and to its embodied reality. Foucault takes theology from its doctrinal closet into its pastoral reality. His work uncovers and destabilizes the unexamined authority of theological discourse and brings Christianity back to the fragility of human struggle. Foucault's methodology disarms the doctrinal by revealing the unconscious of theological knowledge.[7]

The engagement of theology with Foucault has been part of a new wave of theological engagements with French intellectual culture from the 1960s. He has become part of a line of thinkers from the left bank of Paris who have enabled theology to rethink its project in terms of a critique of modernity. This critical consciousness of contemporary culture has enabled theologians to rethink the nature and order of its knowledge. Within this current exploration of post-structuralist thinkers in theology, it is important and revealing to understand the particular location of Foucault in the contemporary theological debate – important and revealing because it shows us the way Foucault is being used by theologians and why other theologians are afraid of employing Foucault's method and insight into theology. Theology becomes a fearful and defensive discourse when its academic exponents become afraid of losing power in the face of the uncontrollable realities of their bodies and their hidden will to power.

Theologians can easily assume a narrow consciousness in the attempt to assert authority through blind intellect, rather than recognizing the dark unconscious of knowledge behind their utterances. They wish to hide in the closet of authority and domination rather than respond with the loving affirmation of shared humanity and a desire to understand the vulnerabilities of themselves and those in their community. Theologians, like any other intellectual group of thinkers, can easily be lost in the regimes of their knowledge-power. They become afraid to listen to those outside their groups or cliques in an attempt to remain blind to the other, whether it be women, people of the two-thirds world, homosexuals or black minorities. Theologians need to take the ethical responsibility to examine their utterances in terms of the regimes of power knowledge they propagate and be willing to suspend such judgment in the face of critique within the Christian community. At a time when the worldwide church, on either side of the denominational divides, faces the politics of exclusion and its collusion with oppression, particularly in response to world poverty, globalization and gay sexuality, Foucault becomes a central thinker for conceptualizing the politics of authority and power in the church. It is precisely at this point that we see the theological lines of engagement with Foucault and understand the sites of resistance, for Foucault's critical methodology is a methodology for the silenced.[8]

WHAT HAS MICHEL FOUCAULT TO OFFER THEOLOGY?

The essays in this volume reflect the multiple forms of engagement between Foucault and theology. The essays embrace Foucault for a critical historical project, as new ways of reading Christian history, they use Foucault to rethink the discourse of the self, the politics of truth, the ideologies of belief, the closure and opening of dialogue and the strategies of embodied knowledge. However, we must not assume that Foucault's relationship is simply a modernist critique of knowledge: it also continually opens up the space of theology and Christian living to new possibilities. Foucault offers theology the critical apparatus to find new inclusive and non-dualistic forms of living; he offers the possibility of imagining ways of rethinking theology, as practice rather than belief.[9]

Foucault's critique is an instrument to examine all forms of knowledge and not simply something opposed to theological knowledge. Foucault certainly assists in developing a self-reflexive critique of theological knowledge, but he also offers a critique of the positivistic knowledge of man and the human sciences. This critique of anthropological man inadvertently opens up the space for theology to empower itself against the claims of humanistic rationalism.[10] It is this which allows Maurice Clavel to claim that Foucault's *The Order of Things* offered a powerful affirmation of the Christian faith.[11] In this sense, far from undermining theological discourse and practice, Foucault establishes ground to develop new forms of negative theology and offers new perspectives for rethinking contemporary body theology.[12]

Given Foucault's concern with the conditions of knowledge, it is not surprising that those theologians fighting for oppressed and marginalized groups have taken up Foucault's entry into the theological world. We find Foucault has been welcomed by feminist theologians, those working on the boundaries of sexuality and theology and also those dissolving the boundaries between politics and theology.[13] If Foucault's method and critique have been used to establish new forms of theology, his later work has also been celebrated by scholars of late antiquity and Biblical studies (see Castelli and Clark in the present volume). Foucault offers a new critical hermeneutics for Christian theology and this has slowly established new readings of the Biblical text, such as in Anthony Thisleton's recent study of Corinthians.[14] What Foucault offers theology is the space to think differently, not by imposing a new dogma for contemporary theology, but allowing his methods to rethink questions inside theology which have previously been suppressed or obscured owing to the interests and attachments to dominant forms of knowledge. As Foucault famously declared in 1984:

> There are times in life when the question of knowing if one can think differently than one thinks, and perceive differently than one sees, is absolutely necessary if one is to go on looking and reflecting at all…. But, then, what is philosophy today – philosophical activity, I mean – if it is not the critical work that thought brings to bear on itself? In what does it consist, if not in the endeavour to know how and to what extent it might be possible to think differently, instead of legitimating what is already known?[15]

Foucault's challenge to theology is to think differently by freeing theology from what it 'silently thinks', to enable Christian theology to recognize its hidden regimes of knowledge power beneath the rituals of its performances.[16]

THE CATHOLIC FOUCAULT: THE SILENT CULTURE OF THEOLOGY

The relation between religion and culture is always a two-sided one.
Dawson, *Religion and Culture*, 1947, p.57.

Religion is the substance of culture, culture is the form of religion.
Tillich, *Theology of Culture*, 1959, p.44.

Most of modern theology reworks past issues for new audiences and in the fetish of the new commodifies its knowledge for a new market and a new generation. We do not have to travel far to see how the present debates about religion and culture are forgotten reincarnations from the past. Indeed, we only have to go as far as the middle of the twentieth century with Christopher Dawson's Gifford Lectures in the 1940s and Paul Tillich's correlation of faith and culture in the 1950s and 1960s to see how Niebuhr's 'enduring problem' occupies the theological landscape of modernity as much as postmodernity.[17] It cannot do otherwise, for the problem of theology and culture is at the heart of humanity's relationship to God. Where the death of God theologians once embraced the liberalism of a changing world, Radical Orthodoxy asserts its rejection of modernity in its nostalgic and elitist conservatism, both failing to see the 'will to theological power' and the imperialism of their projects. The recognition of the games of truth and power in theological discourse provides a new way of reading the successive engagements between theology and culture.

In Foucault's work power is mobile, it is strategic and fluid, refusing to rest by refusing to see 'truth' as given. Truth for Foucault is negotiated and Foucault himself disappears in his own strategic application of knowledge. This strategic knowledge is for Foucault about identifying 'problems'.[18] It is these problems which enable Foucault to see the unconscious of knowledge within certain disciplinary practices. It is wrong to assume, as Foucault made very clear, that he believed power 'could explain everything' or that it was 'sufficient to characterize a society'.[19] It is rather that Foucault examines discursive regimes through the 'relations of power' rather than the 'relations of meaning' in order to examine strategically the politics of truth.[20] Foucault is the great strategist and, when we approach Foucault's work in the field of theology, it may be strategic to ask what forms of theology shape Foucault's own thinking. This is to realize that theology often assumes its efficacy in its silent operation, particularly when it has lost some of its currency as a public discourse.

If the interface of theology and culture is to be taken seriously then we also have to understand that Foucault's critical thinking is born out of his own French Catholic context. Foucault is not exempt from carrying forward his own theological ideas behind his historiographical and philosophical work. It might be possible to ask what theological conditions made Foucault's work possible. Does Foucault's writing hold a distinctively Catholic agenda? While these questions have been raised on the edges of Foucault scholarship, much remains to be documented.[21] It is not the purpose of this introduction to outline the trajectories of such thinking in detail, but if we are to recognize the theological importance of Foucault we need at least to open up this question.

The privileging of certain Catholic concerns can be seen in his discussion of the practices of confession and the examination of conscience and of the place of sexuality in both.[22] Foucault's understanding of pastoral power is never far from the structures of Catholicism. We may also note how the visual qualities of his work hold echoes of Catholic ritual and iconography or what David Tracey identified as the 'analogical imagination' of the Catholic mind.[23] These inferences take on greater weight when we consider Foucault's celebration of Catholic ritual and dress. Foucault had spoken and written of Christian experience with insight and much more of that insight could have been expected if he had had the time to finish his studies of Christianity. Still, his concentration on the role of confessional experience within Christianity may have distorted his interpretation of Christian sexuality. Indeed, his focus might have reflected the legacy of his own Catholic milieu and led him to a similar obsession about sin that John Mahoney had argued to be the negative influence of auricular confession on Catholic moral theology in general.[24]

Foucault's examination of Christian practice was drawn to a sexuality saturated with sinfulness. This was understandable because Foucault did show the historically important role which confessional practice came to exercise in the Christian pastoral governance of souls. More dramatic, though, was his presentation of a modern Christian anatomy of the body which was the fruit of that governance. It was a governance which enmeshed the body within the coils of a rebellious flesh. Foucault's interest in Christianity led him to a fascination with its institution of a 'moral physiology of the flesh' and its 'culpabilisation of the body by the flesh'.[25] His continuing sensitivity to discontinuities had caught the shift in the 16th century from a concern with sins generated out of relationship with others to a sinfulness dominated by one's relationship to the body. Foucault showed a Catholic 'mapping' of the body's sinful sites. The sins of the flesh were the touchings of masturbation, the gazings of desire, the speaking of lusts, the listenings with pleasure.[26]

With the same unforgettable force that Foucault had exhibited in describing the torture at the beginning of *Discipline and Punish*, his studies of Christian sexuality were beginning to paint another dramatic, tortured figure, the Christian as enfleshed. The figure which Foucault's learning and lectures portrayed is certainly not unknown to Christians, so many of whom have been victims of theology's frequent denigration of the body and sexuality. And yet that denigration is certainly not the full story, because there have been so many religious thinkers and spiritualities which have stressed the goodness of creation. To take an example from but one historical period, there is Leo Steinberg's *The Sexuality of Christ in Renaissance Art and Modern Oblivion*.[27] Steinberg's arguments and paintings tell of this other story. From before the 15th century to beyond the mid-16th century, Western art 'produced a large body of devotional imagery in which the genitalia of the Christ Child, or of the dead Christ, receive such demonstrative emphasis that one must recognize an *ostentatio genitalium* comparable to the canonic *ostentatio vulnerum*, the showing forth of the wounds'.[28] If flesh could be inscribed on a register of sin and fault, it was also at the core of Christian faith, the Incarnation. God had become Flesh, had become human, and this incarnation embraced sexuality as well. Perhaps the most striking paintings Steinberg's volume reproduced were those of a naked Redeemer and particularly those of a crucified Jesus who seemed to be in the process of returning to life; it was a resurrection announced in the beginning of an erection, in a flesh revivified. The manifestation of the Redeemer's sexual power showed that there was no shame attached to it and, indeed, that the New Adam had restored the innocence of the original creation, an 'unculpable flesh'. These paintings were works of piety: 'We could say that Christ is shown refuting that tenaciously clinging Docetism which denies the carnality of his body. He is helping the believer overcome a last vestige of doubt about the utterness of his humanation.'[29]

The Catholic incarnational imagination that Steinberg highlighted resonated with the religious faith and spirituality of many contemporary Catholic writers. William Lynch speaks for them, for example, in his *Christ and Apollo*, where he argued that thought and art manifesting Catholic conviction should be in conflict with any facile intellectualism associated with the Apollonian.[30] And Foucault's thought has a similar respect for the limited and finite; its style is incarnational, as it were. His interest was not in some general liberation but in concrete practices, in the ways human agents exercise freedom in particular situations. He appreciated the difference between the analytical verbal confession and the historically earlier public manifestation of sinfulness as a state, the adoption of a 'theatricality' in which verbal expression was subordinated to a way of life which exhibited itself in acts of austerity and attitudes of repentance.[31] The appeal of this ritual, incarnational dimension is demonstrated in an account of Foucault's intense viewing of Pope John Paul II's 1978 papal inauguration. Although he had flown to London to be interviewed on that day, his insistence on watching the televised ceremony made the conversation impossible and so he returned to Paris without any interview.[32] Foucault appreciated that these ceremonies were not ethereal but, rather, that they exercised power. For example, Foucault spoke of the impact of the service which the Archbishop of São Paulo held for a Jewish journalist who was killed by the police. The Jewish community could not hold a funeral so the Archbishop organized an interdenominational service, which

> drew thousands and thousands of people into the church, on to the square and so on, and the cardinal in red robes presided over the ceremony, and he came forward at the end of the ceremony, in front of the faithful, and he greeted them shouting: 'Shalom, shalom'. And there was all around the square armed police and there were plain clothes policemen in the church. The police pulled back; there was nothing the police could do against that. I have to say, that had a grandeur of strength, there was a gigantic historical weight there.[33]

This specific sensitivity to the historically weighty is an important element in Foucault's incarnational style.

His very notion of enlightenment and critique mirrors a religious discernment of spirits. As with the discerner, Foucault wants to understand how the present is different, how the critical question should become a positive one: 'In what is given to us as universal, necessary, obligatory, what place is occupied by whatever is singular, contingent, and the product of arbitrary constraints?'[34] This practice of discernment runs through his writings. His interest was with how knowledges operated in an historical field. His early turn away from psychology as a discipline was motivated by his appreciation of the human being's radical liberty and ability to challenge structures. Foucault strove to grasp not the conditions of possibility but rather the conditions of reality for institutions such as the asylum, the clinic and the prison. His criticism of humanism was a mode of escaping the abstract human sciences that functioned within that ideology. His analysis of power's operation in the strategies of a disciplinary society aimed to grasp how our modern sense of being human was produced by precise technologies and not just the ideas of philosophers. The journey of Foucault's incarnational discernment culminated in his final efforts to restore philosophy to being a way of living, a form of caring for the self and not just a type of knowledge. That effort entailed a new appreciation for spirituality, which Foucault saw as an ensemble of practices that create not the mere consciousness of the subject but the very being of the subject and its paths of understanding.[35] For Foucault, the practices of spirituality do not lead to an isolation from the world but rather a critical immersion into it and a refusal of its immutability. His spirituality is a political exercise, for he recognized that 'one of the first great forms of revolt in the west was mysticism'.[36]

Living in the period that he did, Foucault could not help but encounter the effects of the political faiths that ravaged the 20th century. Although modernity's technological marvels and professed self-descriptions have obscured it, one could claim that the past century was a great Age of Faith. Western democracies, fascist states, the Communist world, all embraced great myths and preached the need for faith: belief in one's innocence, or in the providential destiny of one's race, or in the inevitable progress of class struggle. The continuing relevance of faith in the political realm is easy to appreciate when one takes notice of the contemporary fundamentalisms around the globe. From a Foucauldian perspective, mysticism as 'revolt' may represent a way of leaving the theological positivism and patriotism of the Age of Faith. Problematic as the term 'mysticism' is within the history of religions, particularly as Jantzen has shown from a Foucauldian genealogical perspective, Foucault's model of mysticism as 'revolt' does problematize the private-individualistic reading of mysticism developed in 20th-century psychology.[37] Mystic experience as social and political 'revolt' attaches us to an otherness which limits the claims of any theological categories as well as the unity organized within those concepts. The mystic's intensity of experience is a human revolt against the modern subject and the ideological visions of nature and history that are anchored in that subjectivity. The idea of a Foucauldian mysticism of revolt is an elaboration of a way of relating to oneself differently from modern subjectivity; such practice is a politics of the self which will create new spiritual communities for us to inhabit. And we recognize that these communities will be in critical tension with established faith traditions. Some of the texts in this volume pick up this possibility and open the world and human knowledge to a reality or force that contests the present order of society. There is a constant opening to a transformative presence, something which pushes the human condition to find new possibilities and resists the 'closure' of the theological vision. The site of Foucauldian mysticism is a politically inspired social anatagonism which allows that which is beyond and within humanity to find the hope of transfiguration and resurrection. It interrogates the limits of the human imagination and opens a vision for the possibility of developing new models for human engagement with each other, the world and the divine, a divine present and absent in the fragile and all-too-human theology.

The work of Michel Foucault stands as a significant voice for theology to rethink critically its project. Foucault's work is nonetheless challenging for contemporary theology and the essays in this volume show the rich and imaginative ways his work can bring theology to a new critical understanding. They contribute to the 'enduring problem' of theology and culture and bring theology into the critical space of the politics of living and managing the truth of our being-in-the-world.

THE ESSAYS

The essays in this volume bring together a range of theological engagements with Foucault in the last 14 years and also draw together six new pieces from a range of scholars examining the contemporary engagement between Foucault and theology; the majority of these papers were originally delivered at a special colloquium at Loyola University in Chicago in 2000.[38] The aim of the collection is to give a sense of both the diverse range of theological questions inside Foucault's work and the application of his work to theological concerns shaped by Foucault's critical project. The volume has been divided into four parts according to the broad thematic concerns emerging from Foucault's work. The first part brings together essays examining different aspects of a Foucauldian exploration of the church in late antiquity, the second opens up Foucault's work on the politics of theology, the third draws together a collection of essays showing the interventions of Foucault's work into the nature of theological knowledge and, finally, the fourth part shows the continuing importance of Foucault's work for rethinking work on theology and sexuality. The collection does not attempt to capture every aspect of Foucault's work or present every key piece of scholarship in the area; it rather presents a representative number of past pieces (seven essays) and locates these alongside some important new avenues of exploration (six essays), by both new and more established scholars in the field of Foucauldian studies in theology. If the collection manages to raise a different set of questions and opens new problems for theology then it will carry the spirit of Foucault's work: we hope it will contest the institutional spaces of our knowledge and problematize contemporary theology.

Part One contains three previously published articles, which capture something of the scholarly trajectory of Foucault's work in relationship to the church in late antiquity. The field of late antiquity studies has grown enormously since Foucault's death and these essays can only be representative of the wider engagement. Nonetheless, the essays included are important landmarks and show different facets of the discussion, a corrective reading of Foucault's account of the early church Fathers, a utilization of Foucault's methodology for Biblical criticism and an engagement between Foucault and Augustine. Much of the work takes places in the shadow of Foucault's unpublished fourth volume on Christianity, which still remains an enigma for Foucault scholars.[39]

Elizabeth Castelli's 'Interpretation of Power in 1 Corinthians', written originally in 1992, has become a classic essay in bringing Foucault's analysis of discourse and power to New Testament studies. It explores Paul's discourse in relationship to his 'conversation partners' – the Christians at Corinth – and tries to show the competing site of discourse and power. By playing on the 'lexical coincidence' between Paul and Foucault to develop a 'cultural critique' of Corinthians, Castelli reveals the strategies of power within the text.

Castelli makes power visible in the Biblical text and explores how this operates in Paul's elision of rhetoric and thematics. She uses Foucault effectively to show how power 'refocuses the analysis' of I Corinthians. She wants to reveal the 'multiplicity of discourses inhabiting the text' and how Paul asserts himself as 'privileged speaker'. In addition, she notes how Paul abstracts his power through a discourse of unity over-against the Corinthians who hold 'multiplicity and diffusion'. This analysis is located in a feminist analysis and Castelli reveals how the competing discourses are mapped onto the gendered body. The essay shows the creative and critical value of Foucault's work for biblical hermeneutics and reflects an important shift in such studies towards contemporary critical theory.

Elizabeth Clark's 'Foucault, the Fathers and Sex', written originally in 1988, was one of the first important moves in making Foucault's work on the early Fathers available to the academic theological world. It subsequently opened up a rich engagement between Foucault and church historians. After overviewing the content of Foucault's *History of Sexuality* for a new readership, the essay critically examines Foucault's account of the continuity and discontinuity between the Greco-Roman and Christian attitudes to sex. Clark tests the validity of Foucault's claims, highlights the problems of his historiography and notes the issues requiring qualification. She documents Foucault's concern with the aesthetic of the self, the solitary self-examination and the codified sexual acts according to authority. By taking the focus of the Desert Fathers of Egypt, she qualifies Foucault's argument, not least by suggesting that monastic life was not simply about 'sex in the head' but involved real anxieties about sexual activity. Clark also shows that Evagrius and Cassian do not easily support Foucault's move towards an 'incitement to sexual discourse' or provide an easy road to Freud's Vienna. Clark's other concern is that Foucault makes no distinction between the themes in Clement of Alexandria and Cassian. She nonetheless recognizes that Foucault's treatment of the history of Christianity is dependent on 'scattered references' and whether the unpublished fourth volume of Foucault's *History of Sexuality* would answer these questions is unclear.

J. Joyce Schuld's 'Augustine, Foucault and the Politics of Imperfection', written in 2000, reflects a new interface between Foucault and late antiquity studies. Schuld's work makes an important step in Foucault studies by exploring an issue which will be undoubtedly illuminated much further when Foucault's fourth volume, containing a discussion of Augustine,[40] is – if ever – published. However, Schuld is not limited by the Foucault archive and seeks rather to show how Christian social ethics can benefit from a dialogue between the pre-modern and the postmodern. What Schuld demonstrates is that Augustine and Foucault hold similar political concerns about institutional power and the moral imperfections of human endeavours. She shows how Foucault is not a threat to the evaluative judgments of Christianity, but rather a source for critical understanding with his 'prophetically unsettling methods of scrutiny'.

After examining the problems of a dialogue between Christian social thought and Foucault and discussing the misunderstandings surrounding such an engagement, Schuld shows how Augustine's *City of God* and Foucault's *Discipline and Punish* carry similar political concerns and cross-fertilize each other. Both, she argues, are suspicious of 'culturally privileged rhetoric'. Augustine's concern about the appeals of 'imperial glory' and Foucault's concern about notions of 'scientific progress' are both attempts to question 'self-evident authority'. Schuld reveals how both Augustine and Foucault, even though dealing with different operations of power, attempt to 'shock' their readers in order to collapse the moral order of the day. Both, she argues, encourage a political commitment to the world and hold onto the 'fragility' and 'messiness' of the human condition. They both, according to Schuld, hold an 'antitriumphalist' and 'antiutopian' approach to their respective worlds.

In Part Two, James Bernauer's 'Michel Foucault's Philosophy of Religion: an Introduction to the Non-Fascist Life' examines Foucault's thought as a form of resistance to the fascist glorification and production of the obedient subject as an ideal for human life. For Bernauer, there are three planes that organize Foucault's treatment of religion. First, Foucault's history of the present necessitates an excavation of the continuing role exercised by Christian technologies and problematics in defining modernity. Secondly, Foucault's thought, especially its last stages, provides tools for an effective religious self-criticism, an activity that itself remains a legacy of Christian traditions. Finally, Bernauer sees Foucault's privileging of friendship as an ethical experience to be a counter-force to the fascist project of creating states of permanent enmity. This essay shows how important for understanding Foucault's approach to religion are the yet to be published final lectures from his 1984 course at the Collège de France.

Michiel Leezenberg's 'Power and Political Spirituality: Michel Foucault on the Islamic Revolution in Iran' is one of the few investigations of Foucault's effort to grasp the historic significance of a specific contemporary event, the Iranian Revolution of 1978–79. He shows how various threads in Foucault's thought made him sensitive to the novelty of the calls for change in Iran at a time when many, if not most, Western intellectuals saw those voices as encouraging a mere regression to the pre-modern. He was particularly interested in the spiritual dynamics of the masses which were in revolt against the Shah. Foucault was prescient of the important challenge which Islam's political force posed to customary modern styles of political analysis as well as to modern regimes of government. Since the attacks on New York and Washington of 11 September 2001, there has been wide recognition of the need to map the complex worlds of Islamic culture. More than 20 years earlier, Foucault had posed the task of that mapping before a large audience of readers. Leezenberg shows both the strengths and the weaknesses of those writings.

The title of John Caputo's essay, 'On Not Knowing Who We Are', captures perhaps the most significant and hard-won of Foucault's personal spiritual insights. Foucault renews a respect for a wise ignorance of ourselves. Such unknowing, referred to by Foucault as the 'night of truth', is a refusal of the positive, knowledgable identities that have been fabricated for human beings as ways of mastering them. Caputo portrays Foucault's writings as chapters in a hermeneutics of refusal that rejects an entire series of humanistic knowledges and their products: '*homo psychologicus, homo economicus, homo religiosus*'. For Foucault, all truth about the human is traversed by untruth. Witnessing to this negativity, realizing that we need not be who we are scripted to be is a practice of freedom that welcomes difference and that, for Caputo, could promote a distinctive caring for others in such healing acts as compassion and forgiveness.

In his 'Partially Desacralized Spaces: the Religious Availability of Foucault's Thought', the first essay of Part Three, Thomas Flynn indicates that one route to fruitful dialogue between Foucault and religious thought would cross the philosophical domain of event, space and experience. Foucault's stress on the category of event in his work protects him from subordination to any search for the metaphysical God of the philosophers. His orientation would be to the unrepeatable in history, to a Biblical sensibility. Foucault maintained that contemporary space was still not completely desacralized and his own travels seemed to reflect that argument. As one of his biographers reported, Foucault found in the desert of California experiences of transgression which served to transform his own intellectual trajectory. Finally, Flynn leads us to wonder about the forms of transcendence to which Foucault's restless journeys of mind and body brought him. Does Foucault present a type of secular mysticism in which one's exposure to the mystery of otherness exhibits the whirlwind of one's own 'non-unitary multiplicity'?

In 'Exomologesis and Aesthetic Reflection: Foucault's Response to Habermas', Andrew Cutrofello investigates Foucault's critical approach to modern technologies of the self and his effort to demonstrate their contingency. Cutrofello argues that the injunction of Foucault's last work, the call to care for the self, is part of a deliberately conceived strategy for subverting the triumphant, Socratic tradition of 'know thyself'. Cutrofello claims that Foucault aimed to reverse or transvalue the relationship between visible bodies and articulable speech. His argument takes account of Foucault's deep interest in the distinct forms of early Christian confessional practice: the contrast between the public performance of penance by a sinner (*exomologesis*) and the verbal confession of sins (*exagoreusis*) that was to become the standard Catholic form. Foucault's analysis of the two forms is shown to reflect a common strategy in his work in which items of fascination open spaces for new ways of imagining. In Cutrofello's words, it is 'tempting to read Foucault as regularly attempting to conjure something like an experience of the sublime'.

Thomas Beaudoin enters into another experience of Foucault's life and creativity by considering his interest in music and the potential of that interest for reframing theological knowledge. His 'From Singular to Plural Domains of Theological Knowledge: Notes Toward a Foucaultian New Question' aims to loosen the grip of modern subjectivity on the theological domain. He enters into a conversation with Howard Gardner's effort to theorize a plurality of intelligences and, in the light of that work, Beaudoin presses the question of what is taken to count as theological. Are there subjugated modes of theological knowledge? Is musicality one of them? Beaudoin's contribution is a very suggestive proposal on the necessary pluralism of theological styles of understanding.

Henrique Pinto's 'The *More* Which Exceeds Us: Foucault, Roman Catholicism and Inter-faith Dialogue' develops Foucault's idea of the 'more' in *The Archaeology of Knowledge* to open the infinite possibilities of human becoming in the 'divine'. By locating theology in the decentred subject, historicity and finitude, Pinto seeks to establish a 'non-unitary theology of religious pluralism', which can transform human beings. His work develops an 'ethical sensibility of the other' and offers a critique of the Roman Catholic engagement in inter-faith dialogue. Following the work of Janzten and Carrette, he develops Foucault's theology of language and bridges the divide between the human and the divine. In this critical repositioning theology becomes a 'dialogical practice' and an 'embodied openness to the Other'. His work moves towards a 'Foucauldian mysticism' in creatively developing Foucault's 'more' as a theological concept. The 'more' constantly resists theological closure and marks out the spaces for Christian living in a world of 'open-ended dialogue with the other'. In the end, what Pinto establishes is not just a theological reading of Foucault, but a theological space within Foucault's writing. His engagement with the 'more' shows how Foucault's work, as Maurice Clavel found, can be inspirational to Christian faith – the openness to the 'more' in human life.

Part Four opens with Jeremy Carrette's 'Beyond Theology and Sexuality: Foucault, the Self and the Que(e)rying of Monotheistic Truth' which attempts to rethink theology outside the regime of sexuality, the fixed self and monotheistic truth. It argues that sexuality and monotheistic theology are fundamentally related and control both the body and the understanding of God. By documenting how Foucault's genealogy has been developed in 'queer theory', Carrette seeks to show how Foucault offers a way out of 'sexuality'. He argues that theological engagement with the discourse of sexuality continues an oppressive epistemology, because it anchors reality in a single point. Carrette's essay explores how queer theory can assist theology in overcoming its fascist tendency to control the body and God. In an exploration of Foucault's work on the Christian self, Carrette reveals how Christianity, as opposed to Buddhism, is located in a single truth of self, God and sexuality. Developing Foucault's critical history of the self, he examines the problematic of bisexuality and the multiplicity of desire. He argues that modern theology continues to have a problem with a 'multiple self'. Carrette's essay is an attempt to celebrate the diversity of Christian living and complexity of desire. His challenge to theology is to give up the control of the body by giving up the human–theological control and order of God. The essay shows how theology can liberate itself in the very ambiguity and uncertainty of Christian living.

Taking his starting point from a subtle reflection on Foucault's distinction between the 'sodomite' and the 'homosexual', Mark Jordan leads us into a consideration of the power possessed by Christian rhetorical programmes in regard to sexuality. His 'Sodomites and Churchmen: the Theological Invention of Homosexuality' argues that, contrary to frequent interpretation of Foucault, his history of sexuality does not claim that modern viewpoints on sexuality have simply replaced the Christian rhetoric of sinful identities. Jordan does acknowledge a difference of functions between the two regimes: '"Sodomite" functions as a category for denouncing and excluding, while "homosexual" is a category for managing and regulating.' He shows, however, that both rhetorics endure and, thus, at least in the case of Roman Catholic documents, the 'rhetorical logic of "sodomy" persists under the new term "homosexuality"'. Faced with theologies that may be defunct and yet still devouring, Jordan wonders about the potential for resistance of certain theological categories. Whether that resistance emerges or not, Jordan's analysis forces us to confront the continuing, often unrecognized, influence of Christian churches 'over the imagin-ation of sex in societies that once were Christendom'.

From the perspective of Foucault's approach to ethical formation, Michael Mahon's 'Catholic Sex' examines an important set of popular 20th-century American Catholic moral pamphlets about sex. He finds that they exhibit profoundly modern versions of the self and of manhood. They promote a Cartesian subjectivity aimed at independence from the world and at estrangement from the bodily. They foster a masculinity that is both domineering and suspicious of companionship. Mahon draws a sharp distinction between the ideal of self-control which these texts extol and a Christian path of self-denial and self-sacrificing love.

NOTES

1   The phrase 'postmodern theology' can be misleading. It can imply both a periodization and a philosophical position. In the former sense it is broadly used to refer to theology after modernity, but this is problematic in terms of its modernist assumptions about history. In its philosophical sense the term 'postmodern' is used loosely to include French 'post-structuralists' (Foucault, Derrida, Levinas, Lacan, Kristeva), but more nuanced readings abandon such simple and misleading equations. The term 'postmodernism' still has a currency with reference to the work of Baudrillard and Lyotard. See, for example, David Macey, *The Penguin Dictionary of Critical Theory* (London: Penguin, 2000) and Paul Lakeland, *Postmodernity: Christian Identity in a Fragmented Age* (Minneapolis: Fortress Press, 1997).
2   Preliminary versions of several of these papers were presented at a colloquium, 'Michel Foucault: Religious Explorations', which was held on 26 April 2000 at Loyola University in Chicago (see Acknowledgements). James Bernauer wishes to thank Loyola University, its Department of Philosophy and its Jesuit Community for their support during that year.
3   Hans Frei, *Types of Christian Theology* (New Haven & London: Yale University Press, 1992).
4   H. Richard Niebuhr, *Christ and Culture* (New York: Harper Colophon, 1951).

5   Michel Foucault, 'Who are you, Professor Foucault?' (1967), reprinted in *Religion and Culture by Michel Foucault*, ed. Jeremy Carrette (Manchester University Press & Routledge, 1999, p.91).

6   Michel Foucault, *Discipline and Punish* (London: Penguin, 1975, p.30); Jeremy Carrette, *Foucault and Religion: Spiritual Corporality and Political Spirituality* (London & New York: Routledge, 2000, pp.109–28).

7   Michel Foucault, *The Order of Things* (London: Routledge, [1966] 1991, p.xi); James Bernauer, *Michel Foucault's Force of Flight: Toward an Ethics for Thought* (Amherst, New York: Humanities Press, 1990, pp.61ff).

8   Carrette, *Foucault and Religion*, pp.25ff.

9   Carrette, *Foucault and Religion*, pp.108–28.

10 Bernauer, *Michel Foucault's Force of Flight*, pp.61ff, 178.

11 David Macey, *The Lives of Michel Foucault* (London: Hutchinson, 1993, pp.192, 415); Jeremy Carrette, 'Prologue to a Confession of the Flesh', in *Religion and Culture by Michel Foucault*, p.15.

12 Bernauer, *Michel Foucault's Force of Flight*, p.178; Carrette, *Foucault and Religion*, pp.85–108, 146–7.

13 For example, Bryan Turner, *Religion and Social Theory* (London: Sage [1983] 1991); Grace Jantzen, *Power, Gender and Christian Mysticism* (Cambridge: Cambridge University Press, 1995); Mark Jordan, *The Invention of Sodomy in Christian Theology* (Chicago: University of Chicago Press, 1997); Grace Jantzen, *Becoming Divine: Towards a Feminist Philosophy of Religion* (Manchester: Manchester University Press, 1998).

14 Anthony Thisleton, *The New International Greek Testament Commentary: The First Epistle to the Corinthians* (London: Eerdmans Paternoster, 2000).

15 Michel Foucault, *The Use of Pleasure* (London: Penguin, 1984, pp.8–9).

16 Foucault, *The Use of Pleasure*, p.9.

17 Christopher Dawson, *Religion and Culture* (London: Sheed & Ward, 1947); Christopher Dawson, *Religion and the Rise of Western Culture* (London: Sheed & Ward, 1950); Paul Tillich, *Theology of Culture* (New York: Galaxy and Oxford University Press, 1964); Niebuhr, *Christ and Culture* (1951).

18 Michel Foucault, *Remarks on Marx* (New York: Semiotext(e) [1978] 1991, pp.159ff); Carrette, *Foucault and Religion*, p.130.

19 Foucault, *Remarks on Marx*, pp.148, 170.

20 Michel Foucault, 'Truth and Power', in *Power/Knowledge: Selected Interviews and Other Writings 1972–1977*, ed. Colin Gordon (London: Harvester Wheatsheaf, 1980, p.114.

21 See Laura Penny, 'Catholic, more or less', *Globe and Mail*, 4 March 2000; Carrette, *Foucault and Religion*, p.151. We are also grateful to Paul Morris for his reflections on Foucault's Catholic inheritance.

22 Michel Foucault, *The History of Sexuality: Volume 1* (London: Penguin [1976] 1990); Foucault, 'About the Beginnings of the Hermeneutics of the Self' [1980] in *Religion and Culture*, pp.158–81.

23 David Tracey, *The Analogical Imagination* (London: SCM, 1981).

24 John Mahoney, *The Making of Moral Theology: A Study of the Roman Catholic Tradition* (Oxford: Clarendon, 1987, esp. pp.1–36).

25 Michel Foucault, *Les Anormaux: Cours au Collège de France, 1974–1975* (Paris: Seuil/Gallimard, 1999, pp.180, 188).

26 *Les Anormaux: Cours au Collège de France, 1974–1975*, pp. 174–5.

27 *The Sexuality of Christ in Renaissance Art and Modern Oblivion* (Chicago: University of Chicago Press, 1996, 2nd rev. edn). This was first published as a special issue of the journal *October*, 25 (Summer, 1983). James Bernauer sent Foucault a copy of the issue

which Foucault acknowledged receipt of, expressing his hope of finding a French publisher for it. (Note from Foucault to Bernauer, 5 February 1984).

28   *The Sexuality of Christ in Renaissance Art and Modern Oblivion*, p.3.

29   *The Sexuality of Christ in Renaissance Art and Modern Oblivion*, pp.234, 237.

30   William Lynch, *Christ and Apollo: The Dimensions of the Literary Imagination* (New York: Sheed & Ward, 1960).

31   Foucault, 'On the Government of the Living', in *Religion and Culture*, p. 155.

32   Bernauer owes the story to a conversation with Foucault's partner, Daniel Defert.

33   Foucault, 'On Religion', in *Religion and Culture*, p. 107.

34   'What is Enlightenment?', in *The Essential Works of Foucault, 1954–1984, Volume I: Ethics, Subjectivity and Truth*, ed. Paul Rabinow (New York: The New Press, 1997, p.315).

35   Foucault, *L'herméneutique du sujet: Cours au Collège de France, 1981–1982* (Paris: Gallimard Seuil, 2001, p.17).

36   Michel Foucault, 'What Is Critique?' in *The Politics of Truth*, ed. Sylvère Lotringer (New York: Semiotext[e], 1997, p.74).

37   See Janzten, *Power, Gender and Christian Mysticism;* Richard King, *Orientalism and Religion: Postcolonial Theory, India and 'The Mystic East'* (London: Routledge, 1999, pp.7–34).

38   See note 2.

39   See *Religion and Culture*, where Carrette tries to recover some of the available fragments of this volume.

40   See *Religion and Culture by Michel Foucault*, ed. Carrette, pp.45, note 205; 184ff.

I
FOUCAULT AND THE CHURCH IN LATE ANTIQUITY

Chapter 1

Interpretations of Power in 1 Corinthians

Elizabeth A. Castelli

For the kingdom of God does not exist in talk but in power.

1 Corinthians 4:20

The literature of the New Testament is steeped in the discourse and ideology of power. It imagines a world, indeed a universe, in which power infuses every sort of relationship, social and supernatural. Its narratives and letters are full of descriptions of the highly charged effects of power and prescriptions for comprehending their meanings. The language of power has of course been remarked upon by commentators on these texts, though such commentary has fallen generally into three categories: the apologetic/confessional, in which much is made of the claims about power in order to underwrite theological truth claims; the rationalizing, where claims about power and domesticated by interpreters embarrassed by the discourse's unabashed hierarchical claims; and the sociological, in which models emerging from sociological theory are tested against New Testament evidence, that evidence also undergoing domestication in the process.[1] Notably absent from the interpretive discussion is analysis emerging from the very fruitful area of cultural critique, whose modes of interrogation would appear uniquely helpful for understanding the discourses and ideologies of power in New Testament writings.

Nowhere does this lacuna in the relationship between text and commentary appear more clearly than in the interchange between Paul's discourse and that of his modern commentators. Although a ponderous body of commentary engages Paul's language (worldview, theology, ethics, intentions, and so on), there remain intriguing silences in the chorus of voices attempting to gloss the discourse of Paul, this despite the fact that Paul's own attempt to contain disparate and multiple voices in Corinth has not succeeded in stifling interpretive voices. Yet Paul himself knows the central importance of processes of interpretation, as one can see in his caution to the Corinthians that no one should speak in tongues unless there is an interpreter present to make sense of the power/meaning (*dynamis*) of the language. His own discourse (occasionally as impenetrable as glossolalia) also invites, indeed demands, the presence of interpreters. Yet the nature of Paul's own discourse (*logos*) has only recently and somewhat sparsely been interrogated as a specifically interested discourse, rather than as a normative one. This has left Paul's claims and assertions to be read as indicative declarations, and in the process the multiple voices that must have been part of the conversation 19 centuries ago have been muffled or silenced altogether. When not muted or silenced, these voices tend to be drained of their vibrancy when rendered by the biblical scholar's equivalent of 'the other': 'the opponents'.

This rendering bespeaks the essential continuity of Paul's own discourse and the interpretive discourse that has followed it up, authorizing Paul's discourse and constituting much commentary upon it as mere repetition. One might well argue that Paul's discursive and rhetorical ingenuity and power may be measured in the extent to which he was able to render his contingent language as true. This essay will attempt a different reading of Paul's discourse, one which presupposes the contingency and interestedness of that discourse, and further one which sees in Paul's writing a discursive strategy whose effects close off other competing discourses. This reading does not seek to settle the question of the correctness of the various positions, nor does it presume to set multiple discourses into simple oppositions. The purpose of this essay will be to trace the interweaving threads of rhetoric and thematics in Paul's first letter to the Corinthians, looking at the ways in which claims to power and discourse imbued with power implicate one another and result in the collapsing of argument and content into a singular truth claim about power. In other words, the statement cited as the epigraph to this essay, Paul's claim that the kingdom of God does not exist in discourse but in power, is at some level a disingenuous claim. The thesis of this essay might well be restated as a rearticulation of Paul's claim: 'The kingdom of God exists as a discourse of power.'

My own thinking about early Christian discourse has been shaped by a confluence of interpretive concerns and political commitments, by theoretical conversations in the arena of cultural criticism and by the political and ethical debates falling generally under the umbrella of 'feminism'. Some will no doubt argue that it is inappropriate to interrogate 1st-century texts through the lens of 20th-century theories and concerns; and there is a certain compelling force to the argument that texts should be 'allowed to speak for themselves'. I am more convinced, however, by arguments against the utopian idea that texts can ever simply do that, since they are always already highly mediated articulations, and against the notion that texts exist in a benign, neutral free market which, when left to its own devices, merely allows the best ideas to win. Further, it is not the case that the New Testament possesses privileged status in western discourse by accident. Its normative status as one of the master discourses of western culture and the process by which it attained this privileged status are not the results of an ideological free market, but the effects of much more complex historical processes, and not always laudable ones. The texts themselves are interested, as any interpretation of them must also be. This is not to suggest that every form of discourse, interpretive or otherwise, may simply be reduced to polemic, but to point out the inevitability of perspective in interpretation, the omnipresence of interpretive frames, whether consciously constructed or not. If this were not the case, the work of historians rewriting accounts of remote events that have already been thoroughly narrated would be redundant; and the continuously raging debates within historiography about the nature of historical knowledge and memory, about the continuities and discontinuities of cultural change, and so on, would be without driving force. To varying degrees, we bring present-day questions and interests to bear on history all the time, and not merely in a reductively pragmatic fashion. There is a thrilling expanse of space between the impossible goal of allowing texts to speak for themselves, on the one hand, and the posing of loaded anachronistic questions to texts, on the other. In between is located the evocative, resonant, if often contested, terrain that Foucault calls 'the history of the present'. It is to this kind of history that this essay strives.

Attending to subjugated discourses and producing a 'reading against the grain' have caused me also to be self-reflective about the process by which my own text has been produced. This essay has had multiple, fragmentary incarnations, and I have come to wonder whether the post-structuralist hunch that discourses replicate the processes they claim to narrate has not played out rather dubiously in this attempt to trace the capillary workings of power in the remnants of the discourse we have concerning the early Christian community at Corinth. If power circulates and infuses relationships within communities, it is everywhere and nowhere at the same time. To subject it to scholarly specular intervention is to disrupt its course, to arrest its movement, to reify and objectify what might be better understood as a quality, a resonance or a value (in the sense that color qualifies, has tone and value.)[2] The discursive interactions I have tried to trace have been confounding in their paradoxical nature: the workings of power narrated and deployed in Paul's text have been at the same time conspicuous and elusive. The course of Paul's discourse has never been easy to chart, and discourses of power are all the more perplexing for their apparent and enigmatic invisibility. But we may take heart from Foucault's evocative insight that the imperceptibility of power relations does not mean that they are given, natural or universal; and that to render them visible can have a positive, transgressive effect.[3]

When Paul wrote his first letter to the Christian community at Corinth, he was facing down what he apparently saw as a foundational challenge to his own understanding of how the community was to constitute itself and live out its newly embraced religious existence. The letter betrays a conflict over power and over questions of spoken knowledge (wisdom). These are located thematically in concerns over purity and prophecy, sexual practice and ritual practice. They are addressed through attention to questions of authority (personhood and ideologies of kinship) and in the continuing tendency in the letter to promote unity, oneness and sameness. Power elides and becomes coterminous with the person and discourse of Paul. The multiple and competing voices in the Corinthian community, voices almost muted by the letter's rhetoric, are overpowered by Paul's and are positioned in simple counterpoint to Paul's: the reader is urged to see things from Paul's point of view, to view other positions in caricature, and so on. Paul claims discursive privilege explicitly in the content of his argument and implicitly by the persistence of his use of vocabulary and syntax that render him the active subject of speech and his audience its passive object. Most striking is the degree to which Paul's rhetoric succeeds in producing a thoroughgoing elision of rhetorical discourse (discourse that seeks to persuade) with truth discourse (discourse that claims to represent truth). I do not see the difference between these two forms of discourse as a simple opposition between true and false speech, but rather see the elision of the rhetorical and persuasive into the truth claims grounded in a set of power relations. That is, the elision is a function of power, an interpretation of power. At the same time, the content of the discourse of 1 Corinthians is equally a function of power. One might visualize the relationship between discursive modes and discursive content as a multilayered, mutually implicating complex of relations.

This essay will draw on cultural criticism as it has been informed by two complementary (if sometimes contending) theoretical discourses: the work of Michel Foucault and feminism. It will then provide a brief reading of the discourse of power in 1 Corinthians as a kind of experimental test case.

A BRIEF INTRODUCTION TO FOUCAULT AND A FEMINIST GLOSS

The work of philosopher–historian Michel Foucault has vitally contributed to a new set of conceptual categories and modes of thought now falling, with greater or lesser specificity, under the title 'post-structuralism'. No thoroughgoing introduction to Foucault's work is undertaken here, as there already exist numerous helpful works in this area.[4] Nevertheless, it may prove useful to delineate some of the ways in which Foucault's contributions to modern thought and interpretation have shaped the interpretive frame employed in this reading of 1 Corinthians.

Foucault is best known for his attempt to challenge the naturalness of western categories of thought and forms of social relation. This challenge took root in studies of the intellectual heart of western modernity, the Enlightenment, specifically in the notion of the human self emerging from the epistemic shifts the Enlightenment represents. Two early works, one tracing the development of the concept of 'madness'[5] and a second examining the emergence of the human sciences,[6] argue that categories which modern thought takes for granted as self-evident (sanity and rationality, among them) are conceptual constructions that, while perceived as progressive advancements toward an ever-expanding ground for freedom, are founded on the 'creation' of their opposites (madness and the irrational), function to constrain and confine human understanding and action, and produce forms of knowledge that serve the interests of containing the now dangerous 'other'. Foucault signifies the multiple effects of this new enlightened knowledge about 'man' through his use of the term, 'subject (*sujet*)', the name for the modern human individual. This word, of course, has multiple resonances: it can mean 'subject' in the grammatical sense; it can also mean 'subject' in the psychological sense (possessing a unified and distinguishable identity); and it can also mean 'subject' in the political sense (as in the object of subjection). Foucault's point is that the humanism of the Enlightenment, the refocusing of understanding on 'man' as a knowing subject (condensed in Descartes' *cogito ergo sum*), is no simple advance in human knowledge and reason, but rather an ambiguous shift from one system of subjection to another. Rather than celebrating the emergence of the human sciences that the Enlightenment represents, Foucault goes on to argue that knowledge does not release human subjects from the workings of power, but reinscribes them within a matrix of power/knowledge. He then can pose the question of the relationship between knowledge and power: how does knowledge serve power?[7]

Foucault's interest in the technologies of power that produce the human subject eventually led him away from interrogations of public social institutions and toward questions about the microtechnologies of the production of selfhood and consequently to the heart of the 'private' realm: the history of sexuality.[8] Here Foucault reformulated in a foundational way his understanding of the intersections of power/knowledge on the terrain of the human body, tracing the production of the 'self' not simply to the birth of the modern period, but backwards into classical antiquity whose history, he became convinced, was a history of the present.

To attempt to discern with precision what exactly Foucault means by invoking certain abstract or global terms, such as 'power', can often be a frustrating search for an elusive prize. Foucault himself most often defines 'power' in negative terms. He communicates its meaning by stating at length what he does *not* mean by using the term:

Power in the substantive sense, '*le' pouvoir*, doesn't exist. What I mean is this. The idea that there is either located at – or emanating from – a given point something which is a 'power' seems to me to be based on a misguided analysis, one which at all events fails to account for a considerable number of phenomena. In reality, power means relations, a more-or-less organized, hierarchical, coordinated cluster of relations.... If one tries to erect a theory of power one will always be obliged to view it as emerging at a given place and time and hence to deduce it, to reconstruct its genesis. But if power is in reality an open, more-or-less coordinated (in the event, no doubt, ill-coordinated) cluster of relations, then the only problem is to provide oneself with a grid of analysis which makes possible an analytic of relations of power.[9]

Foucault's unwillingness to define 'power' in positive terms is not to be dismissed as a predictable Parisian wile, as some have characterized it. Rather, the refusal to pin down the notion is a strategic move designed to underscore power's resistance to simple definition. Power is a characteristic of social processes, not a possession of the powerful. Earlier on, in his analysis of the institution of the modern prison, Foucault suggests:

In short ... power is exercised rather than possessed; it is not the 'privilege', acquired or preserved of the dominant class, but the overall effect of its strategic positions – an effect that is manifested and sometimes extended by the position of those who are dominated.

Furthermore, this power is not exercised simply as an obligation or a prohibition on those who 'do not have it'; it invests them, is transmitted by them and through them; it exerts pressure upon them, just as they themselves, in their struggle against it, resist the grip it has on them.[10]

Power, then, is not a simple commodity, something that one group possesses and withholds from other groups. Rather, power is a quality that inheres in social relationships; it flows through the body politic as blood circulates through an organism, capillary rather than controlling. What is most helpful about this conceptualization of power is that it creates the possibility of agency for the occupants of the subordinate position in a hierarchical relationship: that is, rather than theorizing the power*ful* and the power*less*, it suggests that power is multiply figured in social relationships, and creates the possibility for thinking that the weight of the hierarchy might shift.

In the context of New Testament studies, and specifically Pauline studies, the more traditional readings of Paul's writings have tended only peripherally to questions of power/knowledge – an irony when the texts themselves are full of claims to power and articulations of knowledge. Foucault's understanding of power is important to a reading of Paul because it refocuses the analysis: if power is seen as something which circulates within a system, something inhering in relationships rather than as a possession of a person or group, then one can rethink what is going on in the texts this way: rather than looking for Paul's 'opponents', one can look for his conversation partners. That is, rather than assume that Paul is the possessor of truth because he has authority, we can imagine that Paul is claiming authority because he is in a position which is contestable and contested.

In my own theoretical framework, feminism and Foucault come together to argue for the recovery of repressed knowledges and discourses. In feminist biblical scholarship, this has been put forward most often in terms of 'reconstruction' of the historical past;[11] in Foucault, it is a process of reading that promotes the resituating of historical knowledge through the finding of the unsaid. While there is this affinity between these two interpretive discourses, at the same time there are significant differences between feminism as it has been articulated in the United States and Foucault. One of the most salient differences for this discussion is the question of speech as liberation.[12] Whereas for some forms of feminism, speaking in one's own voice or hearing the voices of women has become a privileged signifier in itself for freedom and authentic identity, Foucault would caution that speech is itself not a liberating mode. The clearest example of his position here is articulated in his analysis of the emergence of the confessional as the site of new technologies of power vis-à-vis sexuality.[13] Further, whereas some North American feminism imagines a utopian space devoid of power, Foucault denies that such a space is ever possible.

My own interpretive position takes seriously Foucault's caveat that discourse in its own right is not necessarily a key to liberation. Further, I share the point of view that power is not something that can be strained out of social relationships, but rather is a necessary condition of their existence. At the same time, it is clear that power is not the same thing at every moment, nor does it qualify all relationships in the same ways. Understanding its specific workings can aid in the process of its reformulation, and it is in this sense that Foucault's alignment of knowledge and power has important implications for social change. In the reading of 1 Corinthians that follows, these two interpretive discourses will come together, it is hoped, fruitfully: creating a space for a more complex rendering of the multiplicity of discourses inhabiting the text itself, its own and the more muted subjugated discourses it seeks to replace. In doing this, I hope to complicate the conceptual framework so often imposed on the Pauline corpus, so that it will be less easy to evaluate the early Christian communities to which Paul wrote solely on his terms, setting up Paul as the originary norm and differences from that norm as dangerous deviations. In this, Foucault's insight that 'deviants' are created to authorize 'norms' resonates throughout my analysis of Paul's discourse.

INTERPRETATIONS OF POWER IN CORINTH

The discussion is organized around a series of themes derived from the content of 1 Corinthians, and explores the relationship of two competing sets of discourse: that of Paul and that of Christians in Corinth. There are several interpretive difficulties here, most seriously the problem of skewed evidence. That is, unfortunately, there do not exist texts produced by Corinthian Christians to which one might compare the text of 1 Corinthians. One has to imagine one part of the conversation. My goal is not reconstructive per se; that is, I am not first and foremost interested in sketching out a historical picture of the 1st-century Corinthian Christian community. Rather, I am interested in comparing two competing discursive realms. There have been numerous able attempts at historical reconstruction, and my reading of the text of 1 Corinthians has benefited from these, especially Antoinette Wire's feminist reconstruction.[14] The question posed here, however, is narrower than that of reconstructors of the historical past, and focused differently: what is the nature of power as it is constructed within this conversation? How are certain power relations created and maintained, and how are other understandings of power rendered unthinkable?

Organizing this reading has been difficult because I have cut across the text several times, focusing on different themes and topics which reappear variously throughout the letter. Further, these themes and topics often overlap and imply one another. The reading begins with the question of the primacy of the discursive, and the ways in which talk about language situates Paul as a powerful and authoritative agent in the text. It goes on to look at the language of power and knowledge, and the ways in which those concepts are deployed by Paul and the Corinthians. We then turn to specific spaces and roles in which power is shaped and formulated, battled over and resignified: imagery of the body; kinship metaphors; dualistic imagery (slavery/freedom, strength/weakness); attempts to control unbounded speech; and Paul's advocacy of sameness, unity and oneness. These topics are not all parallel, nor of equal importance, but they join together to undergird a complex and multilayered argument about relationships of and toward power in Paul's discourse, and they become the contested terrain within which the subjugated discourse of Corinthian Christians also finds a kind of voice.

Discourse and the construction of the speaker's privilege

The rhetoric of Paul's letter is remarkable for its subtle but persistent use of language about speech itself. Language, one might argue, is never a neutral medium, for even when it is used simply to communicate, it constructs even as it reflects the world. In a text like 1 Corinthians, where the drive toward persuasion resonates throughout the shape and content of the discourse, language appears to be understood as tremulous with power. Paul constructs himself in the letter and underwrites his authority as an apostle in large measure through the use of self-reflexive language about himself as a *speaker*. The majority of the verbs referring to speech in the letter are cast in the first-person active voice, referring to Paul himself. Further, those referring to Paul's discourse are used to authorize his activities and his demands upon the community. By contrast, when verbs concerned with communication and speech are used in the letter to refer to the Christian community at Corinth or Christians in general, they are derogatory, negative or cast in the passive voice. To put it another way, Paul's discursive strategy appears to be to cast himself as the grammatical subject of speech: he urges (*parakalô*, 1:10; 4:13; 4:16; 16:12; 16:15), says/means (*legô*, 1:12, 7:6; 7:8; 7:12; 7:35; 10:15; 10:29; 15:51; *phêmi*, 10:15; 10:19; 15:50), preaches (*euangelizomai*, 1:17; 9:16: 9:18; 15:1; *kêryssô*, 1:23; 9:27; 15:11), proclaims (*katangellô*, 2:1), speaks (*laleô*, 2:6; 2:13; 3:1; 9:8; 13:1; 15:34), blesses (*eulogeô*, 4:12), admonishes (*noutheteô*, 4:14), teaches (*didaskô*, 4:17), commands (*parangellô*, 7:10), commends (*epainô*, 11:2), directs (*diataxomai*, 11:34; 16:1). Meanwhile, the Corinthian Christians are cast most often as the object of speech, acted upon and not acting. This can be seen in the frequency with which they are characterized through grammatically passive forms (for example, 1:2, 9; 7:18, 20, 21, 22, 24; and so on), subjunctive rather than indicative moods (for example, 1:10, 15; 3:4; and so on), and direct address (*passim*) in which the community is constituted as the object of Paul's discursive activity. When their strong relationship to speech is acknowledged, as it is at the opening of the letter (1:5), the acknowledgment seems to function rhetorically to provide a context for Paul's later attempts to rein in that powerful relationship. When the community is cast in an active role with respect to language, as Paul's polemic against prophetic speech indicates, their speech sets the community at profound risk.

Power and talk are intrinsically linked in Paul's discourse to the Corinthian community. When he wishes to undercut counterclaims about relations to authority, Paul speaks of their *logos* having no power. Furthermore, as he tries to legislate levels of conformity within the worshipping community in Corinth, he does so by trying to rein in unruly forms of speech: speaking in tongues and prophecy. As analysts of rhetoric often point out, there is no reason for a speaker to rail vociferously against a set of circumstances or conditions that does not exist or that is not perceived to exist. Paul's insistence on the powerlessness of forms of speech he finds objectionable suggests that there are equally compelling claims being made that these discursive modes *are* infused with power. Furthermore, one might see in Paul's assertions a moment open to deconstruction: these discursive modes embody power to the same degree as Paul denies their claims to do so. Paul's attempts in the letter to contain and authorize certain forms of talk reflect this close link between notions of power and understandings of language.

Language of power/knowledge

It would be foolhardy to argue that Foucault's use of the terms 'power', 'knowledge', 'discourse' and so on is coterminous with Paul's use of terms that are translated by these English words, and this is certainly not the aim of this essay. Rather, I am taking advantage of the lexical coincidence between two sets of texts in order to make my argument. That is, my interpretation profits from the fortuitous presence of such terminology in Paul's discourse, and then seeks to use such terms and other elements of content as openings into the text and the relationships it seeks to establish rhetorically through the appropriation of such multiply charged terms. The result is that I have bracketed traditional philological and contextual analyses of terms, not because these are not useful, but because my focus is different. 'Knowledge' for Foucault resonates at a number of different levels at the same time; it can refer to everyday knowledge, scientific knowledge or knowledge possessed by superordinate figures in a power relationship. In these multiple meanings, Foucault would emphasize the way in which knowledge characterizes the knower, positions him/her in relation to the known, and permeates that relationship. The possessor of knowledge is also a privileged figure, since knowledge is perceived as a valuable commodity or characteristic of being.[15] The terms 'knowledge' (*gnôsis*) and 'wisdom' (*sophia*) are both used in 1 Corinthians to describe either an undisputed possession of Corinthian Christians or as something claimed as a possession but whose character is called into question by Paul. In other words, they are problematized concepts, disputed and highly charged terms. I have read both these terms to signify forms of knowledge which situate the knower as a privileged figure. Given the rhetoric of Paul's discourse, it does not seem to be a stretch of the imagination to read these terms in this way. Of course, both of these terms are embedded in a dense web of meanings, and both can function as theological technical terms. Paul's own usage suggests that he moves around within the signifying frames of each of these terms, using them in different ways at different moments (sometimes more mundanely, at other times more technically). Paul's usage is not coterminous with Foucault's technical term 'knowledge', though there is a highly meaningful overlap in the two sets of usage. Therefore this reading is pursued from the ground of that overlap.

Interpretations of power/knowledge

The first four chapters of 1 Corinthians articulate a complex interweaving of notions of power and knowledge. From the opening line of the letter ('Paul, called by the will of God to be an apostle') to the closing sentence of Chapter 4 ('Shall I come to you with a rod, or with love in a spirit of gentleness?') Paul's interaction with the Christians at Corinth on the questions of authority and wisdom are framed by a claim to power (his position divinely willed) and an only lightly veiled threat of coercion. In between, one encounters the deep traces of competing discourses of power and knowledge, echoes of whose vehemence resound even as the single surviving discourse (Paul's discourse) claims to stand alone.

Power and knowledge come together in different ways for the women and men of Corinth, on the one hand, and Paul, on the other. In fact, one could argue, insofar as Paul opens the letter's argument with a reflection on his understanding of the relationship between these two forces, that this relationship is the most highly charged of the contested terrain and, at the same time, central to both the Corinthians and Paul. For even as Paul praises the Corinthian power as residing in discourse and knowledge (*pas logos kai pasa gnôsis*, 1:5), ultimately in this section he will invert the conventional understandings of the values associated with discourse, knowledge and wisdom, and argue that any asserted ties between wisdom and power – and any claims to authority emerging from them – constitute only so much talk (4:20), discourse separated irredeemably from power.

The discussion found in 1:18–2:5 is particularly illuminating on this point. In it, Paul begins by connecting a discursive notion ('the *logos* of the cross') with power (*dynamis theou*). The ensuing argument separates conventional notions of wisdom (*sophia*) from this claim to power. A series of rhetorical questions implying the absence of effective power deriving from wisdom is followed by a series of inversions whereby conventional hierarchies are overturned and replaced by their opposites. Then Paul characterizes his own discourse as explicitly lacking in wisdom, and goes so far as to claim ignorance (*ou gar ekrina ti eidenai*) of everything 'except Jesus Christ and him crucified' and, in a remarkable rhetorical turn, locates his own discourse squarely within the realm of divine power (*kai ho logos mou kai to kêrygma mou ouk en peithois sophias logois all' en apodeixei pneumatos kai dynameôs*: 'and my discourse and my message were not in persuasive words of wisdom but in demonstration of spirit and power').

Yet, as the argument moves ahead, Paul remains unwilling to abandon the concept of wisdom, for he goes on to claim wisdom for his own speech (*sophian de laloumen*), not a worldly wisdom but a divine one secreted away in mystery (*laloumen theou sophian en mystêriô tên apokekrymmenên*: 'we speak the wisdom of God, hidden away in mystery', 2:6–7). Though he has claimed ignorance earlier on, he now resituates his own discourse in relation to knowledge and power, effectively authorizing his own speech and wisdom over against 'all discourse and all knowledge' (*pas logos kai pasa gnôsis*) of his audience. The subtle appropriation of wisdom will reappear in the discussion of apostolic authority in Chapter 3, where Paul characterizes himself through the use of a simile of a 'wise designer/builder' (*sophos architektôn*, 3:10) whose work becomes the ground for that of others; eight verses later, he denounces those who think themselves to be wise (3:18–20). Wisdom as it inheres in the person of Paul is the basis for claims to power; others' claims to wisdom are characterized as 'folly with God' (3:19).

Echoes of the competing discourse of Corinthian power resound in this argument. If one is willing to entertain the possibility that what is going on in Corinth is a *different* interpretation of power, rather than an explicit attack on a normative position (represented by Paul), then this argument's logic may be discerned. Knowledge and power are aligned; multiplicities of discourses grounded in wisdom are possible, circulate, and render a diffuse kind of system of power. The opposing views of power here are not understood to be egalitarian/utopian versus hierarchical, but rather as different conceptual models: the Corinthians as knowers and speakers seem to understand power as a fluid, surging quality, occupying different bodies at different moments and with varying intensities. Paul, whose own position is ill-served by such a notion, continues to try to argue for power as inhering in roles and social positions and to claim authority for himself because he occupies these positions (apostle, father, authorized speaker). And, as is the case throughout Paul's discourse, the vehemence with which he insists upon the point suggests only the compelling quality of another point of view.

Body power

The human body provides a central series of images and themes for this text, and one hears the resonances of multiple interpretations of the body's power and power over the body echoing in Paul's discourse. Food practices and sexuality occupy fully half of the letter's content. These discussions are not completely reducible to concern over purity, though purity is clearly implicated in the argument. It is also the case that explicit language about authority and power is used most frequently in the discussion of bodily practices. This may suggest the vehemence of alternative understandings of bodies and power.

Anthropological and social theories have hypothesized, at least since Durkheim, a fundamental relationship between the human body as a signifying entity and articulated social meanings.[16] Theorists influenced by post-structuralism in general and Foucault in particular have advanced a critique of a solely meaning-based analysis of body ideologies, and have suggested that the body functions not simply as a (social or religious) symbol but rather as the site upon which competing discourses are played out. Furthermore, the body itself is seen, not as a blank slate upon which social meanings are inscribed, but as a changing and transitory articulator of multiple (sometimes conflicting and contradictory) identities, discourses and meanings.[17]

Some interpreters of New Testament literature who have been influenced by the work of theorists such as Mary Douglas have seen primarily in 1 Corinthians concern over purity, individual and corporate boundaries, and the mediation of anomalous (dangerous) circumstances.[18] The difficulty with this rendering of the situation is that it sees the body primarily as a problem to be managed, rather than as itself a site of power. That is, it sees the situation primarily through the eyes of the powerful 'informant', Paul, and not enough through the eyes of those whose bodies are being managed.

Furthermore, most unhelpful in thinking about the body/power texts in 1 Corinthians is the language of ethics applied to them by numerous commentators. Not only does this language divert attention away from the concern in those sections for the question of power, but qualifiers like 'libertinism' applied to the Corinthian position serve polemically to reinscribe Paul's discourse as truth while rendering other discourses contingent. Speaking of Paul's discussion of power as concern over ethics also reduces his discourse to a pragmatic level and naturalizes his own claims rather than problematizing them.[19] As with other themes in the letter, the discussion of bodies is approached here as representative of multiple competing discourses of power, rather than as a self-evident set of 'solutions' to 'problems' in the Corinthian community.

Paul's conception of the nature of the human body and its relationship to power is complex and multilayered. From the discussion of *porneia* beginning in Chapter 5 and concluding in Chapter 7, individual human bodies appear as sites of danger and contest, open to the power resignifying force of other bodies. Identity, which is a constant concern for Paul, appears to be thoroughly dependent upon the meanings inhering in individual bodies and always potentially open to controversy and challenge. The imagery of embodiment as tabula rasa, as empty bounded space (that is, *to sôma hymôn naos tou en hymin hagiou pneumatos*: 'your body is a temple of the holy spirit in you', 6:19), as dangerously malleable and open to resignification (*ouk oidate hoti ho kollômenos tê pornê hen sôma estin*: 'do you not know that the one who joins with a prostitute is one body [with her]?' 6:16), invites the view that the issue is, ultimately, a purity issue, as some have argued. That is, the dangerous openness of human bodies comes to signify the danger of pollution of the social body. This reading has merit, but leaves unasked the question of what other interpretations of body power are operative in the situation. If Paul is concerned with the purity of the Corinthian community, apparently his concern exists only in equal measure to some alternative understanding proffered by Corinthian Christians.[20]

Presumably there is significantly less anxiety among Corinthian Christians over questions of identity than one sees reflected in Paul's discourse. From the standpoint of Corinthians, bodies and identities are not rendered less stable by acts Paul believes undermine individual and corporate identity. Bodies are not transformed by interactions with others, in this view, perhaps because the body is seen, not as an empty vessel, but as a site of knowledge. Bodily meanings are not unstable and precarious in this view, as they are in Paul's vision of the effects of certain acts. (Perhaps it is necessary to say that this argument is not for or against the actions in question; rather, it is an attempt to find their logic.)

Gender makes a difference in these competing discourses concerning sexual practice, for it is apparent that the specificities of lived experience in gendered bodies has shaped understandings of body power. From Paul's point of view, there are two different sets of problems about sexual practices among the Corinthians: sexual license among some men, and sexual autonomy (taking the form of renunciation) among women.[21] The apparent egalitarian stance reflected in the syntax of 7:4 (*hê gynê tou idiou sômatos ouk exousiazei alla ho anêr, homoiôs de kai ho anêr tou idiou sômatos ouk exousiazei alla hê gynê*: 'the woman does not have authority over her own body but the man has, likewise the man does not have authority over his own body but the woman has') veils a more complex social reality in which, first of all, men have no particular need to claim authority over their own bodies because they already are granted it unproblematically by the culture.[22] Secondly, men possessing authority over women's bodies and women possessing authority over men's bodies are not parallel lived experiences. One must assume that it is specifically women who are claiming authority over their own bodies, and that the autonomy that their renunciation creates for them has produced powerful effects. Therefore Paul's combined refusal to sanction renunciation within marriage (7:5–6) and his urging for people to undertake marriage if they cannot manage *enkrateia* ('self-control') must, in spite of the apparent egalitarianism of the language, have rather different effects in the lives of Corinthian women and men – rather chilling and potentially devastating effects, one might add, in the lives of women who are called to submit to the authority of a man over their bodies because the man is incapable of exercising self-control (7:9).

Corinthian women, at least, must have had a rather different interpretation of the nature of the body. From their point of view, its boundaries were not perennially at risk, demanding constant vigilance against incursions of pollution. Neither was it an empty site awaiting signification and inscription. Rather, it must have been conceived of as a locus of power and, for those who renounced sexual relations, of autonomy.[23]

Gender further makes a difference in the discussion of embodiment found in 11:2–16, where the veiling of prophesying women is exhorted in the most directly confrontational discourse in the entire letter.[24] Here female bodies are singled out for containment, while the imagery of the 'head' functions multiplies as a site of honor and power, and while the implications of the argument clearly situate the 'head' as the privileged part of the body. The imagery of the head is deployed to undergird a hierarchical arrangement of God, Christ, man, and woman. Subordination is inscribed on social relations through bodily imagery. The piling up of arguments to justify this management of female bodies (arguments from nature, Paul's own refusal to recognize the practice, and the practices of other churches) suggests strong resistance. The competing discourse again shifts the focus away from Paul's own authority and interpretation of power toward a more diffuse interpretation of prophetic power, one in which the body is perceived as the site of power rather than as a threat to it.

The management of individual bodies and the deployment of the body as a resonating symbol in this letter can also be seen in 12:12–31, a text which, along with Romans 12:4–8, is often used to undergird the argument that Paul's notion of the body is not hierarchical but complementary, and furthermore promotes unity through its use of an organic model for social relations. The rhetoric of power implicit in the call to unity will be discussed below in the section on discourses of sameness and multiplicity. The apparently benign nature of the organic model of society, whereby a group is represented through the image of a body, is at the very least problematized by Paul's earlier use of the image of the 'head' as the privileged part of the body. Furthermore, in ancient conceptions of the body as image or microcosm of society – a commonplace trope – the necessity of all parts of the body remains fully in tension with their hierarchically arranged relative importance.[25]

At least two interpretations of body power can be discerned from Paul's discourse and the way he engages his audience: the Corinthians seem to see themselves as embodiments of power, that is, to see their bodies as definers and transformers of external meanings. Meaning is contingent for them, boundaries are fluid and unproblematic, their own power creative of new autonomies and identities. The language of fullness and emptiness suggests that Paul sees bodies as vessels, frames, empty of power and content, only to be filled up by divine action. Just as power abounds in the bodies and identities of the Corinthians as knowing subjects, Paul sees a danger in that fluidity and overabundance, in the multiplicity of meanings that they see. While Paul seeks to contain bodies through an ideology of purity, the Corinthians appear to interpret individual and social boundaries as without resonance or significance. The body resists a simple set of meanings in relation to power in this contest of discourses, though it offers as well an ample space for the playing out of competing interpretations.

The personhood of the apostle and idioms of kinship

In 1 Corinthians, as in other Pauline letters, there is a palpable tension between the image of the writer himself and its relationship to apostolic work more collectively. In this letter, the tension participates in the broader discourse about power. When Paul addresses, for example, the relationship of his own work to that of Apollos, initially the comparison serves the argument of their common identity. He calls them co-workers (*synergoi*, 3:9) and asserts that 'the one who plants and the one who waters are equal' (3:8). The point of this comparison, as is noted frequently, is to contrast the unity of the apostles with the multiplicity of the community. Yet, at the same time, a stringent hierarchy is set in place with the language about apostolic work as farming and building: 'For we are God's fellow workers; you are God's field, God's building' (3:9). The comparison then has a double effect of undergirding the argument for unity and at the same time rendering the women and men of Corinth as passive objects of apostolic working, the products of apostolic production.

As the comparison develops, the language becomes more sharply oppositional, making use of the ongoing strategy of inversion seen first in Chapters 1 and 2. 'We are fools for Christ's sake, but you are wise in Christ. We are weak, but you are strong. You are held in honor, but we in disrepute' (4:10). These statements are at the very least ironic, perhaps even offered sarcastically; they situate the two positions, Paul's and the Corinthians', in sharp counterpoint. The description of the hardships 'we' suffer continues for three more verses, then a remarkable transition occurs in the rhetoric. 'We' becomes 'I', destabilizing the certainty of the referent for the previous few verses: does 'we' refer to Paul and Apollos, or only to Paul?

At the very least, the comparison of Paul and Apollos is at some level strategic and disingenuous, because Apollos does not continue to possess equal status with Paul as the argument continues. For, by the end of Chapter 4, Paul himself becomes the unique model for Corinthian praxis: 'For though you have myriad slave tutors (*paidagogoi*) in Christ, you do not have many fathers. For I became your father in Christ Jesus through the gospel' (4:15). The emphatic use of the subject pronoun *egô* in this sentence, unnecessary by the normal rules of syntax, underscores the elision from first-person plural to first-person singular. Paul occupies the privileged spot.

The use of the idiom of kinship here further undergirds the claims to power that are at the heart of Paul's discourse. That he asserts his paternity is striking, especially at the end of the long comparison with Apollos. As the discourse develops, the parallelism and apparent equality between Paul and Apollos are replaced by a very clear hierarchical distinction drawn between them. 'We' becomes 'I'; Paul's 'co-worker' is transformed into a 'slave tutor', whose relationship to the child could not be more removed from the relationship of a father to a child; [26] and Paul retains for himself the singular position of 'father', a role replete with unique claims to authority. Power continues, then, to be reinscribed by Paul's discourse onto his own position, as speaking subject, as possessor of mysterious wisdom, as apostle and as father.

Dualism and the strategy of apparent reciprocity

Paul's rhetoric often makes use of oppositional pairs which operate in two different ways as a discursive strategy of power. One way is to place two sets of categories, values or positions in clear opposition, and then to allow the distance that separates them or the irony emanating from that distance to undergird his own position. The second strategy is what I have come to call the strategy of apparent reciprocity, in which two opposed elements are arranged as if mirror images of each other. Syntactically or logically, they appear to be parallel, though the parallelism belies real lived differences. This second strategy functions either to bolster a claim otherwise unauthorized or to leave social relations unchallenged.

An example of the first strategy is the inversion of conventional understandings of strength and weakness, wisdom and ignorance, honor and shame, and so on, which reaches its crescendo in 4:8–13. This process of inversion works rhetorically to distance Paul from those he criticizes, only to claim authority for the subordinate position he finds himself occupying.

The second strategy has already been analyzed in the discussion of 7:4, where women and men are both said to have authority over the bodies of their husbands or wives. There, the apparent reciprocity was seen to elide conditions of lived experience and thereby to mask the specificity of the greater demand being placed upon women in the area of sexual practice. A similar elision appears to occur in another set of opposed social roles, that of slave and free person *ho gar en kyriô klêtheis doulos apeleutheros kyriou estin, homoiôs ho eleutheros klêtheis doulos estin Christou*: 'for the one called in the lord as a slave is a free person in the lord, just as the free person called is the slave of Christ' (7:22). The apparent reciprocity erases the differences in the lived realities of slave and free person, and, in so doing, evades a critique of the power relations implicit in the differences of these positions. In the case of sexual authority, a competing discourse of sexual autonomy must have been articulated. In the case of enslavement and freedom, a competing discourse of social freedom may well echo under Paul's rhetoric as the subjugated discourse.

Rhetorical oppositions and hierarchical and reciprocal dualisms have multiple resonances in Paul's discourse, and they function strategically to authorize Paul's vision and position. It is possible to hear still other resonances of how such oppositions were alternately interpreted: in this example, most likely as access to new forms of social autonomy. But, in each case, Paul's assertion of his own authority and his vision are in marked counterpoint to the models of power and autonomy that seem to have been articulated so persuasively within the Corinthian community. Once again, the force of Paul's rhetoric betrays the contingency of his position vis-à-vis other defining discourses.

Interpretations of power in prophetic discourse

The importance of controlling speech is evident already from Paul's attention to situating himself as the privileged speaker. It continues to assert itself in the attempts to rein in prophetic speech in Chapter 14 of the letter. The attention to detail in this section, whereby micro-commands are articulated for the precise management of prayers and prophecies, leads one to suspect that 'uncontrolled' speech was seen by Paul as extremely dangerous and threatening. Inversely, then, it must also have been imbued by the Corinthians with enormous power and authority. Furthermore, the power of speaking in tongues is acknowledged by Paul when, at 14:18, he slips in the self-assertion: *Eucharistô tô theô pantôn hymōn mallon glôssais lalô*: 'I thank God that I speak in tongues more than you all.' Prophetic speech is to be managed, but also claimed, precisely because it can command enormous power and authority. So Paul cannot condemn it, and in fact must claim that he is a privileged user of it.

Prophetic speech, from Paul's perspective, possesses an ongoing dangerous character because it is self-authorizing, mobile and unaccountable to other forms of authority. It is also widely perceived as uniquely powerful. Certainly the discourse of the Corinthian community portrayed it as such.[27] The strident rhetoric of 14:34–6, in which women are silenced in church, explicitly links silence and subordination (*hypotassô*), implicitly speech and power.[28] The chapter ends with the claim that only those who acknowledge Paul's understanding of the place and appropriate performance of prophetic speech are real prophets. Prophecy is fine but *panta de euschêmonôs kai kata taxin ginesthô*: 'all things should occur decently and in order'. The Corinthian prophetic discourse, as with other contested practices, must have paid far less attention to questions of order, asserting itself through bold and powerful articulations and with a certainty that caused Paul's own claims to authority to pale significantly.

Sameness, multiplicity, unity

The rich ingenuity of the rhetoric of 1 Corinthians is seen perhaps never more clearly than in the combined gestures of Paul's claim to absolute powerlessness, on the one hand, and his call for mimetic identification, on the other. I have argued at length elsewhere that the mimetic relationship Paul urges the Corinthian Christians to enter into (4:16; 11:1) within him continually reinscribes his own authoritative position as model.[29] Furthermore, the very notion of multiplicity is characterized as problematic, dangerous and utterly threatening to the communal existence of the Corinthians. Sameness, singularity and unity are advocated throughout the text as pathways to proper existence, and they also serve the function of consolidating Paul's own authority insofar as he calls people to sameness and unity, on his terms.

As the analysis of the counter-discourse of Corinthian Christians all through this essay has suggested, multiplicity and diffusion are not sources of anxiety for these Christians as they are for Paul. The divisions he laments and the 'disorder' of the varieties of articulations of spiritual life he frets over may well be of little consequence to them. Sameness serves the interests of the superordinate in a hierarchical relationship of power. Multiplicity destabilizes the certainty of the very claim to superordinate status. Unity is most often called for by those whose authority will be undergirded by it, and matters most to those for whom identities are problematized and for whom boundaries are at risk. As the discussion of competing discourses of body power suggested, the Corinthians seem not to have been very troubled by questions of identities and boundaries. Power is focused and consolidated in tightly maintained boundaries; it is diffused and circulates more readily when not constrained.

CONCLUSIONS

The argument of this essay has been that competing interpretations of power are to be discerned from the discourse of Paul's first letter to the Corinthians, the interpretations of the Christian women and men of Corinth no less than those of the author of the letter. Rather than starting from the premise that Paul's discourse represents a 'solution' to the 'problems' in the Corinthian community – an interpretive presupposition that operates throughout commentaries on Paul's texts – this reading of 1 Corinthians began from the Foucaultian premise that social discourse is invariably linked to the establishment or arrangement of power relations. Rather than assuming the normativity of Paul's discourse, this reading asked questions about the discourses that were rendered 'deviant' or inexpressible by Paul's rhetorical framing of the issues.

Paul's discourse of power may be read as a complex fiction whereby he asserts the conditions of proper power relations in the Christian community at Corinth as truth. Put perhaps less provocatively, Paul's discourse functions as a form of rhetoric that Antoinette Wire has called (though from a slightly different point of view) 'arguments establishing the structure of reality'.[30] Such arguments are of course the most difficult to sustain, because they do not carry the force of arguments from evidence, but rather advocate what ought to be true by representing it as true.

Paul's discourse and that of some of the Corinthian Christians emerge as two competing imaginings of the workings of power within and among Christians. Where Paul sees danger in the overabundance and multiplicity of the spiritual lives of the Corinthians, they see bold possibilities of yet further access to knowledge and power. The image recurs of Paul reining in what to him is impropriety and disorder, trying to restore order and consolidate the power he understands to belong properly to him. His attempts to reduce what to him is the cacophonous discord of many voices result in his own bellowing tones filling the stage. Nevertheless, there remain crucial echoes of those other voices, heard in the straining tensions of Paul's own discourse. They render Paul's voice less univocal at every attempt to listen, and suggest the rich and exhilarating prospect of re-envisioning the complex discursive contexts that produced this text, its rhetoric and its effects. They are voices suggesting that, once one is willing to render Paul's rhetoric even momentarily contingent, other interpretations of power might reverberate and, for a moment, be rendered possible.

NOTES

1   See Walter Wink, *Naming the Powers: The Language of Power in the New Testament* (Philadelphia: Fortress Press, 1984) for a summary philological study of the language of power in the New Testament. Generally speaking, the sociologically grounded work, especially that on the letters of Paul dealing with power, conflates categories of 'authority' and 'power' without adequately theorizing either category. Alternatively, they are largely derivative of sociological studies drawing on the work of Max Weber or his school. See, as examples, John Howard Schütz, *Paul and the Anatomy of Apostolic Authority* (Cambridge: Cambridge University Press, 1975) and Bengt Holmberg, *Paul and Power: The Structure of Authority in the Primitive Church as Reflected in the Pauline Letters* (Philadelphia: Fortress Press, 1978).

2   This very helpful concept of 'value' drawing on the conceptual world of the visual arts – and thereby complicating its ethical resonances – was introduced to me by Chris Chamberlain, a student at the College of Wooster. I am grateful for his suggestive comments, which led me to think that the specular is not necessarily always bound to objectifying constraints.

3   'The political and social processes by which the Western European societies were put in order are not very apparent, have been forgotten or have become habitual. They are a part of our most familiar landscape, and we don't perceive them anymore. But most of them once scandalized people. It is one of my targets to show people that a lot of things that are part of their landscape – that people think are universal – are the result of some very precise historical changes. All my analyses are against the idea of universal necessities of human existence. They show the arbitrariness of institutions and show which space of freedom we can still enjoy and how many changes can still be made' (Michel Foucault, 'Truth, Power, Self: An Interview with Michel Foucault', ed. Rux Martin, in *Technologies of the Self: A Seminar with Michel Foucault*, ed. Luther H. Martin, Huck Gutman and Patrick H. Hutton, Amherst: University of Massachusetts Press, 1988, 9–15, quote p.11).

4   Hayden White, 'Foucault Decoded: Notes from Underground', in *Tropics of Discourse: Essays in Cultural Criticism* (Baltimore: Johns Hopkins University Press, 1978, pp.230–60); Hubert L. Dreyfus and Paul Rabinow, *Michel Foucault: Beyond Structuralism and Hermeneutics* (Chicago: University of Chicago Press, 1982); Mark Cousins and Athar Hussain, *Michel Foucault* (New York: St Martin's Press, 1974); David Couzens Hoy (ed.), *Foucault: A Critical Reader* (New York: Basil Blackwell, 1986); Gilles Deleuze, *Foucault*, ed. and trans. Seán Hand (Minneapolis: University of Minnesota Press, 1988); James Bernauer and David Rasmussen (eds), *The Final Foucault* (Cambridge: MIT Press, 1988).

5   Michel Foucault, *Folie et déraison: histoire de la folie à l'âge classique* (Paris: Plon, 1961). English translation of abridged edition: *Madness and Civilization: A History of Insanity in the Age of Reason*, trans. Richard Howard (New York: Random House, 1965).

6   Michel Foucault, *Les mots et les choses: une archéologie des sciences humaines* (Paris: Gallimard, 1966). English translation: *The Order of Things: An Archaeology of the Human Sciences*, trans. anon. (New York: Pantheon, 1971).

7   This question is answered through a series of investigations into the emergence of numerous 'modern' institutions where knowledge and power interact in the containment and management of the now marginalized. These studies of the development of the hospital (Michel Foucault, *Naissance de la clinique: Une archéologie du regard médical*, 2nd edn, Paris: Presses Universitaires de France, 1972; English translation: *The Birth of the Clinic: An Archaeology of Medical Perception*, trans. Alan Sheridan Smith, New York: Pantheon, 1973) and the prison (Michel Foucault, *Surveiller et punir: Naissance de la prison*, Paris: Gallimard, 1975; English translation: *Discipline and Punish: The Birth of the Prison*, trans. Alan Sheridan, New York: Vintage, 1979) trace the parallel tracks of increased management of the 'other' (the sick, the criminal) and the development of intellectual disciplines to understand/know them. One might reflect on the very development of the concept of 'discipline' in its multiplicity of significances – an arena of study as well as a form of constraint – within the academic realm to understand Foucault's point here, that knowledge and power are interactive and serve each other's interests.

8   Michel Foucault, *Histoire de la sexualité*, Vol. 1: *La volonté de savoir* (Paris: Gallimard, 1976); English translation: *The History of Sexuality*, Vol. 1: *Introduction*, trans. Robert Hurley (New York: Vintage, 1980); *Histoire de la sexualité*, Vol. 2: *L'usage des plaisirs* (Paris: Gallimard, 1984); English translation: *The Use of Pleasure*, trans. Robert Hurley (New York: Pantheon, 1985); *Histoire de la sexualité*, Vol. 3: *Le souci de soi* (Paris: Gallimard, 1984); English translation: *The Care of the Self*, trans. Robert Hurley (New York: Pantheon, 1986).

9   Michel Foucault, *Power/Knowledge: Selected Interviews and Other Writings, 1972–1977*, ed. Colin Gordon; trans. Colin Gordon *et al.* (New York: Pantheon, 1980, pp.198–9).

10   Foucault, *Discipline and Punish*, pp.26–7.

11   See, for example, *Elisabeth Schüssler Fiorenza, In Memory of Her: A Feminist Theological Reconstruction of Christian Origins* (New York: Crossroad Press, 1983); Antoinette Clark Wire, *The Corinthian Women Prophets: A Reconstruction through Paul's Rhetoric* (Minneapolis: Fortress Press, 1990).

12   There is a considerable body of literature dealing with the intersections of Foucault and feminism. See, for example, Irene Diamond and Lee Quinby (eds), *Feminism and Foucault: Reflections on Resistance* (Boston: Northeastern University Press, 1988); Isaac D. Balbus, 'Disciplining Women: Michel Foucault and the Power of Feminist Discourse', in *After Foucault: Humanistic Knowledge, Postmodern Challenges*, ed. Jonathan Arac (New Brunswick: Rutgers University Press, 1988, pp.138–60); Jana Sawicki, 'Feminism and the Power of Foucauldian Discourse', in *After Foucault: Humanistic Knowledge, Postmodern Challenges*, ed. Jonathan Arac (New Brunswick: Rutgers University Press, 1988, pp.161–78); Nancy Hartsock, 'Foucault on Power: A Theory for Women', in *Feminism/Postmodernism*, ed. Linda J. Nicholson (New York: Routledge, 1990, pp.157–75).

13   Foucault, *History of Sexuality*, Vol. 1, *Introduction*.

14   Wire, *The Corinthian Women Prophets*.

15   Interestingly, Lacan's phrase for the analyst is 'the subject presumed to know', who as such is an object of desire. See Jacques Lacan, *The Four Fundamental Concepts of Psycho-Analysis*, ed. Jacques-Alain Miller; trans. Alan Sheridan (New York: Norton, 1978, pp.230ff). Thanks to Stephen Moore for pointing out the psychoanalytic connection to me.

16 See especially Mary Douglas, *Purity and Danger: An Analysis of Pollution and Taboo* (Washington: Praeger, 1966); *Natural Symbols: Explorations in Cosmology* (New York: Vintage 1970); Victor W. Turner, *The Forest of Symbols* (Ithaca: Cornell University Press, 1967); A. van Gennep, *The Rites of Passage*, trans. M.B. Vizedom and G.L. Caffee (Chicago: University of Chicago Press, 1960); Pierre Bourdieu, *Outline of a Theory of Practice*, trans. R. Nice (Cambridge: Cambridge University Press, 1977).

17 The literature here is extensive. Most helpful for me have been Jean Comaroff, *Body of Power, Spirit of Resistance: The Culture and History of a South African People* (Chicago: University of Chicago Press, 1985), especially the elegant summary of the debate on pp. 6–9; Talal Asad, 'Anthropological Conceptions of Religion: Reflections on Geertz', *Man*, n.s. 18 (1983), pp.237–59; Michael Jackson, 'Knowledge of the Body', *Man*, n.s. 18 (1983), pp.327–45; Jean-Pierre Vernant, 'Dim Body, Dazzling Body', in *Fragments for a History of the Human Body*, ed. Michel Feher with Ramona Haddaff and Nadia Tazi (New York: Zone Books, 1989, vol. 1, pp.19–47).

18 Wayne A. Meeks, *The First Urban Christians: The Social World of the Apostle Paul* (New Haven: Yale University Press, 1983); Jerome H. Neyrey, 'Body Language in I Corinthians: The Use of Anthropological Models for Understanding Paul and his Opponents', *Semeia*, 35 (1986), 129–70.

19 See Hans Conzelmann, *1 Corinthians*, ed. George W. MacRae, trans. James W. Leitch (Philadelphia: Fortress Press, 1975, pp.14–16), for a brief introductory summary of the situation at Corinth through Paul's (and later commentators') eyes, and a good example of the process by which commentary on Paul's discourse approaches it as a 'solution' to a series of 'problems', rather than as problematic itself.

20 This is true not only for the discussion of the sexual practices of Corinthians, but also for their meal practices. Paul's concerns in Chs 5–7 are echoed in the discussion of meals in Chs 8–10 and the competing interpretations of power are structured in the same ways.

21 As Wire, *The Corinthian Women Prophets*, p.74, points out, the charge of frequenting a prostitute must be aimed specifically against men, not simply because the feminine form of the noun *pornê* is used, but also because men were the customers of both female and male prostitutes in Greco-Roman antiquity.

22 See Wire, *The Corinthian Women Prophets*, pp.82–3.

23 Wire, *The Corinthian Women Prophets*, p.182, has reconstructed the position of some Corinthian women, the prophets, rather elegantly, and summarizes their position in this way: 'In contrast to Paul, the women prophets in Corinth's church do not experience in themselves a struggle against God that requires radical restrictions of the body. Instead, the danger seems to be that the spirit poured out might be wasted if fearful people do not allow its exercise in themselves and the community. Many reject sexual relations that involve the authority of one person over the body of another in order to devote themselves to prayer and prophecy. But this does not exclude their support of the sexual bonds of others not ruled by such authority.'

24 The discussion of this passage has been extensive. See the appendix in Wire, *The Corinthian Women Prophets*, pp.220–23, for a summary and bibliography. See also Bernadette J. Brooten, 'Paul's Views on the Nature of Women and Female Homoeroticism', in *Immaculate and Powerful: The Female in Sacred Image and Social Reality*, ed. Clarissa W. Atkinson, Constance H. Buchanan and Margaret R. Miles (Boston: Beacon Press, 1985, pp.61–87).

25 See the classic formulation in Aristotle's *Politics* 1277a: 'Again, the state, as composed of unlikes, may be compared to the living being: as the first elements into which a living being is resolved are soul and body, as soul is made up of rational principle and appetite, the family of husband and wife, property of master and slave, so of all of these, as well as other dissimilar elements, the state is composed; and therefore the excellence of all the

citizens cannot possibly be the same, any more than the excellence of the leader of a chorus is the same as that of the performer who stands by his side.'

26   It may also be significant that Apollos is called a *paidagogos* since that social role is linked with education (the acquisition of knowledge), but it is a role characterized by teaching by rote as distinguished from the teaching role of a *didaskalos*. See Conzelmann, *1 Corinthians*, p.91, n.10.

27   This characterization of prophecy as both powerful and dangerous carries on in the ongoing institutionalization of the church, when movements like the New Prophecy and the prophetic activity associated with martyrdom will be rendered suspect because their claims to authority and power are immediate and diffuse, and circumvent the authority claims of office holders in the emerging hierarchy.

28   The controversy over this passage is summarized helpfully in Wire, *The Corinthian Women Prophets*, pp.229–32.

29   Elizabeth A. Castelli, *Imitating Paul: A Discourse of Power* (Louisville: Westminster John Knox Press, 1991).

30   Wire, *The Corinthian Women Prophets*, p. 35.

Chapter 2

Foucault, the Fathers and Sex

Elizabeth A. Clark

I

After Michel Foucault wrote the first volume of his *History of Sexuality*, he discovered that he could not adequately treat sexuality in modern history without first returning to antiquity. This discovery necessitated a change in approach and so slowed his progress that volumes two and three did not appear for another eight years (Lloyd: 25). The difference in tone between volumes one and two is evident to even the casual reader: the sweeping generalizations and scanty documentation of volume one have been superseded by a respectful approach to texts.[1] Indeed, so carefully does Foucault tiptoe from text to text in the subsequent volumes that admirers of his previous work may find his style plodding. More important, they will find that Foucault's earlier interest in developing an 'archaeological' theory of discourse has been drastically modified by attention to the social practices that link power, knowledge, and the body (Dreyfus and Rabinow, pp.xxiv–xxv, 56, 98, 102–5, 112, 175).

Foucault was impelled to undertake his antiquarian journey by his desire to challenge the prevalent contemporary theory that sexual repression originated in the seventeenth century as an accompaniment to the rise of capitalism, and that from this repression we have allegedly just now, and with much self-congratulation, freed ourselves.[2] Against this conventional assessment, Foucault argues that the early modern and modern eras saw not increased repression, but increased incitements to sexual discourse. In this period, for example, the 'problem' of population was discovered; children's masturbation was for the first time regarded as dangerous and in need of control; homosexuality was invented as a permanent personality state; the medical and the psychiatric examination that required patients to talk about sex was developed (1980a, pp.12–13, 23–30, 38, 42–5, 63). In all these areas, speech and writing about sex greatly expanded. Moreover, Foucault argued, these 'discoveries' and techniques were not first employed repressively against the lower classes as a means of control, as Marxist analysis would posit; rather, they were developed by the bourgeoisie and applied to themselves as a means of enhancing their own life, vigor, and progeny (1980a, pp.120–38).[3]

Foucault described his project for the *History of Sexuality* in various ways. He said, for example, that he aimed to explore how the understanding of the self as a subject of desire had unfolded. Rather than focus exclusively on mechanisms of power and their relation to language, as he had in some of his earlier books, he wished to construct a 'hermeneutics of the self' (1985a, pp.5–6) in which he would explore the ever-changing experience of the self as a sexual being throughout Western history (1981, p.5). How, he asked, had modern people come to believe that the deepest truth about themselves lay 'in the region of their sex?'(1980b, p.214). So keen was Foucault's interest to examine how our understanding of sexuality was related to our quest for 'truth' that he originally planned to name his series *Sex and Truth*, not *The History of Sexuality* (1980b, p.209). His project, however, had a further aim. For not only is there a truth about the self that we believe relates to sex; we also believe that this sexual truth must be talked about. How, Foucault asks, did sexual practices become transmuted into discourse about sex (1980b, p.210), most fully realized in psychoanalysis?[4] To answer his question, he turned back to seventeenth-century pastoral manuals, to eighteenth-century pedagogical treatises, and to nineteenth-century medical handbooks for assistance – but, as his knowledge of Christian antiquity grew, he came to place the origin of the pastoral, pedagogical, and medical techniques in the monastic practice of confession (1980b, p.211; 1980a, pp.19–20, 63, 159).[5] To understand Freud, he believed we must understand early Christian ascetic theory. Denying that Freud represented a cataclysmic break with all past thinking and writing on sexuality, Foucault asked his readers to examine with him 'the machinery of confession, within which in fact psychoanalysis and Freud figure as episodes' (1980b, pp.211–12). The word 'confession' he began to apply to 'all those procedures by which the subject is incited to produce a discourse of truth about his own sexuality which is capable of having effects upon the subject himself' (1980b, pp.215–16). By returning to Christian antiquity and beyond, Foucault thought that he could both overturn the so-called 'repressive hypothesis' *and* explain how the human experience of sex had shifted its locus of intensity from sexual acts to 'sex in the head' (1981, p.5).

After his retreat to study ancient texts, Foucault's second volume of *The History of Sexuality* was published, translated into English as *The Use of Pleasure*. Its subject matter was classical Greece. Foucault projected that in the four volumes to follow he would bring the reader to the early twentieth century and examine the continuities and discontinuities between Plato's Athens and Freud's Vienna. Unfortunately, the project will never be realized, for Foucault died in 1984. By then, three volumes had been published, and materials for a fourth volume on early Christianity were being assembled. Whether these will be published under the title projected, *The Confessions of the Flesh*, still is unclear. Nonetheless, from the published volumes and from essays written and interviews given shortly before Foucault died, we glean some impression of the figures on whom he intended to dwell: Clement of Alexandria, Tertullian, Augustine, John Cassian.

What would have been Foucault's major theme in the projected fourth volume? In a review of volume three (which concerns Rome), historian John Boswell predicts the thesis of the next volume:

> this preoccupation with the well-being of self that Foucault had detailed among the Romans [in the volume Boswell reviewed] becomes the basis for a Christian ethics in which the salvation of the individual soul is the fulcrum of moral activity and thought; Roman advice about how to optimize health and happiness is transformed into absolute rules about how to behave to attain salvation. (1987, p.31)

Foucault himself gives more explicit hints:

> In the Christian book – I mean the book about Christianity! – I try to show that all this ethics [of the Greeks and the Romans] has changed. Because the telos has changed: the telos is immortality, purity, and so on. The asceticism has changed, because now self-examination takes the form of self-deciphering. The *mode d'assujettissement* is now divine law. And I think that even the ethical substance has changed, because it is not *aphrodisia*, but desire, concupiscence, flesh, and so on. (1983b, p.242)

> In the Christian morality of sexual behavior, the ethical substance was to be defined, not by the *aphrodisia*, but by a domain of desires that lie hidden among the mysteries of the heart, and by a set of acts that are carefully specified as to their form and their conditions. Subjection was to take the form not of a *savoir-faire*, but of a recognition of the law and an obedience to pastoral authority. Hence the ethical subject was to be characterized not so much by the perfect rule of the self by the self in the exercise of a virile type of activity, as by self-renunciation and a purity whose model was to be sought in virginity. (1985a, p.92)

To be sure, Foucault also wished to note the continuities between pagan and Christian sexual understanding. The very organization of his project suggested his interest in the continuities. In each volume, he proposed, he would look at four themes: the life of the body, the institution of marriage, relationships between men, and the understanding of wisdom (1985a, p.21). As he announced in *The Use of Pleasure*, he would explore transmutations in these themes as he progressed from volume to volume. He would ask, 'How, given the continuity, transfer, or modification of codes, the forms of self-relationship (and the practices of the self that were associated with them) were defined, modified, recast and diversified' (1985a, pp.31–2, cf. 1981, p.5). In subsequent volumes, Foucault envisioned that he would trace such transmutations, such unities-in-diversities, from the Golden Age of Athens to the Golden Age of psychoanalysis.

My argument will be that, despite the obvious discontinuities between pagan and Christian sexual understandings,[6] there are continuities of theme even beyond those Foucault himself had recognized. To note that the Roman marital ethic – as characterized by Foucault – bears many resemblances to its Christian counterpart constitutes no new scholarly observation. More striking, perhaps, are the ways in which the goals Foucault ascribed to the Greeks' sexual self-cultivation (for example, 'a stylization of attitudes and an aesthetics of existence' [1985a, p.92]) reappear, transmuted, in early Christian asceticism. Before exploring Christian themes, however, we must return to Foucault's Greeks and Romans.

II

According to Foucault's reading of the Greeks, their desideratum was the creation of a beautiful life – a desideratum, that is, for males of a certain class (1985a, p.2; cf. 82). The free male of the upper class (for it is he of whom Foucault writes) governed himself through an 'aesthetics of existence' (1985a, pp.12, 89; 1983b, p.231). He attempted to create 'a way of life whose moral value did not depend either on one's being in conformity with a code of behavior, or on an effort of purification' – both distinctively Christian contributions to the development of sexual ethics, Foucault claims – 'but on certain formal principles in the use of pleasures, in the way one distributed them, in the limits one observed, in the hierarchy one respected' (1985a, p.89). To enhance one's position as a free male (1985a, pp.79, 97), a position from which one could dominate others within both the household and the larger society, the regulation of sexual acts ('the use of pleasures', in Foucault's phrase) was necessary (1985a, p.53). This 'use of pleasures' did not concern itself with distinguishing forbidden from permitted sexual acts, but rather with the prudent calculation of 'more and less' (1985a, pp. 116, 53–4). Consideration should be taken of one's need, the correct timing of the act, one's status in relation to the partner (1985a, p.54). Quantity and circumstances were the decisive factors, not sexual practices per se (1985a, p.114). A prudent self-regulation of the free male's sexual life was in accord with other types of self-regulation he practiced, such as that of food and drink (1985a, pp.50–55; cf. 99–108; 1983b, p.229).[7]

This sexual ethic, Foucault argues, was not universalizable, nor was it meant to be; it was not for *hoi polloi*, but for those elite males who wished to shape for themselves more brilliant lives than those of their fellow men (1985a, p.62). In accordance with such an ethic, sexual 'immorality' concerned only two areas: 'excess' (as just noted) and 'passivity' (1985a, pp.44–7). The theme of 'passivity' leads Foucault to a discussion of Greek homosexual practices, specifically, of pederasty. Foucault notes how many Greek texts that discuss sexual acts, the creation of the self, and the search for truth revolve around the theme of pederasty, no doubt because it was in pedagogical practice that sex and 'truth' were linked (1980a, p.61). According to the ancient Greek ethic, so long as a man were the active sexual partner, it mattered not whether the other were a male or a female; a 'passive' partner of either sex was consonant with his 'moral mastery' of the self (1985a, pp.84–5, cf. 188, 192). The problem of pederasty lay elsewhere: namely, how could a free boy, destined to be a citizen who governed the *polis*, allow himself to have been earlier the *object* of pleasure, to have been dominated and penetrated by another with whom he did not share (according to the received wisdom) a common pleasure? (1985a, pp.220–21, 223).[8] The problem thus lay not with the act per se (as it later would in Christian sexual ethics), but with possible obstacles to the boy's self-realization.

Ancient Greek marriages likewise manifested a dissymmetry of power, but of a different sort. Whereas the wife, always under the husband's control, must restrict her sexual activity to the marital bed, the sexual regulation of the husband rested on quite another principle: if he chose to restrain his sexual pleasures, it was out of no obligation to his wife, but because only thus could he exhibit his self-mastery (1983a, pp.151, 165).[9] His obligation was to himself alone, to his self-cultivation, to the enhancement of his own prestige (1985a, pp. 82–3). Foucault convincingly argues that there was thus for elites in ancient Athens a certain isomorphism between sexual and social relations: whether in the household or in the *polis*, there was always one who penetrates, who demands, who dominates, and one who is penetrated, who is commanded, and who complies (1985a, p.215; cf. 1986, pp.29, 31–2). The foretaste of the future – a future of 'indefinite abstention' for the sake of truth – comes only with Plato, and as Foucault notes, Plato's encouragement to long-term abstention 'could not easily be accommodated in an ethics organized around a search for the right use of pleasure' (1985a, pp. 245–6).[10]

According to Foucault, the breakdown of the *polis* in the Hellenistic and Roman eras occasioned social changes that recast the formulation of sexual ethics (1986, p.84), although he makes much less of the changed historical circumstances than we might expect.[11] (For example, the break in the isomorphism of public and private life is mentioned only briefly [1986, pp.81–97 passim]). The modifications that occurred in Roman sexual ethics were several. For one, there was much less concern than in Greek writings to center the 'problem' of sexual discourse around the topic of boys (1985a, pp.189–90). Foucault notes that even when pederasty is discussed in the Roman texts, the descriptive terms are taken from the model of the marriage relation (1986, p.225),[12] now accorded a centrality it never held in classical Athens (1986, pp.193, 204). In texts dating from the second century B.C.E. to the second century C.E. (especially those by Plutarch and the later Stoics), the personal relationship of the married couple receives major attention (1986, p.148). The 'Greek' model of male dominance and female submission is here replaced by one of mutuality. There is to be a *shared* pleasure between husband and wife; the husband owes respect to the wife, not just to himself (1986, pp.148–9). According to Roman writers, both husband and wife will restrict their sexual relation (in theory at least) to the spouse (1986, pp.173, 175). A man's intense erotic relationship is to be enjoyed with his wife, not with boys (1986, p.180). In addition to procreation, companionship and mutual care are stressed by Hellenistic and Roman writers as central to the marital relation (1986, p.151 [Musonius Rufus]; p.182). Moreover, claims Foucault, these new marital patterns were meant not only for elites who wished to create beautiful lives, but were universalizable: *all* humans can follow the promptings of reason and 'nature', whatever their social status (1986, p.67), and these promptings suggest a more egalitarian model of marriage.

With the Roman relocation of pleasure in the marriage partnership went a greater sexual austerity, a stronger tendency to asceticism, than Foucault believes was characteristic of the classical Greeks (1986, pp.177–80).[13] Medical texts now detail the dangers of sexual activity: the sexual act is compared to disease (for example, epilepsy), and abnormal sexual states (for example, satyriasis) rather than regimens for healthy sexual functioning are stressed (1986, pp. 109–11, 113–17). Another sign of growing ascetic trends, according to Foucault, lies in the themes of the Hellenistic Romances: the virginity of the lovers is brought to the fore. The hero and heroine's abstention reminds us of what was shortly to come, Christian asceticism. Indeed, Foucault characterizes the abstention of these couples in the same words with which he describes Christian asceticism: it 'is modeled much more on virginal integrity than on the political and virile domination of desires' (1986, p.228), the model of restraint that he assigns to Athenian males.

Foucault's treatment of Christian materials requires a more energetic 'leap of faith' than the historian would desire, for only scattered references to specific Christian writers and their theories can be found in his work published to date (1980b, p.211). Yet Foucault's comments in his three volumes of *The History of Sexuality*, in interviews, and in essays, enable the commentator to attempt at least a modest reconstruction of his proposed argument. In a variey of ways, Foucault isolates the changes in sexual ethics brought by Christian teaching. Let me review them briefly.

First, he states, the 'aesthetics of the self', so central to classical Greek ethics, is replaced by an ethic of self-renunciation; according to Christian writers, the 'truth' of the self can be known only by giving it up (1983b, pp.245, 248). Moreover, the problematic center of discussion shifts from the realm of sexual acts and the pleasure derived from them to desire itself. For early Christians, even a married couple's sexual acts – the only permitted ones – should be 'neutral', that is, not prompted by desire. Ideally, pleasure should be completely excluded from consideration. Yet, Foucault notes, although desire was to be excluded in *practice*, it gained a *theoretical* importance in early Christianity as the seat of the 'problem' of sex (1983b, pp.238, 242–3; 1985a, p.254). He writes:

> Classical techniques of austerity which were a means to self-mastery were transformed into techniques whose purpose was the purification of desire and the elimination of pleasure, so that austerity became an end in itself. (1983b, p.255)

In their fear of 'pollution', Christians emphasize purity, not mere self-regulation (1981, p.5; 1983b, p.242). Unwilled sexual desires and their accompanying bodily movements are understood to be inflicted upon a passive subject: the virile and active sexual ideal of the Greeks, Foucault posits, has given way to a passive and 'feminine' understanding of sex. Physical integrity and intactness, a 'female' paradigm, replace the 'male' ideal of domination of self (1985a, pp.82, 92; 1986, p.29; 1983b, p.247; 1981, p.5) – and penetration of others, we might add.

Ultimately, the thematization of sexual issues by Christian writers no longer concerns acts with another person, but the problem of one's solitude. Now, for the first time, masturbation and 'wayward thoughts' are held as central moral problems (1986, p.40; 1981, p.5; 1985b, pp.18–22). And, Foucault posits, as the experience of sex shifts away from acts with other people and toward the privately-felt desire of the individual, an essential new task is defined: self-examination, the raising up of one's sexual thoughts for analysis and 'discrimination'. In a monastic setting, such analysis often involved the advice of an elder monk to a younger one (1983b, p.242; 1981, p.5; 1985b, p.23). Such decipherment and elucidation of thoughts were deemed essential by the monks for ascetic purification (1985a, p.70) – and by Foucault, for later practices involving discourse about sex.

Last, according to Foucault, Christians codified the sexual acts that were deemed necessary to submit to ecclesiastical authority (1985a, p.92), an important step in the development of the confessional (described as a procedure 'for the extortion of truth' [1980b, p.217]).[14] He sees such developments in Christianity as pivotal between Greek and Roman sexual theorizing, on the one hand, and the insights of the psychoanalyst's couch, on the other. Early Christian asceticism, in Foucault's scheme, thus provides the locus for an essential stage in the development of sexual discourse.

III

As a student of early Christian asceticism, I propose several modifications to Foucault's approach. Rather than canvass the vast corpus of early Christian ascetic literature, I focus my discussion on materials pertaining to the desert fathers of Egypt. My first qualification of Foucault's argument is modest: even with the desert monks, we have not entirely left the realm of sexual activity for 'sex in the head'. The textual evidence rather suggests that this upward displacement of the sexual was not always fully achieved. Many women inhabited the desert and many others came on pilgrimages to see the holy men living there. The desert fathers worry whether to meet these female admirers[15] and whether they should visit female relatives living in nearby convents.[16] They tell stories of ascetics who were accused (falsely) of impregnating village girls,[17] of monks who received proposals of marriage,[18] of monks who did 'fall' sexually.[19] They wondered at Amoun, who lived in celibacy for eighteen years with the wife he had been forced to marry in his youth.[20] On a practical level, they questioned whether a woman's body could be touched,[21] and on a theoretical one, whether a monk could lie with a naked virgin and have his heart remain peaceful (the experiment was not recommended).[22] For the monks in Egypt, sex was not something that had to do *only* with oneself in one's solitude – although, to be sure, Foucault is correct in his assertion that the majority of texts center on control of one's mind and desire, not on sexual acts with another.

This point may seem carping, however, since the ascetic literature that most interested Foucault was not so much the sayings of and the stories about the desert fathers, such as those mentioned above, but the monks' 'theoretical' discussions of sexual desire.[23] Thus one of Foucault's central subjects was to be John Cassian, who lived in the Egyptian desert for at least seven years and later reported the advice given by the elders to him and his companion Germanus (Chadwick, pp.13–19). Among the ascetic masters whose teaching informed Cassian's theory was Evagrius Ponticus, and although Foucault does not discuss Evagrius in his now-published works, he surely would have treated him in volume four since Evagrius was the leading 'ascetic theorist' of early monastic Christianity (Chadwick, pp.92–4).[24] Foucault could have drawn much support from Evagrius and Cassian for his argument that in the monasteries of late antiquity, sexual activity became transformed into sexual discourse. Evagrius' own words would give him a key: 'The demons strive against men of the world chiefly through their deeds, but in the case of monks, for the most part by means of thoughts.'[25] Yet both Evagrius' and Cassian's discussions, I would argue, contain themes that call into question too easy a passage from the Egyptian desert to Freud's Vienna.

Central to Evagrius' ascetic theology is the monk's cultivation of *apatheia*, passionlessness or 'lack of feeling'.[26] It is feeling that leads to desire and desire that leads to pleasure,[27] the downfall of the monk. The human memory, with its 'thoughts', poses constant problems for these inhabitants of the desert.[28] In addition, demons attack the monks with phantasms to spur their lust, and they hum suggestive melodies in their ears.[29] From these mental or demonic suggestions, monks must withhold assent.[30] If monks stay on guard while they are awake, there is a better chance that their minds and bodies will stay pure while they sleep.[31] In this much, Foucault would have found support for his thesis in Evagrius' writings.

Evagrius' advice on self-examination, however, leads to some emphases different from Foucault's. For example, Evagrius does not support the notion that examining one's thoughts and desires necessarily leads to discussion about them (except, of course, insofar as Evagrius himself wrote down his insights). To the contrary, dwelling on one's 'thoughts' can be outrightly dangerous, for they impel the ascetic to a state of lust.[32] Although Evagrius advises the monk to note when these 'thoughts' arise and subside and with what associations they come to mind, he does not suggest that the monk talk about them. He advises instead that the monk submit these matters to Christ and await an explanation from him.[33]

John Cassian, too, recognized this problem. Although he explicitly counsels young monks to confess to their elders,[34] who will teach the juniors remedies,[35] he also is aware of how counterproductive the process can be: when an ascetic recollects his own sins or ponders the 'falls' of another, he may feel a delight and an assent that run contrary to his struggle against sin.[36] Indeed, discussing such subjects with an elder or even hearing Scriptural verses about human generation can constitute temptation and lead a monk astray.[37] Thus Evagrius and Cassian's advice provides somewhat less firm a way-station on the road of 'incitements to sexual discourse' than we might have expected on the basis of Foucault's comments.[38]

Moreover, although knowledge of the self may be a goal both for monasticism and for psychoanalysis, the *motivation* differs drastically: for Cassian, the function of confession is to promote humility by subjecting oneself to another's will. The exercise is a cultivation in humility, not an uncovering of the sub-conscious.[39] Not to confess, Cassian claims, means that a monk relies on his *own* judgment rather than on that of someone older and wiser[40] – and self-reliance is a main mechanism by which the Devil is given opportunity for attack.[41] Since mortification of the will is necessary before lust can be bridled,[42] obedience to the elder that is achieved through confession is imperative for the monk's religious cultivation. And yet – still another problem – the desire for perfect obedience carries its own dangers, for it tempts the monk to pride, a worse sin than simple lust ever was.[43] Cassian affords clear proof that Freud has no monopoly on the exploration of the psyche's deviousness.

In addition, Foucault is aware that some transformations of Western sexual ethics took place *within* the framework of early Christianity: the transformation was not simply *between* the Greeks and the Romans, on the one hand, and the Christians, on the other. Thus in writing of John Cassian, Foucault recognizes that Cassian's concerns were not those of Clement of Alexandria, who lived two hundred years earlier. Foucault notes – but only in passing – that Cassian is no longer interested, as Clement had been, in the two major elements of ancient sexual theory, namely, 'the sexual union of two individuals (*sunousia*) and the pleasure of the act (*aphrodisia*)' (1985b, p.20). In his published work, however, Foucault does not reflect on the *meaning* of this difference between Clement and Cassian. If he had, he might have modified his model of difference between Greek and Roman sexual ethics, on one hand, and the Christian, on the other. A more nuanced model of early Christian sexual ethics could even borrow from Foucault's own description of the Greeks and the Romans: one line of development could be posited from Foucault's 'Romans' to married Christians; a second, quite different, line of development from Foucault's 'Athenians' to Christian ascetics. This seemingly enigmatic differentiation requires explication.

The advice and prescriptions given by the church fathers to married Christians follow quite closely Foucault's 'Roman' model. Thus when Foucault states that Clement's discussion of marital sexual ethics in *Paedagogus* II, 10 'draws on a set of principles and precepts borrowed directly from pagan philosophy' (1985a, p.15), he notes a theme discussed by scholars before him.[44] For example, Clement's views that exemplary married persons should perform sexual intercourse without passion, and that sexual faithfulness is incumbent upon the husband as well as upon the wife,[45] are not so different from the sober advice of Musonius Rufus.[46] In prescriptions such as these, we can see an intensification, rather than an abandonment, of the ideals Foucault has labelled 'Roman'.

When Foucault broaches Christian ascetic literature, however, he provides no explanation for the difference in themes discussed by Clement and those discussed by Cassian. His 'non-discussion' is no surprise, however, for there is no straightforward line of development from the one to the other. Rather, some characteristics of Greek (not Roman) sexual experience, as Foucault describes it, reappear in transmuted form in the monastic literature of the late fourth and fifth centuries. Recall Foucault's characterization of these Greek sexual values: a free male practices self-domination or self-mastery in order to create a life more brilliant than that of his fellow humans, and his elitist ethic is accompanied by a quest for self-knowledge, for 'truth'.

The values that Foucault assigned to elite Greek males re-emerge, transformed, in the theorizing of the desert monks. For the monks, combat against the self is the primary task. Self-mastery has been transformed into a holy war. Thus, thoughts of sex must be resolutely combatted;[47] recollections of kin warred against[48] (not to speak of actual relatives);[49] battles must be waged against the desire for possessions,[50] for food,[51] for sleep.[52] As the issue was succinctly put by the desert father Antony, although the solitary has freed himself from hearing, speaking, and seeing, 'yet against one thing shall he continually battle, that is, his own heart'.[53] The 'solo contest' (1985a, p.68) Foucault attributes to the Greek male pursuing an ethic of 'virile self-mastery' fits well in the new arena of monastic combat. Relatively few texts, in comparison, bear out Foucault's claim that the monks manifest a 'feminine' desire for 'intactness'. Self-domination was perhaps even more important for them than for the Greek males to whom Foucault appeals.

Whether through this combat a state of total self-mastery could be achieved was debated by Christian ascetics themselves. Some desert fathers thought that it was impossible *not* to be plagued by 'thoughts';[54] according to them, if a monk did not fight against sin in his mind, he was likely to sin in the flesh instead.[55] Others, such as Evagrius Ponticus, thought that a state of perfect self-mastery could be achieved in which the monk would no longer struggle against disturbing impulses, for he would have none.[56] There were, however, distressingly few exemplars of this passionless state: Evagrius himself is said to have suffered from lust,[57] and the one desert father who was reputed to have conquered desire, Serenus, had achieved his passionless state when an angel removed the 'fiery flesh' from his groin, thus extirpating his sexual desire.[58] Since not many could expect to be rendered 'apathetic' (in the original meaning of the word) by such supernatural operations, the struggle for self-mastery persisted.

The arenas of desire and bodily movement that a Christian monk was expected to dominate were, of course, more extensive than those to which the Athenian male might attend. The monk's problem was often located in areas that seemed indominatable: wandering thoughts, sexual dreams, erections, nocturnal emissions. But even in these seemingly intractable areas, Evagrius Ponticus and Cassian proferred practical advice for the monk that they claimed would lead to success. In addition to keeping close guard over his daytime thoughts, the monk is assisted by a practical regimen: the restriction of food and water ('gluttony' was thought to be closely related to attacks of lust).[59] Cassian himself was advised that if he ate only two pieces of bread a day, took just a few sips of water, and slept no more than three or four hours a night, he could, with God's help, conquer his nocturnal problems within six months.[60] As Aline Rousselle has shown, since even what the monks counted as a rarely-enjoyed 'banquet' consisted in about 1069 calories, their bodies, usually provided with much less nourishment, must have been so physically depleted that sexual desire would fade as a result of malnourishment alone, as modern medical literature demonstrates (p. 223).

Thus Foucault's claim that in Christian asceticism we have moved from the Greek model of self-domination to a 'feminine' model of passivity, that the central theme of sexual discourse switches from 'penetration' to 'intactness' (1983b, p.247), requires qualification. To be sure, although males of the desert are no longer sexually 'penetrating' others and are themselves being 'penetrated' by the Devil's arrows (a common *topos* in monastic literature),[61] they still exhibit that quality of self-mastery that Foucault found characteristic of Athenian male ideals. The model of physical 'intactness' that Foucault deems so important in monastic literature arises relatively late, and is most notably associated with the theme of Mary's perpetual virginity, including her virginity *in partu*. It is no accident that the prime advocates of Mary's perpetual virginity in the late fourth century, Ambrose and Jerome, are the very authors who counsel Christian virgins of their own day to keep their 'gardens enclosed', their 'fountains sealed', language they borrow from the Song of Songs.[62] All in all, however, freedom from pollution and physical 'intactness' are stressed far less than self-domination.

A last point concerning the self-domination theme: unlike the Athenian elite women, described by Foucault as those who were mastered, dominated, and penetrated by another, the women of the desert, like their male counterparts, are described as self-dominating. We hear of a certain Candida, who arose at night to grind corn, fire the oven, and bake bread for the Eucharist in order to subdue her body by manual labor and lack of sleep – and, as she allegedly put it, in order to 'do away with the greedy appetite of Esau'.[63] Of the abbess Sarah, we learn that she contended with the demon of lust for seven years before she finally conquered him.[64] This was probably the same Sarah who reportedly claimed that although she was a woman in sex, she was not one in spirit.[65] 'Virile self-mastery', it appears, was not restricted to males, either of classical Athens or of the Egyptian desert.[66]

A second characteristic that Foucault ascribed to the Athenian male was the desire to create for himself a life more brilliant than that of his fellow men. He would fashion an 'aesthetics of existence' that would set him apart. To achieve this special brilliance, the male would impose various restrictions upon himself, sexual ones included. The creation of the exceptional life, however, is a prominent theme in monastic literature as well. The striving for an exceptional life received (so it was imagined) support from Jesus himself: 'If you would be *perfect*, sell your goods, give to the poor, and come and follow me.'[67] We are told that these words formed the inspiration for Antony's original renunciation.[68] Moreover, Jesus also had allegedly emphasized in his teaching about types of eunuchs that 'not all' would be able to become eunuchs for the sake of the Kingdom of Heaven.[69] Asceticism thus became the preferred mode of life for Christians who strove for a perfection through which they could escape the downward pull of worldly concerns, of family, of sexual activity. That we tend not to associate asceticism with an 'aesthetics of existence' reveals our overemphasis on the material conditions of asceticism – the dirt, the vermin – and our relative neglect of the ascetics' fastidious grooming of their psyches.

As Evagrius Ponticus expressed this Christian elitism, a distinction should be made between 'the righteous' and 'the perfect': 'the righteous' were those who kept free of adultery and other earthly perversities, but not from possessions and the world's business – unlike 'the perfect', ascetics who were free from desire itself and who rose above the entire earthly heritage.[70] As Cassian put it, the commandment 'Thou shalt not commit adultery' was to be interpreted literally by those – but only those – who were 'still in bondage to foul passions';[71] the ascetic had surpassed the need for any such literally-interpreted laws. Those who still lived in the realm of 'law' (that is, the life of reproduction) rather than that of 'grace' (that is, the life of virginity) were prone to slide down the slippery slope from lawful married intercourse to unlawful adultery with alarming alacrity. But for those who renounced even what was 'lawful' (namely, marriage) through their choice of asceticism, 'unlawful' acts could not even pose themselves as temptations.[72] Thus ascetic piety itself created an elite class, the virgins who were equated with the onehundredfold harvest in Jesus's parable – as contrasted with the lowly thirtyfold harvest that represented the married.[73] Moreover – *pace* Foucault – no divine or ecclesiastical law, no pastoral authority, required this striving for a special excellence above and beyond the precepts all Christians were expected to observe; it was a self-imposed restriction.

To be sure, the elitism of 'perfect' Christian ascetics differed in some respects from the elitism of Foucault's Athenian males. Although a surprising number of early ascetic leaders came from privileged backgrounds,[74] the creation of a brilliant ascetic life was open both to those from humble backgrounds[75] and to women, two categories of people deemed incapable of having beautiful lives by ancient Greek standards. Thus a democratizing of opportunity existed in tandem with an elitism based on choice and achievement. Monastic elitism created its own special dangers, however, for if the monks succumbed to pride, the glory of their lives would be ruined: when a monk 'fell', how much the demons loved to chant the Scriptural verse, 'Whoever raises himself up shall be abased!'[76]

The third characteristic Foucault ascribes to the Greek sexual ethic is the pursuit of self-knowledge. Here Foucault's argument founders, for he bolsters his case by an appeal to Plato's view that long-term abstention would assist the quest for 'knowing thyself' (1985a, part 5, esp. pp.245–6), yet he is hard-pressed to find any *other* Greek males who valued sexual renunciation in the quest for 'truth', if they had any interest in such a quest to begin with. Plato stands alone, unintegrated into Foucault's scheme, a harbinger of future ideals but not representative of those of his own day. This point has been scored by other commentators (Lloyd, p.28).[77] As Foucault himself admits, Plato's teaching in the *Symposium* and the *Phaedrus* runs against the grain of traditional Greek wisdom about pleasure, and raises questions that would eventually transform the Greek ethic into one of renunciation (1985a, pp.229–30).[78] 'Indefinite abstention … could not easily be accommodated in an ethic organized around the search for the right use of pleasure' (1985a, p.230). The view that Foucault ascribes to Plato, however unrepresentative of ancient Greek ideals, illustrates well the values of

Christian monastics: the quest for truth, now identified with the quest for God, is the very goal of the monk's *askēsis* (1985a, pp.245–6).

The monk's search for truth, however, was fraught with dangers unknown to an ancient Athenian, for the monk lived in a world peopled by demons who delighted to lead monks astray by appearing as powers of goodness. Thus both Antony and Cassian report that demons can transform themselves into angels of light.[79] They lure the monk to 'holiness' by waking him for prayer and by encouraging him to eat nothing[80] – and this for the sake of causing him to stumble in his renunciation. The Devil tricks the monk into thinking that love of family is praiseworthy – so he can implant avarice in his heart.[81] Demons sing holy songs and recite Scripture, like exemplary monks[82] – but only to get the ascetic in their power. Worst of all, they solemnly pronounce the ascetic to be 'blessed',[83] even predicting that he will attain the priesthood[84] – thus leading him to pride, the deadly sin. The Egyptian ascetic had as many grave problems in discerning falsehood from truth as did the prisoners in Plato's cave who were released into the blinding sunlight,[85] but whereas the eyes of Plato's prisoners would grow accustomed to the light, the monk could exist in lifelong trepidation that he might, at the very end, mistake falseness for truth. Certainty was reserved for the moment of death.

Thus through my reading of the patristic texts, I am prompted to modify Foucault's scheme in several ways, most notably to suggest a double path leading from the ethics of the Greeks and the Romans to early Christian monastic values, on the one hand, and to the ideals of Christian marriage, on the other. These 'Greek' and 'Roman' roads merged in medieval Christianity to the extent that confession became incumbent upon married *lay* Christians, not simply upon monks. But for the late ancient period, I would gloss Athanasius' famous line that the popularity of asceticism had made 'the desert a city':[86] the 'city' it became, I would argue, shares slightly more with ancient Athens, but perhaps somewhat less with *fin de siècle* Vienna, than Foucault himself imagined.[87]

NOTES

1 So noted also by Halperin (p.277).
2 Foucault warns his unwary readers that 'saying yes' to sex does not mean (as is popularly thought) that we have 'said no' to power (1980a, p.157).
3 Foucault emphasizes that if this phenomenon represents *anything* about 'class struggle', it concerns the bourgeoisie's attempt to usurp prerogatives of the nobility (1980a, pp.128–9).
4 The question reveals that Foucault had by no means abandoned his interest in power, for he claims that it is discourse itself that links power and knowledge (1980a, p.100); cf. Foucault's comment in an interview (1980b, p.187) that 'the whole point of the project lies in a re-elaboration of the theory of power'.
5 Cf. Dreyfus and Rabinow, pp.173–8.
6 That Foucault makes no provision for the influence of Jewish sexual ethics on early Christianity will strike students of the period as an odd omission.
7 Halperin (pp.282–3).
8 Cf. 1985a (p.212): can the boy achieve self-mastery in not yielding to others? See also 1983b (pp.232–3).

9   1985a, p.184: 'The wife's virtue constituted the correlative and the proof of submissive behavior; the man's austerity was part of an ethics of self-delimiting domination.'

10   That Foucault underestimated ascetic trends in ancient Greek philosophy seems clear. For example, he nowhere deals extensively with the ethical theory of the Old Stoics. See note 13 below.

11   As noted by critics, for example, Lloyd (p.28).

12   Discussing Pseudo-Lucian's *Affairs of the Heart*.

13   Because Foucault overlooks ascetic tendencies in Greek philosophy that influenced later Roman philosophers as well as the church fathers, he is led to posit a larger gap between Greek sexual ethics and later Roman and Christian ones than seems warranted. Both Zeno and Chrysippus, for example, called for the eradication of the passions: *SVF* I, 205–15; III, 443, 448.

14   Cf. Payer (1985, pp.313–7) on confessionals.

15   *Historia monachorum in Aegypto* I, 4; 7–8 (SubsHag 53, 10, 11); *Verba seniorum* (= *Vitae patrum* V) 2, 7 (PL 73, 858–9).

16   *Vita Pachomii* 27 (Bohairic) (CSCO 89 = Scriptores Coptici 7, p. 26; Latin translation, CSCO 107 = Scriptores Coptici 11, pp. 18–19).

17   *Apophthegmata patrum*, Macarius of Egypt 1 (PG 65, 257, 260).

18   *Questions of the Brethren and Answers of the Fathers* 27 (Martinyana) (Budge, II: 1026–7).

19   Palladius (?), *The Second Book of the Histories of the Fathers* 24 (Stephana), (Budge, I: 400–03).

20   Palladius, *Historia Lausiaca* 8 (Butler, II: 26–8).

21   *Verba seniorum* (= *Vitae patrum* V) 4, 68 (PL 73, 873); Palladius, *Historia Lausiaca* 68 (Butler, II: 163–4).

22   John Cassian, *Conlationes* 15, 10 (SC 54, 220).

23   Whether such concentration on the sexual theme was characteristic of the Coptic-speaking monks or only of the Greek-educated monastic theorists remains a grave historical problem. I thank Coptic scholar David Johnson for reminding me of the discrepancy in the sources (private correspondence of 10/1/87).

24   For Armand Veilleux's assessment of Evagrius' importance, see his essay, 'The Origins of Egyptian Monasticism', in Skudlarek (p.48).

25   Evagrius Ponticus, *Practicos* 48 (SC 171, 608).

26   Evagrius Ponticus, *Practicos* 2; 33: 87 (SC 171, 498, 574, 678).

27   Evagrius Ponticus, *Practicos* 4 (SC 171, 502).

28   Evagrius Ponticus, *Practicos* 34 (SC 171, 578); idem, *De oratione* 46 (PG 79, 1176); idem, *Admonitio paraenetica* 4; 5 (Muyldermans, Syriac: 126–7; French: 158); *Expositio in parabolas et in Proverbia Solamonis* 6 (Muyldermans, Syriac; 134; French: 163).

29   Evagrius Ponticus, *Practicos* 8; 54; 71 (SC 171, 510, 512, 624, 658).

30   Evagrius Ponticus, *Practicos* 75 (SC 171, 662). The withholding of assent was an important epistemological issue as early as Zeno (*SVF* I, 61) and Chrysippus (*SVF* III, 177), became well-known through the Sceptic teaching on *epochē*, and, from there, influenced the Sceptical Academy. That the topic was of concern to some intellectual Christians is shown in Augustine's *Contra Academicos*.

31   Evagrius Ponticus, *Practicos* 55; 56; 64 (SC 171, 628, 630, 632, 648); idem, *Colloquium magistri cum discipulo eius* (Muyldermans, Syriac: 123–4; French: 156).

32   Evagrius Ponticus, *Practicos* 23 (SC 171, 554).

33   Evagrius Ponticus, *Practicos* 50 (SC 171, 614). Antony recommended that the hermit note down his thoughts and the 'movement of his soul': *Vita Antonii* 55 (PG 26, 924–5). Foucault discusses this passage in 1983a, pp. 3–23.

34   John Cassian, *Conlationes* 16, 11; 18, 3; 22, 6 (SC 54, 231; SC 64, 13, 121–2); idem, *De institutis coenobiorum* 11, 17; 4, 9 (SC 109, 444, 132).

35 John Cassian, *De institutis coenobiorum*, 11, 17 (SC 109, 144).
36 John Cassian, *Conlationes* 20, 9 (SC 64, 68–70).
37 John Cassian, *Conlationes* 12, 7; 19, 16 (SC 54, 132; SC 64, 54) (the elders omitted reading Scriptural verses about women when the junior monks were present).
38 Yet if the junior monks were not taught to discuss their sexual thoughts, they themselves would not in later life be well-equipped to advise newcomers to monastic life. The problem, as Terrence Tilley has suggested to me, is structurally parallel to the one Foucault spots in Greek pederasty: how can a boy who is the 'passive' partner emerge into an 'active' adult, both sexually and politically?
39 John Cassian, *Conlationes* 18, 3 (SC 64, 13); idem, *De institutis coenobiorum* 4, 39 (SC 109, 180).
40 John Cassian, *Conlationes* 2, 11; 16, 23 (SC 42, 121–3; SC 54, 242–3); idem, *De institutis coenobiorum* 4, 9 (SC 109, 132). Foucault could have explored the workings of power in this relationship to good advantage.
41 John Cassian, *Conlationes* 18, 3 (SC 64, 13).
42 John Cassian, *De institutis coenobiorum* 4, 8 (SC 109, 130, 132).
43 John Cassian, *De institutis coenobiorum* 12, 1; 12, 3 (SC 109, 450, 452, 454).
44 For example, Broudéhoux, and especially Veyne (1978: 35–63); now see Veyne (1985: esp. 47–59).
45 Clement of Alexandria, *Stromateis* III, 7, 58; 11, 71; 12, 79 (GCS 15, 222–3); idem, *Paedagogus* II, 10, 83; 95; 98; 102 (GCS 12, 208, 214, 215–16, 218).
46 Musonius Rufus XII, XIIIA and B; XIV (Lutz: 86, 88, 90–96).
47 Athanasius, *Vita Antonii* 5; 19 (PG 26, 848, 872); Palladius, *Historia Lausiaca* 29; 38 (Butler, II, 85, 121); *Historia monachorum* 20 (SubsHag 53, 118-19).
48 Athanasius, *Vita Antonii* 5; 36 (PG 26, 845, 848, 896); John Cassian, *De institutis coenobiorum* 4, 36; 5, 32; 6, 13 (SC 109, 176, 240, 242, 276).
49 Palladius, *Historia Lausiaca* 6 (Butler, II, 22–4); Palladius (?), *The Second Book of the Histories of the Fathers* 11 (Budge, I, 332–3); Pachomius, *Regulae* 53–55 (PL 23, 74); John Cassian, *De institutis coenobiorum* 4, 27 (SC 109, 160, 162); idem, *Conlationes* 24, 11 (SC 64, 181–2).
50 Athanasius, *Vita Antonii* 5; 11–12 (PG 26, 845, 848, 860–61); John Cassian, *De institutis coenobiorum* 4, 3; 7, 21 (SC 109, 124, 126, 322); Gerontius, *Vita Melaniae Junioris* 17 (SC 90, 160).
51 Palladius, *Historia Lausiaca* 57 (Butler, II, 150–51); Evagrius Ponticus, *Practicos* 6 (SC 171, 506, 508); idem, *De oratione* 50 (PG 79, 1177); John Cassian, *De institutis coenobiorum* 4, 18; 5, 1–41 (SC 109, 144, 146, 190–258).
52 *Verba seniorum* (= *Vitae patrum* V) 4, 2 (PL 73, 865).
53 *Verba seniorum* (= *Vitae patrum* V) 2 (PL 73, 858).
54 John Cassian, *Conlationes* 1, 17 (SC 42, 98).
55 *Verba seniorum* (= *Vitae patrum* V) 5, 5 (PL 73, 875).
56 Evagrius Ponticus, *Practicos* 68; 87 (SC 171, 652, 678).
57 Palladius, *Historia Lausiaca* 38 (Butler, II, 121).
58 John Cassian, *Conlationes* 7, 2; cf. 12, 7 (SC 42, 245; SC 54, 132, 133).
59 Evagrius Ponticus, *Practicos* 56 (SC 171, 630, 632); *Historia monachorum* 20, 2 (SubsHag 53, 119); John Cassian, *Conlationes* 5, 6; 5, 10; 5, 26; 12, 11; 12, 15; 22, 6 (SC 42, 193–4, 197–8, 216; SC 54, 139–40, 144; SC 64, 121–2); idem, *De institutis coenobiorum* 5, 11; 5, 20; 6, 2; 6, 7; 6, 23 (SC 109, 206, 208, 224, 264, 270, 286).
60 John Cassian, *Conlationes* 12, 15 (SC 54, 144).
61 John Cassian, *De institutis coenobiorum* 4, 9 (SC 109, 132); idem, *Conlationes* 7, 5; 7, 15; 18, 13 (SC 42, 251, 259; SC 64, 25).
62 Song of Songs 4: 12; Jerome, *Epp.* 22, 25; 49(48), 21 (CSEL 54, 178–9, 386); Ambrose,

De institutione virginis 9, 58; 9, 61 (PL 16, 335); idem, *Exhortatio virginitatis* 5, 29 (PL 16, 359); idem, *Epp.* 63, 36 (PL 16, 1250).

63 Palladius, *Historia Lausiaca* 57 (Butler, II, 150–51).

64 Palladius (?), *Counsels of the Holy Men* II, 555 (Budge, I, 773).

65 *Verba seniorum* (= *Vitae patrum* V) 10, 73 (PL 73, 925).

66 Although Foucault allows Graeco-Roman women to apropriate a model of virile self-mastery (1983b, p.247), he does not mention this possibility for Christian women. Foucault's lack of attention to female sexuality has received much comment. For essays on Foucault in relation to women's issues, see now Diamond and Quinby.

67 Matthew 19:21 and parallels.

68 Athanasius, *Vita Antonii* 2 (PG 26, 841).

69 Matthew 19:10–12.

70 John Cassian, *De justis et perfectis* 1; 4 (Muyldermans, Syriac:105, 106; French:143).

71 John Cassian, *Conlationes* 14, 11 (SC 54, 197).

72 John Cassian, *Conlationes* 21, 32–3 (SC 64, 106–8).

73 Matthew 13:8; Jerome, *Epp.* 22, 15; 49 (48), 2; 123, 8 (CSEL 54, 163, 353, 648; CSEL 56, 82); *Adversus Jovinianum* I, 3 (PL 23, 223).

74 Examples: Isidore (Palladius, *Historia Lausiaca* I [Butler, II, 16]); Amoun (*Historia monachorum* 22, 1 [SubsHag 53, 128]); Arsenius (*Apophthegmata patrum*, Arsenius 42 [PG 65, 108]). The Cappadocian Fathers also stand as examples of ascetics from high social backgrounds, as do Western ascetics such as Paulinus of Nola, Ambrose, Sulpicius Severus, Paula, Marcella and the two Melanias.

75 Examples: Paul the Simple, a herdsman; John of Lycopolis, a builder; Sisinnius, a slave; Amoun of Nitria, a balsam grower (Palladius, *Historia Lausiaca* 22; 35; 49; 8 [Butler, II, 69, 100, 143, 27]), among many others.

76 Luke 14:11; 18:14; *Historia monachorum* 1, 35 (SubsHag 53, 21-2).

77 'At many points they [Plato and Aristotle] are typical of no one but themselves.' If the genealogist's task is to show how power, knowledge, and the body relate to each other (Dreyfus and Rabinow, p. 105), Foucault has been less than successful in explicating the 'knowledge' component for the ancient Greeks.

78 Foucault's argument on this point might have been somewhat modified if he had treated the Old Stoics: see note 13 above.

79 John Cassian, *Conlationes* 1, 19; 16, 11 (SC 43, 100; SC 54, 231), citing II Corinthians 11:14; Athanasius, *Vita Antonii* 39 (PG 26, 900). Foucault hints that he is aware of this problem (1985a, p.41).

80 John Cassian, *Conlationes* 1, 21 (SC 42, 105); Athanasius, *Vita Antonii* 25; 35 (PG 26, 881, 893).

81 Palladius, *Historia Lausiaca* 6 (Butler, II, 22).

82 Athanasius, *Vita Antonii* 25 (PG 26, 881).

83 Athanasius, *Vita Antonii* 35; 39 (PG 26, 893, 900).

84 Evagrius Ponticus, *Practicos* 13 (SC 171, 528).

85 Plato, *Republic* VII, 1–2 (514A–517A).

86 Athanasius, *Vita Antonii* 14 (PG 26, 865).

87 I wish to thank Jay Geller, David Johnson, Bruce Lawrence, Terrence Tilley, the members of the Society, Culture, and Religion of Ancient Mediterranean research group, and two anonymous reviewers for their criticisms and comments. I also thank Brenda Denzler for editorial assistance.

ABBREVIATIONS

CSCO   *Corpus Scriptorum Christianorum Orientalium.*
CSEL   *Corpus Scriptorum Ecclesiasticorum Latinorum.*
GCS   *Die Griechischen Christlichen Schriftsteller der ersten Jahrhunderte.*
PG   *Patrologia Graeca.*
PL   *Patrologia Latina.*
SC   *Sources Chrétiennes.*
SubsHag   *Subsidia Hagiographica.*
SVF   *Stoicorum Veterum Fragmenta.*

REFERENCES

Ambrose   *De institutione virginis.* (PL 16:319–48).
                   Epistulae. (PL 16:913–1342).
                   Exhortatio virginitatis. (PL 16:351–80).

Anonymous   *Apophthegmata patrum.* (PG 65: 71–440).
                   Historia monachorum in Aegypto; édition critique du texte grec et traduction annotée, ed. by André-Jean Festugière. Subsidia Hagiographica 10, 11, 53. Bruxelles: Société des Bollandistes.
                   Vita Pachomii (Boharic). (CSCO 89 = Scriptores Coptici 7; Latin translation, CSCO 107 = Scriptores Coptici 11.)

Ariès. P. and G.   *Histoire de la vie privée.* Paris: Editions du Seuil.
Duby, eds.
1985

Arnim, Ioannes von *Stoicorum Veterum Fragmenta,* 4 vols. Leipzig: B.G. Teubner.
1921–1924

Athanasius   *Vita Antoni* (PG 26:823–978).

Boswell, John   'Good Sex at Home in Ancient Rome'. *The New York Times Book*
1987   *Review.* January 18:31.

Broudéhoux, Jean- *Mariage et famille chez Clément d'Alexandrie.* Théologie historique
Paul   11, Paris: Beauchesne.
1970

Budge, E.A. Wallis *The Book of Paradise,* Vols I and II, Lady Meux Manuscript 6,
trans.   London: private printing.
1904

Cassian, John   *Conlationes,* ed. by E. Pichery. *Jean Cassien. Conferences.*
[1953, 1958,   *Introduction, texte latin, traduction et notes.*
1959]   Sources Chrétiennes 42, 54, 64. Paris: Editions du Cerf.
[1965]   *De institutis coenobiorum,* ed. by Jean-Claude Guy. *Institutions cenobitques. Texte latin revu, introduction, traduction et notes.* Sources Chrétiennes 109. Paris: Editions du Cerf.

Chadwick, Owen
1968

John Cassian. 2nd edn. Cambridge: Cambridge University Press.

Clement of
Alexandria
[1905, 1906]

Clemens Alexandrinus, ed. by Otto Stählin. Bd. 1, 2. Die Griechischen Christlichen Schriftseller der ersten Jahrhunderte 12, 15. Leipzig. J.C. Hinrichs.

Diamond, Irene and
Lee Quinby, eds
1988

Feminism and Foucault: Reflections on Resistance. Boston: Northeastern University Press.

Dreyfus, Hubert L.
and Paul Rabinow
1983

Michel Foucault: Beyond Structuralism and Hermeneutics. 2nd edn, Chicago: University of Chicago Press.

Evagrius Ponticus
[1971]

De oratione. (PG 79:1166–1200).
Practicos, ed. by Antoine Guillaumont et Claire Guillaumont, *Evagre le Pontique. Traité pratique ou le Moine ... Introduction, édition critique du texte grec, traduction, commentaire et tables.* Sources Chrétiennes 171. Paris: Éditions du Cerf.

Foucault, Michel
1980a
1980b

1983a
1983b

1985a

1985b

1986

The History of Sexuality. Vol. I. An Introduction, trans. by Robert Hurley. New York: Vintage Books.
'The Confession of the Flesh'; 'The History of Sexuality', in *Power/Knowledge: Selected Interviews and Other Writings 1971–1977. By Michel Foucault*, ed. by Colin Gordon, trans. by C. Gordon, L. Marshall, J. Mepham and K. Soper. New York: Pantheon Books.
'L'écriture de soi', *Corps Ecrit* 5:3–23.
'On the Genealogy of Ethics', in *Michel Foucault: Beyond Structuralism and Hermeneutics*, 2nd edn, ed. by Hubert L. Dreyfus and Paul Rabinow. Chicago: University of Chicago Press.
The History of Sexuality. Vol. II. The Use of Pleasure, trans. by Robert Hurley. New York: Pantheon Books.
'The Battle for Chastity', in *Western Sexuality: Practice and Precept in Past and Present Times*, ed. by Philippe Ariès and André Bégin, trans. by Anthony Forster. Oxford: Basil Blackwell.
The History of Sexuality. Volume III: The Care of Self, trans. by Robert Hurley. New York: Pantheon Books.

Foucault, Michel
and Richard Sennett
1981

'Sexuality and Solitude', *London Review of Books*, 3, 9:3–7.

Gerontius
[1962]

Vita Melaniae Junioris, ed. by Denys Gorce. *Vie de Sainte Melanie; texte grec, introduction, traduction et notes.* Sources Chrétiennes 90. Paris: Éditions du Cerf.

Halperin, David
1986

'Sexual Ethics and Technologies of the Self in Classical Greece', *American Journal of Philology.* 107:274–86.

Jerome   *Adversus Jovinianum*. (PL 23:221–354).
[1910]   *Epistulae*, ed. by Isidorus Hilberg. Corpus Scriptorum Ecclesiasti-
                 corum 54. Vienna; Leipzig: F. Tempsky/G. Freytag.

Lloyd, G.E.R.   'The Mind on Sex', *New York Review of Books*, 13:24–8.
[1986]

Musonius Rufus   *Musonius Rufus, 'The Roman Socrates'*. Ed. by Cora E. Lutz, Yale
[1947]   Classical Studies 10. New Haven: Yale University Press.

Muyldermans, J., *Evagriana Syriaca. Textes inédits du British Muséum et de la
ed.   Vaticane,* in *Bibliothèque Muséon*, 31. Louvain: Publications
1952   Universitaires/Institut Orientaliste.

Pachomius   *Regulae* (PL 23:62–8).

Palladius   *Historia Lausiaca. The Lausiac History of Palladius*. Ed. by Cuthbert
[1894–1904]   Butler, Texts and Studies, 6. Cambridge: The University Press.

Payer, Pierre   'Foucault on Penance and the Shaping of Sexuality', *Studies in
1985   Religion/Sciences Religieuses*, 14:313–20.

Plato   *The Republic*, Loeb Classical Library, trans. by Paul Shorey,
[1942]   Cambridge, MA: Harvard University Press.

Rousselle, Aline *Porneia: De la maîtrise du corps à la privation sensorielle II–IV
1983   siècles de l'ère chrétienne*, Paris: Presses Universitaires de France.

Skudlarek, William, *The Continuing Quest for God: Monastic Spirituality in Tradition
ed.   and Transition*, Collegeville, MN: Liturgical Press.
1982

Veyne, Paul   'La Famille et l'amour sous le Haut-Empire romain', *Annales (ESC)*,
1978   33:35–63.
1985   'L'Empire romain', in *Histoire de la vie privée*. Ed. by P. Ariès and
                 G. Duby, Paris: Éditions du Seuil.

Chapter 3

Augustine, Foucault and the Politics of Imperfection

J. Joyce Schuld

On the face of it, St Augustine's and Michel Foucault's intellectual worlds seem incommensurable. They are not only separated by 15 centuries, but by discordant beliefs, values and loyalties. Whereas one examines finitude in order to help us recognize our creaturely limits and the need to be absolutely dependent upon God as sovereign creator, the other explores it as the key to opening up possibilities for incessant change and novel self-creation. The flourishing of human freedom for one means subordinating ourselves to the constraints of an extrinsic ultimate design, while for the other it means challenging every conceivable limit so as to escape extraneous constraints and definitions and to author one's own creative purposes and direction. Can the works of thinkers with such disparate aims and allegiances be relevant to one another?

This chapter argues that, although Augustine and Foucault seek different final destinations, along the way they paint surprisingly comparable pictures of the social dangers and moral frailties that inevitably arise from finitude and the hazards these pose to all human endeavors. In the background of their analogous descriptions are some general concerns about the extensiveness of asymmetrical relations of power, the ambiguous consequences of human intentions, the vulnerabilities of judgment and the dubiousness of historical progress. In the foreground, Augustine and Foucault share a more particular sensitivity to the tragic possibilities of individuals being ensnared in the morally ambivalent interplay of institutionalized structures of political power.

Both Augustine's and Foucault's accounts show how far they believe all individuals are from reaching any final goal. Indeed, their historical and political observations are precipitated as much by the failure to arrive at a secure and satisfying destination as by the hope of continuously struggling to move forward. It is in having to contend with this persisting failure and yet remaining undaunted in their efforts that Augustine and Foucault have something valuable to contribute to one another. Their cultural criticisms can be usefully related because, at least in the realms of politics and social history, each is dealing, not with the culminating fulfillment of a perfect ideal, but with the unpleasant messiness of present-day human imperfections. Given the practical strain of facing endlessly unfinished business, the empirical observations and conceptual tools of each can instrumentally be of service to the other.[1]

In light of the constraints of an essay of this length, I will be focusing on the resources such a comparison affords to Christian theologians and ethicists. To that end, the essay will be divided into three sections. The first will consider the potential problems facing a Christian who might hope to enter into dialogue with Foucault. Although there are good reasons for Christian scholars to question Foucault's contributions to philosophy and history, these can be addressed in such a way as to make appropriating portions of his work possible. Second, I will explore some conceptual parallels between Augustine's social thought and Foucault's historical analysis that help to situate the latter within a traditional Christian context. Finally, the chapter concludes by examining a specific example that illustrates how Foucault's 'postmodern' and Augustine's 'pre-modern' criticisms of institutional political power can be interpreted as cross-fertilizing and enriching one another. It is my contention that Foucault's philosophy, rather than being a threat to Christian social ethics, should be considered a fertile yet largely uncultivated resource and, further, that one of the easiest ways to appreciate this new resource is to examine it from an Augustinian perspective.

I

Any Christian interested in exploring the usefulness of Foucault's cultural analysis must first assess the merit of two related but distinguishable criticisms of his work and determine how restricting these are to such a project. The primary problem that must be addressed is whether Foucault recklessly challenges certain fundamental moral concepts and thereby undermines normative principles necessary to the regulation and flourishing of civilized communities. Foucault's harshest critics charge that, by investigating truth, reason and knowledge as historically generated and socially malleable constructions, he flippantly relativizes the conceptual underpinnings of modern progressive societies. The radicalness of Foucault's agenda and methodology, from this standpoint, poses both a moral and a political danger to humane ways of life, thought and action to which we have grown accustomed and now take for granted in the west.[2] The secondary problem that needs to be examined and assessed is Foucault's insistence that his histories provide only social descriptions and not evaluative standards and recommendations. Scholars have expressed a twofold concern about his resistance to formulating constructive alternatives to the cultural practices he criticizes. First, they claim that his refusal to supply a normative frame of reference cripples his ability to be a social critic since, without some shared standard, there is no way to judge between more or less humane social patterns, and no way to decide what tools would be of practical use in rectifying identified problems. Second, they conclude that Foucault is logically inconsistent because, even though he professes merely to be describing given states of affairs, he employs normatively loaded terms, such as 'domination', 'subjection' and 'resistance', and confidently relies upon them to anchor his cultural analysis.[3]

The first objection focuses on what Foucault appears to deconstruct in his work; the second on what his critical theory is logically incapable of supporting. While Christians would have reason to be apprehensive about both, the former is more detrimental to the potential usefulness of Foucault's thought because it lays him open to the charge of nihilism. If it is deemed correct, the contributions to Christian social thought would be so severely constricted that they would be of little service. As will become clear, I am persuaded that this objection misunderstands the scope, purpose and consequences of Foucault's political suspicion. The latter criticism can be granted far more credence than the former without hindering the possible benefit of a circumscribed dialogue. Although I believe this criticism to be at least partially justified, it can still be handled in a way that relieves much of its sting. Let me begin by discussing the second problem, since the first will require a lengthier and more detailed response.

When reading Foucault's works, we need to make a clear distinction between ad hoc tools and their normative uses. This allows us to say two things without contradiction: Foucault's research offers analytical instruments that are beneficial to an evaluative critique of culture, and these critical tools by themselves are insufficient for making necessary and corresponding normative determinations and judgments. We can then readily concede that, in order to gain the normative benefit of such interpretive tools, we must employ them within a particular evaluative context and in conjunction with at least a tentative set of shared criteria. However, this does not force us to conclude that ad hoc analytic instruments are themselves somehow illogical and unusable. Such a distinction between tools and uses is not extraneous to Foucault's own philosophical and ethical agenda. It is integral to what he believes to be the right approach to tackling pressing social and political problems. Foucault openly calls intellectuals to the ethical task of fashioning and refining critical instruments, but he counsels that in the end they should leave the strategic and evaluative use of those instruments to the discretion of persons entangled in local and specific situations.[4] One may strongly disagree both with Foucault's focus on particularity and circumstance and with his choosing not to voice his own normative presuppositions, but one cannot say that he is logically inconsistent if he intends to provide only limited ad hoc tools in order to allow those directly on the scene to formulate assessments, criteria and tactics within their own (and not his) evaluative context. It can be argued that even Foucault's most normatively loaded terminology, such as 'domination', 'subjection' and 'resistance', should not be deemed incoherent so long as these descriptions can be interpreted and utilized within particular and concrete normative frameworks. There is no question that Foucault's cultural studies are inherently partial and incomplete, but that does not mean they are inherently contradictory.

If Christian scholars see Foucault as offering useful but limited social descriptions and conceptual tools rather than as presenting a self-contained systematic theory, there should be no logical obstacle to developing a constructive dialogue. We can grant that Foucault's piecemeal approach to political criticism cannot bear the full weight of evaluative judgments while arguing that his methods and descriptions can be used within a different interpretive framework that does make possible normative commitments and justifications.[5] Thus, even though Foucault unquestionably refuses to offer either policy alternatives or standards of appraisal, he can make a significant contribution to social debate, in general, and to Christian social thought, in particular, in a number of ways.

First, his work offers what he calls interpretive grids of intelligibility that attempt to untangle the intricate history of, and interaction between, specific discourses and institutional practices in our society. Clearly, a descriptive analysis elucidating the cultural background of routine practices should be of use in critically assessing distinctively modern moral and political problematics. Second, Foucault renders what we could call 'dissociated' visages by drawing disjointed sketches of a given culture from contrasting temporal perspectives. Analytical tools that provide different angles of vision afford an essential critical service because they can both distance scholars from circumstances they have come to take for granted and assist them in reflecting on their behavior as cultural creatures over a particular stretch of history. The strange unfamiliarity of Foucault's social descriptions have the capacity to shock Christians and non-Christians alike into seeing themselves and their relations to others from fresh perspectives. Third, Foucault is descriptively attentive to the productive and not just the repressive dimensions of power relations, that is, how they can creatively shape and not just how they restrain people. On the one hand, this emphasizes the complex and pervasive dangers asymmetrical power relations pose to both individuals and communities. On the other hand, it encourages a somewhat hopeful view of power relations as opening up possibilities for the constructive employment of various strategies and tactics rather than as merely restricting or inflexibly determining our activities. Fourth, Foucault's carefully interwoven description of individual and social habituation highlights the symbiotic relationship between culture and individuals, and the entangling personal and political consequences that arise from such a close association. By analyzing habits as thickly intertwined personal, social and historical realities, Foucault makes possible a penetrating analysis of the diverse roles habituation plays in the development of individuals and communities. Finally, Foucault's sensitivity to the political vulnerabilities of embodied persons provides greater critical leverage when examining how permeating non-reciprocal power relations can be in constituting particular individuals and when trying to recommend what steps might be taken to monitor and modify the extent of their reach.

Foucault's insistence that his cultural studies propose only limited and incomplete instruments of analysis clears the way, on his own view, to use these prophetically unsettling methods of scrutiny without simultaneously having to adopt all of his personal convictions and aims. In addition to the narrower critical ramifications of remaining unsystematic, one of the distinct advantages of Foucault's refusal to work with an all-encompassing theory is that it helps to mitigate the sharpest difference between Augustine and Foucault, namely, that one is a religious believer and the other an atheist. The fact that Foucault does not advocate a systematized philosophy, as some other atheistic philosophers have done, makes his work comparatively easier to appropriate for Christian scholars because there is no competing metanarrative that must first be deconstructed or dismantled before it can be applied within a new and even dissimilar paradigm of thought and practice.[6] By refusing to tether his conceptual tools and historical methods to his own philosophical values and beliefs, Foucault enables individuals and communities he likely never imagined benefiting to use his work.

Before Foucault's work can be of constructive service to Christians, however, we must answer the most serious charge leveled against his historical projects, that they mount an all-out assault on constitutive normative principles. So far, I have examined only the problem of what seems to be normatively lacking in Foucault's works. The much more alarming concern is with his active deconstruction. Does he conceptually attack so much that is valuable in modern communities that any ad hoc tools would be rendered useless in the face of the resulting damage?

Reading Foucault as broadly indiscriminate in his assault and, thus, potentially creating social havoc is a serious misinterpretation of both the target and the magnitude of his political suspicion. It is fairer to Foucault's historical investigations as a whole to understand his research as exploring rather narrowly circumscribed and contextualized problematics. Foucault repeatedly assures critics that he has no interest in analyzing reason or truth in the abstract. His intent is to explore tangible social patterns that have become embedded in specific cultures over time and that manifest some type of loosely coherent rationality. The primary aim of his research is to discover within such social patterns how particular fields of knowledge and truth claims have been used to bring about distinctly political ends while appearing to be scrupulously neutral, objective and apolitical. Hence it is not impartially regulative moral principles that Foucault addresses and deconstructs, but functioning mechanisms of power that have become gradually entrenched in cultural practices. These are 'depoliticized' political mechanisms, attaining strategic advantage precisely because those who become entangled in them fail to scrutinize how they specifically operate on and through unstable dynamics of power.

In light of their social and historical particularity, Foucault maintains that such concrete apparatuses of power are best examined with respect to delimited fields of study and, if possible, by people actually working within environments where such interrelated practices and discourses of knowledge directly affect the conditions of their life and work.[7] Foucault's own interests are chiefly institutional, examining disciplines of knowledge, truth claims and protocols associated with asylums, hospitals, schools and prisons.[8] As a student and psychiatric intern at the Hospital of Sainte-Anne, Foucault first became aware of how an institutional culture could depoliticize conflicting human interactions and conceal coercive dynamics by clothing them in the armature of modern science.[9] Having witnessed first-hand objectifying physical and verbal examinations, having given batteries of tests to measure exactly how far patients departed from a pseudo-scientific norm, having been expected to make medically certifiable diagnoses and prescriptions, Foucault came to believe that he had participated in strangely inconspicuous and unmonitored rituals of power.

As his career in writing and teaching unfolded, Foucault dedicated his energies to investigating not only the history of asymmetrical interactions exposed in psychiatric facilities like Sainte-Anne's but other complicated networks of power rooted in historically related yet distinct institutional environments. Foucault became convinced that hospitals, medical clinics, counseling centers, schools and prisons all combine a potent mix of authoritative truth claims about pseudo-scientific standards with forceful practical exercises that foster an unreflective but naturally obedient habituation – both among an institution's staff and among those whom the staff are supposed to manage. Although these various institutions have evolved in loose association with one another, Foucault contends that each one has its own cultural dynamics, history and intricate apparatuses of power. Thus, in order to explore the complex evolution and influence of these institutions, they must be examined both in relation to each other and as separate fields of operation. In addition, while these social patterns have been historically shaped by institutionally regulated interactions, they have also developed a social authority independent of such sequestered hierarchical settings and now function as detached and fragmented mechanisms of power within the broader culture. Starting from a specific institutional analysis, then, Foucault traces subtle and complex historical connections that demonstrate how different social environments have adapted and been changed by very particular and concrete instruments of power.

If we had time and space to survey Foucault's diverse historical works, we would find that what most persistently fascinates him in his research is nothing so universal as reason or truth or knowledge.[10] It is not even as general and far-reaching as the field of science considered as a whole. Although it is true that Foucault explores the comprehensive theme of how we privilege scientific discourse in modern culture, his central concern lies with the way such a presupposition is used by specific disciplines that exhibit what he calls questionable 'scientificity'.[11] In contrast to the hard sciences, Foucault refers to these fields of study as 'dubious' or 'pseudo-sciences'. While Foucault is never entirely clear as to what distinguishes 'legitimate' and 'illegitimate' sciences, he tends to describe the hard sciences as examining somewhat more stable objects of study from the natural world, whereas the dubious sciences focus on the ever-shifting and dynamic sphere of human interactions.[12] Foucault does not discount the possibility that the natural sciences could be entangled in a similar manner with unmonitored practices of power, but, on the whole, he believes that the human sciences are more visibly political precisely because their object of study concerns human relationships, interactions and activities.

In sum, by charging that Foucault advances a sweeping assault on normative principles, his critics largely disregard the selective character of his research. Foucault's criticisms are both culturally and historically limited. He does not offer a critique of knowledge or truth in general, but of tangible leverages of power evident in specific cultural patterns. He does not scrutinize reason as a whole, but the operating logic of localized rationalities that have gradually evolved through particular discursive and non-discursive practices. Foucault's analysis is not meant to be global, but circumscribed, piecemeal and ad hoc. When we force Foucault into this foreign universalizing mold, we lose sight of what is actually most interesting about his work and we neglect to explore whether his culturally and historically focused insights have anything novel to contribute to our own efforts at social analysis.[13]

One of the principal reasons for the targets of Foucault's criticisms being so often misjudged is that commentators do not take seriously enough his explicit disinterest in modern philosophical problematics. Especially if Foucault's arguments are read in the context of contemporary epistemological debate with its emphasis on protecting human resources for making rational justifications, the only significance his work would appear to have is negative. For Foucault in no way reassures us about the reliability of knowledge, or judgments of truth, or well-reasoned warrants. He intentionally brackets this modern preoccupation with epistemology and sets it aside. Instead, he focuses his attention on performative encounters, on the historical instability and practical dangers of living in constantly interacting human communities. Foucault no doubt aims at shattering complacency. Rather than inspiring a sense of comfortable assurance, he rouses wariness and caution. Thus, if what frames an analysis of Foucault's writings is the concern to stabilize knowledge in general and rational truth claims in particular, the sole part he seems fit to play is that of the reckless spoiler. Simply in light of the fact that Foucault refuses to participate in this peculiarly modern drama, he gets cast all too easily in the role of the irreverent, disorderly character that the entire drama struggles against. Only if we move away from this modern story line and its preoccupation with epistemic certitude and incorrigible self-confidence can we begin to explore the constructive resources in Foucault's cultural analysis.

II

In leaving to one side our modern epistemological worries, hopes and expectations, Foucault pushes off in a distinctively postmodern direction. Nevertheless, or perhaps because of this, many of his social criticisms can also be profitably explored from a pre-modern vantage point. For apprehending the constantly shifting instabilities of human communities is not the intellectual domain solely of postmodern philosophers, nor is the insight that all relationships and activities are threatened by ambiguous and often imperceptible social dangers. Long before Foucault became aware of muffled disparities of power in institutional settings like Sainte-Anne's, Augustine, in the *City of God*, was wrestling with the interminable moral failings of performative encounters and with the treacherous lack of reciprocity between persons in all levels of human society. Whether writing about the relatively private world of family relations or the more public sphere of civic interactions, Augustine depicted an unsettling uncertainty and insecurity as basic to everyday existence.[14] Although human beings, on Augustine's view, are clearly created to show beneficent concern for one another, because of the damaging effects of the fall, they can only perceive this perfect social harmony as a distant and unattainable ideal.[15] Even in the most loving and noble contexts, human beings perpetually fight against the pull of the *libido dominandi*, their self-absorbed desire to gain power and control over other individuals. Hence, for Augustine, no safe refuge can be found within social life that has been left untouched by agitating tensions and pressures, threats of deception and inequitable uses of domineering force. Some variation of conflict, insecurity and exploitative manipulation are present, at least as hazardous possibilities, in all human projects and interactions.

If we examine Foucault's cultural criticisms through this pre-modern lens, with its sensitivities to the uncertain dangers of daily life, rather than from a more modern perspective, with its prime objective of bolstering our moral self-confidence, Foucault's contributions to social thought begin to come into view. For Augustine, like Foucault after him, consciously deflated the complacent self-assurance of his contemporaries. Rather than enhancing his culture's moral surety, he radically undercut its unquestioned assumptions and comfortable sense of security. In jarring contrast to the Roman empire's self-glorifying narrative of its progress as a just society, Augustine chronicled a pathetic story of overreaching vanity and distorted self-importance. By juxtaposing the heroic lore of Roman society with the unflattering history of Rome's actual moral failures, Augustine challenged his culture's pretensions to social justice and historical achievement. Beginning with the Cain-like murder of Romulus's brother and continuing through brutal incidents like the rape of the Sabine women and the enslavement of Rome's neighboring peoples, Augustine tried to jolt his readers into seeing the moral dissonance between the two contrasting historical depictions.

Central to understanding the moral shortcomings in Roman or any other human culture, from Augustine's point of view, is the ability to discern the dangerously ambivalent role that social institutions play in the dubious progression of political history. Rather than fulfilling the ancient Greek ideal of a polis that provides the means to move its citizens toward a more satisfying state of human perfection and happiness, social institutions merely serve to maintain a minimal level of security and control in communities that are plagued by human imperfection. Since, according to Augustine, political structures of power are wholly a postlapsarian and not a prelapsarian development, and since they rely heavily on coercive measures to meet their goals, they are especially vulnerable to the divisiveness and inequities resulting from the fall.[16] These are not natural institutions dedicated to the right ordering of human fellowship and community, but artificially contrived arrangements of power to which human beings have had to resort in order to preserve some semblance of social order.

From Augustine's standpoint, these institutional structures, although a necessary evil in fallen society, nevertheless exact from their participants a terrible human price. Not only are they often used at the expense of individuals who find themselves under their strict control, but, less obviously, they also impose a cost on those in positions of power. Augustine's depiction of the judge (in book 19 of the *City of God*) who is tormented by his authority to proclaim guilt or innocence best exemplifies just how morally ambivalent social institutions are.[17] The judge must venture determinations to guard against injustices that, if left unchecked, would lead to social disintegration and chaos. But since he must appraise such situations without reliable access to the truth, he always risks condemning, in the name of truth, the very persons he is supposed to protect. This is most poignant in those instances when a suspect's forced confession leads to his execution. In such cases, the judicial process attempts to excavate the truth through the indisputability of coercive force, hoping to escape thereby the perils of uncertainty. But in trying to secure such certitude, Augustine laments, the only incontrovertible fact the judge ascertains is that he cannot know with absolute confidence whether this additional loss of life, which rests solely on his shoulders, is fairly deserved. If the judge is a wise man, writes Augustine, the necessity of pronouncing sentences and the extent to which he can never be sure by how far he misses the mark should forever weigh on his conscience. This is, in Augustine's words, 'something to be bewailed, and, if it were possible, washed away by floods of tears'.[18] Rather than feeling empowered by such a position of authority, therefore, the truly good judge, Augustine concludes, should be sickened and repelled by his duties. Although he knows that, for society's sake, the charge cannot be lifted from his shoulders, he should pray to be delivered from having to make questionable decisions. For Augustine, this moral indeterminacy, which undermines all human achievements, is just as apparent in other institutions, such as the military. Even with respect to the laudable goal of preserving temporal peace, our efforts are always regrettably indecisive and fragmentary. 'The only joy to be attained' from coercive accomplishments, notes Augustine, has 'the fragile brilliance of glass, a joy outweighed by the fear that it may be shattered in a moment'.[19]

The antitriumphalist and antiutopian cast of mind that Augustine shares with Foucault serves as a sobering reminder to ethical theorists of the shifting moral dangers inherent in all social accomplishments. Augustine's most valuable contribution to Christian social thought, however, is not just his vivid suspicion, but also his complementary assertion that human limitations in no way release us from the necessity of remaining politically engaged. That we live in the midst of confusing social circumstances does not lessen the demands placed on us in virtue of living together in society. On Augustine's view, moral and political ambiguities will afflict all persons, all cultures and all times. But despite this ineliminable lack of clarity, citizens must dedicate themselves to tackling practical difficulties in the political realm. Recall the example of Augustine's tormented judge. Although staggered by the weight of his responsibilities, he never tries to squirm out from under them and liberate himself from the heavy moral risks and burdens they entail. As Augustine puts it, 'In view of this darkness that attends the life of human society, will our wise man take his seat on the judge's bench, or will he not have the heart to do so? Obviously, he will sit; for the claims of human society constrain him and draw him to his duty; and it is unthinkable to him that he should shirk it.'[20] By affirming the judge's decision to accept his responsibilities, no matter how toilsome they may be, Augustine places himself squarely against political apathy. Despite never knowing for sure what or how much damage our determinations may cause, we must still wager some response to existing social problems.

In a similar vein, Foucault maintains that he wants his cultural observations to act not only as a restraining check on institutional arrangements of power, but also as a spur that prods individuals to remain politically committed.[21] Thinking over his varied career and the potential impact of his research, Foucault writes, 'My point is not that everything is bad, but that everything is dangerous, which is not exactly the same as bad. If everything is dangerous, then we always have something to do.'[22] His historical efforts, he hopes, will drive readers not to apathy but to an awakened watchfulness and a humbled form of political activism. For both Augustine and Foucault, human beings should always be wary of historically developed social structures, but they must resist the lure of being paralyzed by their pessimism and thus seemingly unaccountable for their existing social condition.

Reading Foucault's cultural analysis with Augustine's political suspicion in mind makes it possible for Christian scholars to use Foucault's disturbing historical observations in their own social criticisms. For if Augustine is correct that our cultural and historical achievements in general and our social institutions in particular are morally ambivalent and radically indeterminate, then they must be left open to all forms of scrutiny. Because what grounds Augustine's political cautiousness and admonitions is a conception of persons, not as obedient believers (ones who confess to and progress towards God), but as self-absorbed, aggressive and reckless creatures, the social problems he addresses do not concern only those who share his faith. As long as the discussion dwells on the inevitable performative dangers and practical quagmires of everyday political life, he seems open to help from all quarters. Since Christians and non-Christians together face the tragic consequences of the ambition to gain power and dominion over others, both must labor to limit the resulting damage. Thus Augustine contends that, even though members of the city of God and the city of earth are clearly differentiated by way of their final destination and will be divided at the end of time, they are, for now, socially and politically 'interwoven'.[23] In no way can they be distinguished by the practical hazards or exigencies of their circumstance; they are separated only with respect to their eschatological vision and hope.[24]

III

Once we establish as the basis of comparison the ambiguities and dangers of our performative world, Augustine's and Foucault's critical observations can be seen to cross-fertilize one another. Augustine's social analysis makes it easier to appreciate Foucault's historical works from a traditional Christian perspective, and Foucault's historical works make it easier to apply an Augustinian social analysis to distinctively modern circumstances. Since the most obvious area of overlap between the two thinkers is their sensitivity to the moral ambivalence of institutional structures of power, one constructive way to explore this cross-fertilization is to look at the way each figure portrays the dubiousness of political power as it extends and consolidates itself institutionally.

What strikes Foucault as the most strategically successful way for institutions to amass political power is to use a culturally privileged rhetoric such that it is able to justify its varied activities and modes of operation without raising any moral suspicions. By attaching themselves to a discourse that makes their social authority appear self-evident and beyond reproach, institutional networks of power can inoculate themselves against political criticism. Even when they resort to base and violent means to realize their immediate objectives, these self-legitimating social structures are able to circumvent all critical reflection that, in other circumstances, might carefully scrutinize and check their excesses. Foucault analyzes the political use of such privileged discourses as though they were characteristically modern techniques of power. But Augustine perceptively describes a similar dynamic operating in his society. For Foucault, contemporary discourses have been able to neutralize social criticisms by cloaking themselves in the rhetoric of scientific progress. Whether they be psychiatric, medical or juridical, such discourses carry out a political agenda without having to face the rigors of political criticism. For Augustine, the language that eludes critical scrutiny is the rhetoric of imperial glory. When immoral acts are perpetrated to the greater glory of the empire, they are not held to the same standard of moral assessment as would be any other human activity. Although these self-legitimating discourses exempt different social authorities, they function similarly in their respective societies because each extends and consolidates institutional power by circumventing critical reflection.

Augustine repeatedly warns his readers in the *City of God* about the blinding effects of the rhetoric of imperial glory and counsels them not to be tricked by its pretentious posturing.[25] 'To help us to form our judgment,' writes Augustine, 'let us refuse to be fooled by empty bombast, to let the edge of our critical faculties be blunted by high-sounding words like "peoples", "realms", "provinces".'[26] According-ing to Augustine, the legitimizing authority such words bestow on even the basest of human activities so warps our critical faculties that we are unable to make adequate moral assessments. Whereas we would not hesitate to condemn unjust aggression and brutality if it occurred between two neighbors in a village, we often fail to criticize the same acts of inhumanity when they transpire for the elevated objective of glorifying the state and advancing its interests.

In order to make his point more emphatically, Augustine recounts the story of Alexander the Great being caught off guard one day while reprimanding a pirate. Questioning the outlaw about his reprehensible acts, Alexander asked him, '"What is your idea, in infesting the sea?" And the pirate answered, with uninhibited insolence, "The same as yours, in infesting the earth! But because I do it with a tiny craft, I'm called a pirate: because you have a mighty navy, you're called emperor".'[27] By reciting this vignette, Augustine highlights the special protection that the privileged rhetoric of imperial glory affords. Acting as a kind of defensive shield, it ensures that there will always be a safe moral distance maintained between the sovereign's accountability and the expected standards that measure the rest of human activities. The story helps Augustine to warn his readers that a sanctified discourse such as this can hinder our normal moral scrutiny and thereby lead us to exaggerate the normative differences that separate what we uncritically think of as the esteemed ruler and the contemptible outlaw. 'Remove justice,' writes Augustine, 'and what are kingdoms but gangs of criminals on a large scale? What are criminal gangs but petty kingdoms?'[28] Augustine claims that, once we examine the behavior of conquering monarchs without the protection of their self-legitimating oratory, we will realize that their acts differ little from those of common pirates or lawless henchmen.

By blurring social distinctions that citizens take for granted in their society, Augustine undermines the self-evident authority of institutional structures of power. This is strikingly reinforced when, in one of his more puzzling passages in the *City of God*, Augustine seems to collapse the moral differences between the institution of slavery and the institutions of political authority.[29] Shifting with ease between the two topics of discussion, Augustine describes them as being similar in origin, in how they manage to retain command and in the 'unnaturalness' of their social power. According to Augustine, institutions of slavery and civil society both are a result of the fall, both involve unnatural dominion and inequality, and both operate on the basis of self-absorbed desires and objectives. As when recounting the story about Alexander the Great, Augustine shocks his readers by failing to note seemingly obvious moral differences. What is normally protected by the rhetoric of imperial glory is stripped by Augustine of its special privileges and placed on a par with sordid and degrading human endeavors. Without the shield of its ennobling discourse, the institutions of political authority can be examined for what they are: regrettably necessary but morally ambivalent structures of power.

Whereas Augustine is concerned with the exalted language that tends to safeguard unjust political power, Foucault struggles with a new problematic involving the privileging of a different cultural discourse. Foucault contends that, in distinct contrast to the traditional rhetoric of imperial glory, modern institutions garner and preserve power most effectively by relying upon a scientific sounding rhetoric of progress.[30] Indeed, rather than seeking protection under the majesty of the political realm, this peculiarly modern discursive force gains its strength precisely by making itself appear as though it is entirely disconnected from all political activities. While the rhetoric of glory blinds our critical capacities through its pretentious splendor, the rhetoric of progress eclipses moral judgments by posing as a coldly antiseptic science. Intrinsic to the self-legitimating and self-evident stature of this discourse in our society is its ability to look as though it is indisputably objective and neutral with respect both to its empirical findings and to its corresponding institutional practices. According to Foucault, how successfully this rhetoric keeps its social power hidden from detection directly corresponds to the degree of its institutional potency. The more it conceals its political leverage, the more it can be effectively political.

Foucault most clearly illustrates the efficacy of this new mechanism of discursive power when he discusses certain social relationships that up to the early modern period had always been considered to be political because they are inherently coercive. In describing how the practices of judicial institutions have been reconfigured over the last two centuries, Foucault demonstrates the ways in which inequitable relations of force can be redefined and concealed by becoming attached to the ennobling purposes of science.[31] Once essentially political interactions are recast as a function of scientific or medical processes, they can be justified in non-political terms as necessary interventions that simply ensure therapeutic progress. What might otherwise appear as morally questionable dynamics of coercive force can thus be draped with the protective mantle of scientific medicine.

To give this historical transformation more specificity, let us look at one way in which, according to Foucault, the criminal justice system has significantly changed. Until the 18th century, only three questions needed to be answered in order to reach a judicial decision. Did a criminal act occur? If so, who is the perpetrator, and what is the appropriate legal sanction?[32] As Augustine has eloquently demonstrated, these determinations were not easy for judges. Because they were at least partially subjective in character and because they carried with them the serious moral risks of error, such institutional judgments were inherently messy and often ugly political necessities. Foucault reports that, partly because of the indignity of having to make such morally indeterminate decisions, and partly in response to the public's concern over arbitrary and excessive uses of power, these well-worn procedures of investigation underwent a gradual but thorough transformation, beginning in the 18th century.[33] In search of more reliable information upon which to base their verdicts and sentencing practices, judges increasingly sought out assistance from the social sciences. By calling on experts from psychiatry, sociology, and criminology, magistrates who once focused almost exclusively on exploring the criminal act began to broaden the scope of their inquest so as to discover with more precision an objectifiable 'delinquent individual'.[34]

Whereas the earlier approach primarily emphasized the factual issues of act and responsibility, this new approach, although not ignoring the crime itself, started to circulate around the criminal as an independent object of scientific inquiry. Ironically, Foucault claims, in the false hope of gaining a firmer grasp on the issues, judges have wound up saddling themselves with a whole new set of problematic questions and uncertainties. Now they must make decisions not only about guilt and punishment but also about kinds and degrees of deviance; about the character of a criminal's past, present and future; and about the quantifiable success of different forms of rehabilitation.[35] Since these determinations require expertise and training that is non-juridical, judges are no longer able to make legal judgments by themselves. As a consequence, Foucault argues, the modern criminal justice system has become dependent on and dispersed throughout a growing army of 'subsidiary judges' –

diverse experts all claiming to have scientifically grounded opinions on relevant criminal questions.[36]

What is especially interesting about this historical development, according to Foucault, is that the transformation is meant to be one-sided. The justice system has taken on these extrajuridical elements, not in order to draw them into the judicial system and its legal power to punish, but to draw the judicial world of legal punishments into the seemingly non-political world of science and medicine.[37] The politically entangled determination of 'guilt' or 'innocence', which was fraught with such danger and anguish for Augustine's judge, now becomes the dispassionate product of what Foucault calls 'a strange scientifico-juridical complex'.[38] Rather than being the morally ambivalent decision maker, the judge takes on the comforting therapeutic role of preparing for the criminal's rehabilitation. The painful indeterminacy so apparent in Augustine's description is, Foucault concludes, a moral shame and a moral burden that modern authorities are no longer willing to bear.

On Foucault's view, the high-minded rhetoric of scientific progress is as unexamined in our culture as was the rhetoric of glory in Augustine's. In order to reawaken our critical capacities, Foucault, much like Augustine, attempts to punch holes in the pretensions of this protective discourse by collapsing certain moral distinctions we now take for granted. Foucault wants to shock his readers in much the same way as Augustine did with his story of Alexander the Great and the pirate. While Augustine sought to demonstrate that the king and the outlaw were different, not in kind, but in degree, Foucault tries to show that supposedly progressive modern verdicts and punishments are no less politically and morally ambiguous than were those of an earlier era. By stepping into the seemingly sterile world of scientific and therapeutic experts, modern judges attempt to distance themselves from the messiness of political force. Although it may appear that this scientifico-juridical approach improves on the past, Foucault wants us to realize that our modern mechanisms of power are no less coercive. In attempting to rehabilitate the whole individual, the modern judicial system uses its own methods of violence and force, only it administers them in such a way that they no longer appear violent or forceful. Indeed, it is in this seeming inoffensiveness that Foucault pinpoints the danger. Intrinsically political interactions are able to free themselves of elements that make them look morally questionable while at the same time employing new technologies that are actually more efficient and powerful. Modern judges and their army of clinical subsidiaries, Foucault argues, now not only have the authority to apply specific sentences and penalties but are justified in intervening in the criminal's life in a much more invasive and enduring manner. Beyond just demanding the restriction of imprisonment, they can govern a person within a meticulous disciplinary environment organized to evaluate and creatively transform every aspect of the criminal – even the most fleeting desires, thoughts and movements. Such political and institutional leverages of power function not simply by restraining and stripping away contingent social freedoms but by permeating, entangling and actively producing new individuals.

According to Foucault, this peculiarly modern illustration of institutional power is protected not simply by a sanctified cultural discourse but by the hidden force of its accompanying social practices. Whereas the political power that Augustine worries over is resplendently in control and constantly on public display, this new mode of power operates almost imperceptibly through inconspicuous details. By intruding itself upon the minutiae of a person's life, by slipping into the individual's most insignificant activities, gestures and habits, its reach can be at once unprecedented in intimacy while paradoxically looking antiseptically distant, depersonalized and withdrawn. The fact that such disciplinary techniques can be so subtle and invisible, and yet so intimately penetrating, gives them the opportunity, Foucault argues, to establish an almost unrestricted domain of social power. To Augustine's precaution that a glorified cultural discourse can hinder our normal processes of moral scrutiny, Foucault would add an urgent warning to be particularly vigilant about accompanying unmonitored social practices.

Augustine and Foucault, in their own ways, intentionally obscure moral and social differences that are unquestioned in their societies. If Augustine sees Alexander's majestic image reflected in the lawlessness of a common pirate, Foucault sees the restrained modern judiciary and its practices mirrored in the invasively violent tactics of medieval executioners. Even though both thinkers exaggerate the similarities between the elevated and the sordid, they do so in order to catch their readers off guard and make them rethink privileged discourses and institutional relations of power to which their respective cultures uncritically subscribe. By provocatively offending established social sensibilities, they shock their audiences into taking at least one more critical look at routinely accepted customs in their societies.

Bringing Foucault and Augustine into conversation can be productive for Christian social thought for several reasons. First of all, an Augustinian political realism with its deep suspicion about human achievements and its particular attunement to the moral ambivalence of social institutions can help to situate Foucault's often alarming cultural critique within a long-standing Christian tradition. Because Augustine is not afraid to confront the moral ambiguities and performative instabilities involved in all historically situated communities, he gives Foucault's extremism a more conventional warrant.

Second, Foucault's historical research employs certain analytical tools that can help to focus an Augustinian critique on the peculiar dangers of modern social accomplishments, especially the uncritically accepted legitimacy of cultural discourses and practices associated with pseudo-scientific progress. With his distinctively postmodern insight about the finely tuned complexity of social power, Foucault constructively amplifies Augustine's pre-modern warnings about the hazards of human divisiveness and the desire to subject others to personal dominion. Whether describing institutionalized or deinstitutionalized networks of power, Foucault demonstrates that subjugation operates in modern society most effectively when it quietly suffuses and creates individuals rather than conspicuously restraining them. Since these mechanisms of power are coercive in a subtle and hidden way, modern patterns of domination may be more difficult to isolate, recognize and rectify than once supposed. At a minimum, the descriptive tools that Foucault develops help to flag previously unseen social dangers and provide some means of analysis by which we can begin probing and untangling the intricate interactions involved in modern relations of power.

Third, both Augustine and Foucault prod us to question the modern preoccupation with establishing grounds for an incorrigible moral self-confidence by reminding us that our moral decisions and efforts can both empower and imperil us. Contrary to present-day hopes, we can never attain a risk-free certainty. Given the precariousness and confusion of our social circumstances, moral hazards will invariably attend human activities, including those we consider to be most high-minded. Augustine's and Foucault's historic contribution to political ethics, then, has less to do with securing indisputable reasons for particular social actions than with keeping us alert to the inevitable imperfections that accompany all human efforts. By making us aware of the fragility of our moral endeavors, and perhaps especially our institutional accomplishments, they encourage us to remain flexible, to remember that our political achievements are provisional and in need of perpetual scrutiny and renewal. Even though their cultural critiques may not be sufficient for determining precisely how to alleviate specific social problems, they are an essential critical complement to our more constructive efforts and, as such, help ensure that we remain politically humble in even our most noble endeavors.

Finally, while Augustine and Foucault deflate the utopian self-assurance of many social reformers, they are equally critical of those who would stand impassively by in the face of injustice. Although all moral efforts entail the threat of soiling our hands with moral failure, we cannot allow this paradox to keep us from being politically engaged. Even if we can never attain a reassuring sense of clarity about the difficult situations that confront us, we must take care that this indeterminacy does not strain our compassion or immobilize our commitment to relieve the sufferings of others. Augustine and Foucault both urge us to venture forth into an ambiguously messy and unjust world. But they try to furnish us with an intricately detailed and cautionary moral map so as to prepare us better for the perplexing and dangerous terrain that awaits us.[39]

NOTES

1   My argument is that, although Augustine and Foucault disagree on what the perfect person and perfect existence would look like, they agree sufficiently on the pervasive social dangers generated by human imperfections for them to be, at least descriptively, of service to one another.

2   For an informative discussion of this first problem, see Charles Taylor, 'Foucault on Freedom and Truth' and Michael Walzer, 'The Politics of Michel Foucault', both in David Couzens Hoy (ed.), *Foucault: A Critical Reader* (Oxford: Basil Blackwell, 1986).

3   This criticism has been articulated most forcefully by Nancy Frazer in 'Foucault on Modern Power: Empirical Insights and Normative Confusions', *Praxis International*, 1 (1981), 272–87.

4   Michel Foucault, *Politics, Philosophy, and Culture: Interviews and Other Writings*, ed. Lawrence D. Kritzman (New York: Routledge, Chapman, & Hall, 1988, p.197).

5   Todd May argues convincingly that philosophers and ethicists can speak of truth and justification in the context of Foucault's work. For anyone interested in pursuing such questions in more depth, May's book, *Between Genealogy and Epistemology* (University Park: The Pennsylvania State University Press, 1993), is essential reading. I would argue that Jeffrey Stout's interpretation of moral justification is most compatible with Foucault's own efforts and can be used without contradicting Foucault's ad hoc and limited critical objectives. See Jeffrey Stout, *Ethics after Babel: The Languages of Morals and Their Discontents* (Boston: Beacon, 1988). Scholars working within a more foundationalist framework could also use many of Foucault's social descriptions and

Michel Foucault and Theology

analytical tools, but they would have to pry Foucault's cultural insights away from his analytical agenda, since any universalizing approach would run counter to Foucault's desire to leave evaluative assessments and strategies to individuals who are entangled in historically situated and locally generated social problematics. Many of Foucault's critics confuse his wariness about our potential to cause suffering in using normative judgments with a nihilistic deconstruction of all forms of evaluation. Charles Scott argues in *The Question of Ethics* (Bloomington, IN: Indiana University Press, 1990) that Foucault does not want to undermine our abilities to make evaluative judgments. He is simply recommending that, as we involve ourselves in specific exercises of judgment, we remain intensely alert to and humble about our capacities to harm others, even when we intend good. 'Our attempts to evaluate and establish a hierarchy of values include forces that run counter to such an effort, forces that put evaluating and hierarchizing in question in the midst of the evaluating process. That does not make evaluation wrong or bad, but it functions as a caution to evaluative processes' (p.7).

6   Indeed, Hubert L. Dreyfus and Paul Rabinow argue that Foucault is not explicitly hostile to metanarratives; he simply is engaged in a different enterprise that, given its parameters, does not take into account any kind of larger overview. 'Foucault is not trying to construct a general theory, nor deconstruct the possibility of any metanarrative; rather, he's [simply] offering us an interpretive analytic of our current situation.' See Hubert L. Dreyfus and Paul Rabinow, 'What is Maturity? Habermas and Foucault on "What is Enlightenment?"', in Hoy (ed.), *Foucault*, pp.114–15.

7   Michel Foucault, *Power/Knowledge: Selected Interviews and Other Writings*, ed. Colin Gordon (New York: Pantheon,1972, p.126), and *Politics, Philosophy, and Culture*, p.59.

8   This is true of all of Foucault's works, except for his last two books, which examine ancient customs and sexual practices.

9   Didier Eribon, *Michel Foucault* (Cambridge, MA: Harvard University Press, 1991, pp.41–9).

10   Foucault's works that best exemplify this are his genealogical writings from the 1970s. However, his earlier studies also confirm a very particular cultural and historical focus. The only book that speaks of 'Reason' as a general term is Michel Foucault, *Madness and Civilization: A History of Insanity in the Age of Reason*, trans. Richard Howard (New York: Pantheon, 1965). This is a practice that Foucault later renounces.

11   Michel Foucault, *The Archaeology of Knowledge and The Discourse of Language*, trans. A.M. Sheridan Smith (New York: Pantheon, 1972, p.187).

12   Foucault, *Politics, Philosophy, and Culture*, p.108.

13   A great chasm generally exists between critics and supporters concerning the aim and consequences of Foucault's work. However, there are also tensions and divisions among Foucault's own followers. Part of the reason for this can be traced back to Foucault himself and the way he granted his numerous interviews. At times, he used the interviewing process to illumine and chronicle the evolution of his thought, and these reflections ended up being particularly helpful in clarifying the changing concerns of his work and in combating widespread misinterpretations. However, as James Bernauer pointed out to me, Foucault also had a penchant for using this venue as a way to be provocative, a way to go beyond expectations and shock the particular questioner in front of him, even if this led him to contradict or obfuscate other statements. The resulting record is a somewhat confusing one. Foucault's historical monographs, in contrast to his quickly executed interviews and essays, are more methodical and less personally interactive, and as a result have left a better, or at least more consistent, record of Foucault's historical objectives. The interpreters I am most confident in on the question of Foucault's philosophical agenda agree that, rather than desiring to have some global impact, Foucault is interested in exploring specifically circumscribed social contexts in

light of localized rationalities and historically developed normative practices. Gary Guting, who has written extensively on such misinterpretations by Foucault's critics, writes in *Michel Foucault's Archaeology of Scientific Reason* (Cambridge: Cambridge University Press, 1989): 'Despite their popularity, such criticisms, based on the charge of global skepticism or relativism, are unfounded. They ignore three aspects of Foucault's work that definitely distinguish it from any universal assault on the notion of truth. First, there is the explicitly local or regional nature of his analysis. His historical critiques of reason are always directed toward very specific applications (psychiatry, clinical medicine, human sciences) with no suggestion that the inadequacies of any one domain can be extrapolated to others. Second, Foucault's focus is always on the domains of "dubious disciplines" ... Third, even for the dubious disciplines that are the objects of his critique, Foucault does not deny all truth and objectivity' (p.273). See also David Couzens Hoy, 'Power, Repression, Progress: Foucault, Lukes and the Frankfurt School', p.129, and Barry Smart, 'The Politics of Truth and the Problem of Hegemony', both in Hoy (ed.), *Foucault*, pp.186–8; and May, *Between Genealogy and Epistemology*, pp.104–5, all of whom reinforce this reading of Foucault's narrowly focused purposes.

14   St Augustine, *City of God*, trans. Henry Bettenson (New York: Penguin, 1972, 19.4–8).
15   Ibid., 22.22–23.
16   Ibid., 19.15. For a detailed discussion of this see, R.A. Markus, 'Two Conceptions of Political Authority: Augustine, *De Civitate Dei*, XIX.14–15 and Some Thirteenth Century Interpretations', *Journal of Theological Studies*, n.s., 16 (1965); 68–100.
17   St Augustine, *City of God*, 19.6.
18   Ibid.
19   Ibid., 4.3.
20   Ibid., 19.6.
21   Foucault does not want to furnish his own evaluative frame of reference to guide individuals in making important decisions about their political commitments. However, he does envision his role constructively as being a political agitator and a provider of critical tools so that people in particular contexts will be both uncomfortably pressured by and better able to recognize complex social problems.
22   Michel Foucault, 'On the Genealogy of Ethics: An Overview of Work in Progress', afterword to Hubert Dreyfus and Paul Rabinow, *Michel Foucault: Beyond Structuralism and Hermeneutics* (Chicago: University of Chicago Press, 1983, pp.231–2).
23   St Augusitne, *City of God*, 1.35.
24   My reading of Augustine favors Markus's interpretation of the political community as one that seriously grapples with the experiences and possible contributions of people who do not share the Christian faith. See R.A. Markus, *Saeculum: History and Society in the Theology of St. Augustine* (New York: Cambridge University Press, 1970, pp.94–104, 173). Since Augustine distinguishes clearly between the required uniformity of ultimate beliefs in the community of faith and the expected variation and otherness of convictions (even if only permitted grudgingly) in the more mundane political community, his work is uniquely able to accommodate Foucault's piecemeal social criticisms without being threatened by Foucault's atheism. Markus argues that part of Augustine's distinctiveness is that his pragmatic and provisional approach to politics is 'compatible with almost any political programme which does not set itself up as an ideology with absolute claims on men's ultimate loyalties' (p.172). As long as Foucault's social criticisms are aimed at this workaday world of performative failures and its many aggravating social tensions, and as long as they do not directly contravene religious beliefs and practices, they can be effectively used in scrutinizing and monitoring established arrangements of power.
25   My analysis of Augustine's 'rhetoric of imperial glory' has been informed by Robert Dodaro's exposition of the *City of God* in 'Eloquent Lies, Just Wars and the Politics of

Persuasion: Reading Augustine's *City of God* in a "Postmodern" World', *Augustinian Studies*, 25 (1994), 77–94. Dodaro's discussion of Augustine led me to reflect on how similarly and yet differently Augustine and Foucault approached sanctified discourses in their societies. Jean Bethke Elshtain also develops an intriguing analysis of the political and critical significance of similar passages from the *City of God*, especially as they pertain to just war, in *Augustine and the Limits of Politics* (Notre Dame, IN: University of Notre Dame Press, 1995, pp.105–12). She persuasively argues, as does Dodaro, that in passages like these, Augustine seems to anticipate modern cultural criticism.

26   St Augustine, *City of God*, 4.3.
27   Ibid., 4.4.
28   Ibid.
29   Ibid., 19.15.
30   Keep in mind that intentionality, in the traditional sense of the word, is a perplexing matter for Foucault. This modern problematic is created by a complicated mixture of moral intentions, unintended and often unforeseen consequences, and a loosely coherent rationality that fulfills a particular social purpose.
31   Michel Foucault, *Discipline and Punish: The Birth of the Prison* (New York: Random House, 1979).
32   Ibid., p.19.
33   Ibid.
34   Ibid., pp.18–19.
35   Ibid., p.21.
36   Ibid.
37   Ibid., p.22.
38   Ibid., p.19.
39   I am here borrowing a metaphor for Augustine's social thought from Elshtain, *Augustine and the Limits of Politics*, p.91.

II
FOUCAULT, POLITICS
AND THEOLOGY

Chapter 4

Michel Foucault's Philosophy of Religion: an Introduction to the Non-Fascist Life

James Bernauer

This chapter considers Michel Foucault's philosophy of religion, for two reasons. As the Cold War's ideologies continue to recede, the more traditional religious cultures of the west are reasserting themselves. It is probably too early to assess the prediction of Samuel Huntington that the major shift in our time is from a world of political states driven by their interests to a globe of clashing civilizations rooted in cultural identities. As he puts the issue: 'While a country could avoid Cold War alignment, it cannot lack an identity. The question, "Which side are you on" has been replaced by the much more fundamental one, "Who are you?"'[1] In dealing with this question of identity, of belonging, and of not belonging, religion seems to be assuming a central role. Secondly, Foucault's philosophy seems to possess particular strengths for the analysis of this new regime; his importance for religious studies is beginning to be appreciated.[2] I will write of what Foucault has to offer us in this realm, especially the very last stage of his work, his consideration of 'speaking frankly', of 'parrhesia'. Facing death, Foucault continued to try to return philosophy to being a way of life and not just a university discipline. Perhaps consideration of his philosophy of religion will strengthen that effort. Another consequence may be the renewal of parrhesia as a religious ideal.

Foucault's thought draws a philosophy of religion on at least three planes. Inasmuch as his project was a 'history of the present', he is necessarily engaged in a religious analysis because the forms of knowledge, power and subjectivity, which he saw as animating our culture, are constructed in decisive ways in argument with or acceptance of religious practices and concerns. This mandated Foucault's scrutiny of Christian writers and customs. In a 1975 lecture he disclosed the insight which would influence his studies of the next decade: 'Now we must ask what happened in the sixteenth century. The period which is characterized not by the beginning of a dechristianization but by the beginning of a christianization-in-depth.'[3] Secondly, Foucault's philosophy offers an effectively critical perspective for a religious self-examination, particularly for Christianity. This strength is shown in the important distinction of his last course, in 1984, between two poles in Christian experience: a parrhesiastic tradition of confident public speech emerging from the tradition of mysticism and the anti-parrhesiastic pole of its ascetic history. A summary of that very last lecture will be presented here. Finally, it is a philosophy which testifies to his decades-long search for the specifically personal dimension of his own life; in reaching it, Foucault walked the shores of the religious domain. The two passages to these shores were provided by the stylization of his erotic life and by his studies of the discourses of self-disclosure. It will not be possible to examine this level of personal search with the detail devoted to the first two planes.

In articulating these planes in this chapter's three sections, I have come to believe that they in effect constitute what he once called an 'Introduction to the Non-Fascist Life'. As a thinker acutely aware of his historical location, Foucault's thought was a critique of our age's three major political cultures: Marxism, liberalism and fascism. Contrary to their frequent self-understandings, he appreciated that these three were not separate species but, rather, were allies at least as much as they were adversaries. Foucault's examination of them may best be approached as his philosophy of religion's confrontation with fascism for he asserted the 'major enemy, the strategic adversary is fascism'. The adversary has three faces: 'historical fascism, the fascism of Hitler and Mussolini'; then there is personal fascism: 'How do we rid our speech and our acts, our hearts and our pleasures, of fascism?'; finally, there is the fascism of sad militancy, the tutelage to the categories of 'law, limit, castration, lack, lacuna' which 'Western thought has so long held sacred as a form of power and an access to reality'.[4] Common to all forms of fascism is the *obedient subject* and Foucault's philosophy of religion is in resistance to that figure.

HISTORY OF THE PRESENT

One of the most significant decisions Foucault's thought took, and a major source of its contemporary relevance, was its double refusal: first, he rejected what he called the 'blackmail of the Enlightenment', that either–or acceptance of it as some new rationality, liberated from the superstitions of a religious past; secondly, he refused to regard modernity as an epoch that had supposedly and definitively moved beyond some dark age.[5] His history of the present came to ignore the customary epochal divisions and concluded that, between different historical eras, the 'typography of the parting of the waters is hard to pin down'.[6] In the case of the early modern period, he refused the typography of a religious era yielding to a secular age. On the one hand, this rejection could involve the claim that the so-called 'religious culture' of the Middle Ages was more legend than reality and that, in fact, it was the modern struggle between Catholicism and Protestantism which made the modern period a religious age. This is the position of Jean Delumeau, whose book on the topic Foucault cites in the just published version of his 1975 lectures at the Collège de France.[7] Foucault's view contains an even more interesting thesis, namely that early modernity was not a tale of growing religious disbelief but, rather, saw the emergence of an energy which drove both the global missionary activities of European Christianity as well as a vast religious colonization of interior life. This colonization is what Michel Foucault refers to in 1975 as a 'christianization-in-depth' or a 'new Christianization'; the effect of this missionary effort was the 'vast interiorization' of a Christian experience which possessed a double center: the practice of confession and the struggle of the flesh with the spirit and the body.[8] Let us take up the former first.

Foucault's 1975 course at the Collège investigated how the general domain of abnormality was opened up for a psychiatric understanding. Foucault attributed responsibility for this development to the articulation of sexuality as a dimension within all abnormality and, most importantly, on the necessity of each individual to avow a sexual identity. His desire to analyze the conditions accounting for the appearance of this obligatory avowal of sexuality prompted him to study the Christian practice of confession.

His initial examination concentrated on its practice after the Council of Trent (1545–63), and the expansion of this 'millennial yoke of confession' to ever-larger numbers of relationships in the period after the Reformation.[9] A special concern took shape that oriented Foucault's approach to the study of Christianity. He focused on the problematic of governance that appeared in the 16th century and that showed itself in the dissemination of discourses on personal conduct, on the art of directing souls, and on the manner of educating children. This intensified Foucault's exploration of the crisis of the Reformation and Counter-Reformation, which provoked in that period an anxiety over the matter of governance by putting in 'question the manner in which one is to be spiritually ruled and led on this earth to achieve eternal salvation'.[10] The exploration of the knowledge–power relations engaged in governance directed him to a treatment of the Christian pastorate, and thus to a confrontation with the ethical formation critical to its way of obtaining knowledge and exercising power. The first major statement of the results of his research in pre-modern Christian experience came with his course 'On the Governance of the Living', which he presented in 1980. He presented a Christian practice that embraced forms of power, knowledge and relation to self very different from pre-Christian practices. It is the continuing vitality of variations on each of these that justifies Foucault's claim of a 'christianization-in-depth' throughout the modern period.

Power

Christian experience represents the development of a new form of individualizing power, that of the pastorate, which has its roots in the Hebraic image of God and his deputed King as shepherds. This power is productive, not repressive. Exercising authority over a flock of dispersed individuals rather than a land, the shepherd has the duty to guide his charges to salvation by continuously watching over them and by a permanent concern with their well-being as individuals. Christianity intensifies this concern by having pastors assume a responsibility for all the good and evil done by those to whom they are accountable and whose actions reflect upon their quality as shepherds.[11] Paramount in the exercise of this pastoral power is a virtue of obedience in the subject, a virtue which, unfortunately, all too often becomes an end in itself. Such obedience is put forward as the antidote to the human condition after Adam's Fall. With the Fall, the original subordination which human nature accorded to soul and will was lost, and the human being became a figure of revolt not only against God but also against himself. This situation was graphically illustrated in the lawlessness of sexual yearnings. Seditious sexuality signals the need for a struggle with one's self, and permanent obedience is essential to this struggle. The obedience that is intrinsic to the exercise and responsibilities of pastoral power involves specific forms of knowledge and subjectivity.[12]

Knowledge

In order to fulfill the responsibility of directing souls to their salvation, the pastor must understand the truth, not just the general truths of faith but the specific truths of each person's soul. For Foucault, Christianity is unique in the major truth obligations that are imposed upon its followers. In addition to accepting moral and dogmatic truths, they must also become excavators of their own personal truth: 'Everyone in Christianity has the duty to explore who he is, what is happening within himself, the faults he may have committed, the temptations to which he is exposed.'[13] Perhaps the most dramatic illustration of this obligation to discover and manifest one's truth took place in those liturgical ceremonies in which the early Christians would avow their state as sinners, and then take on the status of public penitents.[14]

Less dramatic but more enduring was the search for truth served by those practices of examination of conscience and confession that Christianity first developed in monastic life. The Christian campaign for self-knowledge was not developed directly in the interest of controlling sexual conduct, but rather for the sake of a deepened awareness of one's interior life. 'Cassian is interested in the movements of the body and the mind, images, feelings, memories, faces in dreams, the spontaneous movements of thoughts, the consenting (or refusing) will, waking and sleeping.'[15] This endless task of self-scrutiny is accompanied by regular confessions to another, for verbalization of thoughts is another level of sorting out the good thoughts from those that are evil, namely, those that seek to hide from the light of public expression. Through its examination of conscience and confession, Christianity fashions a technology of the self that enabled people to transform themselves. The principal product of this technology was a unique form of subjectivity.[16]

Subjectivity

Christian practices produced an interiorization or subjectivization of the human being as the outcome of two processes. The first is the constitution of the self as a hermeneutical reality, namely, the recognition that there is a truth in the subject, that the soul is the place where this truth resides, and that true discourses can be articulated concerning it.[17] The Christian self is an obscure text demanding permanent interpretation through ever more sophisticated practices of attentiveness, decipherment and verbalization.

The second process is both paradoxical and yet essential for appreciating the unique mode of Christian subjectivity. The deciphering of one's soul is but one dimension of the subjectivity that relates the self to the self. While it involves an 'indeterminate objectivization of the self by the self-indeterminate in the sense that one must be extending as far as possible the range of one's thoughts, however insignificant and innocent they may appear to be', the point of such objectivization is not to assemble a progressive knowledge of oneself for the sake of achieving the self-mastery that classical pagan thought advanced as an ideal.[18] The purpose of the Christian hermeneutic of the self is to foster renunciation of the self who has been objectified. The individual's relation to the self imitates both the baptismal turning from the old self to a new-found otherness, as well as the ceremony of public penance that was depicted as a form of martyrdom proclaiming the symbolic death of the old self. The continual mortification entailed by a permanent hermeneutic and renunciation of the self makes of that symbolic death an everyday event. All truth about the self is tied to the sacrifice of that same self, and the Christian experience of subjectivity declares itself most clearly in the sounds of a rupture with oneself, of an admission that 'I am not who I am.'[19] This capacity for self-renunciation was built from the ascetic power with regard to oneself that was generated by a practice of obedience, and from the skepticism with respect to one's knowledge of oneself that was created by hermeneutical self-analysis. As we shall see, Foucault later came to warn Christianity of the dangers of that obedience.

Fascism

In recent years I have been in the process of exploring the implications of Foucault's assertions regarding modern western culture's christianization-in-depth, especially in the interest of an analysis of fascism. I have come to agree with the judgment of Geoff Eley that Foucault's style of analysis should make him the 'patron saint' for the study of Nazism.[20] I tried to indicate Foucault's strength in this area in an essay 'Sexuality in the Nazi War Against Jewish and Gay People'.[21] That treatment will not be repeated here. Instead, I would like to indicate a complementary analysis, looking, not at the practices of moral formation, but rather at fascism's discourse of political religiosity. If we understand the force of that discourse, we will better appreciate why Foucault sought to rehabilitate parrhesia as a form of speech that was both resistant to the confessional mode which western culture had inherited and alert to the religious categories that had come to be employed politically.

It has long been recognized that fascism cultivated a religious sensibility and frequently it was described as a type of 'religion of nature'. There was a worship of life itself which subverted the old dualism of body and spirit. This sanctification of biological life was transformed into an adoration of national life.[22] Even with this religion of nature, fascism, in both its German and Italian forms, helped persuade its audiences through a utilization of categories from traditional Christian discourses. Political life was sacralized as sacral language was politicized.[23] National Socialist religious mythology made of Hitler a messianic figure, constructed God as a symbol of vital forces, and articulated doctrines of human nature and redemption.[24] I would like to give but one example from a speech of Hitler's which exhibits my claim on how religious discourse was manipulated by him. Hitler's power was tied up with his oratory, better, his preaching. Here is an excerpt from his speech to his political leaders at the 1936 Party Rally in Nuremberg. Within the body of the speech are inserted references to the Biblical texts he is utilizing.

> How deeply we feel once more in this hour the miracle that has brought us together! Once you heard the voice of a man, and it spoke to your hearts, it awakened you, and you followed that voice. [John iii: 4] Year in and year out you followed it, without even having seen the speaker; you only heard a voice and followed it. [John xx: 19–31] Now that we meet here, we are all filled with the wonder of this gathering. Not every one of you can see me and I do not see each one of you. But I feel you and you feel me! It is faith in our nation

that has made us little people great, that has made us poor people rich, that has made us wavering, fearful, timid, people brave and confident; that has made us erring wanderers clear-sighted and has brought us together! [John xvi: 16–17; Luke vii: 22] ... Now we are together, we are with him and he is with us, and now we are Germany! [John xiv: 3][25]

This speech of Hitler's, and of so many other National Socialist leaders who spoke similarly, is in reality a *confession of faith*. The satisfaction in making such confessions is one significant way in which the 'christianization-in-depth' theme comes to outward expression. If psychoanalysis provides a very clear example of how a religious technology of the self migrated into the personal experience of the modern period, fascist discourse shows its survival into collective political articulation. In the light of the historic significance of the struggle between Catholics and Protestants in German lands, it is surprising that it has taken so long for the theme of 'confessionalization' (*Konfessionsbildung* – the intellectual and organizational hardening of the diverging Christian confessions) to become a key theme in analysis of German history.[26] This made sharply opposed identities a major force in modern European history: protected by fortresses of dogmatic truths which generated fierce polemic. The alliance between these confessions and the knowledges of the human sciences helped to forge a regime of knowledge–power–subjectivity that shaped European political culture and that led it to the catastrophe of its 20th-century terrors. The cunning strategy of National Socialism was to have attempted a reconciliation between advanced scientific culture and Germany's inherited religious sensibility and passion. Jeffrey Herf describes the key aspect of this reconciliation as 'reactionary modernism' and maintains that 'Germany, as the country located between East and West, had a unique mission. It alone was able to combine technology and soul.'[27] It is this dangerous cultural complex in western culture that creates the need for a way of speaking which is able to distance itself from the religious regime of dogmatic faith and the production of truth in the modern sciences, both natural and human. It is in the perspective of this problematic and need that we are better able to appreciate Foucault's quest for another way of speaking truthfully in his last lectures on parrhesia.

RESISTANT PARRHESIA

Although Foucault developed analyses that were relevant, explicitly or implicitly, to a critical reflection on Christianity itself, it was in his very last lecture at the Collège de France on 28 March 1984 that he proposed a specific treatment of Christianity in terms of two poles: a parrhesiastic pole which is grounded in the mystical tradition of Christianity and an anti-parrhesiastic pole which emerged from its ascetic history. This latter axis operates through a 'fearful and reverent obedience to God and in a suspicious deciphering of oneself by way of temptations and tests'.[28] We will better understand the importance and efficacy of this distinction if we grasp the movement of the lecture and of the 1984 course it concluded. He announced that this final lecture had a threefold objective. First, he wanted to speak about parrhesia among the Cynic philosophers. This had been the theme of his previous four lectures.[29] Secondly, he wanted to treat the development of the term 'parrhesia' among Christian authors of the first centuries. Finally, he wanted to integrate the 1984 and 1983 courses into the general framework he was giving to these analyses.

Parrhesia

Let us briefly look at the final lectures. Although the first is a general résumé of the previous year's work, I would like to stress a few major distinctions to which he came in 1983.[30] He described his principal purpose for his examination of texts in 1983 as the construction of a 'genealogy of the critical attitude in Western philosophy'.[31] At the heart of this genealogy were the distinct ways in which truth was problematized as a concern. One side of the concern was the approach of an 'analytics of truth' which had the objective of guaranteeing that the process of reasoning was correct in the determination of whether a statement was true or not. The other side of the interest was what Foucault called the 'critical tradition' of the west. That tradition posed other questions. Who is able to tell the truth? What are the moral, ethical and spiritual conditions which entitle one to present oneself as a truth teller? About what is it important to tell the truth? What are the consequences of telling the truth? What is the relationship between the activity of truth telling and the exercise of power? His recovery of the critical tradition led him to a definition of parrhesia as a personal frankness which was different from other modalities of truth speaking (namely, those of prophet, sage or teacher–technician): 'parrhesia is a verbal activity in which a speaker expresses his personal relationship to truth, and risks his life because he recognizes truth-telling as a duty to improve or help other people (as well as himself)'. The parrhesiast articulates 'criticism instead of flattery, and moral duty instead of self-interest and moral apathy'.[32] Foucault's 1984 lectures pursued the critical attitude with an increasing focus upon the philosophy of the Cynics. They were the ones who bound together a style of life with a shameless truth telling; they force the question of what a philosophical life is. Indeed, for Foucault, cynicism is the 'externalization of the theme of the philosophical life in its relation to philosophy itself' (Lecture of 14 March 1984).

The Cynic is distinguished by a parrhesia that functions in various ways. The first is *instrumental*. In order to enlighten humanity, the Cynic must have no ties that would prevent him from accomplishing this task. He must have no family, home or possessions that would distract him from the truth. His style of life is thus the condition of possibility for his parrhesia. The second is *reductive*. The Cynic must lead a life that eliminates all useless conventions, that cleanses his existence in order to reveal the truth. The third is *testing*. The Cynical style of life allows him to find that alone which is indispensable to lead a true life. In this way, rather than separating the soul from life, the Cynic reduces life itself, to itself (Lecture of 29 February 1984). Those who are familiar with the writings of Foucault know that he does not normally encourage people to think that they can return to some earlier perfect model of how to lead a philosophical life. This is also the case with his examination of Cynicism, but in this case that ancient philosophy has been carried into the present by way of three great historical streams: revolutionary movements, especially of the 19th century which demanded not only political change but also required a certain activist style of life; art, which manifests the Cynical principle of life as the scandal of truth: the life of the artist is recognized as different and, in modern times, art has abandoned imitative and ornamental functions and has embraced a violent reduction of life to its elementary existence; finally, there is Christianity, which has been perceived at different times as similar to Cynicism because it presents itself as the visible scandal of truth opposed to institutions, including ecclesiastical ones (Lecture of 29 February 1984). We will now focus on this Christianity which is the major topic of Foucault's last lecture.

Foucault's final lecture (28 March 1984)

In his very last lecture, Foucault returns to his concern with parrhesia. He begins by looking at the inflection that the Cynics gave to it, after which he examines the changing meanings of parrhesia in Judeo-Hellenistic texts, the New Testament and early Christian asceticism.

Cynics and parrhesia

The Cynical scorn for earthly kings had two meanings: it was a critical affirmation of the Cynic as the true king, and it was a reversal of the traditional signs of a political monarchy, in that the Cynics advocated solitude, deprivation and endurance. In this way, the Cynic affirmed himself as participating in the sovereignty of the Gods. This had two consequences. First, Cynical sovereignty founded the possibility of a happy life. This involved a relationship to oneself, in which sovereignty manifested itself through the joy with which one accepted one's destiny. All human troubles became opportunities for positive exercises of endurance. Second, Cynical sovereignty was a manifestation of the truth. The Cynic both told the truth and was a sort of angel of truth. The truth, however, could be manifested in and through the Cynical life in different ways:

1   It could be manifested as conformity with the truth. This could be the conformity of one's conduct with the truth: the Cynic never said one thing while doing another. It could also be the conformity of one's own body with the truth: by the deprivation to which the Cynic submitted himself, as well as by his cleanliness (in Epictetus's version). The Cynic in this way attracts others to the truth. He must be a visible statue of the truth.
2   It could be manifested through knowledge of the self. The Cynic practiced the work of truth on his own self in several ways.
3   The Cynic, like an athlete, assessed himself and his capabilities in order to prepare himself for various tests; that is, for his confrontation with the faults and vices of humanity.
4   The Cynic was in a state of perpetual vigilance towards himself, constantly supervising his soul and its representations.
5   The Cynic constantly supervised the lives of others. He did not, however, indulge in the fault that was despised by the Greeks, that of meddling in the affairs of others. Rather, he only looked after that in others which concerned humanity in general. In this way, then, by looking after others, he was also looking after himself. The Cynic did not interfere with the lives of those he looked after any more than a general interferes with the lives of the soldiers under his command. In both cases, the care for others coincides with the care for the self.

This manifestation of the truth by the Cynics had two consequences. First, it led to a change in conduct. The Cynic showed others that they were in error in their beliefs about the truth, about good and evil, about peace and happiness; that they searched for these truths *elsewhere* than where they really were. This use of the words 'elsewhere' and 'other' were crucial to Cynical practices. Through his *other* life, the Cynic revealed that the ordinary lives of other people were other than the truth.

Second, it led to the need for a total change of the world. The new world could only become the truth with a total change and, most of all, a change in the relationship to oneself.

Pagan asceticism and Christian asceticism

Foucault offers a few guiding principles for a history of the passage from pagan asceticism to Christian asceticism. First, it is necessary to trace the continuity between pagan and Christian ascetic practices. Thus the Cynics practiced deprivation, but in order to achieve a balance; that is, to achieve the most pleasure with the fewest costs and dependencies. For the Christian ascetics, however, deprivation meant the elimination of pleasure altogether. The Christians also continued the Cynical practice of scandal and indifference to the established authorities and to the opinion of others.

But the Christians also introduced important new elements into ascetic practices. Two stand out in particular. In the first place, Christian ascetic practices were not directed at the possibility merely of a different world (*autre monde*), but at a totally other world (*monde autre*). The other life of the ascetic was thus a way of acceding to this other world. The philosophical importance of Christianity is that it is the meeting point between Cynical asceticism and Platonic metaphysics; it brings that metaphysics together with 'the historical–critical experience of the world'.

'The second major difference is of an entirely dissimilar order: it is the importance which is given in Christianity, and only in Christianity, to the principle of obedience, a principle found neither in Cynicism nor in Platonism. This principle must be understood in a broad sense: it is obedience to a god who is conceived of as a despot, a master for whom one is slave and servant. It is obedience to his will which is in the form of law; and it is obedience to those who represent the despot, master and lord, and who retain an authority to which submission must be total.' Christianity stipulated that one could accede to the other world only by obeying the other. Thus the true could occur only through obedience, and only for acceding to the other world.

Thus 'it is impossible to characterize the difference between paganism and Christianity as the difference between a Christian moral asceticism and a non-ascetic morality which would be that of antiquity. Such a vision would be a total day-dream'. The difference is illumined by noting the double relationship between, on the one hand, the other world to which one has access, thanks to this asceticism and, on the other hand, the 'obedience to the other, to the other in this world, the obedience to the other which is an obedience to God and to the men who represent him'. In this way, Christianity inaugurated a new relationship to the self, a new structure of power, and a new regime of truth. This development can be studied by examining the Christian experience of parrhesia.

Christianity and parrhesia

Foucault examines three moments in the Christian experience of parrhesia.

Judeo-Hellenistic texts   Parrhesia appears in three different contexts in these texts. In the same way as it appeared in the Greek context, parrhesia appears in these texts as the courage to tell the truth on the part of those who are pure and noble in spirit. Parrhesia also means the openness of the heart and the transparency of the soul offering themselves to God's gaze. It represents the ascendant movement of the soul towards God, where it will find its joy and its felicity. Finally, parrhesia appears as a property, quality and gift from God himself. It is the very being of God in his manifestation. It is the overwhelming presence of God, in anger and in love. Parrhesia thus signifies the encounter between God and his creation.

The New Testament texts   In the New Testament, parrhesia never appears as a mode of divine manifestation; it only applies to humans. Furthermore, it is not so much the courage to tell the truth as an attitude that does not need to be expressed in words. It is applied to two different groups of people, first to Christians in general. Parrhesia means the unspoken confidence of the Christian in God. This confidence, however, is based on obedience to God's will. Parrhesia signifies the Christian's assurance that he will have the life of everlasting love. 'This is expressed in the First Letter of John, chapter 4, verses 16 to 17: "God is love, and whoever remains in love remains in God and God in him. In this is love brought to perfection among us, that we have confidence on the day of judgment because as he is, so are we in this world."' Foucault continues: 'And so, for Christians in general, parrhesia is this confidence in God's love, the love which God manifests when he hears the prayers that are addressed to him, the love that God shows and will show on the day of judgment.'

Parrhesia is also applied to the apostles. It is the apostolic virtue par excellence. It manifests the personal courage to preach the truth of Christ even at the risk of one's own life. In this way, it is very similar to ancient Greek parrhesia.

Early ascetic texts   In this period, parrhesia acquires a very ambiguous meaning for the Christians. It is invested with both positive and negative significance. On one hand, parrhesia is the attitude of the good Christian towards others. It is the virtue of the martyrs, the courage which one exercises for oneself but also for others, to persuade them or confirm them in faith. In addition, parrhesia is a manner of being before God. It is confidence in God's goodness, and the belief that one can be heard by God. This parrhesia involves the primitive state of humanity, when man could encounter God face to face.

The negative connotation of parrhesia is grounded in the Christian principle of obedience, which became particularly important during this period. This principle required obedience to God, his will and his earthly representatives. It also required one to be suspicious of oneself, and imposed the rule of silence. In this context, parrhesia came to mean presumption and arrogance. A parrhesiast was someone who believed he could find salvation on his own. Parrhesia also meant the pushing away from oneself of the fear of God and divine punishment; the neglect of the self (while previously it had meant the care for the self); confidence in the world; physical familiarity with others; and shamelessness and disrespect (which may or may not be a direct reference to Cynical parrhesia).

In this way, Christianity developed between two poles. There is a parrhesiastic pole, which represents the mystical tradition of Christianity. It involves human confidence in the overflowing love of God, and the belief that God will answer the prayers of the Christian. And there is an anti-parrhesiastic pole, which represents the ascetic tradition. It holds that truth occurs only through the fearful obedience to God and the suspicious examination of oneself through temptations and tests. Any modern movement toward the parrhesiastic pole entails an escape from the positivist, obedient human reality that has been created in the technologies of western thought and practice. The achievement of Foucault's earlier work was to facilitate that escape by problematizing modern human identity.

The death of 'man'

The single idea for which Foucault's philosophy is best known is its announcement of the 'imminence of the death of man', the doom which he has pronounced for the culture of modern humanism: 'you may have killed God beneath the weight of all that you have said; but don't imagine that, with all that you are saying, you will make a man that will live longer than he'.[33] For many, it is Foucault's most infamous statement, betraying his thought as yet another product of a new European pessimism which derives decadent pleasure in a nihilistic destruction of ideas once considered central to western civilization. Foucault's proclamation and welcoming of man's death is interpreted as another sign of the profound perversity into which our age has fallen.[34] Such an interpretation would be an extraordinary misperception of the temper and meaning of Foucault's announcement. The declaration of man's death must be understood on several interrelated levels.

Anti-humanism

First, it both crystallizes in a phrase the central concern that worried Foucault's philosophy and interprets the entire path which Foucault's thought sculpted. For Foucault, modern man and anthropology were prisons: an incarceration of human beings within a specifically modern system of thought and practice which had become so intimately a part of them that it was no longer experienced as a series of confinements, but was embraced as the very substance of being human. The prison from which Foucault seeks escape is nothing other than the modern identity of man himself, the historically constituted figure in that humanism which is both a particular understanding of human reality and a technology for human development: a truth which is power and a power which presents itself as truth.[35] Foucault's various studies represented a relentless campaign against modern humanism and the notion of man which stands at its center. Foucault's work may properly be characterized as an anti-humanism, even if the term provides for many the 'most scandalous aspect' of modern French thought.[36] Although the anti-humanistic accents of Foucault's thought may always offend sensibilities, it is important to recognize that modern humanism represents for him an extraordinary diminishment of the human being. Ethically, Foucault's writings were attempts to demystify the self-professed benevolence of a humanism which, in putting forward its programs for human progress and institutional development, has actually created personal and social conducts of awesome destructiveness.

Negative theology

Secondly, Foucault's thought may be regarded as a modern form of negative theology, his effort to overcome that figure of man whom modernity fashioned as a substitute for the Absolute, and whose quasi-divinization entailed a flight from humanity. The promise of that effort was not a new philosophical anthropology but an invitation to think through our relationship to modern humanism and the view of man and human freedom which it enunciated. Although Foucault never developed the analogy, negative theology is one of the few styles with which he has explicitly compared his own thought.[37] His choice of the comparison is illuminating. It points first of all to Foucault's own experience of a fundamental personal conflict in his intellectual interests as a 'religious problem'.[38] On the one hand, he was passionately involved in the new literary work of such writers as Georges Bataille and Maurice Blanchot which displaced interest for him from a narrative of man to the being of the language within which images of the human are fashioned. On the other hand, Foucault says he was attracted to the structuralist analysis carried out by anthropologist Claude Lévi-Strauss and the historian of religion, Georges Dumézil, both of whom dispersed human reality among cultural structures. That Foucault considers the religious problem as the common denominator for both interests indicates that all four thinkers, although in very different ways, unleashed styles of reflection and forms of experience which overturned for him the accepted natural identity of man.

Foucault's negative theology is a critique not of the conceptualizations employed for God but of that modern figure of finite man whose identity was put forward as capturing the essence of human being. Nevertheless, Foucault's archaeology is best described as a negative theology, rather than a negative anthropology, for its flight from modern man is an escape from yet another conceptualization of God. The project of modernity was a divinization of man, the passion to be, as Sartre saw, the '*Ens causa sui*, which religions call God'. Although Descartes' roots in Scholastic thought and vocabulary enabled him to avoid drawing the implication of his meditations, the discovery of the *cogito* was actually the transference to man of God's function in medieval metaphysics as source of the world's reality and intelligibility: ' "I think" was to become the divine "I am".'[39] After Kant and Hegel had completed the transference and Nietzsche had declared it a cultural fact, it was Foucault who saw that the death of God necessarily entailed the death of the figure who had taken on his role as the Absolute.

Recognizing archaeology as a negative theology permits us to appreciate its strategy, most especially its choice of history as a privileged mode of reflection and its functioning as criticism of that theology of man which humanism is. Parallel to the death of God was a divinization of man. Claiming a firm knowledge of this figure humanism made humanity's happiness its ultimate goal and human perfection its permanent project. The place for humanism's actualization, however, was not the order of the supernatural but rather of the historical. In history purpose and progress could be found and man's victory and beatitude achieved. Uniting the development of modern thought and practice, the order of time became the Sacred History of Man. The religion of the god Humanity, with its priesthood of scientific experts, as advanced in Comte's positivist philosophy, is an integral element of that philosophy and of the modern age itself.[40] Faced with a sacred history constituted by man's revelation to himself of his ever advancing perfection, Foucault has attempted to demythologize the historical reality in which the modern identity of man and the sources of his humanistic knowledges are lodged.

Temporary 'man'

Thirdly, on the level of thought, Foucault's claim of man's death points to a deeper development. It recognizes the fact that the place which man and subjectivity have occupied as the central focus for modern thought has been subverted by a profound change in the direction of our present-day knowledge. While the inadequacy of the category 'man' can already be glimpsed in the structural analysis of Marx or the genealogical investigations of Nietzsche, Foucault indicates that it is the very development of the human sciences which promises that the man of modern humanism is not only finite but also temporary – a figure who will vanish 'like a face drawn in sand at the edge of the sea'.[41] The appearance of psychoanalysis, ethnology and linguistics, to which the human sciences have led, actually sabotages the investigation of man, for they explore the individual and cultural unconsciousness which unveil the fundamental conditions for knowledge about man, for any anthropology. They are, thus, 'counter-sciences' in that they return the human sciences to their epistemological foundations and, thus, they 'dissolve man' and 'ceaselessly "unmake" that very man who is creating and recreating his positivity in the human sciences'.

Foucault defined his own methodological work as an attempt at 'historical analysis freed from the anthropological theme'.[42] In looking beyond man to the cultural crisis from which his specific modern positivity emerged, Foucault restores us to a consciousness of the systems of knowledge and power, whose dominant role in shaping our culture needs to be examined. Victim of this recognition is modernity's false sense of human autonomy and the equally false approach to history which saw it as a passive reality simply to be construed in the pattern of some ideological vision. In renewing a respect for historical events as more than servants of some imaginary human sovereign will, Foucault returns to our sense of history the attitude which Karl Barth saw as precluded by Enlightenment thought: the attitude that the 'historian should take history seriously as a force outside himself, which had it in its power to contradict him and which spoke to him with authority'.[43] The aim of that renewal is not to imprison us within history but, rather, to show how contingent an epoch's order of things actually is, so as to 'show up, transform and reverse the systems which quietly order us about'.[44] This entails a combat with those human sciences whose truth claims are largely defensible in terms of a blind faith in modern humanistic assumptions.

The ensemble of truths in the human sciences currently determines which alternatives for a society's conduct will be articulated and which opportunities will be conceded to human intervention and political action. Because, for Foucault, 'truth is of the world', today's intellectual is summoned to the fundamental task of uncovering how truth operates in our culture, of grasping the uncriticized operation of the 'rules according to which true and false are separated and specific effects of power attached to the true'.[45] In displacing the anthropological focus, Foucault undermines approaches which seek merely to discover patterns of historical continuity, an interest correlative to the presumption that there is a natural, transcultural, ever-identical man. The emphasis of Foucault's thought is on discontinuity, on the question, for example, of how cultures and, thus, human beings in other historical epochs are fundamentally different from the reality fabricated in the modern age. For Foucault, the effect of humanistically inspired histories was to justify the modern age as the culmination of a continuous march of progress: it reduced history to a 'place of rest, certainty, reconciliation, a place of tranquilized sleep' which has made it possible for us to 'avoid the difference of our present'.[46]

Politics of our selves

Finally, on the level of action, Foucault's declaration of man's death is intended as the starting point for a radical politics of our selves, the challenge to our current culture's power to determine our self-identity and lay down a program for our liberation. For Foucault, the many campaigns for liberation from repression (for example, sexual repression) which modernity has been so fertile in generating are often mere diversions from an authentic quest for freedom. For Foucault, that quest begins in the recognition of the human being as an 'agonism', a 'permanent provocation' to the knowledge and power which are allowed to operate on our selves.[47] Although it captures a central insight of his entire work, the specific description of human being as an agonism was owed to his examination of the ancient and Christian texts of his last period.[48] It was meant to engender a new taste of the self, a taste which would be estranged from modern identity.

As a result of his study of Christian practices, Foucault came to grasp a crucial moment in the religious–mystical formation of the self, a moment which sharply differentiated it from the ascetical tradition of both Christianity and modernity. For example, the aim of modern knowledges and practices is to foster the emergence of a positive self in which one recognizes and is bound to the self-knowledge defined through the categories of the anthropological sciences. Modern self-appropriation is the discovery of and attachment to that truth, as the firm basis for encounter with the world. Foucault contrasted the modern vision with those Christian practices which invited a renunciation of the self who was articulated as true. In his view, the key to the Christian's experience of self-discovery and subjectivity was located in the model of martyrdom.[49] One shows who one is by the preference for physical death over spiritual death. The struggle for self-knowledge entails a continual mortification, an 'everyday death' which is a kind of 'relation from oneself to oneself', a relation which becomes a 'constitutive part of the Christian self-identity'.[50] This strategy of renunciation enabled Christian experience to avoid the danger of the spiritual death of positivist self-identity. The effect of this continuing self-renunciation was to open the subject's existence to a field of indefinite interpretation, relativizing any particular anthropology.

As was mentioned at the beginning of this section, Foucault had intended his last lecture to include a more general statement about the framework of his analyses, but he ran out of time before he could do so. I would like to develop a few points in a possible Foucauldian frame for the analysis of parrhesia. Although arguably less influential in the institutional history of Catholicism than the ascetic tradition, the parrhesiastic mystical pole has operated with power: it is the strength of a 'confidence in God' which has subsisted, not without pain, in the margins of Christianity, as a resistance to that forced, ascetic self-disclosure in 'obedience to, and in fear and trembling before God'.[51] The little Foucault says of the mystical parrhesiastic pole is suggestive and provides a fresh vista on some of his most engaging analyses. He appreciated how parrhesia took on a unique feature in Christianity: not the political and moral virtues of the ancient pagan world but rather the power of a courageous openness to mystery. This courage, especially as exhibited in the boldness of the preacher or martyr, was linked to the Christian conviction of God's decisive and full revelation in Jesus of Nazareth and the absolute security of faith in one's personal redemption. This radical openness, parrhesia as exposure to God and mystery, is unique to Christianity in the west and never finds expression in secular Greek: 'in the only passage in Isocrates where parrhesia appears in connection with the gods, it is given the unfavourable meaning of "blasphemy"'.[52]

As Foucault appreciated, mystical parrhesia's courage flows from a confidence not in ideas but in the love of a God who will give special proof of that love on the day of judgment.[53] Two points should be stressed. Mystical parrhesia is a form of communication that is rooted in a love which builds personal community. It is bound up with the language and ideas traditionally associated with Greek visions of friendship as we can see, for example, in Paul's usage in his Letter to the Philippians.[54] The second point to note is how parrhesia operates specifically in the Johannine corpus. While the term appears 40 times in the New Testament, fully one-third of these appearances are in John. In terms of the size of John's text, parrhesia appears there about three times as often as one would proportionately expect. This is important because it transfers the notion of mystery in Christian parrhesia from any tendency to place it on the register of the hidden and obscure. Parrhesia appears in John's Gospel in three distinct meanings: public versus private, plain against obscure, and bold or courageous against timid.[55] John's Jesus is characterized by the determination to speak publicly and plainly.

It may seem that we have wandered far from Foucault in this discussion of Christian parrhesia but, in fact, one may argue that Foucault's own articulation of parrhesia is bound up with its mystical version and that tradition's opposition to any forced disclosure in obedience. At the close of his life, Foucault counseled a 'refusal of this kind of individuality which has been imposed upon us for several centuries', and acknowledgment of the need to sacrifice the identity of the man we had come to know and trust.[56] Foucault's negative theology possesses religious significance, for its effort to dismantle man's prison is also a celebration of the human being's resistant openness. His investigations shatter the silence which the chatter of the trivially knowable has too often forced upon experiences which are signals of the mysterious:

those passionate questions and states of mind which exceed judgments of mental health and illness; the encounter with a sickness unto death that is irreducible to the history of one's body; the self-interrogations which remember Socratic ignorance and are restless with confinements in processes of life, labor, language; the possession of a sexual dynamism which is a product not merely of biology and culture but of life's and love's mysteries. If one stream of Western culture's christianization-in-depth is its dangerous esteem for obedience, a more fundamental and promising current is its confidence that love is the center of the mystery, in exposure to which we live our lives.

FOUCAULT'S SPIRITUALITY OF PERSONS

Our last section will be brief. All who knew Foucault personally or have read his works realize that he was possessed by a profound desire not to be objectivized. He compares the writer to the first Christian martyrs and speaks of the 'sacrifice, the negation of the self' as the 'nucleus of the literary experience of the modern world'.[57] In 1969, he wrote: 'I am no doubt not the only one who writes in order to have no face. Do not ask who I am and do not ask me to remain the same: leave it to our bureaucrats and our police to see that our papers are in order.'[58] The statement is vintage Foucault: an experience of thinking which is identified with an art of escaping the demands of what others consider thought-worthy; a personal pleasure in being different, in not appearing with the face his commentators predicted on the basis of his earlier writings. We are better able to appreciate now that he was on his way to becoming a parrhesiast – affirming his personal spontaneity and character in negation of objectivized identities; in negation of the psychologist and human scientist he had trained to become; in negation of the political ideology of Marxism which had affected his university years; in negation of even the sexual identity of 'homosexual' as a potential trap. These negations served, however, his artistic creation of himself as a person, as a parrhesiast and he acknowledged that 'each of my works is a part of my own biography'.[59]

How might we characterize the life he created? Alexander Nehamas has made the obvious comparison with Socrates. Both were on profound searches which made their philosophy a way of life, one which they trusted would aid their societies. Both needed courage because they confronted their cultures with the dark, shameful side of knowledges which both claimed were often but forms of ignorance.[60] Another author has picked up Foucault's special interest in the character of Creusa in Euripides's *Ion* as an insight into his self-understanding. Creusa had been victimized and had to suffer terribly and unjustly. Did Foucault only become the critic and person he did as a result of the suffering in his own life and his determination to speak truthfully of it?[61] Certainly Foucault's clear sympathy for outsiders and victims came from the difficult experiences his own life endured and which his biographers have recounted with such detail.[62]

Although Foucault was certainly influenced by the Greeks, it is also clear that his style of parrhesia does not disguise the fragments of religious culture, that christianization-in-depth of which we have been speaking, from which it is partly constructed. Who would deny that his personal resistances to objectivizations of himself mirrored closely the mysticism and negative theology he studied? I believe John Caputo has insightfully captured the Foucauldian face of the parrhesiast after the work of a negative theology: our confidence as parrhesiasts is dependent 'on not knowing who we are'. What is recognized is a resistance to 'all secret codes, who has no identity, who is not reducible to one or another of the hermeneutic techniques of pastoral power, who is marked by the "right to be different"'. For Foucault, the freedom of the person is a 'kind of irrepressibility', a 'capacity for novelty and innovation'.[63]

In addition to that powerful non-knowledge, however, there were other traits he respected in Christian parrhesia. Its themes of hope and love are not far from Foucault's personal experience. He possessed a non-ideological hope, a confidence that effective resistance could take place, even against the most entrenched of political or moral systems. Suspicion was an ally of his hope and its protector from ideological fiction and revolutionary excess. This is how he expressed his view in an unpublished part of a discussion with several Americans at Berkeley:

> Despair and hopelessness are one thing; suspicion is another. And if you are suspicious, it is because, of course, you have a certain hope. The problem is to know which kind of hope you have, and which kind of hope it is reasonable to have in order to avoid what I would call not the 'pessimistic circle' you speak of, but the political circle which reintroduces in your hopes, and through your hopes, the things you want to avoid by these hopes.

When one of his discussants noted that his comment seemed 'very Christian', Foucault replied: 'Yes, I have a very strong, Christian background, and I am not ashamed.'[64] His hope is not built on a sense of sin, but who would not see that it reflects a Christian realism about human imperfection?

Even more pronounced than this hope was his commitment to friendship and love, a commitment which reflected the spirituality which had long shaped him. Foucault's capacity for and success in friendship was manifested in the extraordinary grief which met the news of his sudden death. He cherished many and communicated that care to friends, acquaintances, students and readers. In his last years he returned time and time again to the theme of friendship and how it might reorient our current cultures, how it might transform nations, classes, even genders.[65] His thought recognized the mystery and strangeness of human beings and the task of establishing friendship among them was the most important religious task of his philosophy of religion. I have claimed that this philosophy of religion may be regarded as what he called an 'introduction to the non-fascist life'. If anything characterizes fascist ideology, it is its ability to construct enemies with whom no reconciliation could ever take place and so this theme of friendship and the reconciliation that is its core operates as the unmaking of that ideology. In Foucault there was united with receptivity to the difference of others a joy which was a resistance to what he called the 'sad militants' and the 'terrorists of theory'.[66] I believe the joy which was so distinctive of him was rooted in the confidence of a man who had been touched by mystery, however we account for that touching.

Finally, a concluding note which is also a question far beyond my capacity to address. A recent interpretation of Foucault's work claims that running through it is an Oriental subtext and that he appropriates insights from eastern religion and philosophy to resist domination by a western Ratio. Do we see an oriental influence on him in his radical interrogation of western individualism? Is his notion of stylization of life, of an 'aesthetics of existence', themes so crucial in his final thought, owed to Asia?[67] His visits to Japan in 1970 and 1978 were important for him and some of his conversations there, especially those that treated mysticism, spirituality and zen, give a far better indication of how the project of his history of sexuality was developing than anything he revealed in English or French interviews. Is it possible that Foucault's philosophy of religion may serve as a bridge between eastern and western practices of the self?

NOTES

1   Samuel Huntington, *The Clash of Civilizations and the Remaking of World Order* (New York: Touchstone, 1996, p.125).
2   See M. Foucault, *Religion and Culture: Selected Texts*, edited by Jeremy Carrette (Manchester: Manchester University Press, 1999) and Jeremy Carrette, *Foucault and Religion: Spiritual Corporality and Political Spirituality* (London: Routledge, 2000).
3   Course Lecture of 19 February 1975. The lectures from this course have now been published as *Les anormaux* (Paris: Gallimard and Le Seuil, 1999, p.164).
4   English Preface to Gilles Deleuze and Félix Guattari, *Anti-Oedipus: Capitalism and Schizophrenia* (New York: Viking Press, 1977, p.xiii).
5   'What Is Enlightenment?', *The Foucault Reader*, edited by Paul Rabinow (New York: Pantheon, 1984, pp.40–43).
6   'The Battle for Chastity', in *The Essential Works of Foucault 1954–1984: Ethics, Subjectivity and Truth*, edited by Paul Rabinow (New York: New Press, 1997, p.196) and *Religion and Culture*, p.197.
7   *Les anormaux*, p.182, n.18. The English translation of Delumeau's work was published as *Catholicism between Luther and Voltaire: a new view of the Counter-Reformation* (London: Burns & Oates, 1977).
8   Course of 19 February 1975, *Les anormaux*, pp.164, 179, 175.
9   *The History of Sexuality I: An Introduction* (New York: Pantheon, 1978, p.61).
10 'Governmentality', *I & C*, 6 (Autumn, 1979) p.6. This is the translation of an important lecture from Foucault's 1978 course.
11 'Omnes et Singulatim: Towards a Criticism of "Political Reason"', *The Tanner Lectures on Human Values*, 2 (Salt Lake City: University of Utah Press, 1981, pp.228–31, 236–8). Lectures from the 19 and 26 March 1980 course at the Collège de France which I was able to attend.
12 These sections are abbreviated versions of the section 'On Christian Experience' in James Bernauer, *Michel Foucault's Force of Flight: Toward an Ethics for Thought* (Amherst, New York: Humanities Press, 1990, pp.161–5).
13 'Sexuality and Solitude', *The Essential Works of Foucault 1954–1984: Ethics, Subjectivity and Truth*, p.178, and *Religion and Culture*, p.182.
14 Lectures of 5 and 12 March 1980 at the Collège de France; Lecture of 15 June 1982 from Foucault's course at the University of Toronto, 'The Discourse of Self-Disclosure'.
15 'The Battle for Chastity', *The Essential Works of Foucault 1954–1984: Ethics, Subjectivity and Truth*, p.191, and *Religion and Culture*, p.193.
16 'Sexuality and Solitude', *The Essential Works of Foucault 1954–1984: Ethics, Subjectivity and Truth*, p.178.

17 See 'The Hermeneutic of the Subject', *The Essential Works of Foucault 1954–1984: Ethics, Subjectivity and Truth*, pp.95–106.

18 'The Battle for Chastity', *The Essential Works of Foucault 1954–1984: Ethics, Subjectivity and Truth*, p.195, and *Religion and Culture*, p.196.

19 See 'Omnes et Singulatim', p.239; the Toronto course, 'The Discourse of Self-Disclosure', 15 June 1982; *The Use of Pleasure* (New York: Pantheon, 1985, pp.63, 70).

20 'Scholarship Serving the Nazi State I', *Ethnic and Racial Studies* 12.4 (1989), 576.

21 *Budhi*, II,3 (1998), 149–68.

22 Robert Pois, *National Socialism and the Religion of Nature* (London: Croom Helm, 1986, p.91).

23 See Emilio Gentile's *The Sacralization of Politics in Fascist Italy* (Cambridge: Harvard University Press, 1996); Kenneth Burke, 'The Rhetoric of Hitler's "Battle"', *Terms for Order* (Bloomington: Indiana University Press, 1964, pp.95–119); Uriel Tal, 'On Structures of Political Theology and Myth in Germany Prior to the Holocaust' in Y. Bauer (ed.), *The Holocaust as Historical Experience* (New York: Holmes and Meier, 1981, pp.43–74); Friedrich Heer, *Der Glaube des Adolf Hitler: Anatomie einer politischen Religiosität* (Vienna: Amalthea, 1998); and Philippe Burrin, 'Political Religion: The Relevance of a Concept', *History and Memory*, 9, 1–2 (Fall, 1997), 321–49.

24 See Gary Lease, *'Odd Fellows' in the Politics of Religion: Modernism, National Socialism, and German Judaism* (Berlin: Mouton de Gruyter, 1995).

25 See J.P. Stern, *Hitler: The Führer and the People* (Berkeley: University of California Press, 1975, pp.90–91).

26 See Heinz Schilling, *Religion, Political Culture and the Emergence of Early Modern Society* (New York: E.J. Brill, 1992); Robert Bireley, 'Early Modern Germany', in John O'Malley (ed.), *Catholicism in Early Modern History: A Guide to Research* (Ann Arbor: Edwards Brothers, 1988, pp.11–30); and David Warren Sabean, 'Production of Self during the Age of Confessionalism', *Central European History*, 29,1 (1996), 1–18.

27 Jeffrey Herf, *Reactionary Modernism: Technology, Culture, and Politics in Weimar and the Third Reich* (Cambridge: Cambridge University Press, 1984, p.225).

28 Lecture of 28 March 1984, pp.53–4. I am very indebted to James Miller for having made available to me the abstracts and transcriptions of the 1984 lectures prepared in 1990 by Michael Behrent.

29 Lectures of 29 February, 7, 14 and 21 March.

30 For the 1983 course I am using the version prepared by Joseph Pearson who released it as Michel Foucault, *Fearless Speech* (Los Angeles: Semiotexte, 2001). This version is an account of the 1983 material as presented by Foucault at the University of California, Berkeley, Fall 1983.

31 *Fearless Speech*, pp.170–71.

32 Ibid., pp.19–20.

33 Michel Foucault, *The Order of Things: An Archaeology of the Human Sciences* (New York: Random House, 1970, p.342); M. Foucault, *The Archaeology of Knowledge* (New York: Harper Colophon, 1976, p.211). This treatment of Foucault's negative theology draws on James Bernauer, 'The Prisons of Man: An Introduction to Foucault's Negative Theology', *International Philosophical Quarterly*, XXVII, 4 (Dec. 1987), 365–80.

34 As examples of such misinterpretations, see Hayden White, 'Michel Foucault', *Structuralism and Since* (New York: Oxford University Press, 1979, pp.113–14), and Jacques Ellul, *The Betrayal of the West* (New York: Seabury, 1978, p.37).

35 Following Foucault, this essay will employ the term 'man' to designate the specifically modern conception of the person, articulated philosophically most fully in Kant. The term 'human being' is meant to be a broader notion, transcending modernity's image and fabrication of 'man'.

36   Frederic Jameson, *The Prison House of Language* (Princeton: Princeton University Press, 1972, p.139).

37   M. Foucault, *Maurice Blanchot: The Thought from Outside* (New York: Zone Books, 1987, p.16).

38   In a 1967 interview with P. Caruso published in Caruso's *Conversazione con Lévi-Strauss, Foucault, Lacan* (Milan: U. Musia and Co., 1969, p.120).

39   Jean-Paul Sartre, *Being and Nothingness* (New York: Washington Square Press, 1966, p.784).

40   See Erich Voegelin's collection of essays, *From Enlightenment to Revolution*, ed. by John Hallowell (Durham, NC: Duke University Press, 1975), especially 'The Apocalypse of Man: Comte,' pp.136–59.

41   *The Order of Things*, p. 387. For Foucault's consideration of Marx and Nietzsche in this context, see *The Archaeology of Knowledge*, pp.12–13, and 'Nietzsche, Genealogy and History', in *Language, Counter-Memory and Practice* (Ithaca: Cornell University Press, 1977, pp.139–64).

42   *The Archaeology of Knowledge*, p.16.

43   Karl Barth, *Protestant Theology in the Nineteenth Century* (London: SCM Press, 1972, p.58).

44   'A Conversation with Michel Foucault', conducted by John Simon in *Partisan Review*, 38 (1971), 192–201.

45   'Truth and Power', in *Power/Knowledge: Selected Interviews and Other Writings 1972–1977*, ed. by Colin Gordon (New York: Pantheon, 1980, p.132).

46   *The Archaeology of Knowledge*, pp.14, 204.

47   Foucault, 'The Subject and Power', in H. Dreyfus and P. Rabinow, *Michel Foucault: Beyond Structuralism and Hermeneutics*, 2nd Edition (Chicago: University of Chicago Press, 1983, p.222).

48   See *The Use of Pleasure*, pp.65–7.

49   See Foucault, 'Christianity and Confession', in 'About the Beginning of the Hermeneutics of the Self: Two Lectures at Dartmouth', *Political Theory*, 21, 2 (May, 1993, 210–27).

50   'Omnes et Singulatim: Towards a Criticism of "Political Reason" ', p.239.

51   Lecture of 28 March 1984, p.54.

52   W.C. Van Unnik, 'The Semitic Background of Parrhesia in the New Testament', *Sparsa Collecta: The Collected Essays of W.C. Van Unnik*, part 2 (Leiden: E.J. Brill, 1980, p.290). For his own approach to parrhesia, Foucault cites two secondary sources: H. Schlier, 'parrhesia' in the *Theological Dictionary of the New Testament*, edited by Gerhard Friedrich (Grand Rapids, Michigan: Wm. B. Eerdmans Publishing Company, 1967, pp.871–86); S. Marrow, 'Parrhesia and the New Testament', *The Catholic Biblical Quarterly*, 44,3 (July, 1982), 431–46.

53   Lecture of 28 March 1984, p.39.

54   See John T. Fitzgerald, 'Philippians in the Light of Some Ancient Discussions of Friendship', in John T. Fitzgerald (ed.), *Friendship, Flattery, and Frankness of Speech: Studies on Friendship in the New Testament World*, Leiden: E.J. Brill, 1996, pp.141–62).

55   See William Klassen, 'Parrhesia in the Johannine Corpus', *Friendship, Flattery, and Frankness of Speech: Studies on Friendship in the New Testament World*, pp.227–54, especially 239, 242–3.

56   'The Subject and Power', in H. Dreyfus and P. Rabinow, *Michel Foucault: Beyond Structuralism and Hermeneutics*, p.222.

57   Foucault archives, c16: 'Talk with Philosophers 23 October 1980', cited in James Miller, *The Passion of Michel Foucault* (New York: Simon and Schuster, 1993, p.454).

58   *The Archaeology of Knowledge*, p.17.
59   'Truth, Power, Self: An Interview with Michel Foucault, October 25, 1982', *Technologies of the Self: A Seminar with Michel Foucault*, edited by L. Martin, H. Gutman and P. Hutton (Amherst: University of Massachusetts Press, 1988, p.11).
60   See Alexander Nehamas, *The Art of Living: Socratic Reflections from Plato to Foucault* (Berkeley: University of California Press, 1998, esp. pp.157–88).
61   See David McMenamin, 'The Critic's Avowal', in *Critical Essays on Michel Foucault*, edited by Karlis Racevskis (New York: G.K. Hall & Co., 1999, pp.208–32).
62   For example, the Miller biography cited in n. 53 above; also Didier Eribon, *Michel Foucault* (Cambridge: Harvard University Press, 1991); David Macey, *The Lives of Michel Foucault* (New York: Pantheon, 1993).
63   John Caputo, 'On Not Knowing Who We Are: Madness, Hermeneutics and the Night of Truth in Foucault', *Foucault and the Critique of Institutions*, edited by John Caputo and Mark Yount (University Park: Pennsylvania State University Press, 1993, pp.252, 255). Caputo's essay is now included in the present volume.
64   Foucault Archives, Document D250(7): 21 April 1983 discussion between Foucault and P. Rabinow, B. Dreyfus, C. Taylor, R. Bellah, M. Jay and L. Lowenthal, 32 pages, p. 11.
65   Friendship has become the theme of one careful interpretation of Foucault's philosophy: Francisco Ortega's *Michel Foucault: Rekonstruktion der Freundschaft* (Munich: Wilhelm Fink Verlag, 1997).
66   Preface to *Anti-Oedipus*, p.xii.
67   Uta Liebmann Schaub, 'Foucault's Oriental Subtext', *Critical Essays on Michel Foucault*, pp.101–17.

Chapter 5

Power and Political Spirituality: Michel Foucault on the Islamic Revolution in Iran

Michiel Leezenberg

Foucault's writings on the Islamic revolution in Iran have not received the critical attention they deserve.[1] Published in Italian and French periodicals between the autumn of 1978 and the spring of 1979, they may be seen as exercises in modern history or, as Foucault himself called it, 'journalism of ideas'; as such, they form an interesting complement to his other forays into cultural history, which deal with temporally more remote, but specifically European, events and institutions. By and large, however, these articles have been either passed over in a slightly embarrassed silence, or taken as proof that Foucault's enthusiasm for oppositional movements led him to applaud uncritically dictatorial regimes. Both attitudes are mistaken: these journalistic writings indeed have a rather problematic status within Foucault's work as a whole, but not for any such obvious reasons. No apologies are made here for trying, in a perhaps rather un-Foucauldian manner, to locate them in his *œuvre*. Further, not being a specialist on either Foucault or the Iranian revolution, I hope to avoid the two opposing risks of burying difficulties under apologetic exegesis and of merely pointing out alleged 'factual errors' at the expense of more interesting theoretical questions.

A BACKGROUND OF REVOLUTIONARY EVENTS

Although the emphasis here is on Foucault's views on the Iranian revolution rather than the revolution itself, a brief recapitulation of events until early 1979 may serve as background information.[2] Shah Reza Pahlavi's regime had never gained a broad base in Iranian society, but had acquired a measure of legitimacy in the decennia following the CIA-backed coup that had brought him to power in 1953. By the mid-1970s, however, protests against the repressive nature of the regime and the widespread corruption started to increase dramatically. The shah reacted by simultaneously intensifying political repression and introducing half-hearted reform measures – a combination which only exacerbated tensions.

At first, demonstrations calling for reforms were led by secularized and mostly left-wing urban intellectuals, but, in January 1978, a demonstration by seminary students in Qom against a government-sponsored newspaper article criticizing

Ayatollah Khomeini led to a confrontation with security forces that left several demonstrators dead. This triggered the shi'ite Iranian clergy, which until then had remained relatively quiet, into action, and most of the subsequent protests against the shah were centred upon mosques and religious gatherings. The clergy, from the highest religious scholars (*'ulamâ*) to the humblest village mullahs, contributed not only a highly effective mobilizing force, but also an extensive organizational network, to the protests.

On 8 September, or 'Black Friday' as it came to be called, a massive demonstration on Jaleh Square in Tehran was violently crushed, and between 2000 and 4000 demonstrators were killed. This massacre seriously reduced the chances of reconciliation, and henceforth the popular rallying call was for the shah's departure, rather than for reforms. Despite, or perhaps precisely because of, his physical absence, Khomeini was a major source of these more radical demands: he had been exiled from Iran in 1963, and had resettled in the shi'ite holy city of Najaf in Iraq, from where he could afford to be more critical of, and less compromising towards, the shah than other opposition leaders. Another source of inspiration for the revolution was Ali Shariati, a Maoist-inspired (though anti-Communist) shi'ite pamphleteer who had died in 1977.

In December 1978, the shah declared himself ready to negotiate directly with the opposition, but by then his position had become untenable: on 16 January 1979, he left Iran, never to return. A provisional government led by Shahpour Bakhtiar tried to introduce quick reforms, but it was widely seen as too closely associated with the shah for it to have any legitimacy. Upon his arrival in Tehran on 1 February, Khomeini appointed a new government, headed by the moderate opposition leader Mehdi Bazargan, and Bakhtiar's government was subsequently ousted in a three-day uprising, from 10 to 12 February. Among the groups that had headed the revolution, a fierce competition for supremacy now developed. Moreover, in the total anarchy following the collapse of the Bakhtiar government, armed *komitehs* or revolutionary committees had formed all over Iran, a powerful but uncontrolled (and probably uncontrollable), erratic and often violent new force. Khomeini managed to impose a measure of central control on these komitehs, increasing his own power base in the process. He did so, not by trying to curb the revolutionary fervour, but by channelling it to some extent with the installation of revolutionary courts, most of which were quick to mete out capital punishment, thus satisfying the popular desire for vengeance. The courts' violence and lack of adequate standards quickly led to protests both in Iran and abroad, but Khomeini stood solidly behind them.[3] On the whole, however, even as powerful an individual as Khomeini himself was led by events as much as he led them, and his emergence as the victor in the power struggle, let alone the eventual political shape post-revolutionary Iran was to take, was by no means a foregone conclusion.[4]

FOUCAULT IN IRAN[5]

Foucault had long been active on behalf of Iranian dissidents and political prisoners, and, like many others, undoubtedly saw in the popular protests a chance for a change of things for the better, and perhaps even for the ousting of a repressive and unpopular, but apparently solid, regime. Taking up an invitation from the Italian daily *Corriere della Sera*, he set out to write a series of articles on the Iranian protests, based on on-the-spot observations.

He meticulously prepared his Iranian journeys. He received updates on developments and addresses for contacts from Ahmad Salamatian, a left-of-centre, secularized Iranian intellectual who was to become deputy minister of Foreign Affairs in Bani-Sadr's short-lived post-revolutionary government. Further, he read Paul Vieille's sociological studies on Iran, and Henry Corbin's work on Iranian Islamic philosophy and spiritual life.[6] Between 16 and 24 September 1978, one week after 'Black Friday', Foucault paid his first visit to Iran. As it was difficult to get in contact with the religious opposition, Foucault concentrated his inquiries on members of the secular opposition and the military. On 20 September, however, he had a meeting in Qom with the moderate ayatollah Shariatmadari, who opposed the direct participation of the *'ulamâ*, the higher shi'ite clergy, in government. Below, it will be seen how Shariatmadari influenced Foucault's writings about the revolution.

In October, after his return to France, Foucault had discussions with the future president of Iran, Abol-Hasan Bani-Sadr, at that time still in exile; on one occasion, he and a group of journalists also met Khomeini, who had just arrived in France (on 3 October), having been expelled from Najaf by the Iraqi government. It is unknown what was said at this meeting, but at this time, Khomeini was still intentionally vague towards his European interlocutors on precisely what he meant by his call for an 'Islamic republic'.[7] In this period, Foucault published several articles in the *Corriere della Sera*, and one in the *Nouvel Observateur*.

From 9 to 15 November, Foucault was in Iran again; this time, he talked with members of the urban middle class, as well as with oil labourers in Abadan. The same month, a second series of articles appeared, but apart from an interview with Pierre Blanchet and Claire Brière (apparently held in late 1978 or early 1979), he remained silent about subsequent developments. He did not pay any further visits to Iran either, even though he maintained an interest: thus, he went to Paris airport to witness Khomeini's departure on 1 February 1979. Possibly, this silence is due to the many negative, if not hostile, reactions that his articles drew almost from the start; in early April 1979, Foucault was even assaulted in the street, according to some observers, because of his Iranian writings.[8] Only in April and May 1979 did he return to the Iranian revolution in writing, with an open letter to the new prime minister, Mehdi Bazargan, and with two articles of a more general nature,[9] which indeed suggest that he had been badly shaken by his Iranian experiences, and by the many hostile reactions to his writings in the French press. We will return to the significance of this silence below.

JOURNALISM, CONTEMPORARY HISTORY OR PHILOSOPHY?

It should be kept in mind that Foucault's writings on the Iranian revolution are mostly of a journalistic character, and do not directly relate to his philosophical and historical work. Nevertheless, there are some clear, if rather implicit, links to his broader theoretical concerns. First, for Foucault, both journalism and philosophy investigate the nature of the present, and in particular the question of who we are at the present moment.[10] He traces this convergence of interests back to Kant, whose answer to the question, 'What is Enlightenment?' (1784), introduced an entirely new type of question, that of the present as a philosophical event, which thus in a sense defines modern philosophy as a whole.[11] Enlightenment, as captured in Kant's famous slogan, *sapere aude*, 'dare to know!', or even modernity as a whole, is also characterized by the public use of reason, and by a certain type of political rationality that is free of the religious. Significantly, Foucault proceeds to link Enlightenment and revolution: Kant saw in the French revolution, regardless of whether it would succeed, and of whether it would turn out violent and murderous, a sign of mankind's unmistakable progress towards further emancipation and self-determination,[12] and as such, Foucault suggests, 'the revolution is precisely what completes and continues the very process of *Aufklärung*'.[13] A journalistic inquiry into a revolutionary event, especially one which so centrally involves the public and political use of religion as the uprising in Iran, thus implies a philosophical commentary on modernity itself.

Foucault tries to reach a journalistic understanding of the present by means of what he called 'reportages des idées'. The present world, he argues, is replete with novel ideas, especially among suppressed or hitherto ignored groups of people:

> Some say that the great ideologies are in the course of dying. The contemporary world, however, is burgeoning with ideas [...]. One has to be present at the birth of ideas and at the explosion of their force; not in the books that pronounce them, but in the events in which they manifest their force, and in the struggles people wage for or against ideas.[14]

This emphasis on the historical force of ideas is directed as much against the first forebodings of postmodernist claims concerning the end of grand ideologies as against the Marxist dogma that ideology is secondary to economic factors. As a reporter of ideas in Iran, Foucault himself 'would like to grasp what is *in the course of happening*', even though he considers himself a neophyte in journalism.[15]

A second major link is formed by the theme of power and resistance. Foucault was obviously fascinated – and disturbed – by the Iranian population's readiness to risk imprisonment, torture and even death, and tried to discover precisely what gave them this apparently totally unified, and heroic, will. In general, revolt may be seen as an extreme case of resistance against domination, and would thus seem a convenient illustration of Foucault's criticism of a juridical view of power with its domination and state-oriented perspective, a criticism formulated in particular in the first volume of *Histoire de la sexualité*.[16]

Third, Foucault's writings on Iran may be seen as a tentative application of his more theoretical ideas to a contemporary event in a non-western society, whereas his earlier studies had limited themselves to western European, and especially French, historical events and institutions. Some, for example Said,[17] have accused Foucault of an implicit eurocentrism; it is indeed an open question whether the conceptual tools developed in his earlier works can be applied to rather different historical and cultural contexts.

Foucault's first articles in the *Corriere della Sera* show few obvious traces of such broader concerns, as they are no more than preliminary forays into an unknown territory, informed by an inkling that something quite novel was taking place. They try to assess, for example, the role of the army, and the character of the protests against the shah's 'archaic' programme of modernization.[18] The economic reforms introduced in Iran since the 1960s had, for the most part, benefited only a small part of Iranian society, and the increase in oil wealth in the 1970s had only helped to exacerbate the already serious corruption and political repression. In other words, Foucault's critique of the shah's western-inspired modernization programme as 'archaic' is less a relativistic rejection of the idea of modernity in general than a criticism of one specific programme to reach it.

Foucault also notes the apparent absence of any clear social or economical basis for the mass protests, in which both urban workers and bazaar merchants participated,[19] implying, of course, that events in Iran do not allow for a Marxist explanation. At first sight, this observation seems correct, as the Iranian economy had shown a steady growth throughout the 1970s, especially after the drastic increase in oil prices in 1974. The sudden wealth, however, had led the Pahlavi regime to engage in a reckless spending spree, which caused a serious overheating of the economy. The government then cut down on investment and stopped recruiting for the civil services sector, which in turn led to a decrease in business opportunities, mass unemployment and sudden impoverishment among the middle and lower classes.[20] In other words, there *was* a clear economic basis for the protests: for large parts of the population, the supposedly affluent 1970s had only brought new hardships and frustrated expectations, a familiar precondition for the emergence of revolutionary movements.

Foucault gradually shifts his attention towards the peculiar character of Iranian Islam, notably its potential for resistance against state power. At the time, the very idea that Islam, in whatever variety, could be revolutionary, rather than inherently reactionary, seemed anathema; but Foucault correctly saw the decisive importance of political Islam in the protests, both as an ideology for mass mobilization and as providing an institutional and organizational base for the opposition to the Pahlavi regime. This correct assessment is paired, however, with a number of seriously flawed or oversimplified remarks on shi'ism in general. Thus Foucault believes that the shi'ite clergy knows no hierarchy; that shi'ite religious authority is given by the people; and consequently, that clerics can ill afford to ignore popular angers and aspirations.[21] In fact, the shi'ite *'ulamâ* have over the last centuries shaped themselves into a highly organized and hierarchic institution that is to an important extent autonomous from both the state and society. Foucault at once corrects himself by adding that the shi'ite clerics are by no means revolutionary, but that the shi'ite religion *itself* is the form taken by political struggle, especially when it involves mass mobilization. These remarks still sidestep a long history and risk attributing causal power to shi'ite ideology itself, but perhaps one cannot expect detailed historical analyses from a newspaper reportage.

Foucault also gropes at length for an explanation for the fearlessness and 'perfectly unified collective will'[22] of the unarmed demonstrators, which he thinks characterizes not a political movement but a revolt against the existing political order of the whole world: 'the most modern form of revolt – and the maddest'.[23] Aptly, then, it is not a politician, but the 'almost mythical personality' of Khomeini who is able to guide the protests and maintain their momentum. Foucault is well aware of the potential violence of this confrontation: 'the image [of the unarmed saint versus the king in arms] has its own captivating force, but it masks a reality in which millions of dead come to inscribe their signature';[24] he adds that he finds the definitions of Islamic government which he has heard 'hardly reassuring'.[25]

Here, too, Foucault's insight is at odds with the then widespread opinion that Khomeini was merely a figurehead with no power or programme of his own. He explains the intensity of the link between the ayatollah and the people with three facts: Khomeini's not being there, his not saying anything (other than 'no' to every attempt at compromise) and his not being a politician. The last point even led Foucault to state: 'there won't be a party of Khomeini's, there won't be a Khomeini government'.[26] Predictions are always risky, and this one has proved wrong on both counts: on 5 February 1979, Khomeini appointed Bazargan to form a new government, and two weeks later, the strongly pro-Khomeini Islamic Republican Party was formed. Although Khomeini formally stayed outside these new political structures, they unmistakably strengthened his power base, and Foucault's remark suggests a serious underestimation of his political ambitions. Again, however, he was by no means alone in this. Before 1978, nobody outside a small circle of specialists knew of the political ideas among the Iranian shi'ite *'ulamâ*, let alone about the existence and political doctrines of Khomeini, and this circle itself was equally surprised at the course and speed of events in 1978 and 1979. Even such a well-informed observer of Iranian society as Fred Halliday,[27] writing on the eve of the revolution, considered it unlikely that the Iranian clergy was to play a major role if the shah's regime should be overthrown.

Perhaps the main shortcoming of these reportages, apart from such forgivable errors, is that they overemphasize the religious dimension of the demonstrations, at the expense of their unmistakably nationalist element: a clear demand for national sovereignty was expressed in the protest against the American presence and against alleged 'Zionist conspiracies' to undermine the nation. The sweeping character-izations of the social role of shi'ite Islam and of Khomeini's role in the protests are perhaps inevitable with newspaper articles, but at times come dangerously close to idealist explanations.

UNCRITICAL SUPPORT FOR KHOMEINI?

Opposition to Foucault's alleged enthusiasm for the prospect of Islamic government and the person of Khomeini began to be voiced upon publication of the first *Nouvel Observateur* article. It intensified after Khomeini's arrival in February 1979 had triggered off a violent power struggle, accompanied by a wave of summary executions. Thus, in *Le Matin* (24 March 1979), Claudie and Jacques Broyelle accused Foucault of blindly supporting Khomeini, and called on him to 'acknowledge his errors'.[28] More recently, Bernard-Henry Lévy[29] has written that Foucault's judgment on Iran was blinded by his 'hope for a pure revolution', a hope he allegedly shared with many French intellectuals. He construes Foucault's remarks on Khomeini's 'mythical dimension' and 'mysterious link' with the people as signs of a personal admiration. He believes Foucault's main error, 'a practically obligatory stage in this spiritual journey', is an initially boundless and uncritical enthusiasm, which founders on the violence of actual events and leads to an eventual disenchantment with ideals.

Such criticisms, often made with the benefit of hindsight, are not only off the mark but also unfair. Most of them emphasize the violent turn of events from February 1979 onwards, when Foucault had ceased publishing his commentaries; but even in his earlier journalistic articles, Foucault nowhere speaks of the revolt in terms of progress or liberation. He reacted fiercely to these accusations, and forcefully rejected the antagonistic attitude they presupposed: 'The problem of Islam as a political force is an essential problem for our era and for the years to come. The first condition for addressing it with a minimum of intelligence is not to start by confronting it with hatred.'[30]

Indeed, Foucault has to be credited for perceiving the historical importance of this revolution at an early stage, and for repeatedly visiting Iran in order to see for himself what was happening. He was clearly fascinated, and troubled, by this unprecedented assertion of a unified popular will. He may have underestimated Khomeini's political role, but none of his published writings express anything remotely like a blind admiration for Khomeini or an uncritical enthusiasm for the prospect of Islamic government.

More interesting, if hardly less polemical, criticisms have been voiced by non-western intellectuals. Thus Mohammed Arkoun, in an interview with Hashim Saleh,[31] argues that philosophers like Foucault and Derrida, despite their critique of eurocentrism, 'remain within the walls of the European tradition of thought'. In their archaeologies of different systems of knowledge, religion – and in particular Islam – is consistently ignored, despite the presence of millions of Islamic immigrants in Europe. Moreover, when they do write about Islam, as Foucault did on the Islamic revolution, they say nothing but stupidities (*hamâqât*). Foucault, Arkoun concludes, did not understand anything of what was happening in Iran, and would have done better not to have said anything about it at all.[32] On a more moderate note, Darius Rejali argues in his *Torture and Modernity*[33] that Foucault cannot properly account for the persistence of torture in pre- and post-revolutionary Iran, in a state that (at least under the Pahlavi regime) 'slavishly emulated the Western regime of truth', where the need for torture has supposedly been replaced by more disciplinary ways of punishing, such as imprisonment. Such criticisms have considerably more force, as they point to the fundamental question of whether and how Foucault's ideas, which derive from the study of specifically European events and institutions, can be extended to a non-European domain at all. However, they do not apply to all of Foucault's Iranian writings to the same extent.

'POLITICAL SPIRITUALITY' AND ITS ANCESTORS

Foucault's first article for a French audience, 'À quoi rêvent les Iraniens?',[34] is by no means a mere summary of the Italian reportages. It delves much more into the history of Iran and of shi'ite Islam. And it is here that things become problematic. To begin with, his explanation of the call for Islamic government is obviously coloured by the restricted range of his interlocutors:

'What do you want?' During the whole of my stay in Iran, I never once heard the word 'revolution'. But four times out of five, I got the answer 'Islamic government' [...]. One thing should be clear: by [this], no one in Iran means a political order in which the clergy would play a role of ruler or provider of cadre.[35]

This seriously underestimates the character and background of the contemporary debate; most importantly, Foucault was apparently unaware of Khomeini's concept of *velâyat-e faqîh* ('guardianship of the jurist', that is, government by the shi'ite clergy), as Rodinson notes.[36] In his earlier writings, Khomeini had not questioned the legitimacy of the Pahlavi monarchy as such, and merely called for the clergy to play a greater role in political affairs; in the 1960s, he had developed far more radical ideas against the background of the rising Marxist-inspired student activism. But even among the main clerics involved in the revolution, there was no consensus on the nature of an eventual Islamic government. Bani-Sadr, for example, had come close to identifying the shi'ite idea of the *imâm* as the only legitimate ruler with a European idea of popular sovereignty, by developing a concept of *ta'mîm-e imâmat*, or 'generalized imamate'.[37] For him, each member of the community could become a jurist or even an *imâm* through piety and self-discipline; consequently, he saw no need for a separate class of religiously trained jurists. The only religious authority whom Foucault met, Ayatollah Shariatmadari,[38] consistently opposed any role for the clergy in worldly leadership.

Foucault's most controversial remark, however, was his suggestion that those participating in the demonstrations against the shah might be trying to introduce, or reintroduce, a spiritual dimension into political life,[39] and that this might be the ultimate motivation for their heroic and self-sacrificing behaviour:

> At the dawn of history, Persia has invented the State and rendered its services to Islam [...]. But of this same Islam, it has derived a religion that has given its people indefinite resources for resisting State power. Should one see in this desire for an 'Islamic Government' a reconciliation, a contradiction, or the threshold of a novelty? [...] What sense, for the people, in seeking at the price of their very lives this thing, the possibility of which we have forgotten since the Renaissance and the great crises of Christianity: a political spirituality. I can already hear some Frenchmen laughing, but I know they are wrong.[40]

Although the suggestion that all participants were seeking the same spirituality may seem rather implausible, the desire for Islamic government as an end of the Pahlavi regime's sellout to the United States and other foreign powers was undeniably a major mobilizing force. One may wonder to what extent this desire was nationalist or populist, rather than religious, in character, but at least Foucault rightly asks whether this Islamic government might in fact be something radically new, instead of assuming – as many would be tempted to do – that it simply amounts to a step back in time.[41]

In the context of Foucault's journalistic work, the notion of political spirituality should probably not be given too much philosophical weight. Elsewhere, however, it is explicitly linked to his other philosophical concerns. First and foremost, it obviously reflects his intense attempts to come to terms with the apparently novel logic of the early revolutionary events; as seen, he implicitly and explicitly denies the possibility of understanding the revolt in the familiar categories of class struggle and the like.

It seems, however, that Foucault's emphasis on the spiritual dimensions of the uprising derives less from what he observed on the ground than from what he had been reading in preparation. One major source for the notion of political spirituality, acknowledged as such by Foucault, is Ali Shariati.[42] In his pamphlets, Shariati had developed a view of shi'ite Islam as the 'religion of the oppressed', giving the potential shi'ite opposition to any form of worldly government a more revolutionary character. Shariati, active in the 1960s and early 1970s, had been inspired by champions of Third World liberation like Mao, Castro and Fanon, but at the same time he emphasized shi'ite Islamic spirituality as an antidote to Marxist-inspired materialism.[43]

Another, and probably more important, influence is Henry Corbin. According to his editors,[44] Foucault's preparatory reading on Iran included Corbin's important works on Islamic (in particular shi'ite) philosophy and spirituality.[45] Corbin, more than any westerner, had devoted his academic life to the publication and translation of manuscripts from the philosophical traditions of Islamic Iran; his representation of Islamic thought is cast in a distinctly Heideggerian mould, but is simultaneously guided by the essentialist idea that the 'real' Islamic spirituality is to be found in the more esoteric and Gnostic branches of shi'ism in Iran. Thus he concludes his history of Islamic philosophy with an appeal to Iranian Muslims to preserve their 'traditional spiritual culture' against western influence.[46]

Corbin's hermeneutics of Islamic texts stresses the distinction between the superficial exoteric (*zâhir*) meaning and the true, inner (*bâtin*) meaning. In an interview on the Islamic revolt,[47] Foucault also makes much of this distinction, when he describes the Islamic revolution as both an inner and outer experience, as both a timeless and a historical drama;[48] significantly, he also links it to his own theoretical notions when he tries to capture what he calls 'perhaps the soul of the uprising': 'Religion for them was like the promise and guarantee of something that would radically change their subjectivity. Shi'ism is precisely a form of Islam that, with its teaching and esoteric content, distinguishes between what is merely external and what is the profound spiritual life.'[49] Elsewhere, as an explanation of Iranian attitudes to propaganda he writes:

> They don't have the same regime of truth as ours, which, it has to be said, is very special, even if it has become almost universal [...]. In Iran it is largely modeled on a religion that has an exoteric form and an esoteric content. That is to say, everything that is said under the explicit form of the law also refers to another meaning.[50]

We will return to Foucault's appeal to regimes of truth below. His other writings from this period suggest that the formation of, and changes in, subjectivity are processes in which various kinds of power relation are crucial. That political spirituality might also be seen as a form of resistance against a prevailing power with its concomitant form of political rationality is suggested by a passage from the Tanner lectures which Foucault presented at Stanford in October 1979: 'Those who resist or rebel against a form of power cannot merely be content to denounce violence or criticize an institution. Nor is it enough to cast the blame on reason in general. What has to be questioned is the form of rationality at stake.'[51]

For a European audience, then, the concept of political spirituality also suggests an alternative to a kind of political rationality that has been predominant since the

Enlightenment. Such suggestions are certainly interesting and worth exploring further, but it should be noted that Foucault's case rests in part on a rather biased view of what shi'ism amounts to in doctrinal terms. His Corbin-inspired claims notwithstanding, the exoteric–esoteric opposition is not an essential part of shi'ite Islam, not even in its Iranian varieties. In shi'ite Iran, esoteric currents have always remained a minority phenomenon, and most clerics have traditionally been suspicious of such Gnostic and esoteric doctrines that might undermine the *sharî'a* (Islamic law) as the basis of social order.[52]

Foucault not only presents a minority view as the 'real' shi'ite faith, he also speaks consistently of shi'ism *tout court*, as if it were a monolithic and historically stable set of doctrines, or even a 'timeless drama' which has formed a base for opposition to state power 'since the dawn of history'.[53] In fact, Islamic 'spirituality' in Iran has undergone radical transformations over the centuries, both among the population at large and among the shi'ite clergy.[54] Ever since the mysterious disappearance of the twelfth *imâm* in 873 CE, the shi'ite community had faced the problem of legitimate spiritual and worldly authority. Because just rule would only be established at the end of time, when the Hidden Imâm would reappear, all worldly government was in a sense illegitimate by definition; but most shi'ite scholars recommended acquiescing in this cosmic injustice as part of the shi'ites' eschatological fate. This ambivalent attitude towards state power became even more pronounced when law-based 'twelver' or *imâmi* shi'ism became the state religion of the Safavid empire in the 16th century. On the whole, shi'ite jurists and theologians have not developed a consistent and generally accepted theory of the state and of legitimate rule. Before the 1960s, however, none of these thinkers held that monarchy was in itself illegitimate; on the contrary, many of them explicitly considered bad government better than the anarchy of revolution. The development from quietism to revolutionary Islam in this period was itself a revolutionary innovation in shi'ite thought.

Although Foucault undoubtedly would have rejected the idealist position that the shi'ite faith possesses causal historical powers of itself, he faces similar difficulties as the idealist. Thus only by ignoring historical and other variations can he avoid the question of what, if any, is the regime of truth shared by both law-oriented and more mystically inclined Persian thinkers, not to mention the population at large.[55] He also leaves it unclear whether the allegedly sought-for change in subjectivity would amount to a return to a truth regime predating the shah's western-inspired modernization project, or leave the existing truth regime intact. His ignorance of historical developments in shi'ism and his appeal to a presumably timeless drama or a millenarian *zâhir-bâtin* distinction, then, allow for a totally idealist, if not transcendental, reconstruction of his ideas on Iran. This opportunity was eagerly grasped by Corbin's pupil Christian Jambet, who ascribes him a roundly essentialist and ahistorical view, disguised as a spiritual 'metahistory' which seems completely at odds with all of Foucault's other writings:

> Foucault's point is not the politics of a future state but the essence of an uprising, of the 'spiritual' politics which makes it possible [...]. He sees immediately that here history is the expression of a metahistory, or again of a hiero-history, and that the temporalisation of time is suspended in favor of messianic events, whose place is not the world of phenomena understood by science.[56]

Here Foucault's interest in the Iranian revolution as an unprecedented historical event has to make room for an inquiry into the supposed spiritual or transcendental essence of any uprising. The convergences that Jambet perceives between Corbin's 'metahistorical' phenomenology and the archaeology of knowledge seem less the result of any natural affinity than traces of Corbin's direct influence on Foucault's Iranian writings.

But are the essentialist ideas of shi'ism as a force irreducibly opposed to state power, and of a specifically Iranian–Islamic regime of truth, both heavily dependent on Corbin's work, really so at odds with Foucault's more general notions, such as 'episteme' and 'regime of truth'? In a 1977 interview, Foucault suggests that 'each society has its regime of truth [...]; that is, the types of discourse which it accepts and makes function as true',[57] and that the contemporary western European regime of truth (which is centred on a form of scientific discourse and the institutions which produce it) is by and large the same regime operating in the socialist countries, but probably different from that in China.[58] The concept of 'regime of truth', then, seems to play much the same structural role that such notions as 'culture' or 'world view' play in more idealistically inclined authors: it allows for a sweeping characterization of an entire historical period or geographical region. As such, it faces the risk of reducing singular historical events to static and essentialist categories, a risk implicit in any attempt at historical classification or periodization. In short, political spirituality may be quite suggestive as a journalistic notion, but as a philosophical concept it is deeply problematic, indeed indicative of more general problems that Foucault faces.

POWER AND POWER STRUGGLE

The biggest surprises, however, lie in store for those who turn to Foucault's Iranian articles with his 'analytic of power' in mind.[59] After all, the relevance of the Islamic revolution to the concerns of *Surveiller et punir* and the first volume of *Histoire de la sexualité* is obvious. In the latter work, Foucault argues at length against the prevailing juridical view that tends to see power as a kind of institution, and instead proposes to represent power relations as at the same time intentional and non-subjective, as no individual has full control over the directedness of power relations.[60] The juridical view 'from above' sees power merely as domination, or as a purely negative force, thus ignoring its productive capacities: 'the representation of power has remained haunted by monarchy. In political thought, the king's head has not yet been cut off'.[61] As an alternative, Foucault proposes to take the forms of resistance to different forms of power as a starting point. A systematic awareness that power inevitably calls up resistance, that is, that resistance is internal to power relations, opens up the way for an analysis of power relations through the antagonism of strategies.[62] Admittedly, Foucault does not intend his analytic of power as a general theory, but rather as a tool that can open insights into 'a certain form of knowledge about sex';[63] yet it might equally provide new insights into power relations in rather different spheres.

The implications of this shift from a juridical to a strategical view of power do not seem to be sufficiently appreciated by all of Foucault's students.[64] Seen from this novel perspective on power, however, the Iranian revolution, and in particular the chaotic and violent power struggle that erupted when the shah had left and the old institutions of power and government, including the army and the police forces, had collapsed (and, so to speak, the king's head had actually been chopped off), provided an ideal test case for an analytic of power. An analysis of the institutional bases and different strategies of the various actors involved would have proven a worthwhile task, if by no means an easy one; in particular the ways in which Khomeini managed to accumulate political power for himself, by refusing to compromise and by encouraging and at the same time channelling popular action, would have formed an interesting challenge to Foucault's view of power as an intentional relation without an (individual) subject.

But nothing of the sort happened. Instead, Foucault hardly tried to link his initial fascination with the novelty of the protests to his more theoretical interests in power and resistance, and when he did address the violence that marked the post-revolutionary power struggle, he fell back on a universalist position that takes the rights of the individual and the rule of law as a kind of moral rock bottom. This universalist ethics appears clearly in several articles published in April and May 1979. Thus, in an open letter to Mehdi Bazargan, published in mid-April,[65] Foucault argues that political processes against representatives of a former regime are a touchstone regarding the 'essential obligations' of any government. His letter was addressed to precisely the wrong person, however, as Bazargan had already publicly protested against the many summary executions, and against the revolutionary trials, which he called 'shameful', in late March.[66] More importantly, real power at this moment lay with the revolutionary committees and courts as much as with the Bazargan government.

The same theme is picked up in 'Inutile de se soulever?',[67] where Foucault argues that enthusiasm for the Iranian revolution is not a legitimization of (post-) revolutionary violence: 'the spirituality that those who were going to die appealed to has no common measure with the bloodthirsty government of a fundamentalist clergy'.[68] The ethics he defends is not relativist, but rather 'anti-strategic':[69] it involves showing respect when a singularity rises, but being intransigent when power infringes on the universal. Foucault's ethics is clearly universalist in its stress on the rights of the individual, that is, something much like classical human rights. Being 'anti-strategic', it may be opposed to power-as-strategy almost by definition, but its appeal to laws without franchise and rights without restriction almost suggests that such laws and rights are defined without any recourse to power. The question then arises on what *philosophical* basis Foucault can make such an appeal, given his earlier attempts to cast doubt on the universalist aspirations of reason since the Enlightenment; moreover, on earlier occasions, he had explicitly refused to condemn the possibly violent, dictatorial and even bloody power that the proletariat could exercise in 'revolutionary justice' over the vanquished classes.[70]

This problem deserves further attention, but here, the central question is why Foucault reverted to such a classical (dare I say Enlightenment-inspired?) position. Was he really so shocked and surprised at the revolution developing into a violent competition for power? Perhaps he had ignored the political power struggle hidden behind the religious slogans because of his emphasis on the spiritual dimension of the revolt that expressed its supposedly unified popular will. Rodinson[71] argues as much, with his remark that all cases of political spirituality have eventually submitted to the 'eternal laws of politics', that is, the struggle for power, and adds that Foucault more generally has undermined the concept of political power with his constellation of micropowers. Or had Foucault simply lost interest in the revolution as a political struggle *for* power, once the 'spiritual' revolt *against* the shah's power had been successful? This may be suggested by his early remark that 'the phenomenon which has so fascinated us – the revolutionary experience itself – will die out',[72] reflecting his view that his main interest, the unified popular will, was not the result of a political alliance or compromise, but something that stood outside politics, or temporarily transformed it.

Foucault's silence on the complex post-revolutionary power struggle and his subsequently reverting to a universalist ethics based on immutable laws suggest a conceptual inability to move beyond the domination–resistance dichotomy implicit in the juridical view of power which he himself had so strongly criticized. Seen in this light, his ignoring of historical developments in shi'ite Islam, and of internal divisions along lines of political outlook, class, ethnicity or denomination between those participating in the uprising, may not be an accident after all. It points to a far more general difficulty of how to account for variation and change in regimes of truth, or epistemes, or paradigms.[73] In other words, Foucault's conceptualization of regimes of truth and political rationalities, and even his strategy-oriented analytic of power relations, may still be too static and monolithic to allow for a genuine explanation of such drastic changes as occur in revolutionary periods, and of a power struggle in the absence of the effective concentration of power in government and state apparatus.

BY WAY OF CONCLUSION

Let us return to the three links between Foucault's Iranian writings and his broader concerns. First, Foucault's journalistic intuition that something radically new was occurring in Iran has certainly proved correct. He managed to put aside much fashionable prejudice and ask many interesting questions, and intelligently sought for adequate answers at a time when no one quite understood what was happening. Second, however, Foucault surprisingly failed to analyse the revolution in terms of 'power from below' or his strategy-based view of power, and ultimately even reverted to a universalist ethics based on laws and rights that do not seem to allow for compromise or discussion. Third, Foucault's more philosophically loaded remarks on the revolution betray a strong influence of Henry Corbin's work. His explanation of the specifics of the revolt in terms of a distinct Iranian-shi'ite regime of truth and of a desire for a change in subjectivity and political rationality seems less a genuine application of his conceptual tools than a relapse into the conventional text-based idealism of Oriental studies: that is, into precisely the kind of idealist 'history of ideas' which his earlier writings had done much to discredit.[74] Foucault's general works thus do not display the obvious eurocentrism of which he has been accused. At the same time, however, his Iranian writings point to deeper difficulties of his work concerning power relations and intellectual change. They foreshadow the remarkable shift between *La volonté de savoir* (1976) and the last two volumes of *Histoire de la sexualité* (1984), from the microphysics of power to the self-constitution of the individual as a desiring subject, where such power is no longer a central theme.[75] The latter works read much like a conventional exercise in the history of ideas, albeit with an unconventional theme, with their focus on the literate male elite of ancient Greece.

There is little point in biographical speculation as to whether Foucault's sudden reversal on the Islamic revolution is due to his revulsion at the revolutionary violence or to his dismay at the outcry among French intellectuals. His silence on the power struggle and his subsequent reversal to a universalist ethics may not merely be expressive of his shock at the violent turn taken by events, but also reflect his more general intellectual problem of how to account for conceptual change and its relation to changes in power. Depending on one's perspective, then, one may either see Foucault's journalistic writings on Iran as a missed opportunity; as the conclusive proof that his conceptual tools are too static, monolithic and idealist to allow for any practical use; or as a promise, not yet fulfilled, that a Foucauldian vision of cultural history may be extended to non-European territory. Paradoxically, however, Foucault the journalist showed a far greater sensitivity to the specific and novel character of the Iranian revolution as a historical event than Foucault the philosopher. His attempts at a journalistic understanding of the present may yet change our appreciation of modernity, with its entire political rationality inherited from the Enlightenment, and of the protagonists of the present Islamic world, who far from being 'anti-modern' as often thought, are searching for different ways of being 'modern'.

NOTES

1   These articles are now conveniently available in vol. III of Foucault's *Dits et écrits 1954–1988* (Paris: Éditions Gallimard, 1994, 4 volumes, hereafter DE), which contains almost all of his scattered writings and interviews. There are minor discrepancies between the French texts as reproduced in DE III and as quoted by Eribon (D. Eribon, *Michel Foucault*, trans. Betsy Wing, London: Faber, 1992) presumably due to translation differences; but these do not involve any points of importance. Only one of the 1978 articles from *Corriere della Sera*, 'Taccuino persiano: Ritorno al profeta?', dated 22 October was also published in French at the time. It is reprinted in DE III, 688–94 as 'À quoi rêvent les Iraniens?'.

2   For more details, see the excellent political histories by Shaul Bakhash, *The Reign of the Ayatollahs* (London: Unwin, 1986) and Dilip Hiro, *Iran under the Ayatollahs* (London: Routledge, 1985); cf. F. Halliday, *Iran: Dictatorship and Development* (Harmondsworth: Penguin, 1979) for an assessment of Iran just before the turbulent events of 1978 and 1979.

3   Bakhash, *Reign of the Ayatollahs*, pp.59–63.

4   Ibid., p.6.

5   This information is largely taken from Eribon, *Michel Foucault*, ch. 19, and from the editorial introduction to Foucault's Iranian articles (DE III, 662); David Macey's, *The Lives of Michel Foucault* (New York: Pantheon, 1993, pp.406–11) portrait of Foucault in Iran is rather less charitable and well-informed than Eribon's.

6   Cf. H. Corbin, *En Islam Iranien*, 4 vols (Paris: Gallimard, 1971).

7   Bakhash, *Reign of the Ayatollahs*, p.48.

8   *Le Monde*, 4 April 1979; *Le Matin*, 3 and 14 April 1979; *Nouvelles littéraires*, 2681 (1979), 16. Surprisingly, this incident is not mentioned in either Eribon's or Macey's biography.
9   DE III, 780–87, 790–94.
10 DE III, 783.
11 DE IV, 562, 680.
12 *Der Streit der Fakultäten*, ch. II.6.
13 DE IV, 685. Politically, Foucault undoubtedly cherished the prospect of the shah's government being ousted, although philosophically he could (unlike Kant) hardly describe this revolutionary enthusiasm in teleological terms of progress and liberation.
14 DE III, 706–7.
15 DE III, 714; original emphasis.
16 Michel Foucault, *Histoire de la sexualité; La volonté de savoir* (Paris: Gallimard, 1976, pp. 107–35).
17 E. Said, 'Michel Foucault 1926–1984' in J. Arac (ed.), *After Foucault* (New Brunswick: Rutgers University Press, 1988, p.9).
18 DE III, 680–83.
19 DE III, 702.
20 Cf. Hiro, *Iran under the Ayatollahs*, pp.60–63; Bakhash, *Reign of the Ayatollahs*, pp.12–13.
21 DE III, 687, 691.
22 DE III, 715.
23 DE III, 716.
24 DE III, 689–90.
25 DE III, 692.
26 DE III, 716.
27 Halliday, *Iran: Dictatorship and Development*, p.299.
28 Unfortunately, I could not trace this article; cf. Olivier & Labbé, 'Foucault et l'Iran: A propos du désir de révolution', *Canadian Journal of Political Science*, 1991, 24; see p.220, n.4 for its main points.
29 Bernard-Henry Lévy, *Les aventures de la liberté: Une histoire subjective des intellectuels* (Paris: Grasset, 1991, pp.482–3).
30 DE III, 708.
31 H. Saleh, *Al-fikr al-islami: Al-naqd wa'l ijtihad* [Islamic Thought: Critique and Judgment] (London: Dar al-Saqi, 1990).
32 I am indebted to Mariwan Kanie for drawing my attention to this interview.
33 D. Rejali, *Torture and Modernity* (Boulder, CO: Westview, 1994, pp.14–16).
34 DE III, 688–94.
35 DE III, 690.
36 Maxime Rodinson, *L'Islam: politique et croyance* (Paris: Fayard, 1993, p.307).
37 Cf. Bakhash, *Reign of the Ayatollahs*, pp.93–5.
38 DE III, 691.
39 DE III, 693–4.
40 DE III, 694.
41 The implementation of Islamic government has indeed turned out to be something radically new, rather than a return to some 'pre-modern' political order, even if it has in part been legitimized as such. It features a constitutional court, a directly elected president and a supreme leader or 'guide' (*rahbar*), none of which is anticipated in earlier shi'ite political thought, let alone in the original community of believers headed by the prophet Mohammed (Cf. E. Abrahamian, *Khomeinism: Essays on the Islamic Republic* (London: I.B.Tauris, 1993).

42   DE III: 693; cf. Rodinson, *L'Islam: politique et croyance*, p.308. Perhaps Shariati's notion
      of political spirituality had reached Foucault by way of Mehdi Bazargan, when the latter
      two met in Qom in September 1978 (cf. DE III, 781).

43   For example, A. Shariati, *Marxism and other Western Fallacies*, trans. R. Campbell
      (Berkeley: Mizan Press, 1980); cf. Abrahamian, *Khomeinism*, ch.1).

44   DE III, 662.

45   For example, H. Corbin, *Histoire de la philosophie islamique* (Paris: Gallimard, 1986);
      Corbin, *Islam Iranien*.

46   Corbin, *Histoire*, 497ff.

47   DE III, 743–55.

48   DE III, 746.

49   DE III, 749.

50   DE III, 753–4.

51   DE IV, 161.

52   Instead of appealing to the elitist *zâhir-bâtin* distinction, Foucault might as well have
      appealed to the much more widespread politeness principle of *ta'rof*, the Iranian
      equivalent of *comme il faut*, which, for example, requires one to invite visitors to stay for
      dinner for the sake of politeness, even if one has no real intention of actually hosting them.

53   George Stauth, *Revolution in Spiritless Times: an Essay on the Enquiries of Michel
      Foucault on the Iranian Revolution* (Singapore: Dept. of Sociology, National University
      of Singapore, 1991, pp.15–16, 34) had already noted that the concept of political
      spirituality implies a relapse to an Orientalist view of religion as in itself determinative of
      social action.

54   I cannot trace these developments in detail here; see R. Mottahedeh, *The Mantle of the
      Prophet* (Harmondsworth: Penguin, 1985); Abrahamian, *Khomeinism*, ch.1, for the main
      points raised.

55   Significantly, he fails throughout the Brière and Blanchot interview to address the
      questions posed to him regarding ethnic and other cleavages among the protest
      movement.

56   C. Jambet, 'The constitution of the subject and spritual practice', in T.J. Armstrong (ed.),
      Michel Foucault Philosopher (New York: Harvester Wheatsheaf, 1992, p.234).

57   Foucault, *Power/Knowledge*, p. 131; DE III, 158.

58   Foucault, *Power/Knowledge*, p.133.

59   For more detailed discussion of Foucault's views on power, see especially H. Dreyfus and
      P. Rabinow, *Michel Foucault: Beyond Structuralism and Hermeneutics* (Chicago:
      University of Chicago Press, 1982, chs 6, 9); C. Taylor, *Foucault on Freedom and Truth.
      In Philosophy and the Human Sciences* (Cambridge: Cambridge University Press, 1985,
      esp. s.III); J.L. Cohen and A. Arato, *Civil Society and Political Theory* (Cambridge, MA:
      MIT Press, 1990, pt.II, ch.6).

60   Foucault, *La Volonté de Savoir*, p.124.

61   Ibid., 117.

62   Dreyfus and Rabinow, *Michel Foucault*, p.211; DE IV, 225.

63   Foucault, *Volonté*, pp.109, 128.

64   Thus, Taylor, *Freedom* (p.168) seems to mistake Foucault's claim that 'power comes from
      below' for the idea that one should study power in micro-contexts of local dominators and
      dominated, rather than in macro-contexts like state or class; in fact, Foucault rejects the
      domination model at both the micro- and macro-level. Olivier & Labbé (*Désir*: 234)
      likewise attribute to Foucault a state- and domination-oriented view, according to which
      revolt constitutes a limit or obstacle, but not an end, to a given relation of power.

65   DE III, 780–82.

66   Editor's note, DE III, 663; cf. Bakhash, *The Reign of the Ayatollahs*, p.61.

67   *Le Monde*, 11–12 May 1979; DE III, 790–94.

68   DE III, 793. In another article, 'Pour un morale de l'inconfort' (DE III, 783–7), Foucault addresses the difficulty of having to revise one's certainties without giving up one's convictions. Years of experience, he writes, lead us 'not to trust any revolution', even if one can 'understand every revolt'. As Eribon notes, this sounds very much like an acknowledgment that his journalistic adventures in Iran had been a failure.

69   DE III, 794.

70   Witness, for example, the discussion on popular justice as opposed to bourgeois justice and the famous television debate with Noam Chomsky (DE II, chs 108, 132).

71   Rodinson, *L'Islam: politique et croyance*, p.309f.

72   DE III, 750.

73   Cf. Dreyfus and Rabinow, *Michel Foucault*, p.262; Taylor, *Freedom*, p.182.

74   The most famous example of a Foucault-inspired critique of the philological bias and essentialism of much conventional Orientalist scholarship is, of course, Edward Said's *Orientalism* (1978).

75   Edward Said (*Foucault*, pp.8–9) attributes this shift to Foucault's disenchantment with the public sphere, to his pursuit of 'different kinds of pleasures', and to his 'unusual experience of excess' that was the Iranian revolution: 'it was as if for the first time Foucault's theories of impersonal, authorless activity had been visibly realized and he recoiled with understandable disillusion'.

Chapter 6

On Not Knowing Who We Are: Madness, Hermeneutics and the Night of Truth in Foucault

John D. Caputo

This chapter argues that Foucault's thought is best construed as a hermeneutics of *not knowing* who we are. Foucault's work is construed to operate according to what Derrida calls the logic of the *sans*. That means that we get the best results by proceeding *sans voir, sans avoir, sans savoir*, without sight, without savvy, and without seizing hold of what we love. This is a bit of a perversity, turning as it does, not on uncovering the truth or illuminating us, which is the standard hope held out to us by philosophers, but on living with the untruth, with what Foucault calls very early on the 'night of truth'. The night of truth is the truth that there is no capitalized Truth, no 'truth of truth'. In the spirit of a certain Augustine, Foucault is read as himself engaged in a confessional practice, as making a confession in writing, *confiteri in letteris,* from the start, that, as Derrida says, the secret is there is no Secret, no way around the beliefs and practices in which we are steeped, by which we are shaped from time out of mind. His work may be seen as very 'circumfessional', confessing that we are all circumcised, cut off from the heart of unconcealed truth, but this without nostalgia, without concluding, as Rorty attributes to him,[1] that we are thereby lost and have no grounds for hope at all.

So, contrary to the received view of Dreyfus and Rabinow,[2] according to whom Foucault's thought moves 'beyond hermeneutics', it would be better to say it moves beyond a certain 'tragic' hermeneutics toward a more radical one, toward what may be called a 'hermeneutics of refusal'. Foucault rejects a hermeneutics of 'identity' in favor of a hermeneutics of 'difference', negates an assured and positive hermeneutics in order to affirm joyously and positively a *hermeneutica negativa*. I will take my point of departure from Foucault's early writings on madness, although I am also clearly interested in confessions, and so in what he says later on about Christian 'confessional techniques'. At the end an attempt will be made to push out beyond Foucault, to a Foucault without Foucault, in keeping with this logic of the *sans*, by addressing the question of the 'healing gestures' that should accompany all confession. Those who, like us, confess the humility of our condition, should not be left to shiver through the night of truth all alone. I push forward in a direction that, while it was not taken by Foucault, is perhaps suggested by him, is one of the potencies of his thought, belonging to the wake of his passing ship, in which we push past a hermeneutics of refusal to one of response and redress.[3]

TRAGIC HERMENEUTICS: MADNESS AND THE NIGHT OF TRUTH

In his earliest writings on 'mental illness' (*maladie*) Foucault drew a fascinating portrait of *déraison* – 'unreason', the failing or giving way of reason – 'before' it was interned and reduced to silence. By the 19th century, unreason had been constituted as 'mental illness', an object for the 'psychology of madness' (*folie*), which overwhelmed madness simultaneously with the external force of internment and the internal force of moralizing. The effect of this psychology was to foreshorten 'the experience of Unreason', an experience in which, Foucault says, 'Western man encountered the night of his truth and its absolute challenge', which once was and still is 'the mode of access to the natural truth of man'.[4]

What Foucault had in mind at that time might be described as a 'destruction of the history of psychology' that parallels Heidegger's project of a 'destruction of the history of ontology' in section 6 of *Being and Time*.[5] Were psychology to reflect on itself, it would effect a kind of *Destruktion* that would constitute at the same time a *retrieval* of a more essential truth. It would suffer a kind of autodeconstruction, coming under the scrutiny of its own eye. That is because psychology is the alienated truth of madness, the truth in a 'derisory' or alienated form that precisely on that account harbors within itself and maintains contacts with something 'essential'. While deriding madness under the hypocritical veil of moralizing internment, psychology 'cannot fail to move toward the essential', toward that originary point from which it itself arises as a science, namely, 'those regions in which man has a relation with himself'. 'If carried back to its roots, the psychology of madness would appear to be … the destruction of psychology itself and the discovery of that essential, non-psychological because non-moralizable relation that is the relation between Reason and Unreason.'[6] Beneath its moralization by the humanist reformers, viewing madness as somehow a moral failing, an effect of ill will, lies its more essential truth. Psychology cannot master the truth of madness because the truth of madness is the soil from which psychology springs, the prior, anterior sphere of unconcealment of which it is itself the alienating, scientific derivative. Madness is the founding experience from which psychology derives, from the distortion of which it itself arises. Occasionally, Foucault points out, the founding, originary experiences of madness do find a voice (in artists like Hölderlin, Nerval, Roussel, and Artaud) and 'that holds out the promise to man that one day, perhaps, he will be able to be free of all psychology and be ready for the great tragic confrontation with madness'.[7] Lying prior to the scientific truth of psychology, the poetic experience of the truth of madness represents a more radical unconcealment of madness.

'Mental illness' is 'alienated madness', madness in an alienated form. The aim of Foucault's work at this point is to bring us 'face to face' with madness in its unalienated truth, to let it speak in its own voice, which is not the voice of reason or science, to regain 'madness freed and disalienated, restored in some sense to its original language'.[8] But what can this original experience be? What would unreason say were its voice restored? What is the truth of madness, the truth that madness knows but we have silenced? Madness is 'difference', extreme, disturbing difference, inhabiting a 'void'. The Renaissance took the 'risk' of exposing itself to this void. It let itself be put into question by madness, without shutting it away. It allowed itself to be invaded by the 'Other', the 'insane'. It allowed the familiar, the *heimlich*, to be invaded by the strange and *unheimlich*. It allowed reason to be tested by unreason: 'it thought itself wise and it was mad; it thought it knew and it knew nothing'. But in the 17th century there began what Foucault describes as 'the negative appraisal of what had been originally apprehended as the Different, the Insane, Unreason'.[9]

So we have in the last two hundred years constituted *homo psychologicus*, the object of psychological science. Psychological man is a substitute that puts in the place of man's 'relation to the truth' the assumption that psychological man is himself 'the truth of the truth'. By this Foucault means that the 'real' – let us say 'cold' – truth of our divided condition is explained away and forgotten by the 'truth' of psychological science and its purportedly scientific explanations of an inner mental pathology. But the truth of truth, the truth of psychology arrives too late, only after madness in its truth has been closed off. Indeed, psychology itself is constituted as a science only on the basis of having closed off madness and turned it into a phantom of itself. Psychological truth is a way of forgetting the truth and reducing it to silence. Foucault refers to this truth that psychology allows us to forget, and that can be recognized in the modern world only in 'lightning flashes' with names like 'Nietzsche', as a 'tragic split' and 'freedom'.[10]

Foucault thus pursues in these early writings a very original approach to madness. He is not interested in its 'physiological' basis, which he does not deny, or in its 'cure', which he does not oppose, but in the 'truth of madness', in what the mad – shall we say – 'know' or 'experience'.[11] He is not addressing its physiology or its therapeutics but its 'hermeneutics' and the way in which psychological science conceals, represses, forgets and silences the truth of madness (rather the way that Gadamer thinks that 'method' objectifies and alienates 'truth'). In these early writings the mad 'know' something that we want first to diagnose and then to treat (and in recent years simply to anaesthetize with powerful psychotherapeutic drugs), whereas Foucault wants to linger with it for a while, to listen and to learn from it, to hear what it has to say.

What do the mad know? What truth would they speak if we lent them an ear? A 'tragic' truth, the truth of a 'split', let us say, a tragic knowledge. This is the sort of truth that would kill you – or drive you mad – of which Nietzsche spoke. Was Nietzsche's madness a function of what he knew? Was his knowledge a function of his madness? Foucault suspends both alternatives because they are both causal, etiological; he subjects both questions to a kind of *epoche* that puts both physiological and therapeutic questions out of action. His interest is hermeneutic: he wants to hear what one says who has been driven *in extremis*. While Foucault does not cite it here, one is reminded of the passage in *Beyond Good and Evil* in which Nietzsche repudiates the need to have the truth 'attenuated, veiled, sweetened, blunted and falsified', which is pretty much what Foucault thinks happens to madness in psychology. Foucault seems to have in mind what Nietzsche calls the 'elect of knowledge' who are almost destroyed by their knowledge, which carries them off into 'distant, terrible worlds'.[12]

The mad, in these early writings, have experienced a terrible truth; they sail on dangerous seas, have been released from ordinary constraints; they are extreme points of sensitivity to the human condition. They are not truly 'other' than 'us'. That is only the alienating gesture in which 'we' constitute ourselves as sane and normal and constitute 'them' as 'other'. The mad speak of a truth to us for which we have neither the nerve nor the ear, which is the truth of who we are. They instruct us about our hostility, meanness, aggressiveness, combativeness. 'Man has become for man the face of his own truth as well as the possibility of his death.'[13]

Foucault is not saying that the mad are the true philosophers but rather that they are precisely not philosophers at all, that they are the most forceful testimony to the breakdown of philosophy. They speak not with philosophical knowledge but with tragic knowledge. They have broken through the veil that philosophy lays over reality and that, in the form of psychology, philosophy tries to lay over them. The mad speak *de profundis*, from the depths of an experience in which both the reassuring structures of ordinary life and the comforting reassurances of scientific or philosophical knowledge have collapsed. They experience the radical groundlessness of the world, the contingency of its constructs, both social and epistemic; they speak of and from a kind of ineradicable terror. They speak to us from the abyss by which we are all inhabited; they are voices from an abyss.

This discussion, which Foucault inserted as the new 'Part II' of the 1962 revised edition of *Mental Illness and Psychology*, is an incisive summary of *Madness and Civilization*,[14] published a year before, whose 'Preface' and 'Conclusion' it closely parallels. *Madness and Civilization* opens with a reference to the madness of not being mad, the dangerous and unhealthy (*in-sanum*) condition of failing to recognize that 'we' too are a little mad, invaded also by unreason, and that it is mad to want to make reason a wholly insulated and pure region, a seamless sphere of the same insulated from its other. Foucault speaks of the madness of sovereign reason, the madness of a reason that thinks it has purified itself of the madness that inhabits us all, whose exclusion constitutes us as 'us', the madness that speaks in a 'merciless' language of madlessness. The goal of *Madness and Civilization* is to arrive at a zero point, a point *before* madness is divided off from reason, before the lines of communication between the two are cut, before reason looks sovereignly (that is, without risk or threat) upon madness as its pure Other. This is a region where 'truth' and 'science' do not obtain, which is prior to and older than science, which is older than the merciless 'difference' between reason and madness, a region of an originary undifferentiatedness in which reason mingles with and is disturbed from within by its other. Such a return to the original scene of madness will isolate 'the action that divides madness', the 'originative … caesura' by means of which reason and science are made to stand on the side, or better to look on from above, while unreason spreads out beneath its gaze as its object.[15] Then unreason is constituted as madness, crime or mental disease. That deprives madness of its voice, reduces it, in Lyotard's words, to a *differend* in which it is impossible for madness to state its case, and establishes the monologue of reason with itself that we call psychology and psychiatry.[16]

The Greeks, by way of contrast, thought of *sophrosyne* and *hybris* as alternate possibilities – of moderation and excess – within *logos,* but they did not constitute some sphere of exile, of *a-logos,* outside *logos.* The discourse on madness conducted by Europe since the beginning of the Middle Ages gives a 'depth' to western reason that irrupts in some of its greatest artists and poets (Bosch, Nietzsche, Artaud).[17] Reason without unreason is a smooth surface, a superficial transparency; reason with unreason speaks from the depths, *de profundis.* Unreason reduced to its scientific 'truth', constituted as a scientific object, is a surface event, a thin, transparent, placid object. If that depth is still apparent in the 'dispute' conducted between reason and madness in the Middle Ages and Renaissance, the depth is gone and the dispute is hushed in the silent corridors of the mental institution. The task of *Madness and Civilization* thus is one of archeological restoration, a vertical plumbing of the dark sedimented depths from which *homo psychologicus* emerges, of which it still bears a faint trace, reminding us of these hidden depths even as it tries to make us forget them.

What is the 'great motionless structure' (MC, xii) lying beneath the surface that is reducible neither to the drama of a dispute nor to an object of knowledge?[18] Foucault's answer is again the tragic (the tragic category). By the tragic he means a radical breach or split within human being, a profound rupture that makes it impossible for reason to constitute itself as an identity, to close round about itself, to make itself reason and light through and through. Reason is always already unreason; the truth of man is this untruth.[19] The attempt to find the 'truth of truth' is the attempt to expunge this untruth, to take leave of a more disturbing and disturbed region, to simplify and reduce human beings to pure reason by constituting the twin transparencies of reason on the one side and madness as the object of knowledge on the other.

In the 'Conclusion' to *Madness and Civilization,* after tracing the story from the great confinement to the birth of the asylum, Foucault returns again to the theme of the tragic. At the end of the story, by way of a conclusion to his discussion of the asylum, he mentions the advent of Freud. Freud, he says, reproduces in the person of the psychiatrist the confining structure of the institution of the asylum. For that reason, 'psychoanalysis has not been able, will not be able, to hear the voices of unreason, nor to decipher in themselves the signs of the madman'. Psychoanalysis can unravel some of the forms of madness; it is even able to let it speak; but it remains a stranger to 'the sovereign enterprise of unreason'.[20] Were they freed from the fetters of moralizing internment, the voices of unreason would speak of 'human truth' and 'dark freedom', Foucault says. That is the role of the artists who lend unreason an ear, who give it a voice, or lend it a canvas. Of Goya's *The Madhouse*, Foucault remarks: 'within this madman in a hat rises – by the inarticulate power of his muscular body, of his savage and marvelously unconstricted youth – a human presence already liberated and somehow free since the beginning of time, by his birthright'. In *Sleep of Reason*, 'man communicates with what is deepest in himself'. In Goya we experience madness as 'the birth of the first man and his first movement toward liberty', the freedom to dissolve the world and even to dissolve man himself.[21] The madman, Foucault suggests, lives *in extremis,* at the limits of the constitution of the world, where the world threatens to come undone, to deconstitute itself in a kind of pathological parallel to Husserl's famous hypothesis of the thought-experiment of the destruction of the world (*Ideas I,* ss.47–9). But whereas, in Husserl, such a deconstitution would leave sovereign consciousness still standing, Foucault suggests that, in Goya's work, the reduction of the world leads us back to naked unreason.

In Nietzsche unreason acquires a voice of 'total contestation' of the world, contestations that restore 'primitive savagery'.

In Sade we discover the truth of nature, the savage truth that nature cannot act contrary to nature, that every desire arises from nature. As an 'ironic Rousseau', Sade teaches the ethic of a more savage 'fidelity to nature', 'natural liberty'. But Sade pushes on beyond the truth of natural freedom to the 'total liberty' of pure subjectivity that dashes even nature itself by its violence. Sade traverses the terrible path from 'man's violent nature' to the 'infinity of nonnature', thus to a point where nature itself breaks up and reveals its own nature, its dissension and abolition. Sade dwells at that limit point where the world comes undone, where it is unmade, at 'the limits of the world that wounds' the mad heart.[22]

In Goya and Sade unreason finds a way to transcend reason in the path of violence and thus finds a way of 'recovering tragic experience beyond the promises of dialectic'.[23] The tragic always means the split, the rupture of human being, without the dream of dialectical rejoining and reconciliation, and here it means the unmaking and destruction of the world that reason builds around itself.

The final pages of *Madness and Civilization* are devoted to Nietzsche, who represents the tragic voice par excellence, the dominant voice from the abyss. Foucault's early writings are very much keyed to *The Birth of Tragedy* (and not, like the later writings, to *The Genealogy of Morals),* to which, Foucault says, all of Nietzsche's texts belong (MC, 285). Nietzsche is the philosopher of the tragic category, that is, of unreason and of the undoing of philosophy. What interests Foucault about Nietzsche is that his writing fell silent under the blow of madness, that his final word to us after a lifetime of writing was the howl of madness followed by silence.

Foucault is not leading up to the conclusion that madness is, in Heidegger's language, the 'origin of the work of art', but to an opposite conclusion, that it spells its death. 'Pure' madness is not the origin of the work of art but its absence and abolition; there is no work where there is pure madness.[24] Madness is but the parting gesture of the artwork, its final word or non-word just as it subsides into chaos. The work of art springs not from pure madness but from the invasion of reason by madness, from the tension or confrontation between reason and unreason, Apollo and Dionysus. But it is rendered impossible if this tension is broken from the side either of pure reason or of pure unreason.

The work of art carries out a kind of *epoche* of the world, suspending its hold on us, which it does just to the extent that it is 'interrupted' by madness, or exposed to it and held in communication with it. The work of art puts the rationality of the world in question, making the world, and not the madman, guilty, arraigning the world before the work of art. What is the world's fault? What has it done wrong? For what is it to be held responsible? For what does it owe reparation? The guilt of the world is that it has suppressed the world of unreason, and it is precisely the restoration of unreason that the work of art demands or, better, the 'restoration of reason *from* that unreason and *to* that unreason'.[25] So it is not precisely unreason that is restored to itself so much as it is reason that is restored to itself, to its originative belonging together with unreason. Reason is itself only insofar as it is also unreason; otherwise – and this is how *Madness and Civilization* began – it is quite mad. Foucault has turned the tables (or the couch) on the doctor. Now, instead of the madman as patient silently observed by the figure of science, the world itself is put into question by the madman as artist, by a very Dionysiac artist.

These early works of Foucault are not only or even primarily histories of psychology and madness. As archeologies of the silence to which unreason is reduced in the asylum, they offer a positive view of being human, a view best expressed by the 'tragic category'. Human beings are inwardly divided, inhabited by an abyss, by both reason and unreason. We dwell in both the truth and the untruth. In such a view, neither 'science' (the human sciences) nor 'morals' can be what they are (or want to be) all the way through. They are at best limited, incomplete or distortive, and hence in need of correction – the view that Foucault held in the 1954 edition of *Mental Illness and Personality*. At worst, they are useless illusions and even hypocritical attempts to suppress the unreason by which they are inhabited and hence they are beyond correction – the view both of the 1962 edition and of *Madness and Civilization*. The human sciences promote the illusion that unreason is a disturbance to be quelled, an abnormality to be normalized, a cry to be silenced. Ethics promotes the illusion that virtue is a unity, that the law is universalizable, that conscience is God's voice, suppressing the violence and confusion by which we are inhabited. Against the illusions of science and morals Foucault advocates a more originary tragic experience, an experience of reason's undoing and autodeconstruction by unreason, which is the 'truth' of the human condition. This truth is destroyed if it is allowed to evaporate into the 'truth of truth'. The truth is the night of truth, the midnight hour when reason allows itself to be interrupted and invaded by unreason. That happens in certain works of art that flash like lightning in the night of truth, illuminating for a moment a more originary and cragged human landscape.

BEYOND TRAGIC HERMENEUTICS

Foucault's early writings came under fire both by his critics and by Foucault himself. In the first place, these texts are marked by a kind of phenomenological naïveté. The goal of the early writings, which is to find an 'undifferentiated' experience of unreason, before it is differentiated into reason and madness, before the lines of reason are drawn in its virginal sands, perfectly parallels the phenomenological goal of finding a realm of pure 'prepredicative' experience, prior to its being carved up by the categories of logical grammar. To be sure, where Husserl thought to find pure *Sinn* lying beneath the categories of logical *Bedeutung* (in *Ideas Towards a Pure Phenomenology*, ss.124–7), Foucault suggests that we will find a pure *Unsinn*, a kind of perfect, pure, free, natural, undistorted, prepredicative madness, beneath the categories of the prison or the asylum. It was with this in mind that Derrida said it is an impossible dream to think that one could write the history of madness from the standpoint of madness itself. Writing and history already represent the standpoint of reason and are already violent; they have already incised this virginal terrain with their cuts and divides.[26]

This point is well made and Foucault has clearly not avoided this objection. Still we should recall that in the concluding pages of *Madness and Civilization* Foucault makes it plain that pure madness gives rise only to silence, that it leads to the end of the work of art. Now that surely implies that no work of history or of archeology could ever enter the domain of pure madness. The voices of unreason issue in works of art, or works of any sort, only inasmuch as they interrupt, invade, intermingle with and confront reason. So Foucault is aware that there is no access to a 'pure' madness or unreason, to a pure, ante-historical essence of madness, but only to the confrontation of reason and unreason in this or that concrete historical context.

Secondly, in a not unrelated way, Foucault himself criticized *Madness and*

Civilization (he never spoke of the first book, in either edition, on mental illness and opposed its republication) on the grounds that it labored under the 'repressive' hypothesis, that is, the notion that power works by excluding and repressing:

> I think that I was positing [in *Madness and Civilization*] the existence of a sort of living, voluble and anxious madness which the mechanisms of power and psychiatry were supposed to have come to repress and reduce to silence … In defining the effects of power as repression, one adopts a purely juridical conception of such power, one identifies power with a law which says no, power is taken above all as carrying the force of a prohibition.[27]

It is certainly true that in *Madness and Civilization* Foucault thought that unreason is repressed, suppressed, excluded, silenced, denied, obstructed and occulted by reason. On that point he was quite right and, furthermore, virtually the whole power of his book rests precisely on his being right about that. Furthermore, it seems that he does not mean to retract this point. In an interview also given in 1977 he says that the repressive mechanisms of *Madness and Civilization* were 'adequate' to his purposes in that book, that 'madness is a special case – during the Classical age power over madness was, in its most important manifestations at least, exercised in the form of exclusion, thus one sees madness caught up in a great movement of rejection' (P/K, 183–4).[28] However, Foucault was subsequently led by way of his investigations into the history of sexuality to see another mechanism of power, the productive one, which proceeds not by repressing and saying no but which 'traverses and produces things … induces pleasure, forms knowledge, produces discourse'.[29] But this other form of power reflects not so much a change in Foucault's thinking as a discovery about a change that takes place in the later history of power and madness:

> However, in the nineteenth century, an absolutely fundamental phenomenon made its appearance: the interweaving, the intrication, of two great technologies of power: one which fabricated sexuality and the other which segregated madness. The technology of madness changed from negative to positive, from being binary to being complex and multiform. There came into being a vast technology of the psyche, which became a characteristic feature of the nineteenth and twentieth centuries.[30]

One important result of this interweaving is that 'sexuality' assumed the place – as the truth of madness – that Foucault would have earlier said belonged to the 'tragic category'. That is an important point, to which we will return below. The essential thing to see at the moment, however, is that at a certain point, instead of being repressed, unreason is forced to talk. At a certain point, one that Foucault ascribes to the rise of confessional practices in the Church in the 17th and 18th centuries, instead of being doused with water, berated with moral criticism and subjected to a rigorous regimen, the mad are encouraged to say what they have on their mind, to associate freely, to dredge up their dreams, to tell us all about themselves and their parents (especially their parents) and childhood, to reveal their innermost secrets, to bring them out in the public view of the world: in short, to talk, talk, talk, for in the talking is the cure.

Now it would be a mistake to think that the repressive hypothesis is somehow inconsistent with productive power. In fact, the two are quite compatible and, indeed, produce a similar effect. One could even say that the hypothesis of a productive power is a continuation of the repressive hypothesis by another means. The unreason by which reason is inhabited is again silenced, this time not by real, physical, institutionalized silence but, still more effectively, and rather more pleasurably, by talk. The notion that more and more talking is an effective way to silence what requires a voice was noticed early on in the 19th century by Kierkegaard, who found that the idle chatter of the press addressed to the 'millions', and the numerous compendia of Hegelianized Christian doctrine that were being turned out by the dozens, were proving to be an exceptionally effective way to silence the quiet terror of authentic faith.[31] One of the most famous Kierkegaardian pseudonyms bore the name Johannes de Silentio because he was charged with the task of describing the indescribable 'fear and trembling' of Abraham, who was quite unable to explain himself to others and whom everyone else took to be quite – well – mad. Kierkegaard played such silence against the foil of the sane and sensible 'stockbrokers of the finite' with whom he draws a consistent contrast throughout *Fear and Trembling*.[32] In an age of top-down monarchical power, outright repression will do just fine, but in the democratic age of the 'millions', productive power does an even better job of silencing.

The fact of the matter is that, unless power has a univocal essence, unless power means just one thing, it is impossible to sustain the idea that power is only or essentially or primarily 'productive' and not also repressive. Power is only a descriptive category for Foucault and it means many things, in keeping with the plurality of historical situations in which it is deployed. There is no power as such; we can only describe the 'how' of power relations.[33] Power is now repressive, now productive, and now something else that Foucault had not noticed, and later on something else that perhaps has not yet come about. So there is nothing about Foucault's later adoption of the hypothesis of productive power to invalidate his notion that the work of reason is to silence and reject the voices of unreason by which it is inhabited, and hence to invalidate the early notion of the 'tragic category'. On the contrary, the two exist in a continual 'interweaving' and 'intrication'.

The strongest challenge to the continued viability of 'tragic hermeneutics' in Foucault's work is voiced by Dreyfus and Rabinow, who claim that after *Madness and Civilization* Foucault simply disavows any form of 'hermeneutics', and specifically, using Ricoeur's term, the 'hermeneutics of suspicion'. By 'hermeneutics' Dreyfus and Rabinow mean the unmasking and ferreting out of a repressed truth that tells the truth of man. In his 'Foreword to the California Edition' of *Mental Illness and Psychology* (1987) Dreyfus says that even the 1962 revised edition remains under the spell of a Heideggerian conception of '"anxiety" in the face of madness' that is silenced by morality and science. Foucault is convinced that there has been a 'repression of a deep, nonobjectifiable truth'.[34] So there is still a 'conspiracy theory' at work in this book, a notion that something is being suppressed that, if we could just face up to it, would result in liberation (in the way that Heidegger talks about being ready for anxiety). In the first edition of the book, Foucault thought it was a matter of facing up to the alienation produced by social contradiction; in the second edition, he has succeeded only in replacing a Marxist conception of social alienation with a Heideggerian and existential conception of 'strangeness' (*Unheimlichkeit*), but the overall (hermeneutic) scheme of reducing madness into its unalienated, liberating truth remains intact.

In the following years, Dreyfus argues, Foucault came to reject any such 'hermeneutics' and with it the claim that there is some deep truth begging to be deciphered, some latent content that awaits 'commentary',[35] some meaning at once more hidden and more fundamental that demands a "hermeneutics',[36] some interrogation of 'the being of madness itself, its secret content, its silent, self-enclosed truth'[37] that would traverse what is said about madness at any particular historical time. There is no message from the depths. Madness is simply constituted in different ways at different times and nothing is being left out. There is no inexhaustible residue, no cover-up story, no buried saving truth.[38] There is no ahistorical essential structure of madness (analogous to the ahistorical structure of *Dasein* yielded by the existential analytic), but only the changing, historical constitution of human beings. For Dreyfus and Rabinow, the critique made in Volume I of *The History of Sexuality* of the search for a secret self (sexuality) as a 'construction of modern thought', and hence as an important kind of modern power, is to be applied to *Madness and Civilization*. The latter sought to locate that secret, not in sexuality to be sure, but in 'the sovereign enterprise of unreason' that is delivered over to us in flashes of lightning with names like Nietzsche and Hölderlin.[39] But Foucault was led to give up this hermeneutic ontology that locates the transcendental being of unreason behind the play of the historical appearances of madness and *homo psychologicus*. He turns his attention instead to the patient description of the multiple historical forms in which modern man is constituted.

But if that is so, then what difference do the different historical constitutions of madness make? If madness is just produced in various ways, if nothing is repressed, lost, or silenced, why worry about what historical form the historical constitution of madness takes? If nothing is repressed, then nothing is to be liberated. If nothing is repressed, then there is nothing to offer resistance and no historical formation is better or worse than another. As Dreyfus and Rabinow themselves query at the end of their book, 'What is wrong with carceral society? Genealogy undermines a stance which opposes it on the grounds of natural law or human dignity. ... What are the resources which enable us to sustain a critical stance?'[40]

A good deal of what Foucault wrote in the years that followed *Madness and Civilization* raises just those objections. The remaining sections of this chapter will argue that an adequate answer to them turns on understanding what becomes of the hermeneutic impulse that is so clearly evident in the early writings, that it turns, in short, on seeing that Foucault has moved beyond a certain hermeneutics toward another hermeneutics more radically conceived.

THE HERMENEUTICS OF REFUSAL

In 'The Subject and Power', the Afterword to the Dreyfus–Rabinow book, Foucault speaks of the two 'pathological forms' of power, two 'diseases of power – fascism and Stalinism – that the twentieth century has known'.[41] Are we to think that these are 'alienated power', power gone wrong, power that divests human beings of something unalienated or even inalienable? Foucault says they are marked by an 'internal madness', but that such madness is merely the extension of contemporary 'political rationality', of a kind of unlimited rationalization. Are we to think, then, that this is something like a political equivalent of the 'other form of madness' that consists in not being mad, a political analogue of the 'merciless language of nonmadness'?[42] Are we to think that something is lost, repressed or occulted by fascism and Stalinism?

Foucault puts these expressions in scare quotes. They are normative expressions that seem to edge out beyond a felicitous positivism. He is perhaps concerned that he is drifting in the direction of the earlier writings that speak of a more originative sphere. He is worried that he is making himself look like the 'doctor'. In the next paragraph the metaphor switches to Kant, to what Lyotard calls Kant's 'critical watchman', and Foucault speaks of a need for a Kantian-like critique of the limits of political reason that keeps watch for 'excesses'.[44] Still, although it is helpful (this is what the Frankfurt school has already done) it is not enough, he says, to study the Enlightenment and the excesses to which it has led 'if we want to understand how we have been trapped in our own history'.[45]

We are trapped in our history. But *who* is trapped? And how *trapped*? What is the opposite of being trapped? Does being trapped mean that something has been prohibited, occulted, blocked off or repressed,[46] that is, trapped? What would it be like to be untrapped? Who would be untrapped? Who is the 'we' who would be untrapped?

Instead of pursuing the strategy of the Frankfurt school, of analyzing the 'internal rationality' of such excesses, Foucault says that he thinks it would be more instructive to approach such processes of subjection by way of a consideration of the 'resistance' that is offered to them, of the 'antagonisms' that they engender.[47] Insanity and illegality, for example, are (negative) indicators of what a society calls sanity and legality. Consider the 'struggles' we witness nowadays against the power of men over women, of psychiatry over the mentally ill, of bureaucracy over people at large. Such struggles 'assert the right to be different and they underline everything which makes individuals truly individual' and they fight against everything that 'ties [the individual] to his own identity in a constraining way', which reduces the individual to the identity of 'madman' ('mentally retarded'), 'alcoholic', 'handicapped', and so on.

These struggles, he says, 'are not for or against the "individual", but rather they are struggles against the "government of individualization"'.[48] It is not as though Foucault has a positive, affirmative normative idea of what an individual should be in the name of which he thinks these struggles should be waged. What the individual should be in some *determinate* way is none of Foucault's business. More importantly, the very business of coming up with normative ideas of what the individual should be, and of developing administrative practices and professional competencies to see to it that such individuals are in fact produced, is precisely the problem, not the solution: it is precisely what these struggles are struggling *against*.

In sum, he says, all such struggles 'revolve around the question: "Who are we?"'[49] But Foucault's idea is not only *not* to answer this question in a determinate way but to see to it that no one else is allowed to answer it, or rather to answer it on behalf of anyone else and above all to enforce their answer. It is a question that each of us, in our singularity, requires the privacy to raise and answer for ourselves, without sweeping up everyone else in what we come up with, so that, *contra* Sartre, we are not creating an essence for all humankind. It is like Derrida's adaptation of Augustine's question, 'What do I love when I love my God?'[50] Foucault wants to keep this question open, and above all to block administrators, professionals and managers of all sorts from answering this question on our behalf, thereby closing us in on some constituted identity or another that represents a strictly historical, that is, contingent constraint. While the tonality of hope and expectation is stronger in Derrida's slightly atheistic messianic expectation, in Derrida's *viens, oui, oui*, I think that the positions of Foucault and Derrida, their common desire to keep the future open, are very close at this point. That goes some way to explaining what Foucault means by being 'trapped by our history'. There are too many theories 'out there' of what Foucault earlier called 'the truth of truth', of the scientific or therapeutic truth of who we are, too many ready responses to the question 'Who are we?' Foucault's program is to block off or delimit the truth of truth, and to leave us to what the earlier writings called our (simple) truth, to the truth that there is no truth of truth, which is not a statement of despair but a hope for the freedom to invent something new. Foucault wants to defend the impossibility of reducing us to truth, to shelter the irreducibility and uncontractability of being human, its refusal of identity and identification, its refusal of an identifying truth, in order to open up the possibility of new modes of self-invention. Such refusal issues from a felicitous nominalism about the irrepressibility of being human, from its irrepressible capacity for being different, for mutation and transformation.

Like Derrida, Foucault thus has a negative, nominalistic and non-essentialistic idea of the individual. He struggles against any 'positive' theory of the individual that takes itself seriously, that thinks it has the truth of truth, that thinks it can affirmatively say or positively identify who we are. He opposes all 'cataphatic' discourse about the individual, all discourse that tries to prescribe what the individual is or should be, and he does so in the name of a kind of 'apophatic' discourse, of preserving a purely apophatic freedom. The gesture is actually quite classical, reminding us, as James Bernauer argues very powerfully, of negative theology.[51] What you say God is, is not true, Meister Eckhart wrote; but what you do not say God is, that is true. Foucault wants to keep open the negative space of what the individual is not, of what we cannot say the individual is, to preserve the space of a certain negativity that refuses all positivity, all identification, for that is always in the end a historical trap. To paraphrase the Meister, whenever the social sciences tell us who we are, that is not true; but what they do not say about who we are, that is true. Whatever lays claim to being the truth of truth, that is not true; but whatever concedes that we do not know the truth of truth, that is true. Whatever way the individual is historically constituted is not true; but whatever alternatives there are to the way we are constituted, that is true.

The modern exercise of power on Foucault's account represents a peculiar 'double bind' (BSH, 216) that produces individuals (productive power) precisely in order to block off individuality (repressive power). Modern power combines the production of individuals ('individualization techniques') along with the repression of individuality and difference ('totalization procedures').[52] Far from having abandoned the repressive hypothesis, the double bind depends upon the combined and simultaneous effect of both productive and repressive power, upon their 'interweaving' and 'intrication'.[53]

Productive power takes its rise from the spread of 'pastoral power' over the social body.[54] In pastoral power the pastor gives himself over to the production of an individual soul (the 'individual' is an invention of the Christian confessional). The pastor needs to know what is going on in individuals' hearts, to get inside their minds, to have them 'confess' their innermost secrets, in order to give spiritual direction. Pastoral power depends upon producing the truth, the truth of truth, in order thereby to produce good Christians. In the modern world pastoral techniques are multiplied everywhere: among the police, state investigative functions, criminal justice and social work professionals; among medical and health care professionals; among clinical and counseling psychologists and psychiatrists; educationists, demographers and so on. Wherever a 'file' is kept, wherever an individual 'case history' is to be written, the 'individual' is the target of knowledge and power, of power/knowledge.

Against this totalizing, normalizing production of individuals, Foucault holds out for the 'individual'. This is the double bind: not the individual in the sense of the individual case history, of the 'subject' whose secret code we – psychiatrists, moralists or educationists – know, but rather the individual who resists all secret codes, who has no identity, who is not reducible to one or another of the hermeneutic techniques of pastoral power, who is marked by the 'right to be different'.[55] Against the positive production of individuals in keeping with some normative standard, Foucault holds out for the negative freedom of the individual to be different. Whatever the social engineers want the individual to be, that is what the individual wants not to be, what the individual refuses to be in this hermeneutics of refusal.

So what philosophers must do is ask not, like Descartes, 'what am I?', as if there were a general answer, but, like Kant ('what is the Enlightenment?'), who are we *now*, at this particular moment of our historical constitution. Who are we high-tech, late capitalist, mobile, post-Enlightenment – shall we say – postmodernists? And how can we be otherwise? Or better still: 'Maybe the target nowadays is not to discover what we are but to refuse what we are. We have to imagine and to build up what we could be to get rid of this kind of "double bind" which is the simultaneous individualization and totalization of modern power structures' (BSH, 216). The idea is to liberate us not only from the state but from the sort of individualization that the state produces. The idea is 'to promote new forms of subjectivity through the refusal of this kind of individuality which has been imposed on us for several centuries'.[56]

Foucault's position is comparable to Lyotard's call for continual experimentalism, not only in art but in the artwork that we ourselves are, for the formation of new forms of subjectivity, for finding what Lyotard calls new idioms that provide a space for the right to be different. It corresponds, too, to Derrida's call for *l'invention de l'autre*, the coming, the incoming, of something other.

We are now in a position to address the question of just what difference the different historical constitutions of madness make. If madness is just produced in various ways, if nothing is repressed, lost or silenced, why worry about what historical form the historical constitution of madness takes? If nothing is repressed, then nothing is to be liberated, there is nothing to offer resistance, and no historical formation – including fascism and Stalinism – is better or worse than another. It is clear that Foucault does believe that something is repressed, and the very cogency of speaking of a 'double bind' depends on it. The claim that every historical constitution is a contingency that threatens to become a historical 'trap' means that something is being trapped. The idea that no particular historical constitution is exhaustive or totalizing means that there is always a residue, an irreducibility, a fragment that cannot be incorporated.[57] I do not mean a 'transcendental residuum' like Husserl's pure consciousness, or a historical essence or nature of being human, but rather a purely negative, always historical capacity for being otherwise, which is what Foucault means by freedom.

That is the answer to the objection that Foucault's writings provoke after *Madness and Civilization*, that he treats human beings as a kind of pure *hyle* capable of taking on indefinitely many forms, of being historically constituted in an indefinite multiplicity of forms, no one of which is any better or worse than another. Foucault clearly distinguishes the power that is exerted over material objects, for example, by means of instruments, from the power that individuals exert over other individuals, which is not power over things but power over freedom. Power is not a mere violence exerted on an object, like cutting wood or bending a piece of steel. Violence or force are effected on a 'mere passivity'.[58] But the power in which Foucault is interested is exerted over 'the other', over another person who acts and reacts. Power is a set of actions upon other actions. Nor is power *consensus*, a free renunciation of one's own freedom for the sake of a general arrangement. 'Power relations' occur in the space between pure force and free consent, and they may or may not obtain in the presence of either. Power is a matter neither of pushing boulders about with great bulldozers nor of a pure dialogue between Platonic souls.

Power is a way inducing, seducing, conducing (*conduire*, conduct [v.], conduct [n.]), power is conductive. It is stronger (more coercive) than what Husserl calls 'motivation', which is pure intentional freedom, because it is a way we have of being led (*ducere*) around (*con*), but like motivation it belongs in a quasi-intentional sphere of human behavior and is not to be reduced to physical causality. Power is a way of 'governing', shaping, forming – the 17th-century religious orders that Foucault discussed in *Discipline and Punish* called the time of apprenticeship in the order years of 'formation'. Power sets up (*stellen, auf-stellen*) or frames out (*Ge-stell*)[59] a certain preset range of possibilities within which action can take place, broad 'ducts' through which actions are led; power 'structures the field' of actions. Thus 'power is exercised only over free subjects, and only insofar as they are free'.[60] Slavery is not power but constraint because in slavery the range of possibilities has been 'saturated', that is, determined to a specific outcome (*determinatio ad unum*). Power is exerted only over beings capable of being recalcitrant and intransigent. Power implies freedom since without freedom power is just constraint or force. Power and freedom belong together agonistically, in continuing 'agonism', a struggle, in which there are winning and losing strategies, a victorious consolidation of power on the one hand or successful strategies against power on the other hand. If power is cunning and pervasive enough, it will coopt freedom; if freedom is resistant and persistent enough, it will cause power to tremble.

Power is not something that could be removed, the result being a perfectly free society. A society without power would not be a society but a physical aggregate; as soon as human beings come together (and when have they not?), in virtue of their coming together, power relations spring into being. A society is essentially a network of power relations that are more minute than its larger institutional structures. The idea for Foucault is not to abolish power relations – that would make no sense – but to alter them by means of winning strategies, to open up new possibilities, to restructure the field such that something else (being otherwise) is possible.[61] Such an alteration is driven on by the continuing agonism between power and freedom that sees to it that any field of power is an unsteady state, an unstable and hence ultimately open, alterable system. The idea is to keep open 'the free play of antagonistic' relations, to refuse to let the social system harden into place with stable mechanisms that are overeffective in regulating conduct.[62]

So far from excluding or reducing freedom, power over freedom implies resistance. Freedom for Foucault is a kind of irrepressibility, a refusal to contract into an identity, a continually twisting loose from the historical forms of life by which it is always already shaped. Freedom is not a nature or essence but a lack of nature or essence, a capacity for novelty and innovation. Bernauer calls it 'transcendence',[63] the capacity to move beyond a particular historical constitution. That is in keeping with Bernauer's guiding motif of Foucault's 'negative theology' (God transcends whatever we say about God), which is rather a 'high' theology for Foucault, who has in mind a more modest freedom from below, a refusal, a resistance, a certain stepping back, not so much a transcendence, let us say, as a *re*scendence, which seeks to twist free from the trap of the present in order to find a variation.

We are now in a position to evaluate the claim of Dreyfus and Rabinow that, by turning himself over to detailed genealogies of the various ways in which bodies and minds are historically constituted, Foucault moved beyond all hermeneutics. This claim is tied up with the claim that he simply dropped the idea of the repression of something deep and replaced it with the notion of describing the surface of productive relations of power.

This position is partly right. In the early writings Foucault clearly believed in the 'secret' and in finding the hermeneutic key to the secret. The hermeneutics of suspicion he practiced at that point (suspecting psychology of repressing the tragic truth) turned on a positive idea of who we are, a particular – indeed, a Dionysiac – idea of a 'tragic unreason'. The authoritative account of who we are was to be found in *The Birth of Tragedy,* an account the human sciences would like to dismiss or forget. It is clear that by the time of the last works Foucault had given up the idea that there is some *positive* idea of 'who we are' to be recovered, some *particular* identity that is being repressed that needs to be shaken loose ('destruction') and retrieved.

But if he has dropped the idea that there is some particular identity that is being repressed, he has not given up the idea that *something* is being repressed, something much looser, more unspecifiable and indefinite, something negative and unidentifiable. It is no longer an *identity* we need to recover (a secret tragic identity) but a *difference.* It is no longer a positive ideal that needs to be restored but simply a certain capacity to resist the identities that are imposed upon us just in order to set free our capacity to invent such new identities for ourselves as circumstances allow.[64] In short, the movement has not been beyond hermeneutics and repression but beyond a hermeneutics of identity (a positive tragic hermeneutics) to a hermeneutics of difference (a negative hermeneutics of refusal). The later writings turn on the idea that there is always something other than or different from the various historical constitutions of human beings, some 'freedom' or resistance that is irreducible to the several enframing historical forms of life, some power-to-be-otherwise, some being-otherwise-than-the present that radically, irreducibly, irrepressibly belongs to us, to what we are (not). We never are what we are; something different is always possible. As Derrida says in *The Other Heading,* what is proper to the 'identity' of a self or a culture: '*is not to be identical to itself.* Not to not have an identity, but not to be able to identify itself, to be able to say "me" or "we"; to be able to take the form of a subject only in the non-identity to itself or, if you prefer, only in the difference with itself (*avec soi*).'[65] The 'I' or the 'we' is marked by its capacity to be otherwise. That is why Foucault has not dropped the hermeneutic project. He has not abandoned a *certain* hermeneutics, a negative hermeneutics, a hermeneutics of refusal, of what we are not, a kind of 'radical hermeneutics'.[66] In such a hermeneutics there is no question of deciphering a 'master name', of reapprehending through the 'manifest meaning ... another meaning at once ... more hidden but more fundamental'.[67] On the contrary, such a hermeneutics turns on the loss of fixed or determinate meaning, and on an understanding of being human as an abyss that refuses identification, contraction or reduction to a fixed meaning. If Foucault has abandoned the hermeneutics of suspicion, that is because, in my view, he has taken up a hermeneutics of refusal.

Foucault's more radical hermeneutics rejects the idea of the truth of truth, of some nameable, masterable truth of being human. It rejects a whole series of humanisms of truth: *homo psychologicus, homo economicus, homo religiosus*, including his own earlier contribution to this scheme, *homo tragicus*. But he has done so, not in order to skim along the surface of positivistic descriptions, but in order to open a hermeneutic dimension of negativity: that we do not know who we are. He has abandoned the truth of truth, the mastery of knowledge, in favor of the 'cold truth', of the truth that there is no truth of truth, of the truth that our being is always already disturbed by untruth, which means an irreducibility to truth. This is very close to Derrida's notion of the *khora*, that the things we come up with when we describe our condition are written in the sand, a desert sand that is vulnerable to the next storm. The essence of such Foucaultian freedom, were there such a thing, is its untruth, its irreducibility to the truth of truth. Beneath the layers of *homo psychologicus* and of all the 'idols' of the human sciences, of all the 'graven images' of modernity that we might collectively call *homo cyberneticus*, Foucault hears the murmur of a capacity to be otherwise. His is a refusal of the idols of the present, the idolatrous worship we are prone to offer the images that present themselves to us today and threaten to hold us captive. That critique of idolatry is linked to the critical power of the messianic idea in Derrida. The later writings respond to a plea that quietly calls for something different, what Derrida and Levinas call the call of the other. Conductive, productive power is deductive: by leading us along (con) certain paths, it leads us away from (de) others, cutting off, closing off, the capacity to differ. Productive power is interwoven with repressive power. It wants to produce human beings of a certain sort because it is at the same time 'anxious' about the human capacity for being otherwise; it is not a little anxious about difference. Far from giving up on the idea of hermeneutic anxiety, *pace* Dreyfus, the power of Foucault's analyses, early or late, depends on that anxiety.

We do not know who we are, not if we are honest about it. That is a hermeneutic point, albeit a negative one. It is the issue of a certain kind of ruthless facing up to the facts that neither ethics nor the human sciences can tell us who we are or what to do. It is the issue of a certain 'responsiveness' to the abyss that we are, to the capacity to be different. Dreyfus is mistaken to think that Foucault gave up on the hermeneutic idea of 'facing up to the truth' if by that one means the 'cold truth', the truth that there is no truth of truth, the truth that is invaded and fragmented by untruth.[68] Whatever is called 'Truth' and adorned with capital letters masks its own contingency and untruth, even as it masks the capacity for being otherwise. For our being human spins off into an indefinite future about which we know little or nothing, which fills us with a little hope and not a little anxiety, a future to come for which there is neither program nor preparation nor prognostication.

BEYOND FOUCAULT: HEALING GESTURES

I wish to close with a word about madmen and confessors, a word that Foucault does not himself utter but that belongs to the space he opens up, to the potentialities he awakens. Foucault's analysis of the normalization of the mad in psychology and psychiatry, and of the normalization of the faithful in the confessional, addresses the anxiety of modernity about difference and abnormality, and it does so in a most incisive way. But it does not address another issue and another concern, the issue of what *healing* means in such an analysis, since we can hardly think we are all okay. This would represent a final step, from hermeneutics to therapeutics.

Let us return to the question of madness. Madness is a 'disturbance' but in a twofold sense both of what is 'disturbing' and of what is 'disturbed'. Foucault does a masterful job of showing what is 'disturbing' about madness. To put it in the terms of *Being and Time,* Foucault treats madness as a certain way the world is 'understood', not in a theoretical sense, of course, but in the sense of what Heidegger called in *Being and Time* a certain *Weltverstehen,* a practical understanding that is heavily 'mooded' or 'tuned' *(bestimmt).* The disturbing thing about the mad is the nagging fear that they are 'at-tuned' to something, to some deep set dissonance, from which the rest of 'us' seek to be protected. We are apprehensive that, living at the margins of normal life, *in extremis*, the mad have been exposed to something the rest of us prefer to ignore. 'We' are beset by an apprehensiveness that our sane, healed, whole lives mask a deeper rupture, that the settled tranquility of the sane is acquired only by repressing the 'up-set' of the mad. We are disturbed that 'the disturbed' are responding to a certain *turbatio* that is 'there'. 'We' find the 'disturbed' disturbing. Madness is a mirror of ourselves. It tells us who we are. If the mad exhibit 'infantile regressions', it is only because childhood itself is infantilized to begin with, unrealistically insulated from real conflict. If madness takes on the form of 'schizophrenia', it is because the mad reflect the contradictions of a world in which man can no longer recognize himself, because the social world itself is marked by struggle, hostility and foreignness. It is the world that is mad, alienated, unfree, divided and contradictory, and it is such madness that the mad take as their model and in which the world refuses to see itself.[69] That is what gives Foucault's analyses their bite.

But madness is also a being disturbed, *patheia*, a way of suffering that causes *pain*. The mad *suffer from* their attunement, from what they experience/feel/undergo. Their ruptured lives are the site of a wound. It is not as though the lives of extreme manic depressives would be felicitous if we just left them alone or if the world would adjust to them. They live with terror; they wrestle with demons; their works are impaired, ruined, suicidal, brought to halt, reduced to inertia. Their lives are disrupted and destroyed, 'disturbed'. They have fallen prey to madness. They need healing. Their cry of pain is also a call for help. They lay claim to us, we who are whole (enough) to help, we who are perhaps not so much whole and sane as just a little less mad and better skilled at repressing our madness. There are, after all, only a few Nietzsches, Hölderlins and Van Goghs among the mad. It was in the long run better to let Van Gogh and Nietzsche alone, to let mad genius run its course into the dark night of truth. But for the majority madness does not mean genius but pain, and they cry out for help, not for the immortality of the work of art.

I take it that there is nothing in what Foucault says that opposes 'a strategy of cure';[70] it is simply not his subject. Indeed, I see in his work the makings of a certain therapeutic 'direction', let us say of a therapeutic of not-knowing. Such a therapeutic does not come from on high, does not proceed from the heights of science or episteme, and so does not suffer from the illusion that it knows what madness is (when madness is not clearly physiological). Such a therapy of not-knowing would take madness 'seriously', that is, as an Other from which we ourselves have something to learn. Indeed, it undergoes a change of direction by letting the mad come to us from 'on high', in their extreme Otherness. It does not look on the mad as 'patients' in the sense of 'objects' of medical knowledge, but as *patiens*, as ones who suffer greatly, who suffer from their knowledge, as Nietzsche says, and its look is not objectifying but *com-patiens*, compassionate. Such a patient would not be an object of knowledge but an author or subject of knowledge, one from whom we have something to learn. Such patients are not stretched out before the medical gaze as objects but come to us from on high, rather lifted up by their suffering, in the manner of Levinas. We are not panoptical observers of madness, but we are ourselves put into question by the mad, seen and interrogated by them, above all, solicited by them. We have something to learn from the mad, above all that they are not 'they' but who we ourselves are. We are instructed by them; they have set foot where the sane fear to tread. They tell us, unhappily, who we are; they tell us of our own unhappiness. The mad are not the subject of a medical observation but the source of a call that calls upon us and demands our response.

The mad do not ask for analysis and objectification by us but friendship, support, companionship, solace, joy. The healing gesture, the gesture meant to heal their suffering, is not intended to explain anything away or fill in the abyss but simply to affirm that they are not alone, that our common madness is a matter of degree, that we are all siblings in the same 'night of truth'. The healing gesture is not to explain madness, if that means to explain it away, but to recognize it as a common fate, to affirm our community and solidarity, and to divide their pain in half by taking on the half of it in attentive compassion and counsel.

A comparable point can be made about the 'confessional practices' of the 17th and 18th centuries that Foucault has so adroitly analyzed. The meticulous ruminations of an Alphonse Liguori into the most secret recesses of the soul are lurid exercises in a kind of confessional voyeurism, which are useful only as candidates for an inverted, perverted *ars erotica*. But they are also, and more importantly, from a more authentically religious point of view, profoundly insufficient and quite irreligious. The institutionalization, regularization and methodologization of 'confession' is a religious perversity. The confessor (in the sense of *confiteor*, I confess) is a 'sinner'. 'Sin' is like 'madness': it is a larger-than-life term for life *in extremis*, for life that has strayed beyond the safe and reassuring boundaries of everyday life, beyond the wide swaths of normalcy cut by our everyday practices. Sin is not reducible to wrongdoing – no more than madness is reducible to error. It is an expression, perhaps a mythic expression – that is arguably the status of 'madness', too – that provides an idiom for a deeper breach, a profound rupture in the human heart. We are divided against ourselves. Like the madness by which we are all beset and upset, and from which we have something to learn, sin bears testimony to a deep divide. But, unlike madness, sin is a disturbance, not in the sphere of reason and 'truth', but in the sphere of justice and the 'good'. 'Sin' seeks to give words to profound self-diremption, a rupture, a radical unhappiness in our condition.

I believe that sin requires a healing gesture very analogous to madness, a gesture of compassion and commonality. The sinner tells us who we are, tells us of our own unhappiness. Sin is not the object of a Liguorian gaze, not a secret to be ferreted out by confessional techniques, not an object of interrogation. Sin is not an object at all, but the Being of the being we ourselves are.[71] The language of sin provides an idiom for what Levinas calls the 'murderousness' of freedom, the murderousness of our power. We who are free and well fed, we who are whole and hearty, fit and on the move, we who move easily about within the relations of power, are murderous and we cause others to suffer. 'Sin' likewise provides an idiom for our weakness, our infidelities to those to whom we owe loyalty. Sin is not the Other but who we are. Sin is the Other within, the serpent and the apple within our own heart. Sin comes to us from on high and gives us something to understand by telling us about ourselves, by telling us of the abyss within.

The healing gesture handed down to us by the great religious traditions is not analytic objectification, not minute, ruminating subjectification. The great healing gesture that sweeps down over us in Buddhism is called the 'great compassion' and in the New Testament is called 'forgiveness'. Jesus was the discoverer of forgiveness, Hannah Arendt says.[72] Forgiveness loosens the knots of the social network, slackens the ties in the relations of power, even as revenge draws them tighter and makes them more intractable and oppressive. Forgiveness opens the space of the social network; it makes the future possible and denies to the past its role as fate. Forgiveness makes new forms of subjectivity possible, even as revenge condemns us to repeat the past in endless cycles. Forgiveness releases and opens; revenge traps, incarcerates and closes. Forgiveness is not given to minute interior rehearsing of the past and intensive subjectification, but is rather dismissive and forgetting. Go and sin no more! Forget it! Forgiving is active forgetting. Forgiveness does not ask questions, but understands that it has itself been put in question by sin. Forgiveness lets itself be interrogated; it does not interrogate. Forgiveness readily makes itself guilty for the sake of the other. Forgiveness asks who among us can cast the first stone; it looks lovingly on sinners, with whom it consistently consorts to the scandal of the Good and the Just. Forgiveness heals not by analyzing but by holding out a hand of compassion, by offering a forgiving word that affirms and confesses for its own part that we are all sinners, all siblings of the same dark night.

That is the 'truth' of confession, the truth that there is no 'truth of truth', no confessional techniques, no methodological examinations of conscience, no objectification by way of subjectification. That is also why Julia Kristeva thinks that Christian confessional practices have a notable, albeit mystified, healing power. (But then what is more mystifying than the creatures that psychoanalysis invents?) That is particularly true, she thinks, when confession centers on words of forgiveness and not on the rites of 'penance', which is the view of Duns Scotus, whom Kristeva regards as the great theologian of confession.[73] Scotus of course lived before the age of subjectification/objectification, the age of the world reduced to a picture for the subject's gaze *(Weltbild)*, as Heidegger says, and offered an antidote to the Tridentine confessional practices that Foucault has so ruthlessly exposed.

The secret is, there is no Secret. The truth is that we cannot gain the high ground of a capitalized Truth, insulated from violence and unreason, destruction and self-destruction, 'madness' and 'sin'. The truth is what Foucault called, in a wonderfully unguarded moment, the 'night of truth'. His analyses constitute a remarkable hermeneutics of that night of truth, a cold and more merciless scrutiny of the human condition that is, at the same time, bent subtly in a direction not at all at odds with mercy.

NOTES

1   For a discussion of Derrida, Rorty and politics, see 'Parisian Hermeneutics and Yankee Hermeneutics', in John Caputo, *More Radical Hermeneutics: On Not Knowing Who We Are* (Bloomington: Indiana University Press, 2000, pp.84–124).

2   Hubert Dreyfus and Paul Rabinow, *Michel Foucault: Beyond Structuralism and Hermeneutics* (hereafter BSH), 2nd edn, with an Afterword by Michel Foucault, (Chicago: University of Chicago Press, 1983).

3   See the discussion of 'cold hermeneutics' in John Caputo, *Radical Hermeneutics: Repetition, Deconstruction and Hermeneutics* (Bloomington: Indiana University Press, 1987, ch.7).

4   Michel Foucault, *Mental Illness and Psychology*, tr. Alan Sheridan, with a Foreword by Hubert Dreyfus (Berkeley and Los Angeles: University of California Press, 1987, p.74). This is a translation of the 1962 French edition, *Maladie mentale et psychologie* which is an extensive revision of the 1954 edition, *Maladie mentale et personnalité*. The important difference between these editions is examined carefully by James Bernauer, *Michel Foucault's Force of Flight Toward an Ethics For Thought* (Atlantic Highlands: Humanities Press International, 1990, pp.24–36 and Appendix 1).

5   Dreyfus discusses Foucault's interest in Heidegger in his instructive Foreword to *Maladie mentale et psychologie,* pp.ix, xviii–xix, xxviii ff.

6   *Mental Illness and Psychology,* p.74.

7   *Mental Illness and Psychology,* p.75.

8   *Mental Illness and Psychology,* p.76.

9   *Mental Illness and Psychology,* pp.77, 78.

10 *Mental Illness and Psychology,* pp.87, 88.

11 *Mental Illness and Psychology,* p. 86.

12 Friedrich Nietzsche, *Beyond Good and Evil,* tr. R.J. Hollingdale (Baltimore: Penguin, 1972), no.39 (p.50), no.270 (pp.189–90). See my discussion of these texts of Nietzsche in *Radical Hermeneutics*, p.189.

13 *Mental Illness and Psychology,* pp.80–81, 82.

14 *Madness and Civilization: A History of Insanity in the Age of Reason* (hereafter MC), tr. Richard Howard (New York: Pantheon, 1965). This is an abridgment of *Histoire de la folie à l'âge classique* (Paris: Gallimard, 1972).

15 *Madness and Civilization,* p.ix.

16 Jean-François Lyotard, *The Differend: Phrases in Dispute,* tr. G. Van Den Abbeele (Minneapolis: University of Minnesota Press, 1988, p.xi).

17 *Madness and Civilization,* pp.ix, xi.

18 *Madness and Civilization,* p.xii.

19 'Untruth' is an expression used by the later Heidegger in such a way as to say that there is always a radical core of untruth within truth; truth is not truth 'all the way through', concealment is the hidden ground of unconcealment, a wresting of unconcealment from a prior concealment. See 'On the Essence of Truth', tr. John Sallis, in David Krell (ed.), *Martin Heidegger: Basic Writings* (New York: Harper & Row, 1977, pp.132–5. Foucault seems to think of unreason as a prior untruth and concealment embedded in the core of reason.

20 *Mental Illness and Psychology,* p.69; *Madness and Civilization,* p.278.

21 *Madness and Civilization,* pp.279, 280, 281.

22 *Madness and Civilization,* pp.284, 285.

23 *Madness and Civilization,* p.285.

24 See Michel Foucault, 'Madness, the Absence of Work', tr. Peter Stastny and Deniz Sengel, in Arnold Davidson (ed.), *Foucault and his Interlocutors* (Chicago: University of Chicago Press, 1997, pp.97–104).

25 *Madness and Civilization,* p.288.

26 'The attempt to write the history of the decision, division, difference runs the risk of construing the division as an event or a structure subsequent to the unity of an original presence, thereby confirming metaphysics in its fundamental operation' (Derrida, *Writing and Difference,* tr. Alan Bass, Chicago: University of Chicago Press, 1978, p.140); see Foucault's hostile response, 'My Body, This Fire', tr. Geoffrey Bennington, *Oxford Literary Review,* 4(1) (1979), 5–28. For a good account of the acrimonious character of this exchange between Foucault and Derrida and for a sensible appraisal of the convergence of their thought around the themes of power and ethics, which I am also suggesting here, see Roy Boyne, *Foucault and Derrida: The Other Side of Reason* (London: Unwin Hyman, 1990). For Derrida's most recent statement on Foucault, see '"To Do Justice to Freud": The History of Madness in the Age of Psychoanalysis', tr. Pascale-Anne Brault and Michael Naas, in *Foucault and his Interlocutors,* pp.57–96.

27 *Power/Knowledge: Selected Interviews and Other Writings, 1972–1977* (hereafter P/K), ed. Colin Gordon, tr. Colin Gordon, Leo Marshall, John Mepham and Kate Soper (New York: Pantheon, 1980, pp.118–19).

28 *Power/Knowledge: Selected Interviews and Other Writings,* pp.183–4.

29 *Power/Knowledge: Selected Interviews and Other Writings,* p.119.

30 *Power/Knowledge: Selected Interviews and Other Writings,* p.185.

31 See Soren Kierkegaard, *Two Ages: The Age of Revolution and the Present Age,* tr. Howard Hong and Edna Hong (Princeton: Princeton University Press, 1978, pp.68ff, esp. pp.92–102).

32 *Fear and Trembling* and *Repetition,* tr. Howard Hong and Edna Hong (Princeton: Princeton University Press, 1983, p.36).

33 *Michel Foucault: Beyond Structuralism and Hermeneutics,* pp.217, 219.

34 *Mental Illness and Psychology,* p.xxxii.

35 Michel Foucault, *The Birth of the Clinic: An Archaeology of Medical Perception,* tr. A.M. Sheridan Smith (New York: Pantheon, 1973, pp.xvi–xvii).

36 Michel Foucault, *The Order of Things: An Archaeology of the Human Sciences,* tr. Alan Sheridan (New York: Pantheon, 1970) p.373). Dreyfus and Rabinow use this text to set the terms of their own understanding of hermeneutics.

37 Michel Foucault, *The Archaeology of Knowledge and the Discourse on Language,* tr. A.M. Sheridan Smith (New York: Pantheon, 1972, p.32).

38 *Mental Illness and Psychology,* p.xxxiii.

39 *Madness and Civilization,* p.11.

40 *Michel Foucault: Beyond Structuralism and Hermeneutics*, p.206.
41 *Michel Foucault: Beyond Structuralism and Hermeneutics*, p.209.
42 *Madness and Civilization,* p.ix.
43 'Judiciousness in Dispute, or Kant after Marx', in *The Lyotard Reader*, ed. Andrew Benjamin (Oxford: Basil Blackwell, 1990, pp.328 *et passim*).
44 *Michel Foucault: Beyond Structuralism and Hermeneutics*, p.210.
45 Ibid.
46 *Power/Knowledge: Selected Interviews and Other Writings*, p.183.
47 *Michel Foucault: Beyond Structuralism and Hermeneutics*, p.211.
48 *Michel Foucault: Beyond Structuralism and Hermeneutics*, p.212.
49 Ibid.
50 Derrida, 'Circumfession: Fifty-nine Periods and Periphrases', in Geoffrey Bennington and Jacques Derrida, *Jacques Derrida* (Chicago: University of Chicago Press, 1993, p.122).
51 I have found James Bernauer's work (see note 4) to be singularly insightful in its approach to Foucault and quite congenial to my own notion of 'radical hermeneutics', a notion I developed in connection with Derrida, not Foucault. For more on Bernauer's notion of Foucault's negative theology, see his 'The Prisons of Man: An Introduction to Foucault's Negative Theology', *International Philosophical Quarterly* 27(4) (December 1987), pp.365–81, and the excellent conclusion of *Michel Foucault's Force of Flight*, pp.175–84, on 'ecstatic thinking'. For more on the long-range consonance between Foucault and Derrida, which focuses on the question of reason and unreason, see Boyne, *Foucault and Derrida.*
52 *Michel Foucault: Beyond Structuralism and Hermeneutics*, p.213
53 *Power/Knowledge: Selected Interviews and Other Writings*, p.185.
54 *Michel Foucault: Beyond Structuralism and Hermeneutics*, p.215.
55 *Michel Foucault: Beyond Structuralism and Hermeneutics*, p.211.
56 *Michel Foucault: Beyond Structuralism and Hermeneutics*, p.216.
57 The motif of the irreducible residue, the unassimilable fragment, the remains, the leftover that cannot be *relevé*, is central likewise to Derrida's *Glas*, tr. John Leavey and Richard Rand (Lincoln: University of Nebraska Press, 1986), which like so much of recent French philosophy is on the lookout for something that cannot be consumed and incorporated into the Hegelian 'dialectic'. Cf. *Madness and Civilization*, p.285.
58 *Michel Foucault: Beyond Structuralism and Hermeneutics*, p.220.
59 There are late Heideggerian tones in late Foucault: where Heidegger has analyzed the *Gestell* that is the 'essence of technology', in its application to nature, Foucault discusses the *Gestell* that is applied to us in the various 'technologies of the self', or technologies of behavior.
60 *Michel Foucault: Beyond Structuralism and Hermeneutics*, pp.222, 221.
61 *Michel Foucault: Beyond Structuralism and Hermeneutics*, p.223.
62 *Michel Foucault: Beyond Structuralism and Hermeneutics*, p.225.
63 'This ... force of resistance, this Foucaultian spirituality, bears witness to the capacity for an ecstatic transcendence of any history that asserts its necessity' (*Michel Foucault's Force of Flight*, pp.180–81).
64 Foucault does not have a theory of pure or radical freedom, of the sort suggested by his early work on Binswanger, but of a circumscribed, circumstantial (circumcisional!) freedom, a capacity for contextual alteration, for modification of the circumstances one finds oneself by way of refusal. It is also a theory of local revolt as opposed to total revolution. See John Rajchman, *Michel Foucault: The Freedom of Philosophy* (New York: Columbia University Press, 1985, ch. I).
65 Jacques Derrida, *The Other Heading: Reflections on Today's Europe*, tr. Pascale-Anne Brault and Michael Naas (Bloomington: Indiana University Press, 1992, p.9).

66 I have expanded on the notion of a hermeneutics that gives up on the idea of a hermeneutic secret, of uncovering the master name, and that finds itself in an abyss, in *Radical Hermeneutics*, chs 6–7.

67 Foucault, *The Order of Things*, p.373.

68 *Mental Illness and Psychology*, pp.xxviii–xxx.

69 *Mental Illness and Psychology*, pp.80–81.

70 *Mental Illness and Psychology*, p.76.

71 That is fundamentally the argument of Kierkegaard's *The Concept of Anxiety*, tr. Reidar Thomte (Princeton: Princeton University Press, 1980), which is the reason that Heidegger had a fairly easy time of rewriting this concept in a secularized or, as he said, 'formalized' way in *Being and Time*.

72 *The Human Condition* (Chicago: University of Chicago Press, 1958, pp.236–43). 'Trespassing is an everyday occurrence which is in the very nature of action's constant establishment of new relationships within a web of relations, and it needs forgiving, dismissing, in order to make it possible for life to go on by constantly releasing men from what they have done unknowingly' (p.240). Forgiving is releasing, forgetting, and moving on.

73 '*Qui tollis peccata mundi*', in *Powers of Horror: An Essay on Abjection*, tr. Leon S. Roudiez (New York: Columbia University Press, 1982, pp.131–2). Scotus located the essence of the sacrament in the word of the confessor, not in doing penance. Arendt says that *metanoein* (Luke 17:3–4) is better understood as 'change of heart', retrace your steps and sin no more, than as 'repent' (the usual translation), penance, which means of course to revisit yourself with pain. Cf. *The Human Condition*, p.240, n.78.

III
FOUCAULT AND
THEOLOGICAL KNOWLEDGE

Chapter 7

Partially Desacralized Spaces: the Religious Availability of Foucault's Thought

Thomas R. Flynn

To whom life is an experience to be carried as far as possible.

Georges Bataille

Some avowedly atheistic philosophers cannot leave God alone. Sartre fits into this category. To be sure, he confessed in his autobiography, *The Words*, that his atheism was a 'cruel and long-range affair', and he reported he finally 'collared the Holy Ghost in the cellar and threw him out'[1] – a remark that lends Nietzsche's 'death of God' pronouncement a particularly graphic twist. But, in fact, religious concepts and analogies continued to punctuate Sartre's writings to the very end. Indeed, his final interview with Benny Lévy scandalized Simone de Beauvoir in part because of its being 'soft' on religious themes and theses.[2] Bertrand Russell appears to have been another such philosopher. He felt obliged to explain his atheism more than once, as if the questioner were none other than himself.[3]

Yet there are others who seem to feel no need even to raise the question, much less to answer it in the negative. These may be 'anonymous' believers, as some would have it, but they would be surprised by any move to convert them by a definition and would probably insist that the burden of proof rests with those who seek to make the discovery, if not to effect the transformation. Where does Michel Foucault fit into this spectrum of believing nonbelievers and non-believing believers?

Perhaps we should take a hint from the practice of 'stipulative conversion' and examine the meaning of 'religion'. This looks promising at first blush. Even a naturalist like Dewey held 'the religious' in high regard, so long as one kept organized 'religion' at bay.[4] The difficulty with seeking an analogous notion in Foucault or any of the so-called 'poststructuralists' is that Dewey's famous 'sense of the whole' is precisely what they are intent on combating. We operate in fragmented and fragmenting world(s), they insist, whose very limits are there to be transgressed. Still, the concept of *limit* might prove useful. To the extent that it is linked with the *other* and with the 'othering' act of transgression, it may provide a key (but only one among possibly many) for unlocking the topic of religious discourse in Foucault's thought.

Admittedly, the definition of 'religion' like that of 'art' is proverbially elusive. But perhaps we can settle on one commonly accepted sense of the term that would serve to distinguish religious from ethical or aesthetic discourse as we search for some equivalent in the work of Foucault. That his thought, especially in its later stages, gave pride of place to aesthetic considerations is by now a commonplace. That his was an 'ethics for thought' is likewise well documented.[5] But is there any room for the properly 'religious' (on the assumption that we can determine what that is) between Foucault's 'aesthetics of existence' that makes of one's life a 'work of art' in the Nietzschean mode, and his 'ethos of the intellectual' in our day, which is to 'take distance on oneself' (*se déprendre de soi-même*)?[6] If 'to think' is to 'other' in the sense of crossing to the other side of a limit or boundary – the 'thought from outside' (*pensée du dehors*) that so fascinated Foucault – could it be that the space for 'religious' discourse is on the other side, that it perhaps *is* that outside? Two authors whom Foucault highly respects who have written on religion, namely, Georges Bataille and Georges Dumézil, seem to support such a thesis.[7] The 'wholly other' (*totaliter aliter*) of religious philosophers since Rudolf Otto might thereby gain admission or, better, recognition as a possibility worth examining in, and perhaps even on, Foucauldian terms. Besides sketching a few lines toward a possible archaeology and a genealogy of religious discourse, it is chiefly this rather modest proposal that I wish to defend.[8]

THE PROBLEMATIZED OTHER

In an interview concerning his last works, Foucault noted that his thought had come to focus on the 'problematizing' of certain issues, specifically that of the moral self. How did it happen, he asked in genealogical fashion, that sexual conduct became 'problematized' in the genesis of the moral self in Western thought? His strategy has always been to tell the story of the necessities and the taken-for-granted of our received wisdom to uncover the dimension of *chance* and *possibility* that characterizes our past and future, respectively. So the fact that sexual behavior ranked on a par with or somewhat below diet and exercise in the ethical concerns of Athenian theorists in the fifth century BC opens the possibility that we too can think 'otherwise than before' about the determining role that sexual orientation and behavior play in our contemporary view of moral identity and responsibility.

Again and again, Foucault's project of 'thinking otherwise' repeats itself in his works. It appears most regularly in his tendency to inverse the received causal relations in intellectual history. Thus the 'great man' theory of historical causality with its 'tangled network of influences' is overturned by appeal to epistemic shifts such as the one entailing the dissociation of the sign and resemblance in the early seventeenth century. This 'archaeological' shift caused a network of necessities to emerge, namely, probability, analysis, combination and a universal language system, which in turn 'made possible the individuals we term Hobbes, Berkeley, Hume or Condillac'.[9] Likewise, it is the emergence of a 'disciplinary reason' in the early nineteenth century, rendering it commonsensical to incarcerate criminals for whatever offense, that fostered the rise of the social sciences, not the inverse, as is commonly believed.[10] He reminds us that there is always the 'other' of our received opinions, haunting them like the memory of a former resident, dispossessed and exiled in order that we might remain in pacific possession of the 'same'. His early 'archaeology of the silence' to which the insane have been condemned since the Age of Reason, *Madness and Civilization*, was the first of many studies of the ever-present other.

For in Foucault's scheme there is always an 'other'. It may be the 'murmur'of life or being that sounds through the grids of archaeology, the resistances that locate each exercise of power in his genealogies, the spaces of inclusion/exclusion that pervade the 'games of truth' in his retrospective reading of his own work. One has a sense of always being *in medias res*, without well defined beginning or absolute end. Even the epistemic 'breaks' that he adopts from Bachelard mark gaps in two continuities. There is always a 'before' and an 'after', a 'prior' and a 'posterior', a 'here' and a 'there'. If 'religion' is taken to denote a relation (a 'tying fast', *religare*) to the sacred, then Foucault's relation will not be to a metaphysical 'god of the gaps' such as that favored by philosophers in early modernity. For these breaks are descriptive, not explanatory; they delineate formal, explanatory grids, but are themselves simply facts. To question *their* existence in the mode of traditional arguments from contingency, would presuppose another schema, with *its* initial gap, separating and uniting a before and an after, and so on. Of course, there is always the archimedean question, the self-referential challenge to which even the slipperiest relativist is liable: *tu quoque*, where do you stand? But that presumes a certain commitment to more than limited discursive horizons – and it is just such a commitment that Foucaull declines to make. In other words, it looks as if the standard 'approaches to God' are dead ends on the Foucauldian highway. The bridge is out.

THE EVENT

Foucault is a philosopher of the event. Obviously, his focus on 'histories' suggests a profound interest in the historical event. But the term 'event' is far more complex and all-pervasive than that of a mere public, temporal happening. And if the so-called 'new' historians discount the traditional historian's emphasis on individual datable occurrences (what they dismiss as 'battles and treaties'), Foucault's understanding of the term includes the probabilistic, the statistical and the glacial (Braudel's *la longue durée*). Because of the centrality of the event to his thought, I wish to pursue it in some detail in order to consider its possible relevance for religious discourse. *A priori*, one expects that whatever 'god' might fit into Foucault's categories will not be the God of the philosophers (for example, the first or final principle of a metaphysical system) but will be more like that of Hebraism: the God of events, of the unrepeatable, of history. And it may be that a corresponding theological 'positivism' will best meet the exigencies of this self-proclaimed 'light-footed positivist'. In other words, we may discover that the most one can do is *wait* (like Hölderlin and Heidegger) for a theophany of some kind, the upsurge or intervention of the 'other' in some recognizably religious sense.

In a poetic musing that recalls both the negative theologians and the mystics, Foucault observes:

Language, in its every word, is indeed directed at contents that preexist it; but in its own being, provided that it holds as close to its being as possible, it only unfolds *in the pureness of the wait*. Waiting is directed at nothing: any object that could gratify it would only efface it. Still, it is not confined to one place, it is not a resigned immobility; it has the endurance of a movement that will never end and would never promise itself the reward of rest; it does not wrap itself in interiority; all of it falls irremediably outside. Waiting cannot wait for itself at the end of its own past, nor rejoice in its own patience, nor steel itself once and for all, for it was never lacking in courage. What takes it up is not memory but forgetting. This forgetting … is extreme *attentiveness*.[11]

Our initial suspicion about what we may now call 'attentive' waiting seeks confirmation in further consideration of Foucault's notion of 'event'.

Foucault's major work is commonly divided into at least two periods, the archaeological and the genealogical. The former appears more 'structural' in its search for 'a method of analysis purged of anthropologism',[12] one that discounts a set of notions such as origin, tradition, influence, development and evolution, dear to event-oriented historians. But his immediate interest is in the 'statement/event', as he calls it, and he questions, not the grammar of the statement, but 'how it is that *one* particular statement appeared rather than another' (AK 27). His reason for speaking of the statement as event is 'to restore the specificity of its occurrence, and to show that discontinuity is one of those great accidents that create cracks not only in the geology of history, but also in the simple fact of the statement'. In opposition to structural linguistics, Foucault insists that 'however badly deciphered we may suppose it to be, a statement is always an event that neither the language (*langue*) nor the meaning can quite exhaust' (AK 28). We can see in this respect for the factical the root of his 'positivism' as well as the antidote to whatever 'structuralist' proclivities he might have manifested up to that point. In fact, in his most 'structuralist' history, *The Order of Things*, he refers to structuralism as 'the awakened and troubled consciousness of modern thought' (OT 208).

Archaeology is not a form of mental geology. Much less is it the search for beginnings (*archai*). Rather, it is the description of the 'archive', the historical *a priori* of a given period which conditions the practices of exclusion and inclusion that are ingredient in all social exchange: the true and the false, the normal and the deviant, the evident and the unthinkable, and so forth. Obviously, the sacred and the profane could be added to this list. An 'archaeology' of religious discourse would describe the actual discursive and nondiscursive religious practices[13] of an epoch in order to lay bare the grids of intelligibility that condition their exercise.[14] Using the modern 'episteme' as an example, a Foucauldian analysis might focus on the inability of religious discourse in the nineteenth century to bring into viable unity the dualities of phenomena/noumena, relative/absolute, for-us/in-itself, and the like, bequeathed us by the collapse of the 'naming' paradigm in the Classical age. From an archaeological viewpoint, the controversies over form and context (*Sitz im Leben*), for example, that engaged Biblical critics in that period could be read as self-generating and symbiotic, once the Kantian break with the referent is effected.

Of all the 'events' the archaeologist describes, the most important and the rarest are what Foucault calls 'transformations' and 'ruptures', of which the most radical bear on the general rules of one or several discursive formations (AK 177). The famous epistemological 'breaks' analyzed in *The Order of Things* are instances of such ruptures. But the point is that Foucault refers to these radical breaks as 'events' even as he allows that 'archaeology distinguishes several possible levels of events within the very density of discourse' (AK 117).[15]

In the lecture inaugurating his Chair at the Collège de France, 2 December 1970, Foucault distinguishes the critical from the genealogical 'ensembles' of analysis that he proposes for his subsequent work. That same year, he publishes a major essay in which he explains that his 'genealogical method' is concerned, not with origin (*Ursprung*), which he links with Platonic essentialism, but with the course of descent (*Herkunft*) of a series of events.

> Genealogy does not resemble the evolution of a species and does not map the destiny of a people. On the contrary, to follow the complex course of descent is to maintain passing events in their proper dispersion; it is to identify the accidents, the minute deviations – or conversely, the complete reversals – the errors, the false appraisals, and the faulty calculations that gave birth to those things that continue to exist and have value for us; it is to discover that truth or being do not lie at the root of what we know and what we are, but [in] the exteriority of accidents.[16]

As a logic of 'difference', genealogy is an alternative to dialectic (the logic of the same). 'What is found at the historical beginning of things,' Foucault insists, 'is not the inviolable identity of their origin; it is the dissension of other things. It is *disparity'* (NGH, 142, emphasis mine).

Commenting on the work of Giles Deleuze, but expressing his own preference as well, Foucault asks: 'What if thought freed itself from common sense and decided to function only in its extreme singularity? ... What if it conceived of difference differentially, instead of searching out the common elements underlying difference?' In response, he concludes: 'Then difference would disappear as a general feature that leads to the generality of the concept, and it would become – a different thought, the thought of difference – a pure event.'[17] These are the words of a historical nominalist, for whom the drive for *multiplicity* overrides the Hegelian and the Platonizing urge for unity.[18]

The constellation *dispersion–event–chance* hovers over Foucault's nominalistic genealogies just as relations of *power* pervade their every facet. By now it is well known that 'power' denotes not only negative relations of dominance and control but positive ones of creativity and reasoning. Not that Foucault has collapsed 'truth' into 'power', as Habermas and others have insisted. He explicitly denies this is so.[19] But power relations are always present in human exchanges, even in the most detached and cerebral communication. His point is that these events are subject to alternative descriptions along the axes of power or of knowledge. The last phase of his thought, which centers on modes of 'subjectivation' and the constitution of the moral self, adds a third possible axis, namely, the line of self-constitution.[20] So one can chart the advance of a particular topic along each of these lines.

But along the genealogical axis, the events multiply without end. Describing Nietzsche's 'effective history' (*wirkliche Historie*) in terms that anticipate his later remarks about 'eventization', Foucault argues: 'An event consequently is not a decision, a treaty, a reign, or a battle, but the *reversal of a relationship of forces*, the usurpation of power, the appropriation of a vocabulary turned against those who had once used it, a feeble domination that poisons itself as it grows lax. The forces operating in history ... always appear through the singular randomness of events' (IP 154–5, my emphasis). As I noted elsewhere, this last sentence could well serve as the motto for Foucault's genealogical historiography: to search for the 'forces of domination' operating in history by a painstaking and inventive analysis of innumerable heterogeneous events.[21]

GENEALOGY OF RELIGIOUS PRACTICE

Nietzschean genealogy, the inspiration and model for Foucault's enterprise, has long been applied to religious beliefs and institutions. In its attempt to lay bare the descent (*Herkunft*) of religious practice, genealogy in Nietzsche's hands continues the tradition of Lucretius *et al.* in locating the genesis and motor of religion in fear of the unknown. But Nietzsche adds the psychological dimension of *ressentiment* and the metaphysics of will-to-power to his account. In parity with his other genealogies, a genealogy of religious practices and institutions, were Foucault to have undertaken one, would have revealed the relations of power/resistance that lay behind the lofty principles and doctrines of the world's major religions (genealogy as critique). Perhaps the founders of these religions, some at least, would have ranked with Freud and Marx as 'initiators of discursive practices', though Foucault claims that these two were 'the first and most important'. The distinctive contribution of these authors, Foucault explains, 'is that they produced not only their own work, but the possibility and the rules of formation of other texts'.[22] It is crucial that they actually wrote or said what was attributed to them. In this they differ from originators of literary texts or makers of scientific discoveries. Moreover, whereas the founding act of a scientific program 'is on an equal footing with its future transformations ... the initiator of a discursive practice is heterogeneous to its ulterior transformations'. 'In fact, the initiator of a discursive practice, unlike the founder of a science, overshadows and is necessarily detached from its later developments and transformations' (WA 133–4). Moreover, subsequent practitioners of such discourses must 'return to the origin', namely, to a 'text in itself'. As he explains, 'a study of Galileo's works could alter our knowledge of the history, but not the science, of mechanics; whereas, a reexamination of the books of Freud or Marx can transform our understanding of Psychoanalysis or Marxism' (WA 135–6). It seems that something similar could be said of the Bible or the Koran, for example, to the extent that Judaism, Islam and Christianity are religions of the book and that book is attributed to a specific author.

THE SACRED AS HETEROTOPIA

Foucault is also a philosopher of space. In fact, what I have elsewhere called his 'spatialization of reason' is both a positive alternative to dialectical totalization and the mark of his postmodernity.[23] Spatial metaphors abound in his writings. But the concepts of spatial division, exclusion and inclusion are more than rhetorical devices. They enter into the very fiber of the argument itself. This is true of his tables, triangles and quadrilaterals (in *The Order of Things*, in particular), but comes most strikingly to the fore in his use of Bentham's Panopticon. There the model is integral to the reasoning process, just as the artifact is essential to an aesthetic 'argument' that continually refers to it in its singularity and not as a mere instance. In the case of the Panopticon, one is being led by the strategic lines of physical possibility, in this case, visibility, to understand the architectural embodiment of surveillance and control: carceral reason in three dimensions.

In a conference, 'Of Other Spaces', delivered the year after *The Order of Things* was published, Foucault laments:

> Despite all the techniques for appropriating space, despite the whole network of knowledge (*savoir*) that enables us to delimit or to formalize it, contemporary space is still not completely desacralized (unlike time, no doubt, which was detached from the sacred in the nineteenth century).

He admits that a certain theoretical desacralization has taken place since Galileo, but insists that 'we may still not have reached the point of a practical desacralization of space'.[24]

He then distinguishes a category of external spaces or sites 'that have the curious property of being in relation with all other sites, but in such a way as to suspect, neutralize, or invent the set of relations that they happen to designate, mirror, or reflect'. They are linked with all the other sites by the fact that they *contradict* them. There are two subspecies of such contradictive sites, utopias and heterotopias (no-places and other-places, respectively). As we might expect, Foucault proceeds to focus on other-places, suggesting the initial principles of 'a sort of systematic description' of these sites, which, in imitation of Bataille, he calls 'heterotopology' (OS 24).

Unlike utopias, heterotopias are real places, 'something like counter-sites' in the midst of our societies that function 'as a sort of simultaneously mythic and real contestation of the space in which we live' (OS 24). Foucault systematically describes the various forms and functions of these sites, from libraries and museums, barracks and prisons, rest homes and cemeteries, to cinemas and gardens, fairgrounds and ships, the heterotopia *par excellence*.[25] These counter-sites combine the 'othering' character of Foucauldian 'transgressive thinking' with the spatializing nature of his argument. But since they question '*all* the other sites', heterotopias are more 'totalizing' than Foucault seems willing to acknowledge. And since they admix the mythic and the real in this contestant function, they are apt locales for the 'totally other' to be revealed in the spatial contestation of our received modes of living and dealing with each other. One such 'incompletely desacralized' space is the *desert*.

THE DESERT EXPERIENCE

'Going into the desert' has long been synonymous with physical and spiritual removal from the world, its affairs and cares. The desert is the place of theophanies (Moses at Horeb), of spiritual struggle and renewal (Jesus fasting in the desert), of self-discovery and preparation for mission (Paul after his experience on the road to Damascus). The desert, like the mountain, is the paradigmatic 'place apart'.[26]

Whatever one might think of James Miller's biography of Foucault, there is no doubt that it addresses an important problem in the philosopher's life, namely, the change in style and content that marked the last two volumes of his *History of Sexuality* after his visits to California in the 1970s and early 1980s. Miller's case for the close union between Foucault's life and work gives new force to the Foucauldian/Nietzschean injunction to 'make of your life a work of art'. Pivotal to this aesthetico-moral construction was Foucault's own 'desert' experience:

> Night had fallen on Death Valley. Next to a car parked in the lot at Zabriskie Point, a portable tape recorder was playing a piece of electronic music, Karlheinz Stockhausen's *Kontakte*. Near the recorder sat Michel Foucault, alongside two young Americans. … As synthetic blips and bleeps filled the cool desert air, the three men stared silently into space. Two hours before, all three had taken LSD.

> Foucault was about to enjoy what he would later call the greatest experience of his life – an epiphany that climaxed a series of similarly intense 'limit-experiences' in the gay community of San Francisco. As a result of these experiences, Foucault's thought would take a dramatic new turn, transforming, in paradoxical and surprising ways, his continuing effort to illuminate what Nietzsche had called 'the riddle which man must solve' – the riddle of his own singular being.[27]

The desert is a place of extremes, of scorching heat and bitter cold, of parched earth and flash flooding, a site without compromise, wrapped in an immense silence and girded by vast, empty horizons – the void of limitless space, now refracted in the broken mirror of an acid-driven mind. If people for millennia have fled to the external spaces of the desert to free themselves from the distractions of society for whatever revelations awaited them, contemporary space travelers have explored inner space by means of mind-altering drugs in the hope of solving the riddle of existence. 'Contemporary space is … *not completely* desacralized.'

We can only conjecture what Foucault experienced as he gazed into the vast desert sky that May night. Was it akin to what Kant called the 'sublime'? In its riveting of his attention for hours, did it in any way resemble that *mysterium tremendum atque fascinans*, the 'wholly other' that Rudolf Otto finds as the core experience of the holy? 'Contemporary space is perhaps still not completely desacralized.' It is most unlikely that he saw it only as an experience for its own sake, as mere entertainment, a *divertissement* to punctuate his visit to Southern California. He seems to have set aside the 'light-footed' positivism that, in response to a hand pointing toward the sky, would have looked only at the tip of the finger. As Miller notes, these were *limit*-experiences that Foucault was after. And, although its immediate inspiration is doubtless Bataille, the term is an echo of Jaspers' famous 'limit situations' and carries a distinctly onto-theological connotation. And what of *the* limit-experience, the one that, as Miller argues, haunted Foucault all his life? What of *death*? This 'cipher', this 'footstep of God' (in Jaspers' terminology) was certainly ingredient in Foucault's epiphanies at the sado-masochistic clubs and bathhouses of San Francisco that surrounded this desert experience. Did he recognize it as such?

He had long acknowledged the close relation between the 'death of God' and sexuality. As early as 1963, he wrote: 'Undoubtedly it is excess that discovers that sexuality and the death of God are bound to the same experience. ... And from this perspective the thought that relates to God and the thought that relates to sexuality are linked in a common form [as in Sade and Bataille].'[28] But the 'death of God', once one removes its carapace of mere *reportage*, is arguably a *religious* experience, akin to the experience of the 'absence of God' as distinct from the 'absence of the experience of God'.[29] Was not this linkage, sex/death/death-of-God, central to Foucault's limit-experiences in California?

Even to raise these questions, much less to attempt to answer them, runs the risk of 'conversion by definition' that we held under suspicion at the outset. And yet this philosopher of the event and of space, was also, especially in his 'post-desert' writings, a philosopher of *experience*.[30] He could scarcely have missed the awesome encounter with his own potential nothingness that intimates the unqualified Other as such. This is not ad hoc reasoning or baseless conjecture. It simply echoes the testimony that captivated Bergson and so many others: the counter-discourse of negative theologians and mystics through the ages.

THE MYSTICAL

Foucault was not unaware of the 'temptation'. In his brilliant essay on Maurice Blanchot, 'The Thought from Outside', he raises the issue only to dismiss it. But the point is that he senses it is there to be raised.

> Despite several confluences, we are quite far from the experience through which some are wont to lose themselves in order to find themselves. The characteristic movement of mysticism is to attempt to join – even if it means crossing the night – the positivity of an existence by opening a difficult line of communication with it. Even when that existence contests itself, hollows itself out in the labor of its own negativity, infinitely withdrawing into a lightless day, a shadowless night, a visibility devoid of shape, it is still a shelter in which experience can rest. The shelter is created as much by the law of a Word as by the open expanse of silence. For in the form of the experience, silence is the immeasurable, inaudible, primal breath from which all manifest discourse issues; or, speech is a reign with the power to hold itself in silent suspense.

Turning away from this obviously alluring vision, he adds curtly: 'The experience of the outside has nothing to do with that' (FB 53–4).

Does he protest too much? Was not his California pilgrimage motivated in part by the desire to solve the riddle of his singular being? Were not his life-threatening encounters in the city and the initial risk of LSD in the desert precisely ways to 'lose oneself in order to find oneself'? No doubt, that 'self' was more *site* than substance or subject. As Blanchot observed, it was a 'non-unitary multiplicity', something like a phrase in serial music.[31]

James Miller cites the following summary of his book by an unsympathetic critic:

> The ultimate question which Foucault's life poses to Miller is whether various forms of
> radical politics, radical sex, and other kinds of supposed 'limit-experience' actually offer
> the modern subject a real means of self-transcendence.

To which Miller adds, 'Precisely.' His reason for not answering that question, as the
critic challenges him to do, was that he 'wanted to compose a text that would open
the question up – and allow different kinds of readers to respond in different kinds of
ways'.[32] A typically Foucauldian practice.

DIREMPTION AS REDEMPTION: THE DIVINE ABSENCE

Foucault, who once insisted that there has not been an original secular ethics in the
West since the Stoics, exhibited something neo-Stoic, even Camusian, in his own
courageous mixture of life and work, his writing in the face of imminent death, as if
to delay the inevitable by coopting it in the text. His 'ethics for thought' resembles a
kind of self-transcendence. It is a self-distancing (*se déprendre de soi-même*) that is
simultaneously a self-constitution: the self as other. This ethics resists idolatry of all
kinds, even the idolizing of one's previously published works. The image of
Camusian 'secular sanctity' (Can one be a saint without God?) comes to mind in this
context and suggests an analogous one of *secular mysticism* (Can one lose oneself in
the void in order to find oneself?). But this mysticism neither asks nor receives the
consolation and comfort of 'a shelter in which experience can rest'. Rather, it
embraces the whirlwind of one's '*non*unifying multiplicity', intensified by natural or
artificial means.

  The antithesis of 'attentive waiting' referred to earlier? On the contrary, it might
well be a parody of the *via purgativa*, little more than a preparing for the 'event' that
never occurred. Or did it? Could it be that it was happening unnoticed? Could the
seemingly fruitless, even frenzied, repetition be that very multiplicity through which
the Other invades and dissolves one's unity to the point of final disappearance
(*disparition*)?

  This may strike many as meager rations for souls 'athirst for the living God'. Could
one not have achieved the same effect by wiring into a 'virtual reality' mechanism?
Perhaps. As the dying cleric assures us at the end of *The Diary of a Country Priest*,
'Grace is everywhere.'[33]

NOTES

1   Jean-Paul Sartre, *The Words*, trans. Bernard Frechtman (New York: George Brazilier,
    1964, p.158).
2   Simone de Beauvoir, *La Cérémonie des adieux*, suivi de *Entretiens avec Jean-Paul Sartre*
    (Paris: Gallimard, 1981, esp. pp.139–42 and 150–52). Of course, she attributes this to the
    deleterious influence of Lévy himself, who was in the process of rediscovering his Jewish
    heritage.

3   See Paul Grimely Kuntz, *Bertrand Russell* (Boston: Twayne Publishers, 1986), Chapter Eight, 'Russell's Religion'. He cites Katharine Tait's hypothesis 'that her father Bertrand Russell was essentially a religious man', p.135.

4   See John Dewey, *A Common Faith* (New Haven: Yale University Press, 1934, pp.1–28).

5   See James Bernauer, *Foucault's Force of Flight: Toward an Ethics for Thought* (Atlantic Highlands, NJ: Humanities Press, 1990).

6   Interview with François Ewald, 'Le Souci de la vérité', *Magazine littéraire*, 207 (May 1984), p.22.

7   See Georges Bataille, *Theory of Religion*, tr. Robert Hurley (New York: Zone Books, 1989, pp.35–6), and Georges Dumézil, *Mitra-Varuna*, tr. Derek Coltman (New York: Zone Books, 1988, pp.59–60 and 71ff).

    In Bataille's case, the matter is complicated by his distinction between limited and unlimited acts of transgressing a limit. Only the former gives us the 'sacred' in its traditional sense. With the 'death of God', there arises the paradoxical situation of transgressive acts seeking their own limits (to transcend), not unlike the man before the door of the Law in Kafka's famous story. But is not this urge toward 'self' transcendence a way of 'secreting' the sacred (as Sartre might say)? In effect, this is the question I am posing to Foucault.

8   For two other initial ventures into the territory of Foucault and religion/theology, see James Bernauer, 'The Prisons of Man: An Introduction to Foucault's Negative Theology', *International Philosophical Quarterly*, 27, 4 (December 1987), pp.365–80, and John D. Caputo, 'On Not Knowing Who We Are: Madness, Hermeneutics and the Night of Truth in Foucault', in John D. Caputo and Mark Yount (eds), *Foucault and The Critique of Institutions* (University Park, PA: Penn State Press, 1993, pp.233–62).

9   Michel Foucault, *The Order of Things. An Archaeology of the Human Sciences* (New York: Random House, Vintage Books, 1970, p.63); hereafter cited OT.

10 See Michel Foucault, *Discipline and Punish*, tr. Alan Sheridan (New York: Pantheon Books, 1977).

11 Michel Foucault, 'Maurice Blanchot: The Thought from Outside', tr. Brian Massumi, in *Foucault/Blanchot* (New York: Zone Books, 1987, pp.55–6), emphases mine; hereafter cited as FB.

12 Michel Foucault, *The Archaeology of Knowledge*, tr. A.M. Sheridan-Smith (New York: Harper & Row, 1972, p.15); hereafter cited AK.

13 Foucault defines 'discursive practice' as 'a body of anonymous, historical rules, always determined in time and space, that have defined for a given period and for a given social, economic, geographical or linguistic area the conditions of operation of the enunciative function' (AK 117, translation emended).

14 Foucault was already familiar with Georges Dumézil's 'admirably precise study of the Indo-European mythologies by using the sociological model superimposed upon the basic analysis of signifiers and significations' (OT 358, translation emended). In fact, he credits Dumézil with having introduced him to the comparativist method, as distinct from traditional exegesis and linguistic formalism, that he employed in his archaeologies (AK 235).

15 See my 'Foucault and the Career of the Historical Event', in Bernard P. Dauenhauer (ed.), *At the Nexus of Philosophy and History* (Athens, GA: The University of Georgia Press, 1987, pp.178–200), upon which this section of the essay is based.

16 'Nietzsche, Genealogy, History', in Donald F. Bouchard (ed.), *Language, Counter-Memory, Practice: Selected Essays and Interviews by Michel Foucault* (Ithaca: Cornell University Press, 1977, p.146); hereafter cited NGH.

17 'Theatrum Philosophicum', in Bouchard (ed.), *Language, Counter-Memory, Practice*, p.182; hereafter cited TP.

18   In an interview with professional historians apropos his genealogy of the penal system, *Discipline and Punish*, Foucault stresses the centrality of the event by coining the neologism 'eventization' (*l'événementalisation*) to capture his method of multiplying factors of intelligibility with regard to any topic. He wants to inscribe around the singular event analyzed as process a 'polyhedron of intelligibility', the number of whose sides is necessarily without limit. He advises us to proceed 'by progressive and necessarily unfinished saturation', So the analysis of the rise of the prison system, for example, far from focusing on just one item such as Foucault's own 'carceral reason' that emerged as common sense in the second quarter of the nineteenth century, would spin off into a multiplicity of considerations, from the rise of professional armies and a new division of labor to the tactics of response to a particular situation like the disorder provoked by public torture or the application of such theories as utilitarianism to behavior, and so forth (Roundtable discussion of 20 May 1978, in Michelle Perrot (ed.), *L'Impossible Prison* (Paris: Editions du Seuil, 1980, p.45).

19   'Those who say that for me *savoir* is a mask for *pouvoir* do not seem to me to have the capacity to understand' (interview with François Ewald, 'Le Souci de la vérité', p.22).

20   See my 'Truth and Subjectivation in the Later Foucault', *The Journal of Philosophy*, 83(10), (October 1985), 531–40.

21   See my 'Michel Foucault and the Career', p.l91.

22   'What is an Author?', in Donald F. Bouchard (ed.), *Language, Counter-Memory, Practice*, pp.132 and 131; hereafter cited as WA.

23   See my 'Foucault and the Spaces of History', *The Monist*, 74, 2 (April 1991), pp.164–86, and 'Foucault and the Eclipse of Vision', in Michel David Levin (ed.), *Modernity and the Hegemony of Vision* (Berkeley: University of California Press, 1993).

24   Michel Foucault, 'Of Other Spaces', trans. Jay Miskowiec, *Diacritics*, 16(1), (Spring 1986), 23. Translation emended.
      Already in the Preface to *The Order of Things*, he introduces the concept of heterotopia, but with a harsher and more combative function:

> *Utopias* afford consolation. … *Heterotopias* are disturbing, probably because they destroy 'syntax' in advance, and not only the syntax with which we construct sentences but also the less apparent syntax which causes words and things (next to and also opposite one another) to 'hold together'. … Heterotopias (such as those to be found so often in Borges) desiccate speech, stop words in their tracks, contest the very possibility of grammar at its source; they dissolve our myths and sterilize the very lyricism of our sentences. (OT xviii)

25   'In civilizations without boats, dreams dry up, espionage takes the place of adventure, and the police take the place of pirates' (OS 27).

26   Both Sartre and Foucault wrote essays on Flaubert's problematic story, 'The Temptation of Saint Anthony'. This ancient anchorite of Egypt, this 'Desert Father', interested Foucault originally because of Flaubert's use of his story to 'produce the first literary work whose exclusive domain is that of books' ('Fantasia of the Library', *Language, Counter-Memory, Practice*, p.92). Subsequently, he returns to Athanasius' *Vita Antonii* to examine Anthony's temptations in the desert. His interest now is the Christian 'hermeneutics of desire' that modified in major ways the moral problematization of sexual matters inherited from the Greeks (see 'Afterword [1982] to Hubert L. Dreyfus and Paul Rabinow, *Michel Foucault: Beyond Structuralism and Hermeneutics*, 2nd edn, rev. and enl., Chicago: University of Chicago Press, 1983, p.248).

27   James Miller, *The Passion of Michel Foucault* (New York: Simon and Schuster 1993, p.245).

28 Michel Foucault, 'Preface to Transgression', in *Language, Counter-Memory, Practice*, p.33.

29 Pierre Klossowski (another name in Foucault's pleiad) notes that whoever says 'atheology' (Bataille's concept) speaks of divine absence (see his 'A propos du simulacre dans la communication de Georges Bataille', *Critique*, 195–6 [1963]). This thesis is taken up by Mark C. Taylor in his ground-breaking *Erring: A Postmodern A/theology* (Chicago: University of Chicago Press, 1984).

30 I sketch this thesis in my 'Truth and Subjectivation in the Later Foucauld', *The Journal of Philosophy*: 'Two words dominate the horizon of Foucault's later work, "problematization" and "government". When the latter is specified as "government of others" and "of self", we have the three irreducible poles, the three possible domains or axes of genealogical history which constitute [what I am calling his] triangle. The space circumscribed by this figure is "experience", which Foucault characterizes as the correlation between domains of *savoir*, types of normativity (power), and forms of subjectivity (*The Uses of Pleasure*, trans. Robert Hurley (New York: Pantheon Books, 1985, p.4). Although the unwary might be amazed to find Foucault speaking of "experience", any throwback to psychological or epistemological categories is presumably excluded both by the nature of the Foucauldian "self" … and by the other two poles of the relationship. Still, the term is no more precise than the correlates that constitute it' (532–3). I should now add that, having read James Miller's account of Foucault's California experience, my concluding *caveat* is somewhat attenuated, though still not uncalled for.

31 Maurice Blanchot, 'Foucault as I Imagine Him', tr. Jeffrey Mehiman, in *Foucault/Blanchot*, p.75.

32 James Miller, 'Policing Discourse: A Response to David Halperin', *Salmagundi*, 97 (Winter 1993), 97–8.

33 While working for the French government in Sweden, Foucault proposed to offer a course on 'religous experience in French literature from Chateaubriand to Bernanos' (see Jean Piel, 'Foucault à Uppsala', *Critique*, 471–2, August–September 1986, 749).

Chapter 8

Exomologesis and Aesthetic Reflection: Foucault's Response to Habermas

Andrew Cutrofello

I would argue that Foucault's own intellectual practice at this final stage is closer to the specific style of early Christian practice of the self than it is to the pagan.[1]

As far as I'm concerned, the guy was a fucking saint.[2]

Actually the shamanistic cure seems to be the exact counterpart to the psychoanalytic cure, but with an inversion of all the elements.[3]

But the relation of language to painting is an infinite relation. It is not that words are imperfect, or that, when confronted with the visible, they prove insuperably inadequate. Neither can be reduced to the other's terms: it is in vain that we say what we see; what we see never resides in what we say.[4]

In a late lecture, Foucault identifies four distinct social 'technologies', each 'a matrix of practical reason' that 'implies certain modes of training and modification of individuals'. These are technologies of 'production', 'sign systems', 'power' and 'the self'.[5] Although they 'hardly ever function separately', each technology is said to have a specificity and relative autonomy that warrants separate analysis.[6] Foucault's work largely focuses on technologies of power and technologies of the self; the former involve the exercise of force on human bodies while the latter pertain to the formation of thinking, feeling and acting subjects. In tandem, technologies of power and technologies of the self are said to comprise the phenomenon of 'governmentality', that is, practices whose aim is the governance of the lives of individuals. Having hitherto focused on this phenomenon, Foucault now proposes to study the technologies of the self in their own right, that is, to the extent that they can be separated from technologies of power.[7] In tracing the history of practices of self-constitution from Plato to modernity, he hopes to bring to light the contingency of the limits that define how we moderns think, feel and act upon ourselves today. As in all of his work, Foucault's ultimate aim is to show that it is possible to think, feel and act otherwise than we do. Thus there are really two tasks: one is to identify what is peculiar to contemporary technologies of the self; the other is to demonstrate their revisability.

Foucault had more or less completed the first half of this twofold project in the first volume of *The History of Sexuality*, where he defines modern technologies of the self in terms of the 'will to truth'.[8] For we moderns, 'care of the self' requires a constant effort to unearth hidden desires and beliefs that supposedly determine our identity. Under the banner of the 'repressive hypothesis' – the claim that human sexuality has been repressed and must be liberated – psychoanalysis serves as the paradigm of such a practice, its conceit being that the freedom of the individual subject depends upon a painstaking exegesis of its sexual identity. Foucault denounces psychoanalysis, faulting it not only for its links to 'biopower' but also for its failure to reflect on the historical contingency of that specific mode of 'care of the self' to which it gives its allegiance. In its demand that we subject ourselves to endless hermeneutical scrutiny, psychoanalysis merely repeats and so confirms a technology of the self which predates it and of whose history it remains ignorant. Consequently, it cannot claim to be a truly liberating practice.

Having identified modern technologies of the self as hermeneutical, Foucault sets out in the subsequent volumes of *The History of Sexuality* to reconstruct their historical emergence and so to complete his critique of the larger set of critically reflective practices to which psychoanalysis belongs.[9] The ethical imperative to take care of oneself goes back at least to Socrates, for whom the care of the self, as exemplified in Plato's *Alcibiades I*, is connected with an imperative to speak truthfully. This connection persists in Hellenistic and early Christian thought, but its character changes over time. From Socrates to the Stoics, Foucault contends, the imperative to tell the truth about oneself is not associated with a moral demand to fathom the depths of the individual's interior life but with the goal of attaining *eudaimonia*; self-examination aims at 'the transformation of the individual'.[10]

The very idea of the subject's having a radically inward point of view on itself does not arise until the early Christians. Though the idea of an inner sense is sometimes traced back to Augustine, Foucault discerns its genesis in a decisive change that takes place in early Christian confessional practice. In the first century, confession takes the form of *exomologesis*, a practice in which 'the sinner seeks his penance' not through verbal confession but through the public performance of certain acts.[11] These 'obeyed a law of dramatic emphasis and of maximum theatricality'.[12] '*Exomologesis* is not a verbal behavior but the dramatic recognition of one's status as a penitent'.[13] By the fourth century, a significantly different confessional practice emerges. Whereas *exomologesis* had the character of a performance by which the penitent displayed his or her status as a sinner, *exagoreusis* is a purely verbal practice that rests on the experience of inner sense. The penitent must examine his thoughts carefully in order to identify and verbalize the sinful ones.

Foucault had already discerned something similar in Socratic and Stoic self-scrutiny. But in its earlier form, self-examination was a merely hygienic activity directed towards one's well-being; it was not yet conceived as a constant demand to monitor one's interior life, to scrutinize, as it were, the inscrutable depths of one's soul. Exagoreusis is not an occasional act of purification but a lifelong condition; one must forever be engaged in hermeneutical self-reflection whose telos is 'the permanent verbalization of thoughts'.[14]

In both exomologesis and exagoreusis, confession is 'a way of renouncing self and no longer wishing to be the subject of the will',[15] but in the former case the renunciation of self is tied to a practice of *showing*, while in the latter it is a question of *saying*. That is, in exomologesis, I perform or display my sin without saying *that* I am a sinner; no explicit propositional attitude need be involved. By contrast, the whole aim of exagoreusis is to translate felt affects and vague ideas into propositional attitudes, however implicit they might be in the sinner's mind: Yesterday, I wished that…, hoped that…, desired that…, and so on. While the attitude involved in exomologesis suggests that the sinner's sin is a potentially public state that can be displayed, in exagoreusis the sinner must attest to a condition to which only he or she has immediate interior access.

In the shift from confessional showing to confessional saying, from monstration to articulation, the sinner's verbal announcing of his or her status as a sinner exhibits all of the crucial attributes that Foucault identifies in modern technologies of the self, such as psychoanalysis: will to truth, self-analysis, discovery and articulation of inner self-knowledge. To show oneself to be a sinner in exomologesis involved public exhibitions of guilt; the sinner might wear a hair shirt, engage in self-flagellation, or kiss the knees of the priest. Such practices would be of no therapeutic value in psychoanalysis; the patient who did such things in front of an analyst would be described as 'acting out' instead of 'working through' repressed wishes, desires, beliefs and other unconscious propositional attitudes. By contrast, the confessional practice associated with exagoreusis does persist: engaging in endless self-interpretation the results of which one verbalizes to a purported master to whom one has entrusted one's well-being. The shift from exomologesis to exagoreusis would thus represent the decisive turning point whereby modern technologies of the self first appear as such.

Foucault views the legacy of exagoreusis as something that we might want to resist: 'But the moment, maybe, is coming for us to ask: do we need, really, this hermeneutics of the self?'[16] In order to break with the ingrained habit of hermeneutic self-scrutiny, it would be necessary to undo the complicated legacy of exagoreusis. One obvious question that arises is whether Foucault thinks that a retrieval of something along the lines of exomologesis might provide a way of resisting modern forms of exagoreusis. At issue is not so much an ideal to which we might return as a lever by which we might pry apart the dominant technologies that govern – and through which we govern – our bodies. Perhaps, to invoke Marx's *18th Brumaire*, it is possible to change the present only by way of a backward glance, but this backward glance is, paradoxically, the condition for the possibility of doing something truly new.

Both James Bernauer and Jeremy Carrette take Foucault's engagement with early Christian confessional practices to be an attempt at precisely this sort of retrieval. Bernauer starts from what he identifies as 'Foucault's call for a renunciation of the self', arguing that, although Foucault clearly repudiates 'Christian hermeneutics' and 'its project of seeking a hidden self, he also appreciated the "great richness" of the ascetical moment of self-renunciation' found in early Christian practices.[17] Carrette, focusing on the relationship between silence and speech in Christian confessional practices, argues that, although Foucault would oppose the incitement to speak that is associated with exagoreusis, he would have been drawn to the silence that is part and parcel of exomologesis.[18] By linking the relationship between the two forms of confessional practice to the important Foucauldian theme of the relationship between the unsaid and the said, Carrette gives us reason to wonder if elements of exomologesis might even be paradigmatic for a Foucauldian ethic. Bernauer concurs, suggesting that 'Foucault came to esteem and utilise a Christian style of liberty which combined a care of the self with a sacrifice and mortification of that self'.[19]

To see why Foucault would have been drawn to the practice of exomologesis, I would like to situate it with respect to the Foucauldian problematic of the visible and the articulable, which has been admirably discussed by Deleuze. Deleuze reads Foucault's conception of power/knowledge as a way of naming the relations of force that graft a way of speaking (the domain of the articulable) onto a manner of appearing (the domain of the visible).[20] Power/knowledge – or 'order', to use Foucault's earlier term in *Les mots et les choses* – would be located in the relationship between a field of discourse and a field of appearing. Within the bounds circumscribed by a particular power/knowledge formation, it would be possible to say certain things and not others. If correct, this analysis would have two consequences. First, it would imply that the domain of the visible is 'tamed' by language (think of the purported Chinese encyclopedia cited by Borges to which Foucault refers at the beginning of *Les mots et les choses*), with the consequence that the being of the visible is associated with a certain silence; second, it would mean that within the order of the articulable there are certain things that can be said and others that cannot. On one reading, the distinction between the visible and the articulable would be equivalent to the distinction between the unsayable and the sayable. But to put the point this way is to treat the visible as if it were equivalent to a virtual speech, as if things themselves were constantly murmuring, only to be silenced with the imposition of a certain order. Although I would not want entirely to rule out the force of such a reading, it seems to me that Foucault's insistence on the absolute heterogeneity between the visible and the articulable should encourage us to emphasize a second construal, according to which the distinction between the said and the unsaid belongs to the field of the articulable itself. On this reading, what is at stake is not so much the relationship between the sayable and the unsayable as the relationship between structures of sayability and unsayability, on the one hand, and an anterior givenness, on the other. Order, or power/knowledge, is always a relationship between these two disparate fields, a third element that brings them together in what Foucault calls a 'middle region'.[21]

As Deleuze points out, we can read Foucault here as introducing a variation on a Kantian theme. The most important distinction drawn in the *Critique of Pure Reason* is that between intuitions and concepts. Intuitions are immediate presentations of objects of experience that give us direct access to the phenomenal world. Concepts are ways of representing such objects. Unlike intuitions, concepts stand in a mediated relationship to the world; they are applicable not to 'things in themselves' but only to our (actual or possible) intuitions of objects. Kant famously says that neither intuitions nor concepts alone can give us knowledge; only together do they combine in such a way as to determine objects of experience. Crucial to this Kantian model is the claim that intuitions and concepts differ in kind rather than in degree. Against the empiricists, who treat concepts as abstractions from intuitions, and against the rationalists, who reduce intuitions to obscure and indistinct concepts, Kant insists on the utter heterogeneity between the two sorts of representations. Given this heterogeneity, it becomes necessary to identify a mechanism through which concepts can be brought to bear on intuitions, that is, an intermediary through which knowledge becomes possible. He identifies this intermediary under the heading of a 'transcendental schematism', a set of rules which specify a priori how pure concepts of the understanding are applicable to possible objects of experience.

On Deleuze's reading, Foucault's distinction between the visible and the articulable is analogous to the Kantian distinction between intuitions and concepts. Visible bodies and articulable speech are two entirely heterogeneous orders which require some sort of mediation if they are to 'hook up'. Unlike Kantian representations, the domains of the visible and the articulable are not immanent conditions for the possibility of the subject's access to the world but exterior forms of appearance that always already belong to what Deleuze, evidently drawing on Foucault's reading of Blanchot, calls 'the outside'.[22] Provided we respect (and clarify) these differences, it is possible to construe Foucault's conception of power/knowledge, or order, as an account of *something like* a transcendental schematism. The rules in question would be neither transcendental nor a priori; rather, they would be the 'sedimented' consequences of sequences of historical events whose genealogy is Foucault's principal object of inquiry. The primary function of these quasi-schemata would be to *suture* visible bodies with articulable speech. Reading Foucault this way would help to explain why he repeatedly denies, in *Archaeology of Knowledge*, that he is interested in the history of mere linguistic phenomena like words and sentences. Though such phenomena belong to articulable speech, they acquire their suturing function only as 'statements', that is, as potential instruments of power/knowledge (though Foucault's notoriously obscure 'AZERT' example might challenge this point).

For Kant, schematism is only one case of 'hypotyposis', the operation by which we 'exhibit' a concept in intuition. To exhibit a concept is to present an object that either falls under the concept or that stands in for its unpresentable object. Kant thereby distinguishes between two kinds of hypotyposis, 'schematic' and 'symbolic'.[23] While schematism exhibits the object of a concept of the understanding, symbolism is needed to 'present' the unpresentable object of an idea of reason. These two forms of hypotyposis are quite different. Schematism presupposes that intuitions are adequate to our concepts; if they were not, no knowledge of the world would be possible. Symbolism, by contrast, is a device we resort to because our intuitions are inadequate for the presentation of ideas. This inadequacy is smoothed over by the symbol itself, that is, by the presentation of an intuited object which presents the unpresentable. When Kant claims, in the third Critique, that the beautiful is a symbol of the good, he does not conclude that the beautiful object *is* something good. On the contrary, its ability to *symbolize* the good presupposes that no object of sensible intuition, including the beautiful object itself, is an *example* of something good. This point might seem to be contravened by the fact that we can exhibit an action that is in accordance with duty. But strictly speaking we can never show that such an act is truly good, for we could never know if it were performed 'from duty'.

The experience of the beautiful involves a harmonizing of intuitions and concepts, but a harmonizing that stops short of schematic knowing. By contrast, the experience of the sublime involves an experience of disharmony between intuitions and concepts. To experience the sublime is to encounter that in nature which resists conceptualization; this encounter prompts us to recall our possession of ideas to which no object in nature can be adequate. Thus what begins in the experience of the sublime as an awareness of the inadequacy of our concepts ends up being an experience of the inadequacy of the imagination to present an intuition that would be adequate to an idea of reason.

Deleuze (like Lyotard) is drawn to the Kantian sublime because of its account of a disharmonious conflict of faculties. In the experience of the sublime, reason does violence to the imagination by demanding the impossible of it, namely a schematic exhibition of an idea. Put otherwise, the experience of the sublime is the experience of the failure of schematic hypotyposis. This very failure could be said to prompt the shift from schematic to symbolic hypotyposis. Unlike schematic hypotyposes, which Kant takes to be transcendental givens, symbolic hypotyposes are contingent. Though we *can* represent the idea of a despotic state by a handmill (Kant's example), we *need* not. Symbols, unlike schemata, are malleable. By maintaining a sharp distinction between ahistorical schemata and historically mutable symbols, Kant is able to distinguish between those hypotypical features of human experience that are transcendental and unchanging and those that are empirical and changeable. This distinction corresponds to the contrast between the epistemic and aesthetic aspects of experience.

But what if, *contra* Kant, one were to question the rigor of the schema/symbol dichotomy? What if 'schemata' were merely sedimented symbols, 'hardened' as it were over time but in principle subject to revision?[24] We could then characterize the experience of the sublime as threatening to reveal the contingency of hypotyposes in general. Would this not require that fixed epistemic assumptions be treated as contingent aesthetic norms? To ask these questions is to shift from the perspective of Kantian critique to Foucauldian genealogy. One can read Foucault as regularly attempting to conjure an experience of the sublime precisely so as to call attention to the makeshift character of our hypotyposes. Consider the 'unthinkable' taxonomy of animals or the endless frustration of the aphasiac vainly struggling to impose some principle of order on an unruly mass of wool, 'creating groups then dispersing them again, heaping up diverse similarities, destroying those that seem clearest, splitting up things that are identical, superimposing different criteria, frenziedly beginning all over again, becoming more and more disturbed, and teetering finally on the brink of anxiety'.[25]

Obviously, Kant himself deliberately resists the conclusion that the experience of sublimity reveals the contingency of all ways of ordering the world. On the contrary, the conflict between reason and imagination need not affect the harmonious relationship between understanding and imagination, so the message of the first Critique stands firm: there are fixed, 'normal' hypotyposes which every rational subject must perform. Similarly, the experience of the sublime does not undermine the 'normal' hypotyposes in the practical domain, the 'typic' of reason (analogous to schematism in the theoretical domain) through which we determine moral maxims. Yet, at the same time, Kant concedes that the experience of sublimity can occasion a delusional experience of enthusiasm. This takes place when one imagines that mere objects of thought can be exhibited in sensibility. A 'ruleless' imagination can even give way to a more thoroughgoing madness in which the subject is unable to schematize its experience properly. If the analysis of madness presented in Kant's *Anthropology from a Pragmatic Point of View* marks the birth of our modernity for Foucault, it is insofar as the Kantian account of madness is rooted in a distinction between normal and pathological experiences of hypotyposis.

We can think of normal hypotyposis, be it the determination of a particular object of experience in accordance with a category of the understanding or the determination of an action in accordance with a moral maxim, as a way of subjecting visible bodies to articulable rules. Understood in this way, power/knowledge would be a function of what Kant calls 'determining judgment', specifically the determination of bodies by forms of thought. In the third Critique, he contrasts determining judgment with 'reflective judgment', the experience in which an intuited object for which we have no concept occasions an experience of reflection. In the specific case of aesthetic experience, whether of the beautiful or the sublime, reflection disengages imaginable objects from determinations of thought. If power/knowledge is a function of determining judgment, might resistance to power be a function of reflective judgment? This idea, that aesthetic experience might provide us with a paradigm of critical experience, has been an important theme of German political thought from Schiller to Adorno. It is also an implicit theme of the work of Foucault, who attempts to reclaim possibilities of aesthetic experience that have been foreclosed through the sedimentation of practices of determining judgment. At issue is nothing less than a decolonization of the life-world, where 'colonization' is conceived not in terms of the hegemony of cognitive–instrumental rationality (as in Habermas) but in terms of the hegemony of structures of determining judgment that pertain to *all* forms of modern rationality. Foucault's strategy for decolonizing the life-world is to show how these forms of rationality have emerged out of earlier pre-modern European experiences of aesthetic reflection.

In *The Savage Mind*, Claude Lévi-Strauss distinguishes between 'scientific' cultures in which articulable forms of thought determine the visible world and 'savage' cultures in which visible objects in nature can be said to 'reflectively determine'[26] articulable forms of thought.[27] Foucault's various histories can be read as comparable attempts to trace our modern scientific practices back to the 'savage' antecedents out of which they emerged. For example, the Renaissance 'episteme' is said to have been grounded upon perceived relations of resemblance among intuitable objects of experience rather than on the determination of objects of experience in accordance with concepts. The shift from the sort of magical thinking found in Paracelsus to the Cartesian ideal of truth as correspondence or faithful representation is viewed by defenders of modernity as an undeniable cognitive advance. But for Foucault the distinction between the Renaissance and modern epistemes reflects a difference between rival criteria in terms of which the rationality of the shift from one to the other might be assessed.

In the first volume of *The Theory of Communicative Action*, Habermas accepts Lévi-Strauss's distinction between savage and modern cultures.[28] But instead of recognizing Lévi-Strauss's point, namely, that to each form of rationality (savage and modern) there corresponds a different – not inferior or superior – kind of critical stance with respect to norms,[29] Habermas imposes a hierarchical, quasi-Piagetian point of view on the distinction. On his account, to live in a savage or mythological culture is to be unprepared to challenge the norms to which one appeals in making validity claims. By contrast, to live in a modern or Enlightened culture is to be able to call one's own norms into question. Habermas's analysis presumes that, in both cases, we are dealing with cultures whose form of claim making is determining in nature. That is, to make a validity claim, in *any* of Habermas's three spheres, be it cognitive–instrumental, moral–juridical or aesthetic–expressive, is to make a determining judgment of some sort. When a member of a savage culture makes a validity claim he or she is applying a rule to a case just as we do. The savage is perfectly capable of justifying the case with reference to the norm but has not acquired the capacity to evaluate the norm itself. Habermas thus treats the contrast between savage and modern cultures as a distinction between a culture that can determine in accordance with its norms but not reflect on the norms themselves and a culture that can do both of these things.

If we look a bit closer at Lévi-Strauss's analysis, it is clear that he views things differently. For him, a savage culture is one in which the relationship between cases and rules is governed almost exclusively by reflective rather than determining judgment. It is not that members of the culture make determining judgments but then fail to engage reflectively with the norms on which they base these judgments. On the contrary, what look to us like their determining judgments are actually reflective judgments that do engage with the status of the norms in play. If anything could be said to be 'lacking', it would be, not the capacity to reflect, but the capacity to determine cases in accordance with fixed rules. Whence the ease with which rules can be reconfigured; one need not wait for an 'anomaly' that does not fit customary determining judgments for the simple reason that *every* particular is anomalous insofar as it prompts a reflective challenge. On this account, savage thought is hyper-reflective.

Second, and this is the crucial point, Lévi-Strauss's description of savage forms of thought implies that the judging savage is engaged not in 'logically' reflective judgment but in 'aesthetically' reflective judgment. For Kant, a logically reflective judgment is occasioned by an intuition of a particular for which we lack a determinate concept under which we might subsume the particular. It culminates in the discovery or invention of a concept that is adequate to the object, thereby making it possible for us to subsume it under future determining judgments. Determining judgment is thus the telos of logically reflective judgment. By contrast, an aesthetically reflective judgment arises when we encounter an object of intuition to which no determinate concept is adequate. Aesthetically reflective judgment does not have determining judgment as its telos. On the contrary, an aesthetically reflective judgment is its own end; in the case of judgments of beauty it is a stance that tends to perpetuate itself. Now the question is, are norms or rules (that is, concepts) completely absent from aesthetically reflective judgment? The answer, for Kant, is no. When we argue about matters of taste we do so precisely because we feel that an 'indeterminate concept' is at stake in an aesthetically reflective judgment.

Arendt was so impressed with this analysis that she made it the basis of her account of political deliberation.[30] As she conceives it, a debate over matters of taste (or, *mutatis mutandis*, matters of politics) is still one in which we argue about particulars as particulars. But, on her construal, such a debate still has determining judgment as its telos, even if it is unrealizable; we voice our opinions with an eye toward reaching consensus about fixed norms. Arendt arguably remains faithful to Kant's intention here insofar as he too construes agreement as the aim of aesthetic quarrels. Nonetheless, on Arendt's (and possibly Kant's) account, we risk blurring the distinction between aesthetically and logically reflective judgment. In particular, the distinction threatens to become one of degree rather than kind. Indeed, the distinction vanishes completely once we construe all arguments about validity claims, with Habermas, as oriented toward some sort of Peircean 'end of inquiry', for now *all* reflective judgments aim at an ideal consensus that would make definitive determining judgments possible once and for all. The fact that such an end of inquiry is merely a regulative ideal should not prevent us from seeing that aesthetic reflection has thereby been reduced to a kind of logical reflection, albeit one that – like Zeno's arrows – never quite reaches its goal. This is especially evident once we realize that the whole point of Habermas's ideal speech situation (like Arendt's) is to provide us with a workable program for approximating the ideal.

We can read Lévi-Strauss's description of savage thinking as an attempt to reclaim the specificity of an aesthetically reflective judgment that does not have determining judgment as its telos. A savage culture would be one in which norms are perpetually being revised, not with an eye toward achieving rules that would be valid at an imaginary ideal end of inquiry but, on the contrary, with an eye toward a world that is itself inherently resistant to determining judgment: 'Mythical thought … is imprisoned in the events and experiences which it never tires of ordering and re-ordering in its search to find them a meaning.'[31] In such a culture, there would be aesthetic quarrels, but these would be characterized not by a free exchange of 'opinions', or by the 'giving and asking for reasons' in the Sellarsian sense, but by magical and ritual performances which would themselves function as objects of further aesthetic reflection, perhaps governed by something like an 'ideal aesthetic situation'.[32]

Habermas takes the work of critique to consist exclusively in logically reflective judgment – subject of course to the requirements of communicative rationality – whereby we consider the possibility of adopting new norms in terms of which we make determining judgments. From his perspective, it is irresponsible for someone like Foucault to refuse to engage in conversations that seek to identify norms through critical reflection. But we can read Foucault as attempting to think, not like a logically reflective member of an Enlightened culture, but like an aesthetically reflective member of a savage culture. To think like a savage would be to attempt to 'undo' the hegemony of determining judgment itself as an over-arching form of power/knowledge.

Habermas is not unaware of this. He recognizes that Foucault belongs to an 'aestheticist' tradition that would blur the distinction between philosophy and literature. The difficulty is that Habermas's arguments against the aestheticist tradition presume that a savage culture in which there is no practice of logically reflective judgment is inferior to a modern culture in which properly philosophical reflection rests on the 'logical' (in the broad sense) assessment of norms. From this point of view, savage thought lacks a critical skill that we possess. But it is just as plausible to say that savage thought possesses a critical skill that we moderns lack, namely, the capacity to engage in an aesthetic reflection that does not have determining judgment as its telos.

There is no way for the savage to argue against the modernist once the modernist's presumptions about critical reflection are accepted. But this is a truism, equivalent to saying that, from the perspective of modern rationality, savage thought looks 'savage'. Viewed from the perspective of a culture that engages with its norms through aesthetic reflection, it is the modern culture which will appear to be 'lacking' a critical ability that the savages possess. This is the ability to conceive of validity claims not in terms of the application of rules to cases but in terms of the reflective determination of rules by cases. For this reason, it seems parochial for Habermas to describe mythological cultures as 'closed' and modern cultures as 'open'. It is only because of an unthematized prejudice of the modern life-world that we are inclined to view our arguments as legitimation claims and savage arguments as something else.

Both Foucault and Lévi-Strauss can be read as attempting to thematize this background assumption of the life-world. To thematize it is to challenge our conception of what a legitimation claim ought to look like. Obviously the word 'ought' here is problematic since *its* meaning is precisely what is at stake. In particular, we cannot construe the 'conflict' between savage and modern forms of thought as competing validity claims that can be evaluated in terms of statements that each would recognize as 'reasons' or 'arguments'. At least, we cannot do so without violence.

Habermas treats aesthetic–expressive claims as belonging to a domain that sits alongside the cognitive–instrumental and moral–juridical domains. In this way he purports to respect the integrity of aesthetic reflection, that is, to protect the aesthetic domain from colonization by cognitive–instrumental rationality, just as he wants to preserve the other domains from being colonized by aesthetic rationality. But, as he conceives it, aesthetic rationality is still geared toward the marshalling of arguments in support of determining judgments of the sort 'This is beautiful' or 'This is authentic'. That is, he treats 'beautiful' and 'authentic' as cognitive predicates which we ascribe to particular objects of experience. In doing so he fails to capture what is properly aesthetic in Kant's conception of aesthetically reflective judgments. For Kant, the judgment that something is beautiful is not, properly speaking, a judgment about an object in the same sense that a determining judgment is about an object. When we say 'This is beautiful' we are really talking about ourselves; that is, we are reflectively determining subjective states that are prompted by our experience with the form of an object.[33] When Kant claims that we 'quarrel' (*streiten*) rather than 'dispute' (*disputieren*) about matters of taste, he is not merely showing that there are two different kinds of arguments in support of validity claims. More significantly, he is showing that we cannot critically reflect on prevailing aesthetic norms in the way in which we might critically reflect on prevailing cognitive or moral norms. If we apply this point to the argument advanced by Lévi-Strauss and Foucault, we can say that aesthetic reflection does not merely pertain to a domain distinct from that of cognitive and moral reflection. More radically – this point has to be pressed against Kant as much as against Habermas – the claim would be that aesthetic reflection *competes with* the kind of logical reflection whose telos is the determination of cases in accordance with norms. It is this competition between two different kinds of critical reflection that makes the confrontation between 'savage' and 'modern' forms of thought a genuine Lyotardian *différend*.

This, however, is not to decide in favor of Lévi-Strauss and Foucault against Kant and Habermas but only to sharpen a sense of the stakes of the confrontation. At issue is the telos of determining judgment. If we think of modern power/knowledge formations as matrices of determining judgments, we can distinguish between two rival strategies of critical reflection. One would be the Habermasian strategy of striving to make better judgments; instead of determining bodies *this* way, we propose to determine them *that* way. The other would be the Foucauldian attempt to subvert the mechanism of determining judgment altogether. Here the strategy would be 'aesthetic' in the broadly Kantian sense sketched above. Adorno's work is exemplary of this approach. For Adorno, art remembers for us what we lose through Enlightenment, where Enlightenment is to be construed as the passage from mythical immersion in nature to the capacity for self-determination. For Foucault, this task of memory is performed by the archaeologist or genealogist who recalls specific practices that were themselves essentially aesthetic rather than determining in nature. He tries to identify crucial turning points whereby what had been an aesthetic experience of reflection is transformed into an experience of determination. We find such transitions tracked in virtually all of his books, from the change in reason's relationship to madness to changes in medical, penal and confessional practices. In *Discipline and Punish*, the public torture and execution of Damiens is figured as a way in which power *shows* itself, the aesthetic display of a visible body 'reflectively determining' possible articulable thoughts about power. This is in striking contrast to the later practice in which a discourse about delinquency *says* something, thereby determining the manner in which visible bodies comport themselves. In presenting us with 'anomalous' practices like the torture of Damiens, the ship of fools or the scientific works of Aldrovandi, Foucault attempts to 'jump-start' the reader's own aesthetic reflection, providing a kind of critical occasion for us to free ourselves from the present (Marx's *18th Brumaire* point again).

To conclude, Habermas's modernist conception of critical reflection – which, significantly, he bases on psychoanalysis – is the heir to the practice of *exagoreusis*, while *exomologesis* represents a 'forgotten' practice of savage reflection that would link the early Christians to Lévi-Strauss's shamans. The contrast between the two forms of confessional practice provides us not just with a way of imagining something other (determining bodies in a new way) but with a way of imagining otherwise: 'the "bricoleur" also, and indeed principally, derives his poetry from the fact that he does not confine himself to accomplishment and execution: he "speaks" not only *with* things ... but also through the medium of things'.[34]

NOTES

1   James Bernauer, 'Cry of Spirit', in Michel Foucault, *Religion and Culture*, ed. Jeremy R. Carrette (New York: Routledge, 1999, p.xiv).
2   David M. Halperin, *Saint Foucault: Towards a Gay Hagiography* (New York: Oxford University Press, 1995, p.6).
3   Claude Lévi-Strauss, 'The Effectiveness of Symbols', in *Structural Anthropology*, tr. Claire Jacobson and Brooke Grundfest Schoepf (New York: Basic Books, 1963, p.199).
4   Michel Foucault, *The Order of Things*, anonymous translation (New York: Vintage, 1970, p.9).
5   Michel Foucault, 'Technologies of the Self', in Luther H. Martin, Huck Gutman, Patrick H. Hutton (eds), *Technologies of the Self* (Amherst: University of Massachusetts Press, 1988, p.18). It is noteworthy that, in distinguishing technologies of production from technologies of power, Foucault respects the ancient Greek distinction between *poiesis* and *praxis*; yet in classifying both as technologies, and in defining a technology as 'a matrix of practical reason', he complicates matters, since *techne* is traditionally associated with *poiesis*, while practical reason (*phronesis*) is associated with *praxis*.
6   'I wanted to show both their specific nature and their constant interaction' (ibid.).

7   Ibid., p.19.
8   Michel Foucault, *The History of Sexuality, Volume 1: An Introduction*, tr. Robert Hurley (New York: Vintage, 1990).
9   Like Nietzsche, Foucault takes genealogy to be the only proper form of critique, because only a genealogical reconstruction of the conditions of emergence of a technology can put us in a position of freedom with respect to that technology.
10   Michel Foucault, 'Subjectivity and Truth', in *The Politics of Truth*, ed. Sylvère Lotringer and Lysa Hochroth (New York: Semiotext(e), 1997, p.184).
11   Ibid., p.41.
12   Michel Foucault, 'About the Beginning of the Hermeneutics of the Self', in *Religion and Culture*, p.172.
13   'Technologies of the Self', p.41.
14   'Technologies of the Self', p.47.
15   'About the Beginning of the Hermeneutics of the Self', p.179.
16   'About the Beginning of the Hermeneutics of the Self', p.181.
17   James W. Bernauer, *Michel Foucault's Force of Flight: Toward an Ethic for Thought* (Atlantic Highlands: Humanities Press, 1990, p.180). Here one might think of Nietzsche's double assessment of ascetic practices in the third essay of *The Genealogy of Morals*.
18   Carrette does not put the point quite like this, but it is implied when he writes that 'silence (maceration) and speech (verbalisation) operate as political strategies in the organisation of "truth".' Jeremy Carrette, *Foucault and Religion: Spiritual Corporality and Political Spirituality* (New York: Routledge, 2000, p.42). This passage appears immediately after a citation in which Foucault associates *exomologesis* with 'ascetic maceration' and *exagoreusis* with 'permanent verbalisation'.
19   'Cry of Spirit', p.xiv.
20   Gilles Deleuze, *Foucault*, tr. Seán Hand (Minneapolis: University of Minnesota Press, 1988, p.83).
21   *The Order of Things*, p.xxi.
22   'Thinking does not depend on a beautiful interiority that would reunite the visible and the articulable elements, but is carried under the intrusion of an outside that eats into the interval and forces or dismembers the internal' (*Foucault*, p.87).
23   'All *hypotyposis* (exhibition, *subiectio ad adspectum*) consists in making [a concept] sensible, and is either *schematic* or *symbolic*' (Immanuel Kant, *Critique of Judgment*, tr. Werner S. Pluhar (Indianapolis: Hackett, 1987, p.226 [Ak. 351]; Pluhar's brackets).
24   For Kant, something like this occurs whenever artistic practice stagnates. Art is essentially historical insofar as prevailing habits of taste must be constantly challenged by the invention of ever new 'aesthetic ideas'.
25   *The Order of Things*, p.xviii.
26   I borrow this term from Rudolph Makkreel, *Imagination and Interpretation in Kant: The Hermeneutical Import of the Critique of Judgment* (Chicago: University of Chicago Press, 1990).
27   Lévi-Strauss makes the intriguing suggestion that the contrast is between cultures whose knowledge is rooted in a body of synthetic a priori judgments and those whose knowledge is grounded in a body of analytic a posteriori judgments: 'Logic consists in the establishment of necessary connections and how, we may ask, could such relations be established between terms in no way designed to fulfill this function? Propositions cannot be rigorously connected unless the terms they contain have first been unequivocally defined. It might seem as if in the preceding pages we had undertaken the impossible task of discovering the conditions of an *a posteriori* necessity' (Claude Lévi-Strauss, *The Savage Mind*, tr. unlisted (Chicago: University of Chicago Press, 1966, p.35). In my *Imagining Otherwise: Metapsychology and the Analytic A Posteriori* (Evanston:

Northwestern University Press, 1994) I have tried to show how the contrast between the analytic a posteriori and the synthetic a priori might be used to frame the relationship between Kantian and psychoanalytic points of departure. Though there is much in my approach that would require revision, I still regard the basic starting-point as providing a kind of metacritical leverage for posing a question concerning competing conceptions of critique.

28 Jürgen Habermas, *The Theory of Communicative Action Volume One: Reason and the Rationalizaton of Society*, tr. Thomas McCarthy (Boston: Beacon Press, 1984, pp.43ff).

29 'But it is important not to make the mistake of thinking that these are two stages or phases in the evolution of knowledge. Both approaches are equally valid' (Lévi-Strauss, *The Savage Mind*, p.22). 'One deprives oneself of all means of understanding magical thought if one tries to reduce it to a moment or stage in technical and scientific evolution' (ibid., p.13).

30 Hannah Arendt, *Lectures on Kant's Political Philosophy*, ed. Ronald Beiner, (Chicago: University of Chicago Press, 1982).

31 Lévi-Strauss, *The Savage Mind*, p.22. Cf. Foucault's aphasiac, discussed above.

32 One could take Nietzsche to be describing such a culture when he contrasts 'master morality' with 'slave morality'. The 'noble' would be those who simply show themselves as they are in pure visibility, their 'thoughts' being reflectively determined by their bodily comportments (rather than the other way around); by contrast the 'reactive' would be those who, following Socrates' advice, begin to examine possible actions and only *then* act in accordance with what is judged to be good. See Nietzsche's discussion of 'the ancient moral problem that first emerged in the person of Socrates' (Friedrich Nietzsche, *Beyond Good and Evil*, tr. Walter Kaufmann, New York: Vintage, 1966, p.104).

33 For this construal of reflective determination, see Makkreel, *Imagination and Interpretation in Kant*.

34 Lévi-Strauss, *The Savage Mind*, p.21.

Chapter 9

From Singular to Plural Domains of Theological Knowledge: Notes Toward a Foucaultian New Question

Thomas Beaudoin

A beat poised, a crossgrained rhythm,
interplays, imbrications of voice over voice,
mutinies of living are rocking the steady
state of a theme; these riffs and overlappings
a love of deviance, our genesis in noise.[1]

A new mystery sings in your bones. Develop your legitimate strangeness.[2]

INTRODUCTION

In everyday life we employ an astonishing, elusively complex and ultimately non-quantifiable array of resources in working to free ourselves, in attempts both banal and dramatic. Contemporary electronic media multiply these resources for the fashioning of freedom, however ambiguously. Film, music, home video, comic books: who are their authors and how are they used in everyday life? What problems do their uses create that become for us unsettled spiritual and intellectual spaces whose ground we find ourselves devoted to clearing? These concerns are of particular interest among some progressive theological educators. Perhaps chief among our central interests is the inquiry into modern resources for freeing pedagogical practices.

The significance of this inquiry for my life has come from two convergent experiences in the academy. First, I realized that my graduate theological education was not structured to make use of the ways of knowing that I had developed as a musician. There were certain codes about theological knowing that most people at the university seemed to take for granted. Those codes protected the notion of theological knowledge as chiefly verbal, conceptual and linguistic. What I knew, however, after playing bass guitar in rock bands for 15 years, was that my way of 'knowing' musically was in large part nonverbal, nonconceptual and nonlinguistic. I wondered whether theological education, even in the midst of the content of liberationist discourses, was itself not yet liberated in form from a too narrow interpretation of what it means to know theologically.

Moreover, Michel Foucault's work taught me that human ways of organizing or 'constructing' reality – physically, emotionally, intellectually – were always to some degree particular and contingent arrangements or 'productions' of reality, capable of being drained of their seemingly natural inertia through creative historical and philosophical analyses that commence from what we find intolerable about our present and end in a new relationship being taken up to oneself.[3] It was precisely for the sake of a more human freedom that Foucault called into question those structures that had come to be associated with Enlightenment victory: modern prisons, sexual liberation, psychoanalysis. As James Bernauer has argued, Foucault's work manifested an ethic that protests against every historical construction of the human that announces its inevitability, 'bear[ing] witness to the capacity for an ecstatic transcendence of any history that asserts its necessity'.[4]

Yet Foucault's work was not restricted to his books. His own understanding was that 'the work includes the whole life as well as the text'.[5] In seeking to access Foucault as a resource for teaching theology, therefore, it is appropriate to acknowledge that his 'work' includes both his academic texts and his biography. Honoring this, I would like to touch briefly on a rarely examined site of his work: his relation to a nonverbal domain of knowledge, namely music.

FOUCAULT AND MUSIC

That Foucault in fact took much pleasure in music, that he did indeed 'always [have] a soft spot for music',[6] seems indisputable from evidence scattered across several biographies.[7] His tastes often seemed to run to classical music, although the delight apparently was more in the listening than in any technical appreciation.[8] He clearly did not see rock music as an interesting musical form, although he did find noteworthy its ability to generate lifestyles and attitudes.[9] He also seemed to take pleasure, and even find inspiration, in other experimental forms of music. The fact that Foucault and the composer Jean Barraqué were lovers between 1952 and 1956 cannot be overlooked here. In addition, Foucault was personally acquainted with the composer Pierre Boulez in the 1950s and again in the 1970s.[10] (Both Barraqué and Boulez were students of Olivier Messiaen.)

Eribon proposes an important resonance between Foucault's philosophy and Barraqué's music, insofar as the latter described music as 'tragedy, pathos, death. It is the whole game, the trembling to the point of suicide. If music is not that, if it does not overtake and pass the limits, it is nothing.'[11] Eribon further suggests that the music Foucault experienced while with Barraqué 'triggered for Foucault a more general distancing that would permit his escape from the influence of phenomenology and Marxism. This was what he meant when he replied to Paolo Caruso in 1967 that music had played as important a role for him as the reading of Nietzsche.'[12] Macey reports Foucault's comments in stronger terms, asserting that 'the serial and twelve-tone music of Boulez and Barraqué offered him his first escape from the dialectical universe in which he was still living'.[13] Permitting an escape from dialectical thought, and as important as Nietzsche: these are strong claims about and by Foucault. They deserve further thought and research.

In a discussion of Foucault's *Archaeology of Knowledge*, Maurice Blanchot suggests that 'many a formula from negative theology' inform Foucault's style of argument with regard to the uniqueness of 'the statement'.[14] In the following paragraph, Blanchot offhandedly relates this philosophy of the operation of the statement to music, 'seemingly comparable to the perverse efforts (as Thomas Mann put it) of serial music'.[15] Blanchot nowhere hints at an awareness that Foucault had an interest in serial music, or that such an interest may have proved a significant influence on Foucault's philosophizing and his breaking out of dialectical thinking. Blanchot's association of serial music and negative theology – whether or not he knew that Foucault had ever listened to such music (or whether Foucault had read much negative theology, for that matter) – provides another provocation. Why this association in Blanchot between the negative-theological impulse 'behind' Foucault's philosophy and the workings of serial music?

Further research on these questions may not only help us understand the relationship between Foucault's logical–conceptual insights and his musical knowing, but may through such understanding provide further paradigms for thinking about how those of us who teach theology might better dignify theological knowledges that until now have been subjugated.

But how are we to think about the possibility of plural domains of theological knowledge? Any discussion of this question takes place in relation to the work of Howard Gardner, a theorist commonly invoked as authoritative.[16] In my work with theological and religious educators, I have found Gardner's work to be the single most frequently referenced corpus for providing a framework for a more broadly human, and more adequately 'postmodern', sense of what it means to know. Persuaded by the Foucaultian imperative to interrogate popular structures commonly presumed to be liberating, I would like to investigate closely the conceptual basis for this progressive model of learning.

In the remainder of this chapter, I shall attempt to contribute to the problematization of what counts as theological knowledge. My route to doing so will be through a discussion of the influential work of Gardner on 'multiple intelligences'. My aim is to lay groundwork for loosening theological knowledge practices from the grip of the dominant construal of the modern theological subject, a subject formed to accept verbal–conceptual knowledge as the privileged epistemic domain of theology. The present work will not entail a critical discussion of Foucault, but will attempt to honor some fundamental Foucaultian 'dynamics' by rendering their incarnation within a new domain of thought and practice, by contributing to the creation of a new question regarding what counts as theological knowledge.

Jean-Luc Marion suggests that 'theology, of all writing, certainly causes the greatest pleasure',[17] but one need not limit theology to 'writing' in order to find pleasure in it. Marion's claim – that 'to try one's hand at theology requires no other justification than the extreme pleasure of writing'[18] – is true only if 'writing' is writ large, to include music and other domains of knowledge that may be less verbal, though no less at hand.

GARDNER AS RESOURCE

The work of Howard Gardner provides one of the most influential attempts to theorize a plurality of intelligences. The foundational text upon which this progressive pedagogical project is built is Gardner's *Frames of Mind*.[19] Though subsequent works have developed Gardner's ideas, *Frames* is the fullest articulation of his theory and, in my view, remains underanalyzed among progressive theological educators. Thus I will focus primarily on this text with secondary attention to other of Gardner's books and essays.

Frames of Mind, in marshalling evidence from developmental psychology and brain research, sets an impressive standard for a systematic articulation of the plurality of intelligences. Gardner's project is to describe the different types of intelligence existing as a natural part of human development and flourishing variously within different cultures. He is sensitive to the cost to educators, as well as 'nontraditional' learners, of constrictive assumptions about knowing. In pushing back against the 'systematic devaluation of certain forms of intelligence',[20] Gardner is convinced that 'only if we expand and reformulate our view of what counts as human intellect will we be able to devise more appropriate means of assessing it and more effective ways of educating it'.[21]

Frames makes several substantial positive contributions to a theory of multiple intelligences: (1) it risks naming discrete domains of intelligence; (2) it articulates criteria for an intelligence to be counted as such; (3) it creatively interrelates developmental psychology, brain research and cultural anthropology; (4) it attempts to outline the implications of plural intelligences for pedagogical practice. These contributions are offered with a modesty of approach that leaves Gardner's proposal open to further research and critique.

At the same time, Gardner's approach manifests several fundamental unresolved questions and specific deficits in conceptualization. These include (1) an uncritical theorization of the influence of culture on education and formation of intelligence; (2) several problematic criteria in support of what counts as an intelligence; (3) a lack of reflexive consciousness about the power-enmeshed, political–pedagogical uses and effects of delineating a specific set of fundamental human intelligences; (4) specific problems with the conceptualization of each of the intelligences (of which we will focus only on musicality). The strengths and weaknesses of the overall theory will be discussed in turn, seeking to distill a sense of what Gardner's approach provides my task and what work remains after a consideration of his scheme.

Gardner portrays a richly differentiated account of human knowing, divided into seven specific domains of human intelligence: linguistic, logical–mathematical, musical, bodily-kinesthetic, spatial, interpersonal and intrapersonal. These domains are construed as individual cognitive competencies that satisfy what he calls general prerequisites and specific criteria for an intelligence to be counted as such. Gardner defines an intelligence as 'the ability to solve problems, or to create products, that are valued within one or more cultural settings'.[22] He elsewhere discusses an intelligence as a coherent symbolic domain, with development of a particular intelligence being a matter of mastery of that unique symbolic domain.[23]

There are several prerequisites that must be satisfied for an intelligence to be considered a candidate for inclusion in his theory.[24] First, an intelligence must display its power to resolve or create problems, so as to establish 'the groundwork for the acquisition of new knowledge'.[25] Second, an intelligence must prove its nontriviality by being 'genuinely useful and important, at least in certain cultural settings'.[26] Gardner's third prerequisite is that an intelligence display a quality of essentiality, that it not be reducible to some more primary form of knowledge. Fourth, an intelligence must be verifiable empirically. He then adds a sort of meta-prerequisite, which is that knowledges considered by the theory must fairly represent the range of knowledges valued by different cultures.

When moving from 'prerequisites' to 'criteria' for candidate intelligences, Gardner becomes much more specific.[27] His eight criteria include 'potential isolation by brain damage', which is meant to limit intelligences to those forms of knowledge whose neural ground is attested to by their distortion as a result of injury to the brain. Second, the study of exceptional intellect in 'prodigies' yields clues to the existence of unique domains of intelligence. Third, intelligences must exhibit a unique core of cognitive operations traceable to their neurobiological origins. Fourth, a clear developmental path that culminates in identifiable excellences, or 'levels of expertise', is required. Complementary to this developmental history is a fifth criterion, an identifiable history in human biology. That is to say, an intelligence 'becomes more plausible to the extent that one can locate its evolutionary ante-cedents'.[28] Corroboration from research in cognitive psychology and intelligence testing (psychometrics) constitute the sixth and seventh criteria. Gardner's final, eighth, criterion is intelligibility to learners (and researchers): the encodability of an intelligence in symbolic form. His criteria helpfully foreground the terms in which he wants his project to proceed.

Along with these strengths are several problems and a chief conceptual difficulty. Although several of the prerequisites and criteria for intelligences bear the marks of traditional scientific discourse, *Frames of Mind* occasionally hesitates about the scientific status of intelligences. In one passage, Gardner seems to mute the scientific confidence he employs elsewhere, writing that the 'intelligences are fictions … for discussing processes and abilities that … are continuous with one another'. In seeming contradiction of his fourth prerequisite of empirical verifiability, he claims that intelligences 'exist not as physically verifiable entities but only as potentially useful scientific constructs'.[29]

Further, while Gardner's second criterion is a Jamesian utilization of intensi-fications of everyday behavior (in this case, intelligences) for study and interpretation of more commonplace phenomena, it remains very problematic.[30] Gardner approv-ingly cites psychologist David Feldman's assertion that 'the prodigy may be thought of as an individual who passes through one or more domains with tremendous rapidity, exhibiting a speed that seems to render him [*sic*] qualitatively different from other individuals'.[31] One need not dispute the fact of accelerated individual cognitive progress among certain individuals to observe that theorizing the prodigy in this way seems to function to leave the domain boundaries intact between intelligences that Gardner wants to maintain. It is not clear that 'prodigious' behavior, or dynamic and accelerated cognitive abilities, necessarily lead to the maintenance of knowledge domains, or necessarily reveal the 'nature' of intellectual competencies 'in pristine form'.[32] Rather, truly prodigious actions might in fact transgress knowledge boundaries or create new ones. Moreover, not only may Gardner's construal of the prodigy serve to police the boundaries of knowledge already maintained by his (or another) theory, but the focus on prodigies overindividualizes the very concept of 'intelligence',[33] as if prodigious individuals simply rise to the summit of cognitive prowess by force of their own innate prodigiousness. It is troubling that Gardner's interpretation of prodigious intellectuality makes it unlikely that prodigies would ever be epistemologically countercultural, working outside given domains of knowledge.[34] In short, the politically uncritical function of his employment of the prodigy as a criterion disqualifies it as trustworthy.

In addition, it must be said that in some sense Gardner, and any theorist in similar work, is creating a discourse as much as discovering the essence of seven human intelligences; this political dimension of the productive character of such work on knowledge domains is not entertained by Gardner, who focuses on the 'defining' and 'discovery' of intelligence by psychology.[35]

Related to this problem is Gardner's weak sense for the ideological and culturally contested qualities of 'knowledge,' 'culture' or 'symbols'. While Gardner's interpretation of brain research and its implication for intelligences is rich and suggestive, his interpretation of culture, particularly in *Frames of Mind*, relegates culture to serving as midwife to the natural domains of intelligence striving to find their way in the world. But the question of the different cultural powers that may have a stake in producing and defining 'intelligence' itself as a problem remains unaddressed. The undertheorization of the productively powerful role of cultures – in their class, academic, race-ethnic, scientific and gender dimensions – in birthing, shaping and governing 'intelligence' or 'knowledge' represents a significant lacuna. Culture, in his theory, is almost always a benign and secondary force on or support of knowledge.[36] In later work, Gardner and colleagues more complexly theorize the relationship between intelligence and culture, by distinguishing between '*intelligence* as a biopsychological potential; *domain* as the discipline or craft that is practiced in a society; and *field*, the set of institutions and judges that determine which products within a domain are of merit'.[37] Despite the turn toward social and institutional formation of intelligence, the absence of a sufficiently critical social theory remains: a lack of theoretical resources for criticism of dominant knowledges and knowledge brokers, and (thus) for the relationship between cultural authorization of knowledge and the very definitions of and inquiries into 'biopsychological potential'.

Gardner seems in several places to use 'symbol' in the sense of an expressive vehicle of human meaning, with symbol systems as shared repositories of cognitive work.[38] 'Symbols pave the royal route from raw intelligences to finished cultures,'[39] Gardner claims. As culturally influenced organizers of knowledge, he argues that it is 'legitimate to construe rituals, religious codes, mythic and totemic systems as symbolic codes that capture and convey crucial aspects of personal intelligence',[40] but without any account of the danger within or cultural contestation of the construction and use of symbols.

In addition, Gardner's theory overrelies on grounding the intelligences scientifically. It is not self-evident, however, that for linguistic or musical knowledge to be counted as legitimate domains their bonding to a biological limit is required. This is not to say that brain research is irrelevant to, specifically, formulating what counts as doing theology in the classroom. This is, however, to say that – to teach theology, at least – a politically conscious distinction needs to be made between neurobiologically influenced cognitive capacities, on the one hand, and domains of knowledge in which theological formation of the person might render someone fluent, on the other. Each clearly has to do with the other. But each is not the other.

Both need continual denaturalizing, critical investigations as to their conditions and effects. One cannot be made the ventriloquist of the other, else the risk occurs, from one side, of reducing what can and may be known theologically to the rules of knowledge that govern neurobiological discourse; or, from another side, reinscribing modern dismissal of the body's materiality as a locus of cognition by failing to search after the body's own processes. Either approach jettisons the unique and unrepeatable individual cogitating body in favor of a maverick theory of theological knowledges unaccountable to human limits, even while purporting to think them.

Beyond these objections, there remains a major conceptual problem in *Frames*, the tendency to confuse 'intellectual capacities' on the one hand (as what we might call a psychological and medically potentially determinable set of developmental processes and limits), with 'knowledge domains' on the other (as what we might refer to as *styles* of knowledge acquisition and the *contents* of such acquisition). For Gardner, what he interchangeably calls 'intelligences', 'intellectual competences', 'forms of knowledge' and 'knowledge domains'[41] issue primordially from neural and psychological developmental processes of the individual–cultural differences notwithstanding.

But the problem is not only definitional. For to confuse 'intelligence' (as mastery of a discrete realm of knowledge) with 'intellectual competence' or 'proclivity' (as neurobiologically-governed potential for the realization of cognitive capacities) and with 'knowledge domain' (as a unique symbolically coded system of knowledge formed by persons, institutions and cultures) is also a political–pedagogical problem, about who creates or controls what counts as 'knowledge'. Such a conceptual confusion also elides the role of philosophical contributions with respect to the constitution, policing and politics of knowledge.[42] This conceptual problem is crystallized in Gardner's summary of his work at Harvard Project Zero, which attempts 'to arrive at the "natural kinds" of symbol systems: the families of symbol systems which hang together (or fall apart), and the ways they might be *represented* in the human nervous system'.[43] Such a binding of the symbolic character of knowledge (if such character exists) to the nervous system, as if one could be 'read off' the other, represents a leap.

Those of us who teach may not only formulate, as Gardner indicates, a stance about 'the *identity*, or *nature of the intellectual capacities* that human beings can develop'.[44] A fully critical account needs also to formulate a politics of cognitive capacity, which would be the practice of remaining open to and critically articulating the cost of denominating the 'nature' of 'intellectual capacities', particularly as we strive to establish their givenness as natural competence. After all, the desire to open up many domains of theological knowledge in which the student may be formed may tempt any teacher to bind individual differences too readily and firmly to the history, psyche, childhood, anatomy or neurobiology of our students.[45]

To render the conceptual confusion of Gardner's book more clearly as a task for theological educators: we must resist satisfying ourselves with equating what knowledge 'is' with where it 'comes from'. We must also ask what knowledge *does*, how different domains function.[46] What are their effects, who gets to define them, how have they been made possible, what are their situations or roles in various pedagogical contexts?[47]

In short, a distinction must be posited between what might be termed 'cognitive potential' and 'cognitive practice'. Cognitive potentials are the inherent cognitive strengths of each individual that may or may not ever be exercised, whether these be inherited or otherwise present in a person (as Gardner evidences) neurobiologically. Cognitive practices, by contrast, are the actual exercises of knowledge within interrelated personal, cultural and institutional realms (and that always affect the individual's cognitive life, but are surely not reducible to it).[48] (These latter are the practices that populate many of Foucault's texts, from medical knowledge in his earlier work to self-knowledge in his later work.)

The distinction I am proposing between cognitive potential and cognitive practice does not imply a separation between the two. Indeed, Foucault's work would suggest that much, if not all, of the discourses around cognitive potential (such as Gardner's) are always already implicated in cognitive practices. At the same time, cognitive practices rely on cognitive potentials – as elusive to articulate as they remain to the present day – as a condition of their possibility. This distinction serves at least two functions. First, it delineates the primary task of the theological educator: attention to cognitive practices (not, as some appropriations of Gardner's work suggest, to cognitive potentials). Second, this distinction intends to situate both cognitive practices and cognitive potentials within a politics of knowledge.

In sum, what does Gardner's theory provide for a more liberating teaching of theology? It offers a pathbreaking example of a creative collation of psychological and medical evidence for a specifiable plurality of knowledge domains, attentive to forms of knowledge commonly used in practical ways, sensitive to individual and cultural differences in competence and ability within these domains, and rendering any contemporary attempt to continue to educate for one primary or sole intelligence deeply problematic.

What remains is the need for a critical, pedagogically informed and directed, practice-oriented account of the multiplicity of extant and potential knowledge domains. This account could critically invite all disciplinary contributions while avoiding the temptation to overclaim for the relation of knowledges to neurobiological 'origins'. Specifically for the discipline of theology, what is needed is a rendering of this task that furthers the aims of theological work. In other words, becoming a theological 'subject' through the teaching and learning of theology needs to be rendered more adequately as fluency in several domains of knowledge. This move is demanded as an attempt to liberate theological judgment or practices of knowing from the dominant construal of the modern theological subject, formed to accept only one domain (whether we call that domain verbal, conceptual or logical–mathematical knowledge) as *the* privileged epistemological domain of theology.

MUSICAL KNOWLEDGE: A TENTATIVE PROPOSAL

As an initial step toward constructing a new question about the potential diversity of theological knowledges, and building on Gardner's delineation of musical knowledge as an irreducible domain of knowledge, I posit the following theses.[49]

First, musicality is a domain of knowledge irreducible to other domains. In the present terms, musicality is both 'cognitive potential' and 'cognitive practice'. By this I mean that it is both a psychobiological potential, in Gardner's terms, and that it is an area of cultural contestation of meaning, a unique symbolically coded system of knowledge formed by persons, institutions and cultures.[50] Here I can only indicate some promising lines of thought on the topic.

From within the experience of playing music, a few examples may be invoked. Jeremy Begbie examines the practice of musical improvisation to observe that that type of musical experience is a 'thinking in notes and rhythms; not thinking 'before' them, or on to them, or through them[,] but thinking *in* physical sound – notes, melodies, harmonies, meters'.[51] Begbie argues that jazz improvisation affords its own style of knowing through a relationship that one takes up to other musicians, to the music itself and to one's instrument. Improvisation schools one in the skills of collective artistic creation by linking musicality to dialogue with one's fellow musicians, to give-and-take, to attentive listening to others, to a sense for the importance of graceful timing in relation to others and to the shared artistic work.

Jazz pianist David Sudnow gives such arguments phenomenological depth. In his remarkable book *Ways of the Hand*, Sudnow attends in intricate detail to his history of learning to play improvisational jazz at the piano. He relates the changes that took place in his hands during their 'schooling' in formal study with a jazz teacher and in informal experiences of playing in clubs, practicing on his own, and simply watching mature players. The book demonstrates the ways in which hands are able to *know* in a style and content that are unique to the body. The process from beginning lessons to mature jazz playing was one of letting his hands take over their own knowledge of the terrain of the keyboard, not simply carrying out the orders of his conceptual intentions articulated outside his body, but a thinking *through* his hands.

First his hands had to learn the myriad jazz scales. Then he tried simply applying those scales in ways his teacher had modeled. The breakthrough came when he was able to distinguish between how his mentors *talked* about their playing, and how they actually used their bodies while they were playing (in breathing, shoulder rolls, position of the lower back), in order to effect jazz. The latter began to free him to understand that the hand's knowing in jazz was not a matter of repeating his mentor's thinking about jazz, or planning one's playing route conceptually in advance of fingers striking keys, but of thinking through his hands by singing through them. This required conceptual knowledge of jazz musical patterns, but it also required an immersion into his body in order to let the hands practice their own handful knowledge of the musical terrain. He came to call his jazz a 'joint *knowing* of voice and fingers'.[52] This embodied perception in jazz music, which can be trained, he calls an 'incorporated' sense for place and distance, a thoroughly contextualized, felt knowing. It happens that 'finding the named, recognizable, visually grasped place-out-there, through looking's theoretic work, becomes unnecessary, and the body's own appreciative structures serve as a means of finding a place to go'.[53]

Thought as singing through the body would certainly enrich theological thinking were it allowed into the theological classroom, if our thinking were encouraged to be more 'at hand,' and not falsely to attempt to 'partitionalize [the] body'.[54] Teaching theology has not yet come to terms with Heidegger's notion that 'Every motion of the hand in every one of its works carries itself through the element of thinking, every bearing of the hand bears itself in that element.'[55]

From within theological interpretations of music, a few examples are appropriate.

Karl Barth found the music of Mozart to be epistemologically *sui generis*. Mozart functioned for him as theological persuasion against the evil of creation, in favor of its goodness, in and through creation's finitude. For Barth, this was a proof, interestingly enough, 'better than any scientific deduction'.[56] Barth heard in Mozart 'a final word about life insofar as this can be spoken by [humans]' and added that 'perhaps it is no accident that a musician spoke this word'.[57]

From a Catholic perspective, Richard Viladesau has carefully elaborated a case for 'aesthetic theology', defined as 'reflection on and communication of theological insight in a way irreducible to abstract conceptual thought'.[58] He has argued for the facility of music in constructing 'kinetic', as opposed to pictorial, images. He concludes that music's kinetic images

> may not usually represent concepts directly (although in some cases they may do so, functioning as a learned symbolic language). But they are in any case associated with bodily states, emotions, and high feelings (affects), and these in turn embody … implied understandings and visions.[59]

Despite their differences, these different interpretations from Begbie, Sudnow, Barth, and Viladesau share one key insight about the nonverbal character of musical knowledge, namely, 'A solution to a [musical] problem can be constructed *before* it is articulated.'[60]

This position neither implies nor requires that musical knowledge is immune from discursive enmeshment, from the effects of power-knowledge formations operative in and across *all* knowledge domains. There can be no question of uncritically naturalizing musical knowing. Indeed, such discursive enmeshment can be seen in the works cited above. What Begbie's theology selects and interprets as musical knowledge serves to endorse – not undermine or radically correct – prevailing notions of Christian orthodoxy. And *that* music itself may be caught up in and interpreted through contesting ideologies seems missing in Viladesau's claim that 'What distinguishes beautiful music from noise … is precisely its patterns, which create a unity out of disparate elements.'[61] On the contrary (and as Viladesau elsewhere admits), music's own 'images' can become culturally associated with particular symbolic content. What counts as musical knowledge, then, will be heavily mediated by complex vectors of discourse, power-knowledge forces that make musical knowledge no different from other domains of knowledge with respect to its functioning *as* knowledge, its valence in the contestation of truth.

The thesis of the preceding paragraphs, on musicality as an irreducible domain of knowledge, bears resonance to what Theodore Jennings calls 'ritual knowledge'. He writes that

> Ritual knowledge is gained through a bodily action which alters the world or the place of the ritual participant in the world … Ritual knowledge is gained in and through the body … It is not so much that the mind 'embodies' itself in ritual action, but rather that the body 'minds' itself or attends through itself in ritual action. When engaged in ritual action … I do not first think through the appropriate action and then 'perform' it. Rather it is more like this: My hand 'discovers' the fitting gesture (or my feet the fitting step) which I may then 'cerebrally' *re*-cognize as appropriate or right.[62]

Such connection between musicality and ritual knowledge may open new lines of relationship between systematic and liturgical theologians, for example, and the respective teaching of their theologies. Having limned the initial important thesis on musical knowing, I shall describe the following theses more succinctly.

Second, musicality is an irreducible domain of theological knowledge insofar as it functions as a *source of* theology. This thesis follows from the first. It has particularly strong warrant if theology is construed as a revised correlational practice, as David Tracy has argued, and as Kathryn Tanner has helpfully problematized.[63] One side of this correlation, interpreting particular 'operations' or 'uses' of the cultural materials that constitute the 'situation', surely includes uses of musical materials, from popular media culture to classical materials, including those consumed over television or those produced in a local garage band.

Third, musicality is an irreducible domain of theological knowledge insofar as it functions as a *mode for* theology. It is largely accepted by Catholic theology that a plurality of methods, as persuasively articulated by Tracy, need to be put to work for interpreting the 'classic' texts of theology.[64] What is often overlooked is that, not only plural methods are required, but a plurality of *modes* as well. To dwell too intently on the need for a critical pluralism of *methods* has had the effect of reifying one particular mode of theology, the linguistic–logical–conceptual, which all methods eventually must then serve. To limit theology in this way may not only be an unjust exercise of power by its gatekeepers over against others in the academy. Such limiting may also bear negative class and gender biases, as Margaret Miles has suggested, by making the written text the ideal source and mode for theological work.[65] To dignify theology's fragmentation and fissure into a multimodular discipline constructively problematizes what counts as doing theology, refashioning assumptions about what we may interpret as theological work in the past, present and future. Further, it opens us to take seriously the subjugated theological knowledges (again, of past, present and future) and the plurality of theological modes not accounted for within conceptual theology.

What follows from this position is that each knowledge domain may be free to develop its own methodologies and epistemological models (and, importantly for pedagogy, its own practices of critical 'thinking' or critical knowing), open to correction in mutually critical conversations with other domains, to be sure, but not to be conformed or reduced to other domains.[66]

Fourth, musical knowledge can provide knowledge that reworks other theological knowledge domains. It is not enough to say that musicality provides 'language' for other domains, even though that is how I must necessarily express this claim in a written work. While musicality can and does provide language (such as metaphors) for linguistic knowledge,[67] it also can declare its own sense-making logic (such as improvisation) for logical–mathematical knowledge, and offer unique orchestrations of the body (such as the relation between hand and head) for bodily knowledge.[68]

In sum, I propose the following: that in the subject-formation that takes place in pedagogical sites of theology, musicality is a domain deserving of fluency. Indeed, it would seem to be required by a postmodern theological pedagogy that confronts the reality that 'every educational system is a political means of maintaining or of modifying the appropriation of discourse, with the knowledge and the powers it carries with it'.[69]

In concluding this brief discussion of musicality, it is important to note the reformulation of what it means to be a theological 'subject' if theological work is construed as fluency in various knowledge domains, plurisourced and multimodal. This is a very different image of the theological subject than that of the master of conceptual knowledge. At the limit, this reformulation allows theology 'to put into question the signifying subject' by 'try[ing] out a practice … that ends in the veritable destruction of this subject, in its dissociation, in its upheaval into something radically "other"'.[70] Less dramatically, we could say that it is one way to 'develop a form of subjectivity that could be the source of effective resistance to a widespread type of power'.[71]

What follows from this is that it is an inappropriate exercise of power on the part of any one domain to exclude its sources and modes – its practices of truth – from the other domains. The more the domains are allowed to be intercritical, or critically complementary, the more rich and liberative theological subjectification is likely to be.[72] And the more likely theological educators are to honor Psalm 49:4, which raises the possibility of relating verbal and musical knowledge theologically: 'I will solve my riddle to the music of the harp.'

TOWARD PLURAL DOMAINS FOR THEOLOGY

Finally, we may consider here some preliminary implications for teaching theology. What Gardner observes of the modern western school system in general seems an adequate description of many classrooms of theology, investing a 'premium on logical–mathematical ability and on certain aspects of linguistic intelligence'.[73] Gardner and Walters suggest that 'in [US] society we are nearly "brain-washed" to restrict the notion of intelligence to the capacities used in solving logical and linguistic problems'.[74] Certainly, classrooms of theology typically relegate nonverbal or nonlinguistic knowledge to prefatory or satellite status, deploying music, for example, as 'worship', 'liturgy', or some other marginalizing disciplinization. In my own tradition, Catholic academic theology is no exception, as Richard Viladesau summarizes, having been since 'the post-Tridentine period largely dominated by a philosophical and conceptual approach'.[75] Insofar as this is the case, students of theology, like most western students, are subjectified as '*Homo rationalis*, as a coherent, rational, and noncontradictory (i.e. unified) individual; a source of conscious action whose mental capacities can be augmented with technology'.[76]

Regardless of the intelligence or knowledge domain implicitly or explicitly regnant in a theological–pedagogical context, the uncritical privileging of any *single* domain is a dominative power/knowledge practice. Moreover, the privileging of one single domain of knowledge is a restriction on the freedom of theology to do its work, and on the theological subjectification allowed and enforced by a classroom pursuing pedagogical practices of freedom. Respect for a diversity of domains is 'predicated on the assumption that the innate attributes of the individual student', or in the present terms, their cognitive potentials, 'are fundamentally constitutive of her/his identity. These must be explicated and incorporated into the educational process out of fundamental respect for the human dignity of the student.'[77] The theological educator must, then, guard against the 'systematic devaluation of certain forms of intelligence',[78] allowing for what Foucault called the 'insurrection of subjugated knowledges'.[79] A dominative pedagogical power has forced theologically inflected voicings of protest knowledge to operate only on the fringes of theological teaching and learning.

The predominant, modern domains of theological knowledge need not remain untouched by other knowledge domains. Gardner suggests, for instance, that bodily knowing can inform logical knowing. He quotes the research of psychologist Frederic Bartlett to the effect that 'most of what we ordinarily call thinking – routine as well as innovative – partakes of the same principles that have been uncovered in overtly physical manifestations of skill'.[80] By this Bartlett means such skills as a sense of timing, moments of repose and a clear sense of direction. This is an important clue about the possibilities for fruitful interrelationships between domains of theological knowledge.

It is imperative that we consider a reconstrual of the teaching of theology, not for the sake of the maintenance of boundaries of knowledge domains, but for the freedom of critical pursuit of all things 'theological'.[81] Theology may then yet be a practice of freedom, whether positing a diversity of knowledge domains leads to freedom through a powerful 'tear in a dialectical universe',[82] or to a more mundane, careful and subtle redistribution of our intellectual resources for taking up new relations to ourselves and others.

NOTES

1 From 'Cosmos,' in Micheal O'Siadhail, *Hail! Madam Jazz: New and Selected Poems* (Newcastle: Dufour, 1992, p.149), cited in Begbie, 'Theology and the Arts: Music', in David F. Ford (ed.), *The Modern Theologians* (Cambridge, MA: Blackwell, 1997, p.696).

2 René Char, 'Partage Formel,' XXII, translated and cited in James Miller, *The Passion of Michel Foucault* (New York: Simon and Schuster, 1993, p.108).

3 On a 'history of the present', see Foucault, *Discipline and Punish*, tr. Alan Sheridan (New York: Vintage, 1978, p.31).

4 James Bernauer, *Michel Foucault's Force of Flight: Toward an Ethics for Thought* (Atlantic Highlands, NJ: Humanities Press, 1993, pp.180–81).

5 'Postscript: An Interview with Michel Foucault', in *Death and the Labyrinth*, tr. Charles Ruas (New York: Doubleday and Co., 1986, p.184).

6 Jean-Paul Aron, *Les Modernes* (Paris: Gallimard, 1984, pp.64–5), cited in Didier Eribon, *Michel Foucault*, tr. Betsy Wing (Cambridge, MA: Harvard University Press, 1991, p.65).

7 Relevant passages in the major biographies include Eribon, *Michel Foucault*, pp.64–8, 83; David Macey, *The Lives of Michel Foucault* (New York: Vintage, 1995, pp.50–54, 399); Miller, *Passion* (pp.79–81, 89–92, 408 n.68).

8 Eribon describes Foucault in Uppsala as determinedly writing 'always to music. Not an evening went by that he did not listen to the *Goldberg Variations*. Music for him meant Bach or Mozart' (*Michel Foucault*, p.83; also p.66). According to Macey, Foucault 'idolised Beethoven' and enjoyed Mahler and Wagner (see *Lives*, pp.51, 399).

9 See the interview between Michel Foucault and Pierre Boulez, 'Contemporary Music and the Public', in Lawrence D. Kritzman (ed.), *Michel Foucault: Politics, Philosophy, Culture* (New York: Routledge, 1988). Macey reports that Daniel Defert, Foucault's partner of two decades, once took Foucault to a David Bowie concert. Anyone who knows something of Bowie's theatrical gender-bending can only wonder what this experience must have been like.

10   Eribon, *Michel Foucault*, p.65.
11   Cited in Eribon, *Michel Foucault*, p.66.
12   Eribon, *Michel Foucault*, p.67.
13   Macey, *Lives*, p.53. Miller (*Passion*, p.79) quotes the interview: 'the French serialists and deodecaphonic musicians [provided] the first "tear" in the dialectical universe in which I had lived'.
14   Maurice Blanchot, 'Michel Foucault as I Imagine Him', tr. Jeffrey Mehlman, *Foucault/Blanchot* (New York: Zone, 1987, p.74). For an interpretation of the relation of Foucault's thought to negative theology, see Bernauer, *Michel Foucault's Force of Flight*.
15   Blanchot, 'Michel Foucault', p.75.
16   For evidence of this influence, see the list of Gardner's works, works by others, and workshop presenters that defend and elaborate his theories, in H. Gardner, *Multiple Intelligences: The Theory in Practice* (New York: Basic Books, 1993, pp.281–97). As examples of his appropriation in Christian religious education settings, see Carl J. Pfeifer and Janann Manternach, 'The Processes of Catechesis', in Thomas Groome and Michael J. Corso (eds), *Empowering Catechetical Leaders* (Washington: National Catholic Education Association, 1999). Thomas Groome endorses Gardner's seven intelligences in *Educating for Life: A Spiritual Vision for Every Teacher and Parent* (Allen, TX: Thomas More Press, 1998, p.101). For a helpful application of Gardner's multiple intelligence theory to university teaching of religion, see Paul F. Aspan and Faith Kirkham Hawkins, 'After the Facts: Alternative Student Evaluation for Active Learning Pedagogies in the Undergraduate Biblical Studies Classroom', *Teaching Theology and Religion*, 3(3) (October 2000), 133–51.
17   Jean-Luc Marion, *God Without Being: Hors-Texte*, tr. Thomas Carlson (Chicago: University of Chicago Press, 1991, p.1).
18   Ibid.
19   Howard Gardner, *Frames of Mind: The Theory of Multiple Intelligences* (New York: Basic Books, 1993, first published 1983).
20   Gardner, *Frames of Mind*, p.365.
21   Ibid., p.4.
22   Ibid., p.x. This definition is from his introduction to the 1993 edition.
23   Ibid., pp.25–7.
24   I have abstracted these from ibid., pp.60–62. Gardner does not enumerate them.
25   Ibid., p.61.
26   Ibid.
27   The following examples are taken from ibid., pp.63–7.
28   Ibid., p.65.
29   Ibid., p. 70.
30   Hence Gardner's claim in ibid., p.27: 'In monitoring the prodigy as he advances, one glimpses a "fast-forward" picture of what is involved in all educational processes.' See William James, *The Varieties of Religious Experience* (New York: Vintage, 1990, first published 1902, p.436), wherein observation of the most intense form of a religious phenomenon becomes the ideal mode for its study.
31   Gardner, *Frames of Mind*, p.27.
32   Ibid., p.28.
33   There are many examples of this overindividualization of intelligence in *Frames of Mind*. See, for example, p.148, where Gardner ignores any social or cultural influences that may have functioned to allow or disallow the 'faith in the power of one's own intuitions concerning the ultimate nature of physical reality' in certain prodigious scientists; or p.289, where Gardner claims that, with respect to truly original thinking, 'it is up to the skilled practitioner himself [*sic*] whether he in fact produces original work or is simply satisfied with realizing a prior tradition'.

34 See, for instance, Gardner's alarming statement in ibid., p.311: 'It is given to only a few individuals in most cultures to reach the apogee of symbolic competence and then to move off in unanticipated directions, experimenting with symbol systems, fashioning unusual and innovative symbolic products, perhaps even attempting to devise a new symbol system.' While this observation may be statistically 'true' ('a few individuals'), it fails to investigate critically why so 'few' exhibit this creativity with respect to experimentations with knowledge – other than presupposing the tautology that prodigious individuals are rare.

35 Among other places, see ibid., p.xii, 'efforts to *define* intelligence', and p.xvi: 'intelligences are always *expressed* in the context of…' Further, see Gardner (with Joseph Walters), 'A Rounded Version', in *Multiple Intelligences*, p.16: 'the biological proclivity to participate in a particular form of problem solving must also be coupled with the cultural *nurturing* of that domain'. (All italics in these quotations are mine.)

36 For example, see Gardner's interpretations of culture in *Frames*, pp.57, 98, 164, 242. Typical is the claim in *Frames*, p.242, that 'symbolization [is] of the essence in the [intra- and inter-]personal intelligences. Without a symbolic code supplied by the culture, the individual is confronted with only his [*sic*] most elementary and unorganized discrimination of feelings: but armed with such a scheme of interpretation, he has the potential to make sense of the full range of experiences which he and others in his community can undergo.' Gardner's assertion that several of the intelligences are essentially acultural is thus equally problematic. He argues that musical and linguistic intelligence, for example, are 'not closely tied to the world of physical objects', having 'an essence that is equally remote from the world of other persons' (ibid., p.98). He argues that only logical–mathematical, spatial, and bodily intelligences are formed through interaction with objects in the world (ibid., p.235).

37 Gardner and Walters, 'Questions and Answers', in Gardner, *Multiple Intelligences*, p.37. See also, in *Multiple Intelligences*, Gardner, 'The Relation of Intelligence', pp.50–51, and 'Assessment in Context', pp.172–3.

38 Gardner's definition of symbol is too thin to do the work he wants it to do (defining it as 'any entity (material or abstract) that can denote or refer to any other entity') and frequently vague, lacking a critical sense ('a symbol can convey some mood, feeling, or tone … just so long as the relevant community chooses to interpret a particular symbol in a particular way'). See Gardner, *Frames*, p.301.

39 Gardner, *Frames*, p.300.

40 Ibid., p.242.

41 Gardner argues (ibid., p. 284) that 'What is crucial is not the label but, rather, the conception: that individuals have a number of domains of potential intellectual competence which they are in the position to develop, if they are ["]normal["] and if the appropriate stimulating factors are available'. From this definition, the 'domains of competence' seem to exist prior to and may 'develop' largely independent of external power–knowledge relations.

42 Gardner in many places gives an uncritical and politically agnostic reading of the history of intelligence tests in the past, muting their socializing and normalizing functions. See, for example, ibid., pp.14–17, and Gardner, 'Intelligences in Seven Phases', in *Multiple Intelligences*, pp.215–30. A more critical view appears in Gardner, Kornhaber and Krechevsky, 'Engaging Intelligence', in Gardner, *Multiple Intelligences*, pp.238–43.

43 Gardner, *Frames*, pp.28–9, italics mine.

44 Ibid.

45 Educators must not only enter the conversation by merely receiving the authorized foundation statements of science, 'build[ing] upon a [scientific] knowledge of … intellectual proclivities and their points of maximum flexibility and adaptability' (ibid., p.33), but must undertake a constant criticism of them as well.

46   *Contra* Gardner in ibid., p.68: 'Intelligences are best thought of apart from particular programs of action.'
47   In this respect, the politics of Gardner's own text often protects reigning knowledge brokers of society: 'Those individuals most directly charged with the maintenance of cultural knowledge and tradition … are well[-]equipped to know, and to evaluate, the dances, dramas, and designs fashioned by members [of a culture]' (ibid., p. 300).
48   This distinction relates 'cognitive potential' to Gardner's more recent definition of intelligence as 'a *biopsychological potential*', in Gardner and Walters, 'Questions and Answers', p.36.
49   My initial thinking in this area was influenced by many helpful verbal and musical conversations and nonverbal musical collaborations with theologian and percussionist Loye Ashton.
50   Gardner discusses the evidence for musical intelligence in *Frames*, pp.99–127.
51   Jeremy Begbie, 'Theology and the Arts: Music', in David F. Ford (ed.), *The Modern Theologians: An Introduction to Christian Theology in the Twentieth Century* (Cambridge, MA: Blackwell, 1997, p.695).
52   David Sudnow, *Ways of the Hand: The Organization of Improvised Conduct* (Cambridge, MA: Harvard University Press, 1978, p.150), italics mine. 'Joint knowing' is a pun: much musical knowing depends on unselfconscious attention to physical sensations at the joints – of fingers, arms, shoulders.
53   Ibid., p.13.
54   Ibid., p.152. Sudnow's book also shows how new domains of knowing have political implications for the institutional identity of academic theologians. One mentor 'enabled me to realize the consequences of allowing the keyboard, and not an academic discipline, to tell me where to go' (ibid., p.viii).
55   Martin Heidegger, quoted in ibid., p.ix.
56   Karl Barth in Richard Viladesau (ed.), *Theological Aesthetics: God in Imagination, Beauty, and Art* (New York: Oxford University Press, 1999, pp.4–5).
57   Barth, *Final Testimonies*, ed. Eberhard Busch, tr. Geoffrey W. Bromiley (Grand Rapids, MI: Eerdman's, 1977, pp.20–21).
58   Viladesau, *Theological Aesthetics*, p.x. For Viladesau, music does not necessarily constitute a distinct 'domain' of knowledge. Rather, he frequently turns (via Thomism) to 'feeling' and 'affect' as other 'modes' of intelligence, cutting across the boundaries of more familiar formulations, such as Gardner's, of bodily, musical, personal intelligences and so on (see Viladesau, ibid., p.85).
59   Ibid., p.180.
60   Gardner and Walters, 'A Rounded Version', p.20.
61   Viladesau, *Theological Aesthetics*, p.149.
62   Theodore Jennings, 'On Ritual Knowledge', *Journal of Religion* 62 (1982), 115, cited in Richard Gaillardetz, *Transforming Our Days: Spirituality, Community and Liturgy in a Technological Culture* (New York: Crossroad, 2000, p.117).
63   See David Tracy, *The Analogical Imagination: Christian Theology and the Culture of Pluralism* (New York: Crossroad, 1991), and Kathryn Tanner, *Theories of Culture: A New Agenda for Theology* (Minneapolis, MN: Fortress Press, 1997).
64   Tracy, *The Analogical Imagination,* pp 112–13.
65   See Margaret Miles, *Image as Insight: Visual Understanding in Western Christianity and Secular Culture* (Boston: Beacon, 1985, pp.xi, 9).
66   Musicality may fail to appear to most theologians as a mode for theology not because of music's inherent deficiencies as a cognitive practice, but because of the reigning knowledge paradigms in which modern theology and theological education are invested. Of pivotal importance here is the often biased pedagogical training of academic

theologians. The question of the possibility that musicality and bodily knowledge, for example, may manifest or develop their own unique critical practices, analogous to linguistic-logical 'critical thinking', cannot be adjudicated, indeed can hardly get a fair hearing, under current norms for theological work, under the distortions present by the powers of musical–bodily restriction and linguistic–logical production and domination in modern subjects of theology.

67 For example, the musical concept 'overtone', derived from musical experience, can function as an alternative to the hermeneutical concept 'correlation', as in Begbie, 'striking theological overtones emerge in any study of improvisation' ('Theology and the Arts', p.693). Viladesau wisely observes that 'Unless they take refuge in a totally negative theology … neither philosophy nor theology can do without metaphor – and metaphor cannot be controlled or communicated without art of some kind' (*Theological Aesthetics*, p.209).

68 Viladesau summarizes the work of neurologist Antonio Damasio, whose survey of brain research, recalling that of Howard Gardner, indicates that 'knowledge, "which exists in memory under dispositional representation form, can be made accessible to consciousness … virtually simultaneously" in *both verbal and nonverbal versions*. Hence the coexistence in individual minds of different kinds of symbolic mediations of thought – heuristic and conceptual, pictorial and verbal, felt and formulated – allows for *comparison and dialectic between our various symbolic "languages", so that no one of them can be absolutely determinative of our interpretation of experience*' (Viladesau, *Theological Aesthetics*, p.81, citing Antonio Damasio, *Descartes' Error: Emotion, Reason, and the Human Brain* (New York: Avon Books, 1994, p.166), italics mine. Note that Viladesau's claim here touches only upon cognitive operations in general – not upon theological knowledge in particular. However, it seems to me appropriate to find in the construction of theological knowledges an analogical relationship to what can be known neurobiologically about human cognitive operations (mindful to avoid the conceptual confusion of which I accuse Gardner's work). This appropriateness issues from at least two sides: from the side of responsibility to the body's own unique learning processes manifest in the mind/brain; and from the side of the legitimate (natural and cultural) diversity of human ways of knowing, ways that take on a heightened significance when viewed as rooted in some sense in the dignity of being created in the image of God – an argument for another time and place.

69 Foucault, 'The Discourse on Language', in *The Archaeology of Knowledge*, tr. A.M. Sheridan Smith (New York: Pantheon, 1972, pp.226–7).

70 Foucault, in Miller, *Passion*, p.93.

71 James Bernauer and Michael Mahon, 'The Ethics of Michel Foucault', in *The Cambridge Companion to Michel Foucault*, ed. Gary Gutting (New York: Cambridge University Press, 1994, p.147).

72 There arises here the important question of whether verbal–linguistic–conceptual knowledge does and should have a priority in the work of academic theology. A full treatment of this important question is beyond the scope of this chapter. Let me briefly note that the reasons for *granting* such a priority, and therefore for relegating all other domains of knowledge to a secondary status, include the following:

(1) the traditional priority of linguistic, verbal or conceptual knowing for theology's dominant modes of practice;
(2) the purported immediacy of non-linguistic, non-verbal domains of knowing to 'originating' religious experience, rendering them inadequate in serving the necessity of a critically systematizing, 'second-order' dimension for theology, or, at the limit, a 'metaphysical' task, which is most adequately carried out in linguistic–conceptual modes.

As Viladesau writes, 'Thematically reflexive, discursive thought is the exceptional mode of rationality – one to which we refer when doubt is introduced, when critical control is needed, or when system is desired' (*Theological Aesthetics*, pp.85, 86–9). Viladesau endorses Paul Ricoeur's case for the priority of linguistic expression and perception in the adequate rendering of meaning. He recalls Ricoeur's argument that 'the word can generally represent absent realities, abstract ideas, analogies, and judgments in a more clear and direct way than spatial images'. Further, the 'capacity of the word to express judgments of being and of doing make it the normal (although not exclusive) medium of ontological and ethical thought'. And finally, 'word's unique ability to express negation directly makes it capable of expressing inverse insight and transcendence' (Viladesau, *Theological Aesthetics*, p.89, summarizing Ricoeur, *Fallible Man*, tr. Charles Kelbley, New York: Regnery, 1965, p.27);

(3) the broadly public (and hence accessible to general argument) character of linguistic or verbal knowledge, a character that does not obtain with respect to other domains, such as the musical;

(4) the training of contemporary theologians, which precludes facility with nonverbal knowledge domains.

For myself, these positions are very nearly persuasive for the priority of verbal, linguistic or conceptual knowledge for theological work, and so for theological pedagogy. However, reasons for *questioning* such a priority can be formulated as problematizations of the aforementioned claims:

(1) While a theology in service of a tradition must take particular methodological care to foster exposure to that tradition's orienting claims, it is the question of what in fact constitutes the orienting claims of a given theological tradition *and the knowledge domains mediating those claims* that is raised by the positing of nonverbal ways of knowing as legitimate theological knowledges;

(2) it seems an open question whether musical knowing, as discursively situated, is any closer to 'originating' religious experience than (discursively situated) linguistic–verbal knowing. Moreover, there may be forms of dialectic and criticism unique to nonverbal domains, such as the tendency toward the dialogical 'undistorted communication' that may be immanent in improvisatory instrumental work (Begbie, 'Theology and the Arts', p.694). It bears asking whether the modern tradition of critical thought has been too narrowly restricted to the realm of the verbal, and whether Viladesau and Ricoeur overclaim for the precision of the word. There is a need for research on quasi-metaphysical operations in the domains of music and the body;

(3) I take the need for critical and publicly accessible language for theology to be the greatest challenge to the epistemologically leveling prospects of my proposal. At the same time, proficiency in nonverbal knowing, such as the capacity for perfect pitch, may be more widespread than is recognized in the general population. Such proficiency may be a cognitive potential in our students to a greater extent than we typically assume. We lack critical pedagogical means to inquire whether the dominant domains of theological knowledge merely mirror (while developing and intensifying) the dominant knowledge domains in the larger culture in which theology takes place;

(4) work on the three questions above has implications for the training of theologians. Certainly, academic fragmentation and intratheological balkanization have not provided conditions favorable to the present proposal. The lack of intimate work between contemporary liturgical and systematic theologians is just one example of a hindrance in this regard. A much greater fluidity among the modern divisions of theology would be necessitated by my approach.

In sum, the dialectic expressed in this note suggests that the present proposal needs further exploration as a new question. What seems to be needed is much more time to allow nondominant domains of knowledge an extended opportunity to make real contributions to theology. Some sort of 'affirmative action' for these heretofore nondominant domains may be programmatically required in order to give them a fair chance at proving their truth-bearing possibilities. Only then can the many quandaries raised in this note be adequately answered.

73   Gardner, *Frames*, p.353.
74   Gardner and Walters, 'A Rounded Version', p.14.
75   Viladesau, *Theological Aesthetics*, p.20.
76   David Shutkin, 'The Deployment of Information Technology', in *Foucault's Challenge: Discourse, Knowledge and Power in Education*, Thomas S. Popkewitz and Marie Brennan (eds), (New York: Teachers College Press, 1998, p.207).
77   Aspan and Hawkins, 'After the Facts', p.134, referencing Cleo Cherryholmes, *Power and Criticism: Poststructural Investigations in Education* (New York: Teachers College Press, 1988, p.171).
78   Gardner, *Frames*, p.365.
79   Foucault, 'Two Lectures', in *Power/Knowledge: Selected Interviews and Other Writings 1972–1977*, ed. Colin Gordon, tr. Alessandro Fontana and Pasquale Pasquino (New York: Pantheon, 1980, first published 1977, p.81).
80   Gardner, *Frames*, pp.208–9, quoting Frederic Bartlett, *Thinking* (New York: Basic Books, 1958, p.14).
81   It is worth noting the way in which critical pedagogies and critical forms of religious education, that rightly prize critical reception of knowledge, may unwittingly reinscribe the authority of logical-mathematical and/or verbal domains of theological knowledge, insofar as those may be the domains most appropriate for such critical pedagogies. *Other domains may not conform neatly to such a critical epistemological model.* For example, Gardner argues that bodily–kinesthetic intelligence is developed through practices of mimicking and imitation, which may imply that 'imitative teaching and learning may be the most appropriate way to impart skill in this domain'. The problem for some critical pedagogies is that 'the ability to mimic, to imitate faithfully, is often considered a kind of arrogance or a failure to understand, rather than the exercise of another form of cognition which can be highly adaptive' (see *Frames*, pp.228–9, taking cues from John Martin's *Introduction to the Dance*, New York: Dance Horizons, 1965). Overall, Gardner and Walters provide a helpful warning:

> The kind of thinking required to analyze a fugue is simply different from that involved in observing and categorizing different animal species, or scrutinizing a poem, or debugging a program, or choreographing and analyzing a new dance. There is little reason to think that training of critical thinking in one of these domains provides significant 'savings' when one enters another domain … [*Each form*] *of critical thinking must be practiced explicitly in every domain where it might be appropriate.* ('Questions and Answers', p.44)

This signal insight needs much more development if the project I am describing here is to have merit.
82   Foucault, in Miller, *Passion*, p.79.

Chapter 10

The *More* Which Exceeds Us:
Foucault, Roman Catholicism and
Inter-faith Dialogue

Henrique Pinto

NEITHER GOD NOR MAN BUT THE *MORE*

One of the great insights of Foucault's work was the realization that human consciousness was not Husserl's *raw material*[1] and that scientific discourses were not *ousiodic* unities.[2] On this discovery, Foucault rejected those aspects of the Enlightenment project that made 'human reason a final authority and effective agent of change'.[3] He also turned away from the 'traditional goal of ultimate, fundamental truth',[4] precisely because 'truth and its original reign' lay at a place of inevitable 'countless lost events, without a landmark or a point of reference'.[5] The postulation of a *centre*, of a truth that 'remains always the same',[6] condemned one's thinking to a self-enclosed, sterile, hermeneutical practice of the same, and assimilated, absorbed and reduced otherness 'to a mere instantiation of one's categories'.[7] In looking beyond a *totalizing historical dialectic*, so as 'to dispense with "things"'[8] and liberate silenced and subjugated *differences*, Foucault restored us 'to a consciousness of the systems of knowledge and power'.[9] In such a place, the essence of God and man were not to be found, and there was no *centre* from which to comprehend the world.

Instead of developing a fixed point within knowledge to comprehend the world, what Foucault offered, in his 1969 work *The Archaeology of Knowledge,* was an appreciation of the *more*. The *more* renders discursive practices 'irreducible to language (*langue*) and to speech', it opposes unitary metaphysical visions and the suppression of otherness, and it is, according to Foucault, that which 'we must reveal and describe'.[10] It is not a some*thing* beyond or before history, but a 'thought that is rightfully Being and Speech, in other words, Discourse, even if it is the silence beyond all language and the nothingness beyond all being'.[11] The *more* resides at the heart of a 'deep contingency', in a 'lack of necessity in things', and in a 'background of emptiness'[12] – a space created precisely by the death of both God and man. This means that Foucault's *dismantling of the subject of knowledge* is not, in any way, the restoration and strengthening of the credentials of 'models of religious transcendence'.[13] The rumbling silence and nothingness of the *more*, is not, in Foucault's thought, a 'restored transcendence nor a way that has been reopened in the direction of an inaccessible origin'.[14] Rather, it is the *finite infinity of discourse*, the *alterity* inhabiting and overflowing every arrest of itself.[15] The philosophical mechanics of Christianity in the west sacrificed such an understanding, in order to comply with the demands of a detached reason, and to deal with rival religious traditions.[16] For the *other*, to modern thought, was not only a 'disturbance', an 'abnormality' and a 'cry',[17] it was also a theological embarrassment, which disturbed and haunted Christianity. It was a provocation, therefore, which the Roman Catholic Church (hereafter RCC) always tried to quell, normalize and silence, in all its attempts to unify and totalize a 'history adrift in an oceanic void'.[18]

What I wish to show in this essay, considered from the perspective of Foucaut's critique of Christianity, is that by 'reclaiming the Other, the excluded or denied aspects of Western thought',[19] the *more*, in Foucault's 'history of truth',[20] delegitimates the RCC's totalizing thinking. I intend also to point out that, in Foucault's return to history, to the agonistic constitution of reality, the *more* provokes not a negation but a new understanding of religion, demanding a new exercise of religious authority and dialogue. This means that in Foucault's account of the historical and social field as a 'multiplicity of force-relations',[21] the *more* not only takes religions out of their 'privileged realm' into the 'body politic' and 'heart of culture',[22] it also legitimates the existence of all religious traditions as a 'political force'.[23] While making a distinct contribution to the discussion on inter-faith dialogue ('the chief religious arena of debate, in the twenty-first century'),[24] this essay also seeks to move towards a non-unitary theology of religious pluralism and an open-textured process of self-transformation.[25] This work is a transgression of the limits of Christian and scientific humanism, or an askesis of genuine becoming beyond good and evil. It constitutes an ethical sensibility to the other, in which differences, in agonistic dialogue, are not for elimination but for self-transformation. The absence of a fundamental meaning is not a denial of meaning as such, but a negation of the 'limit of the Limitless'.[26] This means that the *lieu vide* is now the 'space in which it is once more possible to think'[27] the *more* exceeding us, as gratuity and nothingness.

ROMAN CATHOLICISM AND THE IDEOLOGICAL WORK OF COMPASSION

Embedded in a belief in an 'ousiodic structure',[28] the RCC assumes that there is an Ultimate Real or Truth of existence binding everyone, a truth linked to a univocal conception of language, capable of expressing truth in absolute terms. It believes in a reason enlightened by truth in advance and raised above all its prejudices and limitations.[29] It assumes that, 'once recognized as truth', it must be also 'acknowledged as true in an enduringly valid sense'.[30] Being *Christ-centred* (that is, a society in which 'Christ is both the (objective) truth, and the (subjective) way' to truth itself)[31] entails fundamentally the orientation of all its dialogue partners towards the 'depth of its *a priori* Christological difference'.[32] Dialogue implies a return to the 'foundational sources of church teaching' (that is, to 'Scripture and tradition'), in which Jesus 'must always be the measure and not what is measured', and the church's tradition a much more accountable interpretation of the truth, than any other of its subjective representations.[33] Likewise, in the encounter with other faiths, 'two truths' must always be kept together, against 'the relativist dissolution of Christology' and 'ecclesiology', namely, 'salvation in Christ for all mankind and the necessity of the Church for this salvation'.[34] The recognition and appreciation of the good in every religion has certainly urged the RCC, since the council of Trent, to abandon the exclusivism entailed in the dogmatic axiom '*Extra ecclesiam nulla salus*'.[35] The insistence, however, that religions, apart from Christianity, are not divinely inspired, that the 'elements of goodness and grace which they contain' cannot be understood except in relation to the mystery of Christ, and that only the church is the 'universal sacrament of salvation', dissolves other traditions into a 'single divine economy'.[36] It reaffirms the illegitimacy of all non-Christian religions as paths in their own right to salvation and the role they are to play as *praeparatio evangelica*.[37] But such a position denies today's claim that 'meaning has no resting place'.[38] It rejects pluralism as a 'basic law of religious life', in which 'religion thrives'.[39] It leaves no room for Dupuis' claim, that 'to be religious' nowadays implies necessarily 'to be interreligious'.[40] Finally, it ignores O'Leary's remark, that 'one cannot erect a historical figure, carrying the mark of all the contingencies of human existence, and subject to the play of interpretations to which everything historical lends itself, into a transcendent signifier, pure sign of the ultimate transcendental signified, God'.[41] Indeed, for the RCC, the 'full force and necessity' of inter-faith dialogue does not derive from the fact that it wishes to be challenged, affected and possibly transformed by what the *other* has to say, but from the fact that 'salvation' and 'conversion to the Lord Jesus Christ' must be unconditionally proclaimed.[42]

Theologians from both Catholic and Protestant circles, unhappy with the church's Christocentric and ecclesiocentric approach to other religions, sought to acknowledge, in different ways, how non-Christian religions are independent paths of salvation.[43] Bound, however, to a unifying form of thinking and acting, most of these paradigms, such as Hick's theocentrism, Lindbeck's linguistic culturalism, Tracy's prophetic mysticism, O'Leary's perspectivism, Knitter's and Dupuis' regnocentrism, have ended up either by affirming the supremacy of Christianity or by pronouncing religions as exclusive cultures or languages. They assert a notion of God and the complementary uniqueness of all religions based on what we have in common. In this way, religious differences are constantly captured, dissolved, eliminated or declared incommensurable.

Against the assumption that 'all positions are equally valid',[44] the RCC emerges in this 21st century, determined to work for a more 'coherent account of the universal and transcendent value of revealed truth'. They aim to fight against relativism and nihilism by asserting Christianity's 'universal and epistemological value'.[45] If, as Bauman says, submission to a '*supreme* authority' to end 'all other authorities' remains always a possible option in this postmodern time, then no doubt the RCC does offer to those who find 'the burden of individual freedom excessive and unbearable' a sense of security, certainty and stability.[46] In reaffirming a God-given, eternal and absolute truth, the RCC seeks to free humanity from the anxiety of the here and now, as it intends also to establish the enduring validity of the Christian truth, beyond any historical and cultural context.[47] The question, however, with not only Christianity, but with most religious traditions, is that they easily overlook the fact that we exist 'inescapably in the midst of dialogue'.[48] This means that every time they attempt to resolve once and for all the mystery of existence, they actually deny the fact that we can only live by *being-with-in-dialogue*, as will be shown later. But then, having produced, against what 'Durkheim called a state of *anomie*', a certain stability and order, they have also created, as Berger rightly points out, a '"false consciousness" and a sense of "alienation"'.[49] Can religions ever claim to be 'the repository of Truth',[50] of the ultimate meaning of existence, and of the unerring practice that leads to it? And can their function be to protect us from the anxiety, the suffering and the agonism intrinsic to the practice of living? Is it not the imposition of one voice upon another (found in all religions to some degree) which is at the heart of the hatred, injustice and violence operating in the world?[51] Was it not this which in Italy gave 'preference to Catholic immigrants over Muslim ones',[52] which killed Christians in Southern Sudan, and dismissed 'Hinduism as a religion of superstition and crass idolatry'?[53] And was it not also this which, at a more internal level, kept women both in church and society 'under male domination',[54] which silenced Jacques Dupuis, condemned Paul Collins, killed Yitzak Rabin and murdered the Sikhs in the 'Holocaust of the Punjab'?[55]

SELF, DISCOURSE AND TRUTH

As history became, in the modern era, the 'unavoidable element of our thought', language could not *represent* and *exhaust* the meaning of the internal relation between elements.[56] Having become a historical reality itself, and an object of study, language also decentred the sovereign subject, and fractured incessantly 'the unity of its discourse', as it mirrored itself to infinity.[57] Historicity and finitude would in effect disrupt the Enlightenment's idea of Pure, Universal Reason. It is history – 'the confluence of encounters and chances',[58] and not an immutable necessity – which defines the birth of both the empirical and the subject of knowledge.[59]

In a 'decentring that leaves no privilege to any centre',[60] Foucault's genealogy brings to light that *man*, as both a subject and an object, is the product of endless battles and disagreements, of actions upon other actions.[61] It is what Foucault calls 'power-knowledge relations',[62] or 'strategic games between liberties',[63] which transform, strengthen or reverse one another. For Foucault, reason is not a substance – the 'illusion of the theologians'[64] – but a 'form'.[65] A form, 'not primarily or always identical to itself',[66] but a 'base of human practice and human history'.[67] Such a form cannot exist, or care for itself, except in an embodied, dialogical relation to others. Its proper mode of existing is to be decentred or to *be-with-in-dialogue*. This means that if the *self* cannot exist without the *other*, neither can *otherness* ever be excluded from the dialogical processes through which we exist. Foucault's announcement of the *death of man*, in the footsteps of Nietzsche's proclamation of the *death of God*, intends, in fact, as Visker observes, not to state man's disappearance, but simply to pull him 'out of the centre which it traditionally occupied'.[68] For, dependent on 'what can be said' (the network-conditions of its existence) and also traversed and troubled, in the constitution of itself as an identity, by the *unthought* or the negation of what it says,[69] the subject is 'neither fully constituting nor fully constituted'.[70] We are not masters in our own houses,[71] for meaning 'does not simply originate in us',[72] but in the pressures 'through which the movements of life and the processes of history interfere with one another', and which Foucault calls 'bio-history'.[73]

The idea of a 'state of communication', free of 'constraints or coercive effects', appears to be in effect, a mere utopia.[74] For, as Foucault remarks, a society 'without power relations' is not possible.[75] If on the one hand, subjects in conversation cannot unify and totalize meaning, on the other, they cannot evade its endless production. For what else should we do, having discovered that the self is 'not given to us', if not 'to create ourselves as a work of art',[76] by way of becoming, in answer to the *more*, 'what thought has yet to think?'[77] This 'exercise' of ourselves, which Foucault calls *'askesis'*, is not the elaboration of a programme for a new man or society.[78] It rather means to 'think differently, instead of legitimating what is already known';[79] it does not constitute a high point, or a point of completion, but always a local 'loss which makes for transformation',[80] beyond binaries.

Official discourses, found in science and theology, are 'practices that systematically form the objects of which they speak'.[81] They are not the manifestation of a secret voice running and animating them from within, neither are the objects of which they speak the 'visible and prolix objectivity' of pre-existing entities, 'held back by some obstacle at the first edges of light'.[82] Instead, discourses are the outcome of a 'complex group of relations', established between 'institutions, economic and social processes, behavioural patterns, systems of norms, techniques, types of classification, modes of characterization'.[83] This means that *truth* too, as Foucault asserts, is not 'the reward of free spirits, the child of protracted solitude, not the privilege of those who have succeeded in liberating themselves'.[84] Truth, in effect, is not 'outside power, or lacking in power'.[85] It is a 'thing of this world', produced 'only by virtue of multiple forms of constraint',[86] by those who, as Jantzen puts it, are 'able to assert the power to do so'.[87] Hence, it does not refer to a 'disembodied discourse', to 'a voice as silent as a breath, a writing that is only the void left by its own trace',[88] waiting to be captured in the shadows, through a hermeneutical search for depth. It is rather a *practice* never localized in an 'agency' or 'prime mover' (hence in nobody's hands), which articulates *body* and *history*, in the search for meaning.[89] Because 'the course of history', as Veyne says, 'does not include eternal problems, problems of essences or of dialectics', then it cannot but offer 'valorizations that differ from one culture to another and even from one individual to another, valorizations that, as Foucault was fond of saying, are neither true nor false: they are'.[90] They are what people value as most appropriate and worth living, in the resolution of local problems, and in the government of themselves. They are specific strategies that can never claim universality, precisely because they are rooted, not 'in the silent depths of a choice that is both preliminary and fundamental', but in the interplay of historical and contingent power forces.[91] In the historical analysis of the statements of a discourse, one does not 'question things said as to what they are hiding, what they were "really" saying, in spite of themselves, the unspoken element that they contain, the proliferation of thoughts, images, or fantasies that inhabit them', since 'there is not a profusion of things half said, sentences left unfinished, thoughts half expressed, an endless monologue of which only a few fragments emerge'.[92] Instead, 'it questions them as to their mode of existence, what it means to them to have come into existence, to have left traces, and perhaps to remain there, awaiting the moment when they might be of use once more; what it means to them to have appeared when they and where they did – they and no others'.[93]

To sum up, we could say that if the historicity and finitude of existence reveal, on the one hand, that things have 'no essence or that their essence was fabricated in a piecemeal fashion from alien forms',[94] on the other hand, they disclose that things are always open, that is, never finally delimited. This means that, as they were made, they can also be unmade, and thought differently. For this reason, Foucault's denaturalization of the present, which was to become 'one of the sharpest critiques of Western thought',[95] is not merely 'an abandonment of the history of ideas',[96] of all its unifying and totalizing projects. Having unveiled 'the radical groundlessness of the world', the historicity and contingency of all its constructs, 'both social and epistemic',[97] Foucault's work is 'an attempt to practise'[98] a new way of thinking and writing history. The substitution of a *philosophy of relation* for a philosophy of the subject and object demands, in fact, that, in the fight against local evils, we 'think problematically rather than question and answer dialectically'.[99] If within dialectical and totalizing forms of thought otherness was to be always recaptured and returned to the knowing subject, in Foucault's *acategorical* or *decentred* form of thinking, neither thought nor unthought are to be excluded, dissolved or eliminated. For *otherness* is the unreason of reason, the 'tragic', the 'radical breach or split within human being', which, in Caputo's terms, 'makes it impossible for reason to constitute itself as an identity'.[100] Because 'reason is always unreason', and because 'the truth of man is this untruth',[101] each then is to constitute, affect, resist and transform the other by *being-with* in an open-ended dialogue.

Obviously, something must be said. Indeed, the 'best', as Derrida would say. Yet it must be 'the best as example'.[102] This means that, as a system of constraints, the 'best' has always to leave individuals the liberty to resist and transform themselves.[103] If to be genuinely the best, a form of government has to be, on the one hand, the outcome of a 'permanent critique of ourselves', on the other, it has also to contain the means to resist and transform itself, in a never-ending dialogue with the *other*.[104]

FOUCAULT'S THEOLOGY OF LANGUAGE

With the claim, in Caputo's terms, that 'reason is itself only insofar as it is also unreason',[105] Foucault has not only contributed to the 'breakdown' and 'dispersion' of philosophical subjectivity, he has also dispersed theology. Foucault, as Carrette rightly notes, disperses theology 'into the space of the "Other", the forgotten dimensions of religious discourse',[106] and, in so doing, he has repositioned 'religious discourse in the spaces of the body and the political rather than in the transcendent hierarchies of Dionysius'.[107] He does not take religious experience back into that 'pneumatic immediacy' in which, according to O'Leary, 'religious traditions draw nearest to each other'.[108] Instead, he situates 'this experience in the politics and strategic relations of human struggles',[109] thus lending support to Katz's view (against Forman's notion of pure consciousness), that '[t]here are No pure (i.e., unmediated) experiences'.[110]

Born, therefore, against the background not of silence but of discursive practices, language does not take us into the essence of things, but into the materiality and messiness of history, in which relations, though not 'hidden', are not 'visible' either.[111] For as a 'ceaseless activity – an *energeïa*', language never stops talking.[112] As Foucault says, 'language always seems to be inhabited by the other, the elsewhere, the distant; it is hollowed by absence'.[113] Hence, where it 'pours and loses itself',[114] it multiplies and repeats itself to infinity, in an untamed and enigmatic exteriority. '*Words* are deliberately absent as *things* themselves',[115] where *no-thing* exists, 'since in history,' as Veyne points out, 'everything depends on everything else,'[116] although, 'marked by the sacred', this void 'opens the space where the divine functions'. As Foucault states:

> it should not be understood as the promised return to a homeland or the recovery of an original soil that produced and will naturally resolve every opposition. In introducing the experience of the divine at the centre of thought, philosophy has been well aware since Nietzsche (or it should very well know) that it questions an origin without positivity and an opening indifferent to the patience of the negative. No form of dialectical movement, no analysis of constitutions and of their transcendental ground can serve as support for thinking about such an experience or even as access to this experience.[117]

As that which renders reality irreducible to language, this rumbling emptiness is not a 'region beyond knowledge' or 'something prior to the sentences we speak', but the space, as we could say in a theological appropriation of Foucault's thought, of the human/divine relation in western history.[118] It is the place where we have stopped believing in grammar, as ceaselessly fomenting the metaphysical God in the shadows of its laws.[119] This fact not only denies the RCC, and most religious groups, access to a deeper truth (since the scriptural texts are not vessels of a more precious truth hidden in them, as to require an exegete to bring it to light, through a rigorous process of interpretation), it also dislodges revelation from a 'privileged arena free from human prejudice and bias'.[120] It relocates revelation in 'the ambiguities of human living',[121] not 'in some binary incarnational theology' but in 'an embodied and lived reality'.[122] Here the divine is human, and the human divine, the spirit is body and body spirit, the kingdom is society and society kingdom. This means that theology, no longer in the hands of an inspired Kantian or Hegelian subject, is, as Carrette argues, a discourse about what individuals do with their sexed and gendered bodies, 'with whom and where they are doing it', and not about a cold, abstract and unworldly entity.[123] According to Carrette's understanding of practice as embodied belief, 'doctrines become disciplines of the body' and 'rituals and religious architecture are reconfigured as constraints and venerations of sexed-bodies in space and time'.[124] Quoting Hart, we could say then, that 'the God whom Nietzsche's madman declared dead' can only return 'as a fully incarnate divinity, a god of earth'.[125] This means that, 'no longer separable from the world, our souls are to be mixed with nature; while the notion of a divine spark in humankind is to be renounced as firmly as the human longing to return to God'.[126] For *what we are* (the actual form of the self, praised and admonished) and *what we are yet to become*, as a possibility (that which is worth becoming, the beautiful life) are not givens, but the historical outcome of an existence constantly trying to come to terms with the *more* which exceeds, disrupts and negates its embodiments.[127] Indeed, 'we finally realize,' as Hart says, that this thought of the outside, this unreason of reason, this untamed exteriority, this unconscious of knowledge, this transcendence, this *more*, which is 'neither transcendental nor anthropological',[128] 'is all about us, in simple things and ordinary acts. It is a truth which had long been in us, hidden by our longings for excarnation, which are at odds with human love and complicit with writing.'[129] Hence theology is not a discourse about a reality outside of us (the *ens causa sui* of metaphysics), but, according to Carrette, a statement 'about the politics of human living at the limits of knowing and at the limits of life itself'.[130]

Here then, unlike in Feuerbach, the human and the divine do not exclude each other.[131] Read in theological terms, we could say that, in Foucault, the human is divine and the divine human. Although (fused in the materiality of existence), one is inseparable from the other, the divine (the *neither this nor that* of existence) is distinct from the human (the *this and that* of existence), insofar as the latter's becoming divine is never exhaustive of the endless murmuring of the *more*.[132] This means that, insofar as this finite infinity of discourse 'effaces every determinate meaning and even the existence of the speaker', the *more* shows itself as though the 'always undone form of the outside'.[133] Yet this distinction does not create a dualism in the world, for the *more* (precisely because it 'never solidifies into a penetrable and immobile positivity') is 'neither truth nor time, neither eternity nor man', to which we could compare ourselves.[134] Instead, it is the experience of ourselves at the limits of living, a 'formless rumbling' held in 'silent suspense', whose power resides in dissimulation.[135] It is an event, therefore, which decentres us, while disclosing, as the *centre* of all that *there is*, the mystery, the gratuity and nothingness of existence, to which we have no access, and from which we cannot break free. For this is what 'makes us who we are', what 'resonates within us and for us', whenever the *other* passes by.[136]

In the projection of ourselves, and in addressing the problems of the *here* and *now*, life is summoned to become that which is *not yet*. We are not moving back, unlike in Pseudo-Dionysius, 'to the Unity of the One',[137] which, in Foucault's terms, has 'survived for a millennium or so in the various forms of negative theology'.[138] Instead, we are losing ourselves (a loss constantly subverting the union it seeks) in that to which we are attached, that is, the pure gratuity and nothingness of an undifferentiated plurality of interactive voices, from where not only us (the *same*) but they too (the *other*) – indeed, all reality – come to life.[139]

THE BEST AS EXAMPLE, THEOLOGY AND THE RELIGIOUS SELF

With the rejection of metaphysics, based precisely on the fact that there is no divine mind whose meaning must be interpreted,[140] Foucault's return to history takes religion, predominantly loaded with heavenly concerns and binary oppositions, back into the historical figures and practices associated with their emergence. Contrary, however, to what is often asserted about them in most religious traditions, in Foucault, these icons cannot be said to be the bearers of a universal and ultimate meaning, neither can they be raised against each other. Carrying the mark of the historicity and contingency of human existence, these embodied beliefs are always exceeded, in the discourses they speak, and in those which comment on them, by 'the existence of another language that also speaks', a language that 'strives, fails, and falls silent'.[141] Hence they are not coincident with the *more*, but historical coagulations of its rumbling absence – *forms, players in conflict* and not the means to its resolution.[142] Even though Jesus, Buddha, Muhammad, Confucius and others may be the 'best' embodied expressions of how we ought to *be-with-in-dialogue*, these historical images of the divine are not to be idolized, or imitated, since they are not the *acting*, nor the revelation of any thing existing before or beyond history.[143] Life, in effect, in relation to them, is not about finding the divine hidden in them and conforming to it. Instead, and precisely because they are the 'best as example', they are a *force* with whom we ought to be in conflict, in the never-ending constitution of ourselves, and making of society.

Obviously, this necessarily implies a return to their narratives: a return, however, not to the interpretation of their dogmatic and fixed meanings, but to the telling and retelling of the practices in which they first came to life, and of the styles of living through which, in conflict with them, peoples have managed, in the course of the years, not to solve the ambiguity, pain and uncertainty of existence, but to live meaningful lives. This means that theology is no longer a science which needs to postulate and interpret dogmatic formulations, as if understanding was a 'way leading from the outer word to its inner meaning and ultimately to the one eternal word of God'.[144] Instead, having given up the idea that there is an ultimate truth, the search for a deeper understanding of itself and the practice of one's conformity to it, theology is to account for the problematization of the forms of the divine to which individuals or populations have subjected themselves, in the shaping and ordering of the world.[145] But then, theology has also to unmask and denounce, whenever this appears to be the case, the ideological and idolatrous arrest of the *more* in them, so as to free not only the metaphorical from the univocal, but also the *not yet* from these and other historical embodiments of itself.[146] If, in Cupitt's words, a dogmatic theology 'seeks closure and enclosure', if it 'includes by excluding, encourages hostility and (to an astonishing degree) inhabits thought',[147] then a metaphorical one honours and worships the mystery of existence, through surrendering to the *more*. In this way, it encourages a critical thinking, and promotes a coexistence of differences mutually transforming one another.

Thus, as a critical and subversive language, theology is not a discourse on truth, on the '*adaequatio rei et intellectus*', but a discourse on the never-resolved letting be of the *more*. Hence what should characterize, and grant respectability to, the work of the theologian, is not the *obedience of faith*, nor the submission of will and intellect to a set of timeless truths, as these have been established by the religious authorities, but faithfulness to the *more*. It is a faithfulness given by means of a permanent critique of one's theological positions, in 'agonistic respect'[148] for the *other* of one's religion, and the *other* of other faiths. It is precisely the awareness, as I have pointed out before, that our discourses on the divine are historical and contingent, and so '*contestable* and *questionable*',[149] which demands that we not only get free of any atemporal order of things and fixed selves, but that we never give up dialogue with the *other* who, as a 'partner', has also the 'right to speak'.[150] Thus, if the theologian cannot absolutize, as in Milbank, the 'Christian *mythos*', and reduce the '*saeculum*' to a bastardized or a failed realization of itself,[151] he or she can in no way state, as in Cupitt, the irrationality of traditional beliefs, and create for themselves a 'universal human kind of religion', taking them, so Cupitt believes, to 'salvation' or 'blessedness'.[152] With the relocation of religious discourse 'in the very fabric of the "secular" – in the absence',[153] as Carrette has stated, faiths and identities do not need to search for the foundation of revealed truths, or the choice of what we think is good for us, but the *more* exceeding every local present, the edge, the abyss, from where we are to shape and transform our lives, endlessly.[154]

The decentring is not, unlike in the Christian renunciation of the self, a negation of our concrete embodied selves, but a denial of ourselves as the *centre of things*, hence, an affirmation of what we truly are: *infinite becoming*, calling for a never-ending experimentation and transformation of ourselves.[155] It is the *askesis* of the death of self, thus the constant acting on others, and ourselves, 'with as little domination as possible', which grants genuineness and value to our becoming divine.[156] For no genuine truth of the self, though being the truth of *no-thing* at all, is without the sacrifice of the totalitarian tendencies of the provisory practices of the self.[157]

THE DIALOGICAL PRACTICE OF BECOMING DIVINE

In a time when modern thought has been set at odds with the 'nonself-identity of human reality', the 'limited validity of analytic rationality' and the 'absence of any transcendental foothold in the cosmos',[158] it is 'human presumptuousness of the highest order', as Kaufman rightly observes, 'for any individuals or groups to make claims to special knowledge' on matters such as 'the ultimate meaning of human life'.[159] If what has characterized 'much traditional religious thinking and practice', until now, was the 'property-model of truth' and 'authoritarian relationships',[160] then, from now on, there can be no ultimate form of government, and every style of life must be the outcome of a dialogical interplay of bio-historical forces, freely affecting, resisting and transforming one another.

Back 'into history', into the 'immanent struggle of identity and subjectivity', the RCC has to understand that the *religious other* is not only the difference of itself, but a voice in its own right, with which it must be in a constant agonistic dialogue, if it wishes to be faithful to the divine, and live genuinely.[161] The challenge lies, precisely, in being dialogists and not polemicists, that is, in trying not to 'bring about the triumph of the just cause', which one has manifestly upheld from the beginning.[162] For this reason, dissent can only mean one's refusal of dialogue and not one's breaking with the truth. In the church, differences are not to conform to some official and indisputable teaching. Instead, they are to be acted upon, resisted, appropriated and transformed, through 'ceaseless struggles and confrontations'.[163] There is in fact no better *magisterium*, or better transforming fire, than the network of power-knowledge relations, in which all comes to life.

This means that, rather than spending time fighting error, and checking the orthodoxy of its members' views and practices, the RCC should always do its best to ensure that, in trying to address and solve local problems, people have the means to resist both their selves and the truth of the day. To come to a situation where the Christian narrative means infinitely more, the church's authority is not to be shaped by an 'internal Church ideology',[164] but by social and political issues, in which the laity is not simply acted on, but is also an actor. 'Conversion to the acceptance of a loss of power, to being stripped down and having less influence',[165] is, according to Gaillot, entirely necessary.

The question remains as to how this situation has to come about, especially when, at the beginning of a new millennium, the RCC insists on resolving the postmodern religious situation, the problems concerning its own exercise of power and its practice of dialogue, through a reconsecration of its own 'hierarchic–bureaucratic organizational structure' and 'inquisitorial authority'.[166] To those who, as *masters of truth*, have in the RCC the authority to 'judge, punish, forgive, console and reconcile',[167] Foucault has shown that neither centralization nor the dogmatization of religious narratives will sustain itself. It is only through participation, metaphoricity, and the practice of an embodied openness to the other, that we can be faithful and honour the finite infinity of the divine in history.[168] If this has to be said in relation to the church's dialogue with the *other of itself*, how much so in relation to the encounter between religions. For, no matter how meaningful and internally coherent, a religious tradition can exclude neither itself nor others from the encounter between faiths. No language, no context in fact, can serve as the ground on which to claim absolute exclusivity, because, as historical and finite realities, they also affect other languages and contexts.[169] This means that, if to be a Hindu in India, a Muslim in Indonesia, a Christian in Europe and a Buddhist in Tibet is not a necessity, then, *being-with-other-faiths* is an inevitable fact of our existence, besides being also, in the end, a tribute to the *neither this nor that* of the *more*.

Contrary to what is still very much the view today, inter-faith dialogue is not the space in which religions are to compare, or measure against one another, the accuracy of their truth-claims, for there is no substance, *no-thing* with which they can compare themselves.[170] Although they may agree on certain issues, and join forces in the combating of 'common' problems, the scope of religions in dialogue is not the overcoming, but the telling and sharing, of differences and experiences. The goal is not to find more inclusive and universal ideas of the divine, for the *more* is not the total sum of all religions. The goal is rather to celebrate who they are and become who they are not yet, by mutually affecting, resisting and transforming each other, in faithfulness to the *more*. In such an affirmation and transgression of limits, inter-faith dialogue entails the worshipful surrender of all religions to the *more*. The *more* engulfs and constitutes existence as the mystery of *no-thing* at all, wishing nothing more for itself than to become that desert of non self-subsistent relations, so as to listen to its murmuring voice, and be filled by it. As a service to the mystery of existence, inter-faith dialogue is then, in the end, a safeguard and affirmation of individual freedom, against all sorts of domination and manipulation.

THE THEOLOGICAL DISTINCTIVENESS OF FOUCAULT'S THOUGHT

'Foucault's work has no vision of a religious faith.'[171] He does not sustain, as Carrette rightly observes, 'a traditional theological worldview'.[172] Yet, Foucault's *déprise de soi*, or Foucault's refusal to fill the space left empty by the death of God and man, is one of the most remarkable and fascinating aspects of his *rapport à soi*. For in his seeking to 'free the history of thought from its subjection to transcendence',[173] neither God nor man became the centre of his thought, but '*l'espace d'une extériorité sauvage*',[174] where existence is denied 'the eternal and visible body of truth'.[175] Although the absence of an 'alternative',[176] of a 'theory as the final refuge of resistance',[177] was to become for the foundationalists synonymous with total relativism and nihilism, the truth is that Foucault's refusal 'to convert our finitude into the basis for new certainties' has not left us with a 'deficiency' or a 'lacuna', neither has it thrown existence into the total fragmentation and dispersion of incommensurable languages and cultures.[178] Instead, it 'offers our skeptical age the hope that, even without the Truth, we may still be free',[179] as Gutting rightly remarks.

Having exposed the holders of an ideological hope to the 'contingent mysteries of themselves and others',[180] freedom for Foucault would never be the transparency of reason in one's search for foundations, nor the reward of one's total submission to an authority to end all other authorities, but the mastery of one's self, by means of an open-ended dialogue with the other.[181] It is this openness to the *more* in the other which takes us beyond relativism and reveals, in the end, that nihilism can never be posed as a problem. For in a local struggle for human liberation, through a mutually transforming dialogue, truth can, in Foucault, be more than power games, and so be a genuine and meaningful valorization.[182] Even though, in faithfulness to the finite infinity of which man is 'both the negation and the herald', Foucault could in no way suggest an ideal of the human/divine relation, he certainly proved that it is possible to conceive of a liberating critique of finitude, in which the here and now of ourselves 'is not an end, but that curve and knot of time in which the end is beginning'.[183]

For this reason, 'Foucault's work,' as Carrette points out, 'provides us with a critical apparatus in which to challenge the epistemological assumptions of religious and theological thinking. He provides us with new ways to reconceptualise and "think differently" about religion.' Above all, however, 'he provides us with ways to allow "difference" and the "Other" a voice'.[184] Unlike the unifying and totalizing epistemology of the RCC, which demands of its *other* faithful adherence to the fundamental teachings of the church's *magisterium*, and reads other faiths as a *praeparatio evangelica*, the distinctiveness of Foucault's relocation of religion lies precisely in the fact that it brings back to flesh the divine. In reinstating its finite, unlimited and irreducible nature, Foucault's work not only frees the *more* from all fixed and reified conceptualizations of itself, it also creates the space where human existence is no longer coerced to repeat itself in subordination to a perennial *verbum externum*.

Foucault is left free to explore ad infinitum other possibilities of being-with, through openness to other styles of living. If the magnitude of Foucault's death of man is to open decentred venues of negotiation and mutual transformation, then it surely functions as a subversive critique of the way we open ourselves to what the *other* has to say. Foucault's death of man tells every religion that we can only be sure of the genuine quality of our openness to the *other* when the agonistic encounter with difference has expelled us from our rest, and has not left us the same.[185] And this is why 'religion after Foucault can never be the same'.[186] The task ahead is to be open 'to widening horizons and possibilities of becoming divine',[187] without a fixed objective or an immutable postulate. The task is to be faithful to the *more* and to follow, with 'patient labor', the theological practice of 'giving form to our impatience for liberty'.[188]

NOTES

1   See Foucault (1983), 'Structuralism and Post-structuralism', pp.441–3, reprinted in *Aesthetics: Method, and Epistemology, Essential Works of Foucault 1954–1984*, Volume Two, ed. James D. Faubion, tr. Jeremy Harding, Penguin Books, 2000, pp.433–58.
2   See Foucault (1969), *The Archaeology of Knowledge*, tr. A.M. Sheridan Smith, Routledge, 1997, p.49.
3   Keith Ward, 'The Decline and Fall of Reason: From Modernity to Postmodernity', p.27, in *Faith and Praxis in a Postmodern Age*, ed. Ursula King, Cassell, 1998, pp.15–27.
4   Gary Gutting, *Michel Foucault's Archaeology of Scientific Reason*, Cambridge University Press, 1989, p.xi.
5   Foucault (1971), 'Nietzsche, Genealogy, History', pp.80, 89, in *The Foucault Reader: An Introduction to Foucault's Thought*, ed. Paul Rabinow, tr. Donald F. Bouchard and Sherry Simon, Penguin Books, 1991, pp.76–100.
6   International Theological Commission, 'On the Interpretation of Dogmas', in *Origins: CNS Documentary Service,* 17 May 1990, 20(1), pp.1, 3–14.
7   Christopher Falzon, *Foucault and Social Dialogue: Beyond Fragmentation*, Routledge, 1998, p.18.
8   Foucault, *The Archaeology of Knowledge*, p.47.
9   James Bernauer, 'The Prisons of Man: An Introduction to Foucault's Negative Theology', p.378, in *International Philosophical Quarterly*, XXVII, no.4, Issue 108 (December 1987), pp.365–78. See Foucault (1975), *Discipline and Punish: The Birth of the Prison*, tr. Alan Sheridan, Penguin Books, 1991, pp.27–8. And in so doing, he construed philosophy not as an instrument for asserting objective and universal truths, but 'for realizing concrete and local objectives in the struggle for human liberation', entailing also 'the possibility of going beyond them [*de leur franchissement possible*]' (Gary Gutting, *Michel Foucault's Archaeology of Scientific Reason*, p.xi); Foucault (1983), 'What is Enlightenment?' p.319, reprinted in *Ethics: Subjectivity and Truth, Essential Works of Foucault 1954–1984*, Volume One, ed. Paul Rabinow, tr. Catherine Porter, Penguin Books, 2000, pp.303–19).
10 Foucault, *The Archaeology of Knowledge*, p.49. Although the *more* is not a central concept in the philosophy of Michel Foucault (in effect, it only gets some attention in *The Archaeology of Knowledge*), what it stands for, namely, what *there is yet to say* in every *said*, and what *there is yet for us to become*, as a possibility, is one of the most remarkable and important experiences in his thought. It is this experience, which, as a *thought of the outside*, continuously demands the *de-centring* or the *death* of both God and man, in the understanding of the world, and in the process of human becoming. As a concept, therefore, the *more* translates quite well Foucault's *finite infinity of discourse*, its material and concrete nature as well as its endless network of relations. For this reason, it is not a marginal but a central term in this essay.
11 Foucault (1966), 'The Thought of the Outside', reprinted in *Aesthetics: Method, and Epistemology*, tr. Brian Massumi, pp.147–69.
12 William Connolly, 'Beyond Good and Evil: The Ethical Sensibility of Michel Foucault', in *The Later Foucault*, ed. Jeremy Moss, Sage Publications, 1998, pp.108–28.
13 Jeremy Carrette, *Foucault and Religion: Spiritual Corporality and Political Spirituality*, Routledge, 2000, p.5.
14 Foucault, *The Archaeology of Knowledge*, p.113.
15 See ibid., pp.111, 113.
16 See Peter Henrici, 'Modernity and Christianity', in *Communio: International Catholic Review*, tr. Albert K. Wimmer, 17 (Summer 1990), 141–51.

17   John Caputo, 'On Not Knowing Who We Are: Madness, Hermeneutics, and the Night of
      Truth in Foucault', in *Foucault and the Critique of Institutions*, ed. John Caputo and
      Mark Yount, The Pennsylvania State University Press, 1993, pp.233–62.
18   Thomas R. Flynn, *Sartre, Foucault and Historical Reason: Toward an Existentialist
      Theory of History*, Volume One, The University of Chicago Press, 1997, p.263. See
      Henrique Pinto, *Foucault, Christianity and Interfaith Dialogue*, Routledge, 2003. For
      this reason, Foucault's critique of dialectical thought is also a critique, in the west, of the
      silencing, normalizing and controlling powers of Christianity, in the fight against
      heretics and dissenters, and 'in the demand for confession' (Jeremy Carrette, *Foucault
      and Religion*, p.4). The influence of Christianity in the west, the fact that often, in
      support of what was believed to be 'invincible in reason', Christianity constituted 'the
      concrete form of what cannot go mad', and the spreading of its pastoral power over the
      entire social body, all became so determinant, in the constitution of the western self, that
      Foucault's history of the present could not but be a 'philosophical critique of religious
      ontology', as Carrette points out (see Foucault (1961), *Madness and Civilization: A
      History of Insanity in the Age of Reason*, tr. Richard Howard, Routledge, 1997, p.244;
      Jeremy Carrette, *Foucault and Religion*, p.3).
19   Jeremy Carrette, *Foucault and Religion*, p.49; see also p.4.
20   Foucault (1984), *The Use of Pleasure: The History of Sexuality, Volume 2*, tr. Robert
      Hurley, Penguin Books, 1992, p.6. The 'history of truth' is not the history of 'what might
      be true in the fields of learning', Foucault says, 'but an analysis of the "games of truth",
      the games of truth and error through which being is historically constituted as
      experience; that is, as something that can and must be thought' (ibid. pp.6–7).
21   Foucault (1976), *The History of Sexuality, Volume 1: An Introduction*, tr. Robert Hurley,
      Penguin Books, 1990, p.92. See Christopher Falzon, *Foucault and Social Dialogue*,
      p.44.
22   Jeremy Carrette, *Foucault and Religion*, p.xi.
23   Foucault (1978), 'On Religion', in *Religion and Culture by Michel Foucault*, tr. Richard
      Townsend, ed. Jeremy R. Carrette, Manchester University Press, 1999, pp.106–9.
24   *The Tablet*, 9 September 2000, p.1179.
25   Here, unlike Schrag, I do not favour 'self-constancy' and 'existential continuity' in
      relation to a particular lifestyle, but to existence as *infinite becoming*. Consequently, the
      turning of one's religious self can never be towards an 'open-textured *process of
      unification*', as Schrag sustains, but towards an open-textured process of self-
      transformation (Calvin O. Schrag, *The Self After Postmodernity*, Yale University Press,
      1997, pp.65, 63, 133; see also pp.42–75).
26   Foucault (1963), 'A Preface to Transgression', reprinted in *Aesthetics: Method, and
      Epistemology*, tr. Donald F. Bouchard and Sherry Simon, pp.69–87.
27   Foucault (1966), *The Order of Things: An Archaeology of the Human Sciences*, tr. Alan
      Sheridan, Routledge, 1994, p.342; see (1976), 'Two Lectures', in *Power/Knowledge:
      Selected Interviews and Other Writings (1972–1977)*, ed. Colin Gordon, tr. Kate Soper,
      New York: Pantheon Books, 1980, pp.78–108.
28   John McCumber, *Philosophy and Freedom: Derrida, Rorty, Habermas, Foucault*,
      Indiana University Press, 2000, p.9. See International Theological Commission, 'On the
      Interpretation of Dogmas', in *Origins: CNS Documentary Service*, 17 May 1990, 20(1),
      pp.1, 3–4.
29   See Walter Kasper, 'Postmodern Dogmatics: Toward a Renewed Discussion of
      Foundations in North America', in *Communio: International Catholic Review*, tr. D.T.
      Asselin and Michael Waldstein, 17 (Summer, 1990), pp.181–91.
30   International Theological Commission, 'On the Interpretation of Dogmas', p.4, §4.
31   David Schindler, 'On the Catholic Common Ground Project: The Christological
      Foundations of Dialogue', in *Catholic International* 8(8), August 1997, pp.360–66.

32 Ibid., pp.362–3, §4.
33 Joseph Bernardin, 'Questions and Answers: The Common Ground Project', in *Origins: CNS Documentary Service*, 29 August 1996, 26(11), pp.204–6. According to Ratzinger, 'the faith, together with its praxis, either comes to us from the Lord through his church and the sacramental ministry, or it does not exist in absolute' (Joseph Ratzinger, 'Relativism: The Central Problem for Faith Today', in *Origins: CNS Documentary Service*, 31 October 1996, 26(20), pp.309, 311–17). Because Roman Catholicism is 'founded on divine revelation', the church, as Dulles asserts, has a 'public faith that is not subject to debate' (in Gary Culpepper, 'Dialogue Within the Church', in *Communio: International Catholic Review*, 24 (Summer 1997), pp.339–46). Which means, 'it is divine and not merely human authority that establishes the unity and catholicity of the Church in situations of conflict and division', as Culpepper explains (ibid., p.346). This is why, for cardinal Law, 'dissent from revealed truth or the authoritative teaching of the church cannot be "dialogued' away".' For as he says, 'truth and dissent from truth are not equal partners in ecclesial dialogue'. So, 'dialogue as a pastoral effort to assist in a fuller appropriation of the truth is laudable. Dialogue as a way to mediate between the truth and dissent is mutual deception' (Bernard Law, 'Response to "Called to Be Catholic"', in *Origins: CNS Documentary Service*, 29 August 1996, 26(11), pp.170–71). For Law, 'dissent either yields to assent or the conflict remains irresolvable' (ibid., p.171). According to Cardinal Bernardin, however, the 'call to dialogue within the church no more legitimates dissent than does dialogue with the other faith traditions' (Joseph Bernardin, 'Questions and Answers', p.205). On the church's monarchic exercise of power, see Jacques Gaillot, 'The New Europe: A Challenge for the Churches', in *Concilium (1992/2), The New Europe: A Challenge for Christians*, tr. John Bowden, ed. Norbert Greinacher and Norbert Mette, London: SCM Press, 1992, pp.87–95; Paul Collins, *Papal Power: A Proposal for Change in Catholicism's Third Millennium*, Fount, 1997.
34 Congregation for the Doctrine of the Faith, *Dominus Iesus*, Vatican Press, 6 August 2000, §20; Joseph Ratzinger, 'Relativism', p.312.
35 Except for the more positive approach to other religions by some of the early apologists of the second and early third century AD, the postulate 'outside the church no salvation' had been for centuries, as Dupuis points out, 'the symbol of the church's negative stand on the possibility of salvation for members of other religions' (Jacques Dupuis, *Toward a Christian Theology of Religious Pluralism*, Orbis Books, 1997, p.21). See Francis Clark, *Godfaring: On Reason, Faith and Sacred Being* (London: St. Pauls, 2000, pp.65–9).
36 Congregation for the Doctrine of the Faith, *Dominus Iesus*, §8, 12, 20; see also §21.
37 Ibid., p.21; see also pp.4, 22. See Jacques Dupuis, *Toward a Christian Theology of Religious Pluralism*, p.11.
38 Kenneth L. Schmitz, 'Postmodern or modern-plus', in *Communio: International Catholic Review*, 17 (Summer 1990), 152–66. See Congregation for the Doctrine of the Faith, *Dominus Iesus*, §15.
39 Joseph S. O'Leary, *Religious Pluralism and Christian Truth*, Edinburgh University Press, 1996, p.16; see also p.x.
40 Jacques Dupuis, *Toward a Christian Theology of Religious Pluralism*, p.11. See Congregation for the Doctrine of the Faith, *Dominus Iesus*, §22.
41 Joseph S. O'Leary, *Religious Pluralism and Christian Truth*, p.253.
42 Congregation for the Doctrine of the Faith, *Dominus Iesus*, §22.
43 See Paul Knitter, 'Catholic Theology of Religions at a Crossroads', in *Concilium – Christianity Among World Religions*, ed. Hans Küng and Jürgen Moltmann, Edinburgh: T. & T. Clark Ltd., 1986, pp.99–107.
44 See John Paul 11, *Fides et Ratio* (Encyclical Letter), Vatican Press, 14 September 1998, §5.

45   Ibid., §83, 94; see also §96.
46   Zygmunt Bauman, 'Postmodern Religion?', in *Religion, Modernity and Postmodernity*, ed. Paul Heelas with the assistance of David Martin and Paul Morris, Blackwell Publishers, 1998, pp.55–78. There are those who, in the words of Duquoc, look at the role played by the institutional church in relation to its members, as a work of compassion, for, as Duquoc tells, the church is what 'frees us from having to confront the void or the night, the suffering of profound desire, the intolerable pressure of a burning presence'. Because the mystical wandering is too hard to bear, 'the institution smoothes over the breaks', providing security and certainty (Christian Duquoc, 'Postscript: The Institution and Diversion', in *Concilium 1994/4 – Mysticism and the Institutional Crisis*, ed. Christian Duquoc and Gustavo Gutiérrez, tr. John Bowden, SCM Press Ltd., Orbis Books, Maryknoll and London, 1994, pp.101–6. On the church's role as *mater* et *mediatrix*, see Kenneth L. Schmitz, 'The Authority of Institutions: Meddling or Middling', in *Communio: International Catholic Review*, 12 (Spring 1985), pp.5–24. Bauman argues, however, that postmodern men and women need 'neither the carrot of heaven nor the stick of hell' to address, with serenity and confidence, the 'ontological insecurity', and the 'identity-focused uncertainty' of the present. What de-legitimates Bauman's view, however, that 'religious fundamentalism is a legitimate child of postmodernity', is precisely the understanding of ourselves as *being-with-in-dialogue*, as I explain later (See Zygmunt Bauman, 'Postmodern Religion?' pp.68, 74).
47   See Congregation for the Doctrine of the Faith, *Dominus Iesus*, §4; John Paul II, *Fides et Ratio*, §80–99.
48   Christopher Falzon, *Foucault and Social Dialogue*, p.4; see also pp.30–35.
49   In James Thrower, *Religion: The Classical Theories*, Edinburgh University Press, 1999, p.197.
50   Bruce B. Laurence, 'From Fundamentalism to Fundamentalisms: A Religious Ideology in Multiple Forms', in *Religion, Modernity and Postmodernity*, pp.88–101.
51   Levinas did show in fact, against *dialectical metaphysics*, that peace does not go hand in hand with totality, and violence does not stop with unity. Which is also to say that communion and peace do not necessarily mean the sharing of a human element common to all. For, 'to be in communion', as Schroeder comments on Levinas's thought, 'is not to be one in any transcendent or quasi-mystical sense, nor is it subjection to the greater will of the state'. Instead, 'it is the ability to accept the radical difference of the other and to coexist in spite of the infinite distance or separation that will always remain between the same and the other' (Brian Schroeder, *Altared Ground: Levinas, History and Violence*, Routledge, 1996, p.64). See E. Levinas (1971), *Totality and Infinity: An Essay on Exteriority*, tr. Alphonso Lingis, Pittsburgh: Duquesne University Press, 1979, p.18).
52   *The Tablet*, 23 September 2000, p.1247.
53   K.L. Seshagiri Rao, 'Conversion: A Hindu/Gandhi Perspective', in *Religious Conversion: Contemporary Practices and Controversies*, ed. Christopher Lamb and M. Darrol Bryant, London: Cassell, 1999, pp.136–50.
54   Rosemary Radford Ruether, 'Gender, Equity and Christianity: Premodern Roots, Modern and Postmodern Perspectives', in *Faith and Praxis in a Postmodern Age*, pp.60–74.
55   Bruce B. Laurence, 'From Fundamentalism to Fundamentalisms', p.97.
56   This was the loss of the old certainties and the breaking of knowledge's 'old kinship with *divinatio*' (Foucault, *The Order of Things*, pp.59, 219).
57   Foucault, 'A Preface to Transgression', p.83; see (1963), 'Language to Infinity', reprinted in *Aesthetics: Method, and Epistemology*, tr. Donald F. Bouchard and Sherry Simon, pp.89–101.
58   Foucault, 'Structuralism and Post-structuralism', p.450. See Christopher Falzon, *Foucault and Social Dialogue*, p.46.

59   See Foucault, *The Order of Things*, p.219; 'Structuralism and Post-structuralism', p.438.

60   Foucault, *The Archaeology of Knowledge*, p.205.

61   This subject and object is the 'empirico-transcendental doublet' of modernity (Foucault, *The Order of Things*, p.319).

62   Foucault, *Discipline and Punish*, p.27. In Patton's terms, one must understand Foucault's concept of power, first of all, 'in its etymological sense, as the capacity to become or to do certain things', and then, in the exercise of itself as an act of 'individual or collective human bodies' upon the actions of one another. So, while 'power over' is 'an inescapable feature of any social interaction', domination is an effect of relations of power, which emerges whenever 'the possibility of effective resistance' has been removed from the field of relations between subjects (Paul Patton, 'Foucault's Subject of Power', in *The Later Foucault*, pp.64–77).

63   Foucault, 'The Ethics of the Concern for Self as a Practice of Freedom'; see pp.291–2, 296–9, in *Ethics: Subjectivity and Truth*, tr. P. Aranov and D. McGrawth; *The History of Sexuality, Volume 1*, pp.92–6; 'Afterword: The Subject and Power', pp.216–26, in H. Dreyfus and P. Rabinow, *Michel Foucault: Beyond Structuralism and Hermeneutics*, University of Chicago Press, 1982, pp.208–26.

64   Foucault, *Discipline and Punish*, p.30.

65   Foucault, 'The Ethics of the Concern for Self as a Practice of Freedom', p.290. Already Nietzsche, before Foucault, could have not been more devastating, when, with regard to the idea of a pre-given autonomous subject, he says that not only 'there is no such *substractum*, there is no "being" behind doing, working, becoming', but that we are also only in action, since 'action', in Nietzsche's words, 'is everything' (F. Nietzsche, *The Genealogy of Morals: A Polemic,* ed. Oscar Levy and T.N. Foulis, tr. Horace B. Samuel, Edinburgh, 1910; see pp.43–4). And then, that 'all that we know about an act is never sufficient to accomplish it'. It is in fact 'universal folly and presumption', as he says, 'that knowledge exists concerning the essence of an action'(F. Nietzsche, *The Dawn of Day,* ed. Oscar Levy and T.N. Foulis, tr. J.M. Kennedy, Edinburgh, 1911; see pp.120–22). Thus, in rejecting the idea of an 'abstract', 'ahistorical', 'ghostly' and 'disembodied' self, Foucault, in Falzon's words, 'restores a human, concrete understanding of human beings as embodied, corporeal beings' (Christopher Falzon, *Foucault and Social Dialogue*, pp.43, 44).

66   Foucault, 'The Ethics of the Concern for Self as a Practice of Freedom'; see pp.289, 291–2.

67   Foucault, 'Structuralism and Post-structuralism', pp.443, 450.

68   Rudi Visker, *Truth and Singularity: Taking Foucault into Phenomenology*, Kluwer Academic Publishers, 1999, p.3. See Foucault, 'Structuralism and Post-structuralism', pp.448–9.

69   Foucault, *The Archaeology of Knowledge*, p.129; see 'The Thought of the Outside', pp.149–51.

70   Rudi Visker, *Truth and Singularity*, p.3. Foucault does not question the importance of critical reason in any epistemological endeavour, but the place generally given to the knowing subject, in the formulation of 'truth', and, for that matter, also the view which asserts that 'truth' is intimately linked to the *dialectical* exercise of reason. In the past, in the tradition of Hegel, Husserl and Heidegger, the adequation of *logos* to *eidos* might have served quite well the idea of truth understood as unconcealment, coming-to-presence or conceptual adequation. Nowadays, the plurality of meaning not only reveals the non-originarity of particular presence, but also the impossibility of an adequation of *logos* to the *real*. Thus, in the understanding of meaning, not only is the position of the knowing subject to be revised, but also the very function of the exercise of thought is to be considered anew (see Foucault, 1984, 'Polemics, Politics, and Problematizations', p.117, reprinted in *Ethics: Subjectivity and Truth*, tr. Lydia Davis, pp.111–19).

71   See Foucault, *The Order of Things*, p.323.

72   Rudi Visker, *Truth and Singularity*, p.4.

73   Foucault, *The History of Sexuality, Volume 1*, p.143.

74   Foucault, 'The Ethics of the Concern for Self as a Practice of Freedom', p.298.

75   Ibid.

76   Foucault, 'On the Genealogy of Ethics', p.262.

77   Foucault, *The Order of Things*, p.332.

78   Foucault, *The Use of Pleasure*, p.9; see Foucault, 'What is Enlightenment?', p.316.

79   Foucault, *The Use of Pleasure*, p.9.

80   Mark Vernon ' "I Am Not What I Am" – Foucault, Christian Asceticism and "Way Out"
     of Sexuality', in *Religion and Culture by Michel Foucault*, pp.199–209. About
     transformation as the goal of one's self-discipline, see Foucault (1982), 'Michel
     Foucault: An Interview by Stephen Riggins', reprinted in *Ethics: Subjectivity and Truth*,
     pp.121–33; (1978) 'How an "Experience Book" is Born', in *Remarks on Marx:
     Conversations with Duccio Trombadori*, tr. R. James Goldstein and James Cascaito,
     Semiotext(e), 1991, pp.25–42.

81   Foucault, *The Archaeology of Knowledge*, p.49.

82   Ibid., p.45.

83   Ibid.

84   Foucault (1976), 'Truth and Power', in *The Foucault Reader*, tr. Colin Gordon,
     pp.51–75.

85   Ibid.

86   Ibid., pp.72–3.

87   Grace M. Jantzen, *Becoming Divine: Towards a Feminist Philosophy of Religion*,
     Manchester University Press, 1998, p.192.

88   Foucault (1968), 'On the Archaeology of the Sciences: Response to the Epistemology
     Circle', reprinted in *Aesthetics: Method, and Epistemology*, pp.297–333.

89   Paul Veyne, 'Foucault Revolutionizes History', in *Foucault and His Interlocutors*,
     ed. and introduced by Arnold I. Davidson, tr. Catherine Porter, University of Chicago
     Press, 1997, pp.146–82. See Foucault, 'Two Lectures', p.98. Practices are, in effect, a
     relation of bodies imprinted by history (see Foucault, 'Nietzsche, Genealogy, History',
     p.83).

90   Paul Veyne, 'The Final Foucault and His Ethics', in *Foucault and His Interlocutors*, tr.
     Catherine Porter and Arnold I. Davidson, pp.225–33. See Foucault, 'Truth and Power',
     p.60.

91   Foucault, *The Archaeology of Knowledge*, p.69.

92   Ibid., pp.109, 112. The discovery of hidden 'exclusions, limits or gaps' must be
     analysed, in effect, not in relation to a '*lack*', but to the conditions of possibility of a
     statement and its object (ibid., p.110; see also p.45).

93   Foucault, *The Archaeology of Knowledge*, p.109.

94   Foucault, 'Nietzsche, Genealogy, History', p.78.

95   Jeremy Carrette, *Foucault and Religion*, p.7.

96   Foucault, *The Archaeology of Knowledge*, p.138.

97   John Caputo, 'On Not Knowing Who We Are', p.238.

98   Foucault, *The Archaeology of Knowledge*, p.138.

99   Foucault (1970), 'Theatrum Philosophicum', reprinted in *Aesthetics: Method, and
     Epistemology*, tr. Donald F. Bouchard and Sherry Simon, pp.343–68.

100 John Caputo, 'On Not Knowing Who We Are', p.239.

101 Ibid.

102 Jacques Derrida (1991), 'Post-Scriptum: Aporias, Ways and Voices', in *Derrida and
     Negative Theology*, ed. Harold Coward and Toby Foshay, tr. John P. Leavey, State
     University of New York Press, 1992, pp.283–323.

103 See Foucault (1982), 'Sexual Choice, Sexual Act', reprinted in *Ethics: Subjectivity and Truth*, tr. James O'Higgins, pp.141–56. Jacques Derrida, 'Cogito and the History of Madness', in Jacques Derrida, *Writing and Difference*, tr. Alan Bass, Routledge & Kegan Paul, 1981, pp.31–63. As Simons underlines, 'limits are historical and contingent rather than universal and necessary' (Jon Simons, *Foucault & the Political*, Routledge, p.17). Critique, therefore, as Foucault remarks, must not but 'separate out, from the contingency that has made us what we are, the possibility of no longer being, doing, or thinking what we are, do, or think' (Foucault, 'What is Enlightenment?', pp.315–16).

104 Foucault, 'What is Enlightenment?', p.313. And it is this *work of the self on the self*, what makes the *truth* that is born of its relations, so central to the constitution of the ethical subject (see Foucault (1984), *The Care of the Self: The History of Sexuality, Volume 3*, tr. Robert Hurley, Allen Lane Penguin Press, 1988, p.68).

105 John Caputo, 'On Not Knowing Who We Are', p.242.

106 Jeremy Carrette, *Foucault and Religion*, p.107.

107 Ibid., p.106; see 'Mystical Archaeology', in ibid. pp.85–108.

108 Joseph S. O'Leary, *Religious Pluralism and Christian Truth*, pp. 30–36.

109 Jeremy Carrette, *Foucault and Religion*, p.146.

110 Steven T. Katz, 'Language, Epistemology, and Mysticism', in *Mysticism and Philosophical Analysis*, ed. Steven T. Katz, London: Sheldon, 1978, pp.22–74; also in Robert K.C. Forman, 'Introduction: Mysticism, Constructivism, and Forgetting', in *The Problem of Pure Consciousness: Mysticism and Philosophy*, ed. Robert K.C. Forman, Oxford University Press, 1990, pp.3–49. Against 'the notion that there is an inner experience of God common to all human beings and all religions', Lindbeck asserts also that 'there can be no experiential core because, so the argument goes, the experiences that religions evoke and mould are as varied as the interpretative schemes they embody'. So 'it seems implausible to claim that religions are diverse objectifications of the same basic experience' (George Lindbeck, *The Nature of Doctrine: Religion and Theology in a Postliberal Age*, London: SPCK, 1984, pp.40, 41).

111 Foucault, *The Archaeology of Knowledge*, p.110.

112 Foucault, *The Order of Things*, p.290.

113 Foucault, *The Archaeology of Knowledge*, p.111. See Grace M. Jantzen, *Becoming Divine*, pp.186, 188.

114 Foucault, 'A Preface to Transgression', p.83.

115 Foucault, *The Archaeology of Knowledge*, p.48.

116 Paul Veyne, 'Foucault Revolutionizes History', p.170. Indeed, this is the space, as Foucault tells, 'in which no existence can take root'. Mallarmé had taught us, in effect, as Foucault underlines, that 'the word is the manifest nonexistence of what it designates' (Foucault, 'The Thought of the Outside', p.166).

117 Foucault, 'A Preface to Transgression', p.75.

118 To have a more general significance, the human/divine relation (still meaningful in the west) may need to be translated into the notions which speak, in other parts of the world, of the 'thrownness' of existence (existence ordered to the other), namely, of *what we are*, and of *what there is yet for us to become*, as a possibility.

119 Foucault, *The Order of Things*, p.298. Although the death of God is a rejection of the metaphysical postulation of the divine, as *divine simplicity*, in Foucault, as in Nietzsche too, this 'is not a statement of the non-existence of God but the "now constant space of our experience" where we face the limits of our existence', as Carrette observes (Jeremy Carrette, *Foucault and Religion*, p.82). See Foucault (1966), 'Philosophy and the Death of God', in *Religion and Culture by Michel Foucault*, tr. Elisabeth Ezra, pp.85–6.

120 Jeremy Carrette, *Foucault and Religion*, p.146.

121 Ibid.

122   Ibid., p.147. Foucault does not treat religion as a transcendent, privileged domain
      beyond culture, but as a force 'inescapably bound up with cultural practices ' (ibid.,
      p.145).
123   Ibid., pp.146–7.
124   Ibid., p.127.
125   Kevin Hart, 'The Impossible', in *Religion, Modernity and Postmodernity*, pp.314–31.
      See *Nietzsche and the Divine*, ed. John Lipitt and Jim Urpeth, Manchester: Clinamen
      Press, 2000; Tyler T. Roberts, *Contesting Spirit: Nietzsche, Affirmation, Religion*,
      Princeton University Press, 1998.
126   Kevin Hart, 'The Impossible', p.324.
127   In Foucault, human existence ordered to the other is a condition experienced in local
      struggles, in the acting of individuals or groups affecting, resisting and transforming
      each other. But, rather than implying, as in Blondel, a turn towards what is beyond
      ourselves, that is, the 'Unique Necessary Being', *potentiality-for-being* implies a turn
      towards the difference of ourselves (the *not yet*), precisely because it does not carry
      within itself an 'insufficiency', a lack, but the absence of an origin, of a reason to
      conform to (Charles Davis, *Religion and the Making of Society: Essays in Social
      Theology*, Cambridge University Press, 1994, p.8). See Maurice Blondel, *Action (1893):
      Essay on a Critique of Life and a Science of Practice*, tr. Oliva Blanchette, University of
      Notre Dame Press, 1984, pp.345–57; John Milbank, *Theology and Social Theory:
      Beyond Secular Reason*, Oxford: Basil Blackwell, 1990, p.216. So, if in ancient Greece
      the self, as Hadot observes, was to conform to nature or universal reason, then, in
      Foucault, the self has no universal *telos*, neither has it to conform, unlike in Christianity,
      to a revealed, atemporal truth. The beautiful, therefore, namely that which people, in
      their daily regional struggles and negotiations, value as worth becoming, is not in
      Foucault, unlike in Milbank, an 'ever greater depth of harmony', but a mode of
      existence, an art of living (Foucault's *déprise de soi*, and the *Parrhesia*), beyond what
      conventions have transcendentally naturalized as the *good life* and the *beauty* of it –
      hence a life beyond any name, any synthesis, any arrest of itself, which is to say, an
      endless becoming *neither this nor that* (John Milbank, 'Sublimity: The Modern
      Transcencent', in *Religion, Modernity and Postmodernity*, pp.258–84. See Pierre Hadot,
      'Reflections on the Notion of the "Cultivation of the Self"', in *Michel Foucault
      Philosopher*, tr. and ed. T.J. Armstrong, Routledge, 1992, pp.225–31; Barry Allen,
      'Foucault and Modern Political Philosophy', in *The Later Foucault*, pp.164–98; John
      Rajchman, *Truth and Eros: Foucault, Lacan and the Question of Ethics*, Routledge,
      1991, p.13).
128   Foucault, *The Archaeology of Knowledge*', p.113.
129   Kevin Hart, 'The Impossible', p.324.
130   Jeremy Carrette, *Foucault and Religion*, p.146.
131   See Denys Turner, 'Feuerbach, Marx and Reductivism', in *Language, Meaning and
      God*, ed. Brian Davies and Geoffrey Chapman, 1987, pp.92–103. Also in Foucault, *what
      bodies are yet to become* does not rest, as in Heidegger and Sartre, on a more authentic or
      essential form of the self (see Martin Heidegger, 1926, *Being and Time*, tr. John
      Macquarrie and Edward Robinson, Oxford: Basil Blackwell, 1967, p.224; Jean-Paul
      Sartre, 1943, *Being and Nothingness*, tr. Hazel E. Barnes, Routledge, 1993, p.32;
      Foucault, *The Order of Things*, p.327).
132   See Derrida's distinction between the 'infinite idea of justice' and 'law', in Grace M.
      Jantzen, *Power, Gender and Christian Mysticism*, Cambridge University Press, 1995,
      pp.351–3.
133   Foucault, 'The Thought of the Outside', p.168.
134   Ibid.

135   Ibid., pp.166, 167.
136   Rudi Visker, *Truth and Singularity*, p.376.
137   Jeremy R. Carrette, *Foucault and Religion*, p.97.
138   Foucault, 'The Thought of the Outside', p.150.
139   See John McCumber, *Philosophy and Freedom,* pp.151–2.
140   See Foucault, 'Nietzsche, Genealogy, History', p.86.
141   Foucault, 'A Preface to Transgression', p.79.
142   On the 'subject in battle' and 'law', see Duncan Ivison, 'The Disciplinary Moment:
      Foucault, Law and the Reinscription of Rights', in *The Later Foucault*, pp.129–48.
      Speaking of Jesus of Nazareth as a subject in conflict, and as a practice worth living, that
      which has always caught up the attention, as well as the veneration and trust of many
      generations, was the subversive character of his words and deeds, in defence of
      mistreated otherness, hence, in resistance to self-enclosed institutions, beliefs, customs
      and practices. As Aichele observes, Jesus, according to the synoptic gospels (especially
      the gospel of Mark), is a 'violent man', a man 'who contests violently with others
      (Pharisees and scribes, his own followers, the crowds, and perhaps even the Romans).
      Jesus fights with these others over his own role and identity, over the meaning of the
      scriptures, and also over the kingdom of God', forcing them, as Doran rightly says, 'to
      rethink their assumptions' (George Aichele, 'Jesus' Violence', in *Violence, Utopia and
      the Kingdom of God – Fantasy and Ideology in the Bible*, ed. George Aichele and Tina
      Pippin, Routledge, 1998, pp.72–91; Robert Doran, *Birth of a Worldview: Early
      Christianity in its Jewish and Pagan Context*, Rowman & Littlefield Publishers, 1999,
      p.3). Also for Sobrino, the 'most fundamental gesture' of Jesus was precisely that of
      'taking sides with human beings in a concrete situation where the existing politico-
      religious structure has dehumanized people' (Jon Sobrino, *Christology at the
      Crossroads: A Latin American Approach*, SCM Press Ltd., 1978, p.92). In resisting what
      Sobrino calls 'structural injustice', which 'has turned those with power into brutes,
      while alienating and oppressing everyone else', and in 'challenging the idolatrous use of
      power to oppress people and the idolatrous conception of God that justified such use',
      Jesus reveals that 'God's will is historical rather than eternal and universal' (ibid. pp.92,
      129, 214). And in so doing, he does not resolve the practice of human existence. Instead,
      'the whole context of the moral subject becomes very complex, going far beyond any
      straightforward search for what is obviously good and what is obviously evil' (ibid.
      p.129).
143   Also according to Girard, 'the teaching of Jesus and the Passion in the Gospels constitute
      the strict development of a paradoxical logic. Jesus wants nothing to do with all that
      makes someone divine in the eyes of men: the power to seduce or constrain, the ability to
      make oneself indispensable' (René Girard, 'The God of Victims', in *The Postmodern
      God: A Theological Reader*, ed. Graham Ward, tr. Yvonne Freccero, Blackwell
      Publishers, 1997, pp.105–15).
144   International Theological Commission, 'On the Interpretation of Dogmas', p.9/4.
145   See Bauman's new understanding of the sociology of religion, based, precisely, on
      Foucault's work, in Zygmunt Bauman, 'Postmodern Religion?', p. 7.
146   With the recapture of the body as the 'central site' of theological thinking, Foucault
      opened the way, not for 'models of religious transcendence', but for 'models of religious
      immanence' (Jeremy Carrette, *Foucault and Religion*, pp.5, 127). So, if up until now, as
      Cupitt observes, the history of the church has been the 'history of the clergy, and, with
      them, of the few other "ecclesiastical persons"'; if theology has always been 'the
      clerical ideology by means of which the professionals justify and seek to extend their
      power'; and if 'theologians are perceived on all sides as persons employed to work as
      spin-doctors in the service of the clerical power-structure', then, today's real challenge,

according to Gaillot, is that the church 'should become truly lay', and theology a critical description of its becoming divine (Don Cupitt, *The Revelation of Being*, SCM Press Ltd, 1998, p.91; also p.92; Jacques Gaillot, 'The New Europe', p.90).

147   Don Cupitt, 'Post-Christianity', in *Religion, Modernity and Postmodernity*, pp.218–32.
148   William Connolly, 'Beyond Good and Evil', p.122.
149   Ibid., p.123 (italic mine).
150   Foucault, 'Polemics, Politics and Problematizations', p.112.
151   John Milbank, *Theology and Social Theory*, pp. 9–26, 389–92; see also *The Word Made Strange: Theology, Language, Culture*, Blackwell Publishers, 1997, pp.123–68. Contrary to what Milbank asserts, the *saeculum* is not the result of a failure, namely that of the Christian interruption of history. Instead, it is the *alterity* which has always been 'out there', exceeding dogmatic identities, and which the church has always tried to lock up, dissolve or eliminate (see John Milbank, *Theology and Social Theory*, p.432).
152   Don Cupitt, *The Revelation of Being*, pp. 4,12,13; also *After God: The Future of Religion,* Weidenfeld & Nicolson, 1997, pp.xiv, 128.
153   Jeremy Carrette, *Foucault and Religion*, p.152.
154   The *more* is not only that which, in the arrest of every possible signification, gives every individual freedom a sense of purpose, and a concrete realization of itself, but also that which, in the dialogical encounter with other faiths, frees the practice of ourselves from the danger of falling into existential nausea, boredom and self-enclosure, to set it towards other equally charming and fulfilling experiences of ourselves.
155   See Teodros Kiros, *Self-construction and the Formation of Human Values: Truth, Language, and Desire*, Praeger, 2001.
156   Foucault, 'The Ethics of Concern for Self as a Practice of Freedom', p.298.
157   See James Miller, *The Passion of Michel Foucault*, HarperCollins Publishers, 1993, p.324.
158   Thomas R. Flynn, *Sartre, Foucault, and Historical Reason*, p.263.
159   Gordon Kaufman, *In Face of Mystery: A Constructive Theology*, Harvard University Press, 1993, p.65.
160   Ibid.
161   Jeremy Carrette, 'Prologue to a Confession of the Flesh', in *Religion and Culture by Michel Foucault*, pp.1–47.
162   Foucault, 'Polemics, Politics, and Problemizations', pp.381–3.
163   Foucault, *The History of Sexuality, Volume 1*, p.92.
164   Gene Burns, *The Frontiers of Catholicism: The Politics of Ideology in a Liberal World*, University of California Press, 1992, p.17.
165   Jacques Gaillot, 'The New Europe', p.90.
166   Hans Küng, *Theology for the Third Millennium: An Ecumenical View*, Harper Collins, 1991, p.10.
167   Foucault, *The History of Sexuality, Volume 1*, pp.61–2.
168   See Charles Davis, *Religion and the Making of Society*, p.122. Paul Collins, *Papal Power*, p.217.
169   See Sheila Greeve Davaney, 'Judging Theologies: Truth in a Historicist Perspective', in *Pragmatism, Neo-Pragmatism, and Religion: Conversations with Richard Rorty*, ed. Charley D. Hardwick and Donald A. Crosby, Peter Lang, 1997, pp.129–47.
170   See *Religion*, ed. Jacques Derrida and Gianni Vattimo, Polity Press, 1998.
171   James Bernauer, 'The Prisons of Man', p.379.
172   Jeremy Carrette, *Foucault and Religion*, p.xi.
173   Foucault, *The Archaeology of Knowledge*, p.203.
174   In James Miller, *The Passion of Michel Foucault*, p.30.
175   Foucault, 'The Thought of the Outside', p.167.

176   Foucault, 'On the Genealogy of Ethics', p.256.

177   Barry Smart, *Foucault, Marxism and Critique*, Routledge & Kegan Paul, 1983, p.136.

178   Foucault, *The Order of Things*, p.342. 'The vision of fragmentation', as well as the vision of total relativism and nihilism, 'far from representing a break from metaphysics', are, as Falzon correctly points out, 'a perpetuation of metaphysical thinking'. In effect, these visions reflect a 'nostalgia for vanished metaphysical unities' (Christopher Falzon, *Foucault and Social Dialogue*, p.18).

179   Gary Gutting, *Michel Foucault's Archaeology of Scientific Reason*, p.288.

180   James Bernauer, 'Cry of Spirit', in *Religion and Culture by Michel Foucault*, pp.xi–xvii.

181   It is 'this opening up to the other' which plays, in Kristeva's words, 'a decisive role in the evolution of species as well as in the maturing of each generation, or in every individual's particular history' (Julia Kristeva, *Tales of Love*, tr. Leon S. Roudiez, Columbia University Press, 1987, p.14).

182   See Foucault, 'The Ethics of the Concern for Self as a Practice of Freedom', p.296.

183   In David Macey, *The Lives of Michel Foucault*, Hutchinson, 1993, p.89.

184   Jeremy R. Carrette, 'Prologue to a Confession of the Flesh', p.9.

185   'Unlike the typical revolutionary,' as Gutting observes, Foucault 'does not see one all-pervading enemy, whose existence corrupts everything and whose elimination will solve all our problems. Rather, he thinks the liberation of human beings requires an unending series of local battles against an ever changing series of particular evils' (Gary Gutting, *Michel Foucault's Archaeology of Scientific Reason*, p.288).

186   Jeremy Carrette, *Foucault and Religion*, p.xi.

187   Grace M. Jantzen, *Becoming Divine*, p.18.

188   Foucault, 'What is Enlightenment?', p.319.

IV
FOUCAULT, THEOLOGY
AND SEXUALITY

Chapter 11

Beyond Theology and Sexuality: Foucault, the Self and the Que(e)rying of Monotheistic Truth

Jeremy Carrette

Where religions once demanded the sacrifice of bodies, knowledge now calls for experimentation on ourselves, calls us to the sacrifice of the subject of knowledge.

Michel Foucault (1971) 'Nietzsche, Genealogy, History'[1]

One of the central insights of Michel Foucault's work on religion was to establish a link between the emergence of the discourse of sexuality in the West and the history of Christian ideas and practice. Foucault recognized that in order to understand the 'cultural facts' account had to be taken of religious history (perhaps even questioning the whole distinction between religion and culture).[2] However, scholars both inside and outside the fields of religion and theology still appear to ignore the full impact of the interrelation between Christianity and sexuality. Scholars outside the fields of religion want, for example, to extend Foucault's work on sexuality in the development of queer theory without reference to religion or theology, and scholars of religion and theologians fail to appreciate fully how these developments of Foucault's work in queer theory may subsequently challenge religious thinking. Despite Foucault's work, those writing on either religion or sexuality seek to maintain an isolationist agenda. It seems that Foucault's archaeological and genea-logical interweaving of the discourses of religion and sexuality has opened a Pandora's box few wish to explore; it appears to threaten both those inside and outside religious worldviews. If Christianity is implicated in the discourse of sexuality, then the so-called 'secular' body can never be free of its religious boundaries and Christianity can never escape the sexual body. Perhaps, even more alarming for both conservatives and radicals, on either side of the divide, is the unsettling implication of fusing sexuality with theological concepts. Foucault had exposed the 'queer' world of Christianity and sex.

This chapter seeks to unravel the relationship between Christian theology and sexuality in Foucault's work by examining recent developments in queer theory, and to show that Foucault's critique of sexuality is simultaneously a critique of a certain type of theological thinking constructed on an essential model of the self. In effect, the chapter opens the space for a theology, not without self, but with multiple selves. It will be argued that Christianity and sexuality are anchored in the same religious symbolic of dualism and monotheism. This epistemological framework, however, is broken in queer theory, which results in, and indeed demands (and here my claims become stronger), the death of the imperialistic regime of theology.[3] The argument here is that the cultural mindset arising from Christian claims for a single (orthodox) truth about salvation anchors an ideological oppression of a single (heteronormative) sexuality. It is my claim that to liberate ourselves from sexuality is simultaneously to liberate ourselves from certain dominant forms of orthodoxy in the history of Western theology; that is, the proliferation of sexuality in our culture is coterminous with a hegemonic Christian discourse, which restricts the 'truth' of Christianity in a desire for certainty and power.

My argument will follow two main lines of enquiry: first, detailing Foucault's genealogical project and examining its final stages of creative analysis so often ignored in queer scholarship; and second, showing how Foucault's genealogy of the modern self reveals a problematic of self in queer studies which arises from the location of the theological truth of self in sex. My argument is that Christian theology supports the modern emergence of sexuality because it is grounded in a politics of unity and the obligation to confess the truth of sexual identity. Such a monotheistic grounding of self-identity and the demand to say what you are (a penitent and a homosexual) is unable to hold the discourse of 'ambiguity', 'desire' and a 'fragmented self' found in post-structuralist-inspired queer theory. To overcome the discourse of sexuality we need, as I have said, to overcome the symbolic foundations of Christian theology and the monotheistic politics of ourselves.

Monotheism in this chapter is seen as a symbolic system of thought which attempts to obliterate the possibility of difference and diversity. It anchors truth within a single point of reality rather than holding multiplicity within its sphere of lived experience. The struggle between orthodoxy (monotheism) and heterodoxy (polytheism) is the struggle for a purchase on the truth, as defined by the dominant social order. Theological orthodoxy and sexuality are dominant discourses that silence difference and conceal the implicit relationship between theological utterances and bodily acts. This domination is maintained by the symbolic system of monotheism, which secures a single theological truth and a dominant sexuality. This link between monotheism and sexuality was tentatively explored in Howard Eilberg-Schwartz's creative study of masculinity, *God's Phallus: and Other Problems for Men and Monotheism*. In this work Eilberg-Schwartz set up a series of imaginative readings of the Hebrew Bible and sought to show the relationship between monotheism, masculinity and homophobia. Taking his lead from Freud's *Moses and Monotheism*, he argues that 'there are reasons at the outset to assume that the classic treatment of monotheism serves very strong apologetic and theological interests'.[4] Irrespective of the hermeneutical validity of Eilberg-Schwartz's reading of the Biblical text, he recognizes a central link between sexuality and divinity that Foucault had already identified. While Foucault did not specifically explore the nature of monotheism, there are important issues related to the structure of monotheism and heteronormative social structures that are worth exploring in relation to queer theory. Indeed, Eilberg-Schwartz's appeal for a 'polymorphously perverse theology' is recognition that queer theory demands new conceptions of divinity. The reason for this is that the religious symbolic holds in place bodily practices. I want to explore such ideas through the work of Foucault and queer theory and examine one aspect of a cultural mindset that seeks 'closure' in terms of the body and the religious symbolic.[5] Moreover, I want to show how Foucault is able to illuminate the interdependence between the discourses of theology and sexuality. Such a move is to recognize that it is only by changing the Christian discourse about God that we can also change the discourse of our bodies. But before examining how Foucault's work challenges both sexuality and theology, as partners in the crime of essentialism and binary knowledge, I want to outline the nature of queer theory as an intellectual perspective.

QUEER PERSPECTIVES: A FUNCTIONAL VIEW

In her review of a series of books on lesbian sexuality and queer theory for the *Journal of Gay and Lesbian Studies*, Carolyn Dever suggests an 'either/and' scenario in regard to the emergence of queer theory inside gay and lesbian studies. She begins her review by stating: 'Either: queer theory is elitist, incomprehensible, narcissistic, tautological, hopeless as a political engine ...' (she goes on to list a whole series of negative possibilities). 'Or,' she states more positively, 'queer theory is the logical extension of a rigorous thirty-year feminist interrogation of the limits of language, identity politics, and social control. Its attack is levelled at the most fundamental premises of epistemology itself.'[6] She suggests that, if nothing else, queer theory is 'an overdetermined site of multiple, and multiply conflicting, desires'. However, what is striking about her critical review is the way she goes on to suggest, somewhat in passing, that this overdetermination 'suggests less about what queer theory *is* than about what it *does*'.[7] It is precisely this focus on the function of knowledge in a particular historical space that I want to pick up in relationship to the question of theology.

According to Dever, in the unclear horizon of what queer theory may turn out to be, it is necessary to explore what queer theory has done to the 'constitutive paradigms informing feminist and lesbian studies'.[8] Rather than asking the question of whether queer theory is an elitist academic discourse, or even whether, like the tension between feminist and gender theory, it distracts from the activist programme from where it emerged, we need to ask how it functions in the intellectual space. What, we may ask, is the intellectual task of queer theory? Like its sister concept, that declining amorphous idea, 'postmodernism', it may disappear as a temporary conceptual space on the journey to more refined analysis. As postmodernism 'fades' into a more specific appreciation of the critical insights of particular post-structuralist thinkers, we are able to see the more nuanced intellectual insights behind the sensations of commodified knowledges.[9] Queer theory may disappear, but what we may learn from it and what it conveys as an intellectual project may have more lasting effects. In the attempt to understand the geography of queer theory it will perhaps be useful to return to one of its sources of inspiration, the works of Michel Foucault. (I state one source of inspiration, for, as Jonathan Katz has indicated, the emergence of queer theory has more to do with activists programmes from Christopher Street (New York) to the Castro (San Francisco) than the icon of Michel Foucault, central as he may be to such texts now declared as mapping the space of queer theory.)[10]

I want to take Dever's passing suggestion of the need to explore what queer theory is *doing* inside the critical genealogical exercise of Michel Foucault's work, particularly, as just indicated, because it grounds so much of contemporary queer theory. This exercise assumes even greater significance in the light of the fact that Foucault's work can be seen to focus precisely on the 'constitution' and 'function' of ideas in the historical space.[11] While queer theory is indebted to Foucault's genealogical project, with its emphasis on the social and historical construction of knowledge, there seems to have been little analysis of the strategic stages of the genealogical project and of the function of this type of discourse. I want, in effect, to wander around in the intellectual landscape of genealogy in order to show that it is the intellectual strategies behind queer theory that transform religious or theological discourse. The function of queer theory as an intellectual task following post-structuralism is, in part at least, a strategy to break essentialist categories and constructs. The queerness of queer theory is that it challenges us, not only to leave the discourses of the closet and 'coming out' (both essentialist constructs), but also to redraw the entire epistemological map of Western thinking about not only sexuality and the politics of identity but the very space of religion.[12] Queer theory blurs boundaries and institutional discourses that privilege the normative. Such intellectual moves lead us to recognize that the contemporary epistemological 'performance' (to use Butler's enigmatic term) of Christianity needs to be reconfigured in the contemporary cultural practices of sexuality. What I am suggesting is that the dis-course of sexuality is part of a Western Christian epistemology and that the complex cultural sites of sexual practices, including gay and lesbian identity, fetish culture, the power relations of sadomasochism and the leather scene, continue and perpetuate, despite being simultaneously points of internal resistance, the dualistic ideology of Christianity. Sexual subcultures are in this sense parasitic on the cultural inheritance of Christianity, they are manifestations of suffering and points of healing in the attempt to overcome the binary division of body and soul.[13]

GENEALOGY AND QUEER THEORY

Queer theory, particularly as represented in the work of Judith Butler and David Halperin, not surprisingly, carries forward a series of operations from Foucault's genealogy. Writers within queer theory attempt to produce a 'counter-history' or a 'counter-memory' in opposition to the heteronormative paradigm.[14] As part of this project, Foucault's genealogical method was used to identify the 'deployment of sexuality'; it revealed sexuality as an 'historical system of discourse and power'.[15] Sexuality was seen as an historical construction and the inadequacy of the essentialist terminology of homo- and heterosexual is revealed. Genealogy, like archaeology before it, revealed the 'ruptures and discontinuities' in the history of ideas; it uncovered, suspended, questioned, disconnected, broke up and interrogated the discourse of sexuality.[16] As Foucault recommended in 1969:

> We must examine those ready-made syntheses, those groupings that we normally accept before any examination, those links whose validity is recognised from the outset; we must oust those forms and obscure forces by which we usually link the discourse of one man [*sic*] with that of another; they must be driven out from the darkness in which they reign.[17]

Queer theory, using the methods of genealogy, revealed the 'failure of representation' and the 'silencing', as de Lauretis indicates, of the 'specificity' of desire, not least in terms of gender, race and cultural location. The work of queer theory also revealed, as Garber and others have indicated, the problematic of 'bisexuality'.[18] Foucault's genealogical methods proved effective in transforming and transgressing the hegemonic structures and destabilizing the essentialism of heterosexuality.

What Foucault's work offered was a discourse for the multiple sites of sexual expression which had been unleashed into the polymorphous landscape of 'queerness'. It was the signifier 'queer' which brought together and marked out such groups as 'lesbian, gay, bisexual, transgendered, and friends'; and for those who were unhappy in the queer location (the 'queer's queers', to use the Carol Queen and Lawrence Schimel expression) there were the 'pomosexuals' (postmodern sexualities), transsexuals and others 'who can't be fenced in'.[19] However, this destabilizing of terms within identity politics and the history of sexuality was not without its problems. Writers such as Butler and Spivak both recognized that non-essentialist discourses may have to be strategically suspended in the face of political and legal struggle.[20] In the contemporary political world there was no space for nuanced readings of bodies. The Western symbolic, guided by a Christian epistemology, could not allow for the 'truth of sex' to be ambiguous. As Foucault wrote in 1969, in response to his imaginary interlocutor:

> I know how irritating it can be to treat discourses in terms not of the gentle, silent, intimate consciousness that is expressed in them, but of an obscure set of anonymous rules. How unpleasant it is to reveal the limitations and necessities of a practice where one is used to seeing, in all its pure transparency, the expression of genius and freedom.[21]

As with the mad, categories were imposed upon bodily practices to regulate and order the social space. Foucault, along with others, such as Jeffery Weeks, had begun to show that sexual identity was not liberating but a means of control.[22] Indeed, the category of the homosexual was constructed through and maintained the domination of heterosexuality. It was, as Foucault had indicated, not enough to liberate sexuality, what was required was to 'liberate ourselves ... from the very notion of sexuality'.[23]

These arguments, based on Foucault's archaeological and genealogical methods, are now textbook material for queer studies. But what is often neglected in exploring Foucault's work on sexuality is the attempts to move outside this discourse. Sex for Foucault was a boring subject, it was not the real problematic which preoccupied his later work.[24] Few studies in queer theory have appreciated how, in the final stages of the genealogical project, Foucault attempted to move outside the 'discourse of sexuality'. There is in fact a continual tension in Foucault-inspired writings on queer theory between references to sexual specificity and the simultaneous attempts to mutate such a discourse. Foucault attempts to move beyond the discourse of sexuality into a new imaginative space of human relations. He does this in a number of ways: first, by discussing a new economy of bodies and pleasure in order to move outside the regime of sexuality. As Foucault remarked in 1976:

> It is the agency of sex that we must break away from, if we aim – through a tactical reversal of the various mechanisms of sexuality – to counter the grips of power with the claims of bodies, pleasure, and knowledges, in their possibilities of resistance. The rallying point for

the counterattack against the deployment of sexuality ought not to be sex-desire, but bodies and pleasure.[25]

This discourse has been picked up by David Halperin in his discussion of sadomasochistic practice and it forms a new basis for rethinking desire and erotic sensation.

Foucault's second attempt to move outside the discourse of sexuality was the reconfiguration of the ideas about sex in terms of 'technologies of the self'. He examined the underlying dynamic of sexual discourse where 'the truth of what we are is found in sex'.[26] (This discussion will form the basis of my critique of theology and I will therefore return to the subject in more detail below.) Finally, as James Bernauer, Mark Vernon and Herman Nilson have recently pointed out, Foucault offered a third way out of sexuality, the attempt to rethink human relations in terms of 'friendship'.[27] As Mark Vernon writes, in appreciation of the politics of friendship:

> Friendship is strategically important because it opens up new spaces for affection, tenderness, fidelity, camaraderie and companionship and so reveals the emotional emptiness of the tyranny of sexuality ... In this way friendship is politicised and might create a 'way out' [of sexuality] through an offensive of affection.[28]

This problematic of friendship opens up a whole series of non-essentialist questions about human relations and desire. It brings to light Andrienne Rich's idea of a sexual continuum in female friendships.[29] When does the touching and holding in female friendship become sexual? And for men, when does the homosocial become the homosexual? When does intimacy and closeness become a question of sexual practice? Its seems that the attempts to regulate the ambiguities of human relations is problematic for legal observers, because fundamentally you cannot police and lock away in the grey areas of life. This is not to say that some legal apparatus is not required in society, but that the construction of 'justice' and 'truth' in a hegemonic world of patriarchy and heterosexuality is often not representative of queerness.

In the attempts to move outside the discourse of sexuality, Foucault problematized what he calls an 'apparatus of knowledge' (*dispositif*), the substructure, if you like, of our thinking. For Foucault the 'emergence' of sexuality as a discourse is grounded in a Christian epistemology. Sexuality is anchored in the Western symbolic and functions to 'orientate', as Mary Keller and I have argued elsewhere, one's places in the world.[30] In its extreme form, one could say that theology is part of the technology which maintains heterosexuality, monotheism and capitalism: it functions to maintain the relations of power and the epistemological frameworks of Western imperialism. As Grace Jantzen has shown in her groundbreaking study of the Western symbolic, we have hardly begun to understand what it might be like to think outside the categories of the binary logic of Christianity.[31] Theology has only just started to enjoy celebrating the discourse of sexuality which emerged from its history, never mind the rejection of such a discourse as a part of its imperialistic project. Indeed, theology can embrace sexuality as a discourse because it is grounded in the same problematic of self, the same 'apparatus of knowledge' or symbolic; it functions in the same way. To queer sexuality is therefore simultaneously to queer theology and, as Dever recognized, to queer epistemology. This will become clearer if we return to

Foucault's genealogy of the modern subject, for sexuality and theology are totalizing discourses of the self.

SELF AND SEXUALITY

According to Foucault, Christianity introduced a new technology of the self where the truth of what we are was related to sex. Judith Perkins, developing Foucault in a study of the discourse of the suffering self in the second century, even goes as far as to suggest that the triumph of Christianity arose in part from the 'triumph of a particular representation of the self'.[32] The shift in sexual morality from the Greco-Roman period was not, according to Foucault, related to a different model of austerity but to a change in one's relationship to oneself. This relationship to oneself was grounded in the processes of self-examination and confession. For Foucault, Christianity was a 'confessing religion', there was an obligation first to acknowledge oneself publicly as a sinner (Tertullian's 'exomologesis'), the dramatic ritual performance through which one's status as a sinner was confirmed, a kind of 'coming out' as a Christian.[33] Foucault also identified a second form of confession in monastic practice of the fifth century, which was known as 'exagoreusis' (according to Foucault 'an analytical and continuous verbalisation of thoughts').[34] The verbal act of confession was the verification of the 'truth' of oneself. In order to discriminate between different thoughts (discretio), to test whether they were of Satan or of God, the monk had to verbalize the thought processes, not least because thoughts which resisted verbalization were dangerous. As the founder of Western monasticism, John Cassian wrote:

> A bad thought brought into the light of day immediately loses its veneer. The terrible serpent that this confession has forced out of its subterranean lair, to throw it out into the light and make its shame a public spectacle, is quick to beat a retreat.[35]

The key insight for Foucault was that Christianity held a paradoxical self, insofar as verbalization was an act of self-sacrifice. The self in Christianity was found in a self-sacrifice. As Foucault points out:

> We have to sacrifice the self in order to discover the truth about ourselves, and we have to discover the truth about ourselves in order to sacrifice ourselves. Truth and sacrifice, the truth about ourselves and the sacrifice of ourselves, are deeply and closely connected.[36]

What we find in the earliest texts of Christianity is an ordering of the self according to the dynamics of truth, sex and confession. It was this dynamic of self which triumphed in the Western world and paved the way for the emergence of sexuality. But this demand for the utterance of truth was not limited (as in Foucault) to statements of bodily desire in confession. What Foucault did not explore was the related political struggles surrounding Christian doctrine and the emergence of creedal performances of truth. Christianity also demanded the utterance of truth in terms of metaphysical belief. This can be seen in Richard King's problematization of the idea of 'religion' as a theological construct derived from a particular politics of truth. He notes the theological transformation in the third century of the Latin term 'religio' from an idea of practice to an idea of belief, a shift from orthopraxy to orthodoxy.[37] In the political discourse of Christianity it becomes important to discriminate 'truth' and 'falsity' through verbal acts.[38] In this sense, we can see how Western Christianity is preoccupied with the truth of belief and truth of self through creed and confession. What Foucault suggests is that at the heart of Christian theology is a model of truth and self which is carried over into modern sexuality. Christianity creates a fetish out of the truth of what we are, it demands an utterance. The discourse of sexuality in the modern consciousness mirrors this demand to utter the truth of oneself in terms of sexuality. However, this was not, according to Foucault, through a sacrificial self but through what he called 'a positive self' (the assertion of the modern Western anthropological subject). It was in the 18th and 19th centuries that all those figures who had been happily silent in the past had to be identified. The positive self did not confess the sins of the flesh but rather ordered the body and its desires. As Foucault indicated, 'it was time for all these figures, scarcely noticed in the past, to step forward and speak, to make the difficult confession of what they were.'[39]

Theology now responds to this positivity of self with studies that affirm sexuality as a part of spirituality. These studies, valuable as they are in overcoming sexual guilt and ignorance in Christianity, uncritically support and sustain the oppressive discourse of sexuality.[40] But what is striking about Foucault's analysis is not only that sexuality and the theological demand for truth are linked, but that sexuality and theology are grounded on a fixed model of the self. There is a notion of a coherent self (usually the rational male) from which a position of truth can be established in terms of both sexuality and theological belief. Theology stabilizes the self by fixing a singular 'truth' (monotheism) and a singular 'sexual' identity (heterosexuality over against homosexuality). The liberal attitude of modern spirituality is therefore able to embrace the truth of a whole range of sexual identities as long as the categories are 'straight' forward and the monotheistic ideal is preserved. Such studies neatly preserve the tradition because they realize that supporting sexuality inadvertently maintains the hegemony of theological values. If we are therefore to find a way out of sexuality we have simultaneously to find a way out of the theological constructs that anchor an essentialist notion of the self. What I am suggesting is that there is some interdependence between the discourse of sexuality and the discourse of theology, grounded in an epistemology of self and truth as coherent and fixed. Christian theology and sexuality share the same epistemological foundations; they both demand an utterance of the self. In this respect, if Christianity is to overcome its oppressive regime of knowledge it needs to reject not only its model of self and God, but also the discourse of sexuality, which it so powerfully supports.

RELIGIONS OF SOUTH EAST ASIA, THE SELF AND SEXUALITY

The correspondence between models of the self in Christian theology and sexuality appears to be confirmed when we reflect on notions of the body, pleasure and desire in non-Christian traditions. In one of the few studies to use post-structuralist analysis to reflect on Buddhism and sexuality, Bernard Faure attempts to explore the Buddhist origins of 'sexuality'. He questions the idea that there was such a thing called 'sexuality' in Buddhist thinking. Although modern discourses of sexuality are to be found in Japan and China these are more to do with the influence of the West. According to Faure's study, unlike in the Christian tradition, 'there has never been in Buddhism a full-fledged discourse on sexuality'.[41] (Sexuality here is understood in terms of Foucault's 'scientia sexualis'.) In Buddhism, sexuality was not 'the central, organising principle around which the self crystallised'.[42] This is not to say there were no discourses about sex in South East Asia; there were obviously different types of discourse about desire and the body.[43] However, what we find in Buddhism is that the 'self' is not as much of a problem (given its illusory nature) as the problem of 'desire' or 'craving'; it is sensual misconduct in any form which can lead to attachment.

These cross-cultural comparisons, as Jolly and Manderson indicate, need to caution themselves against the dangers of 'exoticism' and 'overemphasizing difference'.[44] While it would be wrong to presume a universal discourse about sexuality, there are 'cross-cultural *exchanges* in sexualities' through processes such as colonialism.[45] However, what is never explored in Faure's work is the way the hermeneutics of the self in Buddhism differs from Christianity (something which engaged Foucault in his own explorations of Buddhism) and how this in turn shapes the discourse about sex.[46] This analysis seems important because of the way sexuality emerges out of a Christian hermeneutics of self.

The hermeneutics of self is central to the discourse of sexuality and once we question the Christian self from which sexuality emerges we can begin to unravel the complexities, not only of sexuality, but of the very nature of theology. As Foucault argues:

> Maybe the problem of the self is not to discover what it is in its positivity, maybe the problem is not to discover a positive self or the positive foundation of the self. Maybe our problem is now to discover that the self is nothing else than the historical correlation of the technology built in our history. Maybe the problem is to change those technologies which we have inherited from the first centuries of Christianity.[47]

Queer theory destabilizes the essentialism of sexuality but, as I have also tried to argue, it also destabilizes the essentialism of the self and very truth of Christian theology. When the self is fragmented historically we also fragment our desires and the truth of theology. Religion becomes queer when it breaks up the desiring self, when it refuses to confess an identity, when it refuses to say who we are, and acknowledges a plural self with polymorphous desires. To queer religion is to queer the foundations of theology, its monotheism, its monosexuality and its monopoly of truth. In the queer spaces of theology we find 'ambiguity' and 'not knowing', a performative self, which can, as Grace Jantzen indicates, imaginatively recreate the symbolic.

Grace Janzten's post-structuralist inspired analysis opened a new imaginary for women, but related to this and acknowledged in a number of places in her work is the importance of race and sexual orientation.[48] The challenge to the 'masculine' symbolic is also a challenge to the 'heteronormative' symbolic and the symbolic of white supremacy. These critical indexes do not exist in isolation and theology needs to be taken into account for developing ways of thinking that have encouraged monotheistic models of ourselves. Foucault challenges the very nature of Western thought by identifying how the Western symbolic anchors and orders sexuality and how it is necessary to find new imaginative spaces beyond 'sexuality'. This may mean we have to leave the foundations of theological certainty. Nietzsche's call for the death of God was not a call for rejecting the existence of God; it was a call for the death of a way of thinking – the death of imperialistic theology. Foucault's work is likewise a call for a new way of thinking about our bodies, our desires and our conceptions of God. This does not leave us with a nihilistic wasteland, as some may fear, for out of the ruins of imperialistic theology and sexuality the phoenix of a queer world, as yet unknown, will arise to celebrate the heterodox.[49] Foucauldian queer theory reveals how Christian theological doctrine and practice shape the overarching Western symbolic. It highlights how theology permeates the flesh and how it seeks unity rather than diversity. Orthodox theology, like sexuality, frames reality in terms of the singularity of 'identity', rather than multiplicity of bodily 'acts' and pleasures and the complexity of desire; it seeks a fixed self rather than a plural self with changing and multiple desires.

IDENTITY WITHOUT SELFHOOD

Foucault's response to the problematic of the self emerges out of his study of Christianity and he sought to offer an 'aesthetics of self'.[50] But such a position was not without its problems. It has been seen as not only privileging the 'self's relation to itself', and those who have the economic status to perform such pleasures, but also maintaining a coherent and fixed self which 'frees' itself.[51] As Marian Fraser indicates: 'Foucault's "solution" to the "problem" of the self appears to be bound by the very theory (his own) which precedes it.'[52] The central problem here is how to break the links between representation, identity and selfhood. Fraser attempts to do this in her study of Simone de Beauvoir and bisexuality, using Deleuze and Guattari's idea of 'bodies without organs', a body without image, depth or productivity and where there is 'no longer a Self that feels, acts and recalls'.[53] Desire here is a series of forces or acts without representation. According to Fraser, the BwO (bodies without organs) bisexuality is a position which 'deterritorialises the lines which stratify and produce identities organised around individuality, possession (of identity), material corporeality, visibility and sameness'.[54] The success of Fraser's intriguing argument depends largely on whether the notion of 'bisexuality' can be seen as existing outside the realm of 'narrative identity'. She believes that the effect of bisexuality 'is to mimic the stratifications of identity'.[55] It holds stratification (of identity) and at the same time it overcomes a fixed position through movement and contingency.[56] Intriguing as this argument may appear, it ignores the history of the referent bisexuality and its binary construction. There is some tension in maintaining the term 'bisexual' in the 'body without organs'.

   Bisexuality, as Firestein and others have shown, has a narrative history, emerging with the construction of homosexuality.[57] However, what emerges from Fraser's work is not just Garber's recognition of the 'fluidity' of sexual desire, but the whole problem of a self without identity.[58] What we need is a more complex hermeneutics of desire which questions Christian models of selfhood and opens the space for a cross-cultural reinventing of ourselves. If, as Elspeth Probyn indicates, desire is not restricted to the individual body or a fixed self, then desire can be liberated from bodies and selves and can be seen as the very process of becoming 'orientated' in life.[59] In this way religion can become a form of 'desire' without identity or a single selfhood. How do we take the discourse of religion out of the discourse of self, and has Christianity the resources to do so? If we question a sexual self do we in turn not only question a fixed self but also question a fixed 'truth'? As Foucault recognized in his foreword to Deleuze and Guattari's *Anti-Oedipus*, we have to ask: 'How do we rid our speech and our acts, our hearts and our pleasures, of fascism? How do we ferret out the fascism that is ingrained in our behavior?' We need to pursue and root out, as Foucault went on to acknowledge, 'the slightest traces of fascism in the body'.[60] We need to be aware of the fascist within us all and within theology, that is the desire to control desire in the other and the understanding of God. Queer theory at least unveils the fascist regimes of Christian theology and sexuality in the bondage of a fixed self.

MULTIPLE SELVES AND THEOLOGICAL AMBIVALENCE

Theologians, of course, are not immune to thinking through the problematic of the so-called 'postmodern' self. Anthony Thiselton, for example, acknowledges that theology has much to learn from Foucault and other post-structuralist writers.[61] But such accounts are attempts, as in the moral philosophy of Charles Taylor, to hold on to a position of unity from the fragments of a multiple self.[62] Theology remains in a position where multiplicity is contained or countered by a greater unity in the Godhead, if it is not simply eradicated. In two very different theological accounts given by Anthony Thiselton (*Interpreting God and the Postmodern Self*) and David Ford (*Self and Salvation*) the multiple self is reconciled in a similar way: either through a theology of promise, following Moltmann (Thiselton), or through a worshipping self transformed in the face of Christ (Ford).[63] In both cases multiple selves are acknowledged as very real postmodern phenomena which call for Christian theology to respond to a crisis of the self through a redemptive theology. There is no doubt about the creativity of theologians to address the shifting intellectual tides, but such moves continue the imperialistic project of theology by simply repackaging the subject in a teleology of salvation. The future hope neatly obscures the ambiguity of our queer living and the complexity of our desires. As Ford confirms through his reading of Levinas and Jüngel, 'faith in this God secures the self in trust in a way which liberates it from the compulsion to find other good or bad absolutes or inappropriate forms of certainty.'[64]

The technique of self in such work still conforms to Foucault's understanding of Christianity in late antiquity as a 'paradoxical self', a self found in the sacrifice of self; the only difference is that, in the pre-modern world, the sacrificial self held a greater unity. The self in salvation is still unified in a way which takes no account of the queer desiring self, principally because such a position is a worldly pleasure to be purified in a higher unity. Not only is such theology an insult to queer pleasures, it remains a superficial valorization of our bodily selves. Not surprisingly, such accounts never address Foucault's alignment of Christianity and the history of sexuality. The gendered sexual body only appears at the point of defining the postmodern self for Thiselton (as if Foucault wrote about power with no reference to sexuality) and Ford hides his most telling omissions in a footnote, where he confesses:

> Five topics in particular have been frequently on my mind but have not been discussed at any length: Christianity in relation to other religions; gender in relation to self and salvation; physical and psychological healing; the politics and economics of self and salvation; and, perhaps most insistent of all, the Shoah, or Holocaust.[65]

But surely, it is precisely this list of omissions which is central to the contemporary readings of the self and, more importantly, it is these features (other religions, gender, the physical, the psychological, the political, the economic and the horrors of the Holocaust) which raise the very question of our multiple selves. To speak from multiple sites is to have multiple selves, as Malcolm Bull's account of Du Bois's double consciousness of American Blackness demonstrates so well.[66] The queer self, like the racial self, has more than one site from which to speak. But theology in the 'face' of this fragmentation still seems to insist on imposing a future unity because it holds a fundamental nostalgia for a pre-modern imperialistic truth of what we are and what we may become. It appears to concede to 'looking through a glass darkly', but is never prepared to alter its central precepts in a blind hope of future victory in the unity of monotheistic truth and theological orthodoxy. The so-called 'radical theologians' may pay lip service to queer theory, the multiple self and the crisis of postmodernity, as long as it does not infect the basic laws of the pre-modern Christian gospel. Foucault's genealogy of Christianity and sexuality does not allow for such theological immunity. *If Christianity is entwined with the discourse of sexuality then to queer sexuality is simultaneously to queer the symbolic of theology, it is to fragment the self and the theos.* If I am not a single self, a single set of desires, I have no single truth. I am body in motion and constantly disrupting the selves I have been in the past. The question remains as to whether theology can exist without the certainty of self, whether theology can allow for multiple selves.

Thiselton touches on the key to such a question when he notes Moltmann's concession that theism 'runs the risk of appearing to give "a *fixed form* to reality" '.[67] But if, as Thiselton suggests, it is 'love' that provides a way for 'movement and change' then why is it not the 'apparatus' of theology that is open to transformation rather than our fragmented selves? Could theology become fragmented in the fragmentation of our desires? Could it not be that to queer sexuality may be in turn to queer the truth of theology? Could theology become more ambiguous than it already appears to be? Could we develop a theology that speaks from many sites and performs many roles? Could we dress theology in drag and become aroused by the polymorphous theism of ourselves? To have one God is to have one sex, one leader, one choice. Monotheism anchors heterosexuality. To have more than one desire is to have more than one symbolic of divinity, more than one truth. To be polymorphously perverse is to be open to the polytheism of desire. It is to take self and desire out of the epistemology of monotheism to create a diversity of truths.

Perhaps, as Butler suggests in relation to sexuality, we could hold on to our 'displays of ambivalence' in certain forms of debate.[68] This underlying dynamic of ambiguity is part of an attempt to find a new intellectual space from which to explore the ruins of sexuality (and, we may add, theology) and the attempt to build a place from which a specific non-essentialist politics of desire can emerge. Butler, in her preface to the tenth anniversary edition of *Gender Trouble*, wants to refuse the 'erasure of bisexuality' and the 'irreducible complexity of sexuality' and in turn, following Foucault's work on religion, we may see such a 'refusal' as a simultaneous rejection of the unity of self in theology.[69] To hold the ambiguity of sexuality is to hold the multiplicity of self and the 'irreducible complexity' of religious and theological belief and practice. It is to take the humbling position that the truth of what we are is, as Foucault noted, 'nothing else than the historical correlation of the technology built in our history'.[70] We have no more right to normalize theology in the oppression of orthodoxy than we do to normalize sexuality in the oppression of homophobia. The truth of what we may become may not be so much the sacrifice of ourselves as the sacrifice of the knowledge we have of ourselves – it is 'the sacrifice of the subject of knowledge' – the sacrifice of sexuality and hegemonic theology. The question remains as to whether we have the courage to embrace the creative possibilities of Foucault's work in order to 'think differently' about theology.[71] If Christianity can move beyond its ideology of monotheism, it may just be possible to move beyond sexuality and homophobia. The challenge to the Christian church is to give up its control of the body by giving up its control of God.

NOTES

1 Michel Foucault 'Nietzsche, Genealogy and History', in *Language, Counter-Memory, Practice*, ed. D.F. Bouchard, Ithaca, New York: Cornell University Press, pp.139–64.
2 Michel Foucault (1967), 'Who are you, Professor Foucault?', in *Religion and Culture By Michel Foucault*, ed. Jeremy Carrette, Manchester: Manchester University Press/New York: Routledge, 1999, p.91.
3 In this chapter I often refer to a 'Western Christian symbolic' as part of an imperialistic regime of theology. While this may in some sense homogenize very diverse traditions and historical periods, it acts strategically to highlight the hegemonic constructions of orthodoxy by church authorities in Western history. Such constructions seek to separate body and spirit, politically suppress diversity in both the self and God, and refuse dialogue with other religious traditions. Nonetheless, I accept that the phrase 'Western Christian symbolic' needs to be 'queered' (the process of questioning unity and exposing multiplicity and fragmentation). Christianity needs to be seen as holding many disparate strands. This chapter follows Foucault's homogenization of Christianity as a strategic move that seeks to question the normative structures in both sexuality and theology. It also seeks to destabilize a certain dominant paradigm in Western thinking. Christian theology, in this sense, holds a responsibility to critique its patterns of thought as part of its theological practice.
4 Howard Eilberg-Schwartz *God's Phallus: and Other Problems for Men and Monotheism*, Boston: Beacon Press, 1994, p.9.
5 For a discussion of the idea of 'closure', see Hilary Lawson, *Closure: A Story of Everything*, London: Routledge, 2001.
6 Carolyn Dever, 'Either/And: Lesbian and Gay Sex Identities', *GLQ: A Journal of Lesbian and Gay Studies*, 5(3), 1999, pp.413–14.
7 Dever, 'Either/And', p.414 (emphasis my own).
8 Dever, 'Either/And', p.414.
9 Brian Knauft, *Genealogies for the Present in Cultural Anthropology*, New York: Routledge, 1996, p.239.

10   Jonathan Ned Katz, *The Invention of Heterosexuality*, New York: Plume, 1996, p.10.
11   Michel Foucault (1967]), 'Who are you, Professor Foucault?', reprinted in *Religion and Culture by Michel Foucault*, ed. Jeremy Carrette, Manchester: Manchester University Press, 1999, p.98; Jeremy Carrette, *Foucault and Religion: Spiritual Corporality and Political Spirituality*, London: Routledge, 2000, p.9.
12   See Eve Kosofsky Sedgwick, *Epistemology of the Closet*, Berkeley: University of California Press, 1990; Marion Fraser, *Identity without Selfhood: Simone de Beauvoir and Bisexuality*, Cambridge: Cambridge University Press, 1999, p.46; David Halperin, *Saint Foucault: Towards a Gay Hagiography*, Oxford: Oxford University Press, 1995, pp.34ff.
13   See Jeremy Carrette, 'Radical Heterodoxy and the Indecent Proposal of Erotic Theology: Critical Groundwork for Sexual Theologies', in *Theology and Literature,* 15(3), September 2001, pp.286–98.
14   Foucault, 'Nietzsche, Genealogy, History', p.160.
15   Judith Butler, *Gender Trouble: Feminism and the Subversion of Identity*, New York: Routledge, 1990, p.95; Halperin, *Saint Foucault*, p.40.
16   Michel Foucault (1969), *The Archaeology of Knowledge*, reprinted London: Routledge, 1991, pp.22–6. Cf. Carrette, *Foucault and Religion*, p.94.
17   Foucault, *The Archaeology of Knowledge*, p.22.
18   Teresa De Lauretis (ed.), *Queer Theory: Lesbian and Gay Sex Identities*, Providence: Brown University, 1991, pp.5–7; Marjorie Garber, *Vested Interest: Bisexuality and the Eroticism of Everyday Life*, London: Penguin, 1995; Fraser, *Identity without Selfhood*.
19   Carol Queen and Lawrence Schimel, *Pomosexuals: Challenging Assumptions About Gender and Sexuality*, San Francisco: Cleis Press, 1997, p.23.
20   Judith Butler, *Gender Trouble: Feminism and the Subversion of Identity*, 10th anniversary edn, London: Routledge, 1999, p.xxvi; Fraser, *Identity Without Selfhood*, p.5.
21   Foucault, *The Archaeology of Knowledge*, p.210.
22   See Jeffrey Weeks, *Coming Out: Homosexual Politics in Britain from the 19th Century to the Present*, London: Quartet, 1977; Jeffrey Weeks, *Sexuality and its Discontents*, London: Routledge, 1986.
23   Foucault, in Halperin, *Saint Foucault*, p.96.
24   Michel Foucault (1983), 'On the Genealogy of Ethics: An Overview of Work in Progress', reprinted in *The Foucault Reader*, ed. Paul Rabinow, London: Penguin, 1984, p.340.
25   Michel Foucault (1976), *The History of Sexuality: Volume 1*, London: Penguin, 1990, p.157.
26   See Foucault, *The History of Sexuality*, pp.77–8; Michel Foucault (1980), 'About the Beginning of the Hermeneutics of the Self', in *Religion and Culture*.
27   See Michel Foucault (1981), 'Friendship as a Way of Life', in *Foucault Live: Interviews 1961–1984*, ed. Sylvère Lotringer, New York: Semiotext(e), 2nd edn, pp.298–301; James Bernauer, 'Cry of Spirit', Foreword to *Religion and Culture*, p.xvi; Mark Vernon, '"I am Not What I am" – Foucault, Christian Asceticism and a "Way Out" of Sexuality', in *Religion and Culture*, pp.207–8; Herman Nilson, *Michel Foucault and the Games of Truth*, London: Macmillam, 1998, pp.109–12.
28   Vernon, '"I am Not What I am"', p.208.
29   Andrienne Rich, 'Compulsory Heterosexuality and Lesbian Existence', in Snitow, Stansell and Thompson (eds), *Powers of Desire: The Politics of Sexuality*, New York: New Feminist Library, Monthly Review Press, 1983, p.192.
30   Jeremy Carrette and Mary Keller, 'Religions, Orientation and Critical Theory: Race, Gender and Sexuality at the 1998 Lambeth Conference', in *Theology and Sexuality*, 11, September 1999, pp.23–31.
31   Grace Jantzen, *Becoming Divine: Towards a Feminist Philosophy of Religion*, Manchester: Manchester University Press, 1998, pp.59–76.

32 Judith Perkins, *The Suffering Self: Pain and Narrative Representation in the Early Christian Era,* London: Routledge, 1995, p.11.
33 Foucault, 'About the Beginning of the Hermeneutics of the Self', pp.171–3.
34 Ibid., p.179.
35 Quoted in Foucault, 'About the Beginning of the Hermeneutics of the Self', p.178.
36 Ibid., p.179.
37 Richard King, *Orientalism and Religion: Postcolonial Theory, India and 'The Mystic East'*, London: Routledge, 1999, pp.35–41.
38 Ibid., p.39.
39 Foucault, *The History of Sexuality*, p.39.
40 See, for example, James Nelson, *Body Theology*, Louisville, Kentucky: Westminster/John Knox Press, 1992.
41 Bernard Faure, *The Red Thread: Buddhist Approaches to Sexuality*, Princeton, New Jersey: Princeton University Press, 1998, p.281.
42 Faure, *The Red Thread*, p.10.
43 Faure, *The Red Thread*, p.9.
44 M. Jolly and L. Manderson (eds), *Sites of Desire: Economies of Pleasure: Sexualities in Asia and the Pacific*, Chicago: University of Chicago, 1997, p.xiii.
45 See Jolly and Manderson, *Sites of Desire*.
46 For Foucault's brief discussion of Buddhism and the self, see Michel Foucault (1978), 'Michel Foucault and Zen: A Stay in a Zen Temple', in *Religion and Culture*.
47 Foucault, 'About the Beginning of the Hermeneutics of the Self', p.181.
48 Jantzen, *Becoming Divine*, pp.26, 122, 126.
49 As I have defined elsewhere, heterodoxy is 'the play of truth silenced by power', see Carrette, 'Radical Heterodoxy and the Indecent Proposal of Erotic Theology', p.287.
50 See Foucault, 'About the Beginning of the Hermeneutics of the Self'; Michel Foucault, *The Use of Pleasure: The History of Sexuality Volume 2*, London: Penguin, 1984; and *The Care of the Self: The History of Sexuality Volume 2*, London: Penguin, 1984.
51 Fraser, *Identity without Selfhood*, pp.166–7.
52 Ibid., p.165.
53 Ibid., p.160.
54 Ibid., p.161.
55 Ibid., p.162.
56 Ibid., p.162.
57 Ronald Fox, in Beth Firestein (ed.), *Bisexuality: The Psychology and Politics of an Invisible Minority*, London: Sage, 1996, p.4. See also Merl Storr (ed.), *Bisexuality: A Critical Reader*, London: Routledge, 1999.
58 Garber, M. (1995), *Vice Versa: Bisexuality and the Eroticism of Everyday Life*, London: Penguin, p.66.
59 See Carrette and Keller, *Religions, Orientation and Critical Theory*.
60 Michel Foucault (1977) 'Preface' to *Anti-Oedipus: Capitalism and Schizophrenia* by Gilles Deleuze and Félix Guattari, reprinted, London: Athlone, 1984, p.xiii.
61 Anthony Thiselton, *Interpreting God and the Postmodern Self*, Edinburgh: T&T Clark, 1995, p.14.
62 Malcolm Bull, *Seeing Things Hidden: Apocalypse, Vision and Totality*, London: Verso, 1999, pp.256–61. Cf. Charles Taylor, *Sources of the Self: The Making of the Modern Identity*, Cambridge: Cambridge University Press, 1989.
63 Thiselton, *Interpreting God*, pp.145–52; David Ford, *Self and Salvation: Being Transformed*, Cambridge: Cambridge University Press, 1999, pp.73–164.
64 Ford, *Self and Salvation*, p.71.
65 Ford, *Self and Salvation*, p.13, n.9; Thiselton, *Interpreting God*, p.11.

66   Bull, *Seeing Things Hidden*, p.145. See also W.E.B. Du Bois (1903), *The Souls of Black Folk*, reprinted, New York: Dover, 1994.
67   Thiselton, *Interpreting God*, p.145.
68   Judith Butler, *The Psychic Life of Power*, Stanford: Stanford University Press, 1997, p.10.
69   Butler, *Gender Trouble*, 10th anniversary edn, p.xxvi.
70   Foucault, 'About the Beginning of the Hermeneutics of the Self', p.181.
71   Foucault, *The Use of Pleasure*, p.8.

Chapter 12

Sodomites and Churchmen: the Theological Invention of Homosexuality

Mark D. Jordan

On different pages within the ever-revised project of the *History of Sexuality*, Foucault makes two suggestions about the history of Christian moral theology. The first suggestion is incidental to the notorious discussion of the 'homosexual' as a category invented in the 19th century. It is the claim that there is a decisive difference between a 'sodomite' and a 'homosexual'. The second suggestion is central to the project of the unfinished analysis of sexuality in the early and medieval Christian churches. It is the claim that what distinguishes Christian teaching about sex is not specific ideals or prohibitions, but rather 'new mechanisms of power for inculcating' moral teachings about sex.[1] The term Foucault borrows for the ensemble of these mechanisms is *le pastorat*, the pastorate or, more colloquially for Catholic ears, pastoral care. These two suggestions will be discussed, not as stages of revision, but as points where Foucault engages or fails to engage the Christian 'mechanisms' for creating sex-linked identities.[2] The comparison between the 19th-century category of the 'homosexual' and the medieval theological category of the 'sodomite' will be pursued back to a deeper comparison, one between state power and church power. It will then be argued that this comparison of powers misleads us in at least one important way: it encourages us to overlook the extent to which 'homosexual' is both the product and the plaything of Christian theology – which hardly disappeared with the waning of the Middle Ages. The chapter concludes by trying to show why the theological contribution to 'homosexuality' ought to matter very much to us, whether we are Christian or not.

NEW 'HOMOSEXUAL' AND OLD 'SODOMITE'

We begin with the bitterly contested set of lines from Foucault's *History of Sexuality*, vol. 1, even if I seem to redo what David Halperin has recently done in his retractation, which is not a retraction.[3] It will be seen that the passage leads me in other directions. The passage begins:

> The sodomy of the old civil or canonical laws was a category of forbidden acts; their perpetrator was nothing more than the juridical subject of them. The nineteenth-century

233

homosexual has become a personage: a past, a history and a childhood, a character, a type of life; also a morphology, with an indiscreet anatomy and possibly a mysterious physiology. Nothing of what he is in totality escapes his sexuality.[4]

Now this passage is so often contested because it is so badly misread. It is taken to mean, for example, that there were no males before the 19th century who preferred to copulate with males rather than females (the emphasis in Foucault remains on males); that there were no earlier homoerotic habits or institutions or artworks or discourses; and so on. The passage is thus regularly taken to be 'refuted' by citing examples of same-sex preferences, habits, institutions, artworks, discourses – evidence from the Dutch persecutions of 1731, say, or the 'Mollie Houses' of 17th-century London, or Florentine and Venetian 'subcultures' of the 15th and 16th centuries, or 12th-century clerical networks. And then Foucault is damned for being a bad scholar, or a philosopher rather than a historian, or a bad philosopher, a self-loathing homosexual or, in the ever-restrained language of Camille Paglia, 'a glib game-player who took very little research a very long way'.[5]

I will pass over the ferocity of these misreadings of Foucault – and Halperin's diagnosis of them – in order to describe how he might actually have spoken the controversial lines. What precisely is the historico-theological narrative that Foucault means to tell about the difference between 'sodomite' and 'homosexual'?

By 'The sodomy of the old (*ancien*) civil or canonical laws', does Foucault mean the civil codes of late antiquity and their analogues in the early medieval church? If so, he writes sloppily.[6] The category 'sodomy' does not appear in the late ancient codes or the early medieval penitentials, which are in any case very different types of discourses. Nor is it helpful to emphasize that Foucault speaks only of 'premodern *legal* definitions', since the distinction between canon law or penitential practice and moral theology cannot be applied to the most important medieval treatments of same-sex desire.[7] Christian moral theology has its origins in canon law and the confessional, as these in turn depend on extracts from the principal theological authors of the early church. In many texts of medieval Latin Christianity, canon law *is* moral theology, and moral theology law.

Perhaps Foucault means by '*ancien*' not ancient, but before the French Revolution, in which case he is making a point that seems to be both true and important. Catholic casuistry of the 16th to 18th centuries is notable for its zeal in isolating the act of 'sodomy'. It strives to abstract 'the metaphysical notion and definition of sodomy' or 'the notion and metaphysical essence of sodomy', to quote the Carmelites of Salamanca.[8] The individuals behind these reified acts do appear chiefly as the 'juridical subjects' of them – of the punishments to be meted out for them. But if Foucault's contrast means only to cover the discourses of 16th- or 18th-century casuistry,[9] it would not support his larger claims in *History of Sexuality*, vol. 1 about a distinctively contemporary compulsion to speak sex. It would certainly not cover the theological discourses of the Middle Ages and their afterlives.

Perhaps Foucault's next sentence will help: 'The nineteenth-century homosexual has become ... also a morphology, with an indiscreet anatomy and possibly a mysterious physiology.' Foucault may be using the terms 'morphology', 'anatomy' and 'physiology' quite precisely, as names for sciences newly constituted in the 19th century.[10] Perhaps he presupposes his own narratives in *Birth of the Clinic* or *The*

Order of Things (as we call it in English) about the origin and character of the modern life sciences. Before the 19th century, the 'sodomite' could not have had 'a morphology, with an indiscreet anatomy and possibly a mysterious physiology', because those sciences did not yet exist. The modernity of the 'homosexual' is the modernity of the scientific discourses in which the 'homosexual' is described.

This way of delimiting the passage does respond to part of Foucault's meaning, but at the price of shifting interest from 'homosexuality' or 'sexuality' to a (prior) narrative of the history of sciences. The homosexual appears with a physiology in the 19th century because the homosexual is an artifact of the new science of physiology that appears only with the 19th century.[11] So this reading, while attractively historicized, risks reducing *History of Sexuality*, vol. 1 to a footnote for Foucault's earlier works. It can also become tautological. The homosexual is a 19th-century identity because it depends on concepts created in the 19th-century sciences. Of what medical or forensic identity deployed in the 19th century would that statement not be true? We need a better reading of the passage.

Perhaps the key to the passage is one we have passed by, the term 'personage' (*personnage*): 'The nineteenth-century homosexual has become a personage.' The word can mean individual, but also celebrity or figure, as in a painted tableau, or character, as in a performance. The 19th-century homosexual has become an individual, a celebrity, a stylized figure, a performed character. This is what Foucault means by 'a new specification of individuals'; that is why he interchanges *personnage* with *caractère*, *visage* and *figure*.[12] It is not that 19th-century discourses were the first to link certain genital acts with other behaviors or mannerisms, say effeminacy or secrecy or fashion-sense, or that they were the first to bring together legal, medical and religious prohibitions around certain genital acts. Neither of these combinations would be news to Christian theologians. What Foucault means to contrast with earlier discourses is the *kind* of 'personage' being constructed around the genital behavior, the totality and necessity of the 'character', its being now 'a singular nature', 'a species' and yet also a type, a character, a role.[13]

If this is the historical narrative Foucault means to tell, it would seem just to be false on standard notions of historiography. Before the abstractions of counter-Reformation casuistry and the consequent criminal codes, and long before the totalizing strategies of the 19th-century theory of perversions, we find in high medieval theology a figure totally informed by his taste for male–male copulation, a figure with a personal and tribal history, a distinct physiology and pathology, and even 'a certain quality of sexual sensibility'. We find a figure that has both a deviant morphology and a deviant subjectivity, who has a same-sex-desiring identity.[14] I mean the figure of the sodomite. There are many discourses in which this figure appears, but none so emblematic as the 11th-century *Liber Gomorrhianus* or *Gomorran Book*, by Peter Damian, sometime cardinal, ardent hermit and zealous reformer of priestly morals, from which let me briefly construct a comparison with Foucault's description of the 'homosexual'.

Foucault says that the 19th-century homosexual has a 'morphology', with an 'anatomy' and 'physiology'. Peter Damian speaks at length about specifically sodomitic bodies, which are for him only male bodies. The sodomite's body is a morbid or pathological body. Sodomy is likened to the cause of plagues or plague itself, to a tumorous growth, a wound or wounded member, a raging contagion, an aggressive contagious disease.[15] It is compared at length, in its attendant rituals and consequences, with leprosy.[16] Homoerotic desire is madness.[17] Indeed, as Peter Damian repeats, sodomites are rightly classed with the insane – a Foucauldian analogy if ever there was one.[18]

Foucault says that the 19th-century homosexual has 'a past, a history' that is a series of gender inversions. So too do Peter Damian's sodomites. Their history is the history of their dreadful tribe, which escaped astonishingly from God's fiery wrath. Their past is a life of continually disputing natural boundaries. On the one hand, Peter reports with disgust that sodomites would, if nature permitted, do to the male body every act that men can do to women.[19] They would treat the male body as female. On the other hand, sodomites seem to forget what organs their own bodies have. They seek out in others what they already possess.[20]

Foucault says that the 19th-century homosexual has 'a character, a type of life'. So too do Peter Damian's sodomites, who strive to draw this kind of life into an inverted community. The sodomites are violently attacked for committing spiritual incest with their own children. Sodomitic bishops and priests 'beget children' by preaching and baptism, only to corrupt them by copulation.[21] Their habits of begetting also infect their reason, their speeches, so that they scramble bodies while constructing the theological arguments by which they attempt to justify themselves. Their authoritative texts are monstrous hybrids.[22]

I could go on – there is a certain masochistic delight in quoting Peter Damian – but the point will have been made already. What do we have in this 11th-century theological polemic if not a personage of the sodomite, whose self, whose soul and body, morphology and subjectivity, are wholly formed by the sin? In what way does Peter Damian's 'sodomite' fail to satisfy the criteria Foucault establishes for the 19th-century 'homosexual'?

I have chosen the counter-example carefully, of course, and Foucault goes some way towards agreeing that its 'sodomite' is historically related to the 'homosexual'. Foucault himself describes a series of extensions by which the monastic discipline of chastity was applied to larger and larger groups – to the clergy as a whole; then to all religious, male and female; then to pious laypeople; then to laypeople simply.[23] Foucault even suggests that we can discern the birth of the modern notion of sexuality in the kinds of surveillance practiced within seminaries, religious colleges and convents since the counter-Reformation.[24] The sexualities of 19th-century psychiatry can seem a pastoral theology by other means. The therapy of the modern clinic looks like Christian morality for the secularized bourgeoisie. But these are resemblances and analogies. Foucault cannot let the homosexual become only a generalization of the medieval sodomite. To do so would be to give up the central claims of *History of Sexuality*, vol. 1 for the distinctiveness of the modern notion of perversion – which is to say, of the key discourses that now multiply around and through sexuality.

What, then, would Foucault reply to my paraphrase of Peter Damian? He might reply that he is less concerned with an exact chronology for the invention of the 'homosexual' than with the changes in modern rhetoric that make it possible to describe the 'homosexual'. After all, in earlier works Foucault himself had put the invention of the homosexual in the 17th century, not the 19th.[25] Moreover, and as we have seen, Foucault is quite willing to describe a slow transfer of materials from Christian and specifically Catholic theology into modern legal and clinical speech.

What matters to Foucault is a difference in function between a Christian discourse about inveterate sin and a clinical discourse about perversion. It may be that elements from the discourses of medieval monastic or clerical spirituality enter into the discourses of 19th-century forensic medicine (or 17th-century proposals to incarcerate the insane), but they do so only by entering the service of a different kind of power. To judge the adequacy of Foucault's contrast between homosexual and sodomite, we have to be able to judge the different powers enacted in the modern rhetoric of perversions and the medieval rhetoric of sin. But this cannot be just a contrast between modern powers and medieval ones, because there are still churches now. It must rather be a contrast between two competing modes of power, the one secular, the other churchly. How are we to understand this deeper comparison, the difference of these two powers over same-sex desire?

NEW 'HOMOSEXUAL' AND PERSISTING CHRISTIANITY

Foucault compares homosexual and sodomite so far as they condense different sorts of power, which is to say, so far as they are fashioned to produce different kinds of power effects. He juxtaposes the effects or consequences of their discursive deployments, which means, the speech of the apparatus of power that each term serves. This sort of contrast can find interesting differences between sodomite and homosexual. There is, for example, a difference in how the terms register visibility. When Peter Damian comes 'face to face' with the sodomite – the image of faces is his – the only thing he can say is: 'Sodomite, whoever you are.'[26] Peter Damian can stand face to face with the sodomite without being able to recognize him because the sodomite's morphology is curiously concealed. Every characteristic he ascribes to the sodomitic body is anticipatory. However much one might wish for the sodomite's body to betray itself, it remains equivocal until named. The homosexual body is, by contrast, 'indiscreet'. It already betrays itself in physical and physiological attributes. Long before there is a confession, before there is even an overt genital act, the cunning clinician can diagnose the hidden causality of homosexuality.

A related rhetorical difference can be found in how the terms prescribe speech or silence. In the *Gomorran Book*, Peter Damian calls out to the sodomite whom he cannot see, whom he could not recognize even if they were standing 'face to face'. He must persuade the sodomite – he must beg, flatter, bully the sodomite – to admit to being named. The sodomite must convict himself by speaking. Of course, once the sodomite begins to weep over his sin, once he confesses his crime, he is sent into a permanent exile of solitary repentance. The moment the sodomite names himself, he is to be silenced. By contrast the category 'homosexuality' is meant to elicit a steady stream of speech from the pervert, even if it is the speech of denial. The category is imposed by an astute clinician or judge with or without the subject's agreement. It does not require assent. It does require response. Being named 'homosexual' is an invitation to a lifetime of speeches, of reports about one's condition, of endless therapeutic exchange. Refusals to accept the imposed name are just so much more evidence for clinical or juridical inspection.

There are other rhetorical differences between the categories, but they tend to converge around a contrast that Foucault describes throughout *History of Sexuality*, vol. 1 and suggests in the controversial passage. 'Sodomite' functions as a category for denouncing and excluding, while 'homosexual' is a category for managing and regulating. The rhetorical presumption of the category 'sodomite' is that the sin can be, if not repented, at least obliterated. The rhetorical presumption of the category 'homosexual' is that the perversion can be, if not cured, at least managed.

These differences of rhetorical effect have been chosen to illustrate the kinds of contrasts Foucault wants most to register in his own rhetorical forms. But the distinctness of these rhetorical forms can be maintained in the end only by invoking a deeper distinction between state power and church power. While this distinction is emphasized in Foucault's lecture, it is not applied, there or in the other published material, to a reconsideration of the theological bases for the 19th-century sex-identities. Nor do we see it applied in the latest and most elegant re-reading of Foucault by Halperin.[27] Among many other things, Halperin proposes to save Foucault's claim for the newness of the category 'homosexual' by arguing that it combines in a novel way features that can be found in a variety of earlier homoerotic identities, including the identity of the sodomite. Halperin refers to several kinds of medieval materials in making his argument, including Bruneto Latini's retelling of a story from Apuleius. The comparison between Bruneto Latini's version and the version in the Greek novel reveals much about differences between medieval Christian and ancient pagan views of same-sex desire. It does not address the persistent power of medieval Christian rhetorics to elicit and superintend contemporary sexual identities. Indeed, Halperin sometimes supposes what Foucault sometimes suggests in jest – that medieval Christian rhetorics are just as rhetorically inert, just as dead, as ancient Greek novels.

State power and church power have long existed side by side, in a complex system of mutual influence and violent competition. It is a remarkable fact that Christian theology has been lavish in making identities around sex – and perhaps even in making the very templates for our sex-linked identities. It is more remarkable (and more urgent) that Christian rhetorical programs retain so much of their power over such identities.

Certainly Foucault was interested in the distinctiveness of church power. Indeed this interest become central to the program for the whole of the *History of Sexuality*. In a 1978 lecture before the University of Tokyo, for example, Foucault presented the 'state' of some of the 'hypotheses' that structured the project for the history of sexuality as he was then revising it.[28] One of these hypotheses is that Christianized western society, since Augustine at least, has overproduced discourse about sex. Another is that this discourse 'very quickly and very early took what can be called a scientific form'.[29] A third hypothesis holds that what is distinctive about Christian sexual science is not the content of its prohibitions, but the form of its imposition. 'It is then along the way of the mechanisms of power much more than along that of moral ideals or ethical interdicts – it is along the way of the mechanisms of power that one must do the history of sexuality in the western world after Christianity.'[30] The name for this power is the pastoral, and the origin of this 'science of sex' is distinctly Christian.

In the lecture, Foucault summarizes the distinctiveness of Christian pastoral twice, first in terms of the character of its power, then in terms of its significance or implications. The four characteristics of its power are that it is not territorial; that it is concerned with nurturing its own rather than vanquishing others; that it entails responsibility to the point of self-sacrifice; and that it is exercised over individuals, one by one.[31] The four implications are that the individual is obliged to seek salvation; that seeking is not done alone; that it requires an absolute obedience; and, finally, that there will be a 'series of techniques (*techniques*) and procedures (*procédés*) concerned with truth and the production of truth'.[32]

What has happened to this Christian power? Sometimes Foucault does speak of Christian pastoral in the past tense. For example, in a series of originally anonymous conversations with a young hitchhiker, Foucault recalls nostalgically what church power used to be.[33] He jokes that he is the only one who remains interested in the daily operation of the Catholic church in France.[34] I can only reply: would that he were right. In reality, we still inhabit extremely powerful 'religious' rhetorics, not least in regard to same-sex desires or acts. We may even be living through a great reassertion of the power of 'religious' judgment over the secular management of sex-linked identities – and not only in Christianity. Certainly church power is still with us, and not only as appropriated or adapted by the modern clinic. It projects its identities in ministry, in liturgy, in doctrine – not to say, on radio talk-shows and televangelists' broadcast preaching.

Indeed, we should remember that many early and medieval Christian sex-identities are assumed and performed daily right around us. Some individuals confess that they have been doing just what the Christian scriptures or the theological authorities described, and then they resolve to exchange sinful sex-identities for other sex-identities, for example to go from being sodomites to being penitents or preachers or monks. These individuals perform and exchange these identities, not on their own, but in communities, some of which have elaborate discourses for elicitation and conformation as well as large bureaucracies for surveillance and punishment. The sodomite is still on stage, with new performers appearing daily.

Foucault most have known much of this, so I assume that he would not want to endorse any simple notion that modern rhetorics have simply replaced Christian rhetorics. But then what becomes of the claim that a new discourse of homosexuality has appropriated elements of Christian pastoral generally and of the medieval discourses of sodomy in particular? How do we show that a new rhetoric, a new regime of power, has taken over elements from an older regime that still exists? In fact, the discourse of sodomy continues to flourish today in certain Christian groups right alongside the discourse of homosexuality.

Foucault might reply that the invention of the homosexual has altered or substantially changed present performances of the sodomite. For example, some Christian denominations have recently abandoned the term 'sodomy' in favor of 'homosexuality'. But the substitution is ambiguous. In the documents of the Roman Catholic *magisterium*, for example, the rhetorical logic of 'sodomy' persists under the new term 'homosexuality'. The category of 'homosexuality' brings some of its own ideas, some of its particular legal and medical respectability, but it has to fit these within a logic of definition and condemnation set in place long before it was coined. In such cases, how do we determine who controls the term 'homosexual', who really runs power through it? If the term is now being used by both clinical regimes and 'conservative' theologians, who is appropriating what? Has the newness of the modern identity been lost because it is now used as a synonym for older identities?

And was the new identity, built out of Christian materials, ever really free from the power of Christian rhetorical regimes?

In and after *History of Sexuality*, vol. 1, Foucault dismissed the easy programs of sexual liberation, straight or queer, in order to propose a more radical refashioning of new selves. We do not need to avow ourselves homosexuals, he would say, 'We have to create a gay life.'[35] To which I say, Amen. But if we are to refashion our selves and cities, we ought to try something other than *bricolage* in the basements and attics of defunct and yet still devouring theologies. 'Homosexual' is a theological riddle. It cannot be unriddled by pretending that theology is dead.

MAKING AND REMAKING SEXUAL IDENTITIES

Christian rhetorics still use their distinctive power to project identities built around sex. Pastoral power is exercised daily in words arranged into scripts. By 'scripts' I mean the ways in which the words impose not just terms for self-description or self-evaluation, but the role for a personage, the stage directions for an identity. Pastoral scripts can be found in every Christian genre: in sermons and scriptural interpret-ations, treatises and compendia of cases, confessional interrogatories and inquisitorial trials, marriage manuals and pamphlets of prayer. What runs through these genres – and what runs through Foucault's four characteristics or implications of pastoral power – is the power of words to elicit and enforce the performance of certain roles or identities.

Of course, the scripts of Christian pastoral care are not just words – certainly not just didactic words. We may think of ritual actions (the sacraments or sacramentals, liturgical and para-liturgical rites) or places (the confessional, the pulpit, the churchyard, the town square) or punishments (fasting, flogging, exile, execution). Medieval words and practices about being a sodomite enacted distinctive notions about what identities were and how they could be assumed, repented or exchanged. In medieval Latin liturgy, for example, there are multiple substitutions of identity: at the Mass, a priest becomes Christ, but also Christ's spouse; a nun at her veiling becomes the virgin martyr Agnes, but also Christ's bride. In baptism, the new believer puts on Christ; in the Eucharist, she or he consumes Christ as bread and wine in order to be united with Christ. In much Christian doctrine, the central claim of vicarious atonement requires multiple exchanges of identity. The Lord's sacrifice on the cross can be applied for salvation only by a sort of substitution of persons, without regard for their sexes or genders. Christianity is a religion of exchanging identities without sex. It can do this only by a series of repressions and aversions. So of course Christianity produces another series of strongly sexed identities in antithesis, as sin.

The very successful projection of sexual identities in Christian pastoral practice depends on a gender-suppressing dogma that is performed in liturgy and sacraments. Gender suppression implies gender ambiguity, which must be policed by stigmatization. I have been speaking of the role of the Sodomite, but we should remember as well the Lascivious Widow, the Witch and the Self-Abuser, who was a figure of theological imagination before he – less often, she – was an object of clinical attention. Against such sin-identities, we can place the Angelic Monk, the Virgin Martyr, the Chaste Wife and the Priest with Pure Hands. When I reach out to touch the bodies of these figures, I touch theological artifacts. I touch them still when I touch the body of a modern Homosexual. Christian rhetorics of identity enforcement were infused into the category from the very beginning, in ways that Foucault does and does not admit. It may be that the identity of the Pervert really is just a variation on Christian scripts for stigmatizing sex-identities. The Pervert responds to a sort of power that is a variation of Christian pastoral (as Foucault admits), but she or he also carries an identity that makes sex morally central and personally defining in just the way Christian sin-identities did. The Pervert is child to the Sodomite. The Sodomite reverses sexual nature, but thus also emphasizes it, insists on its fixity at the core of the person. He thus blocks exchange with the Body of an incarnate God whose genitals are necessarily erased. For the Sodomite, as for other Christian sex-identities, the content of the genital acts are not so troubling as the negation of Christian wishes for genderless moral exchange, for vicarious atonement through unsexed substitution, Body for bodies.

Christian churches have been able to project sin-identities, not just because of their political power, but because of essential features of their doctrine and worship. If this is right, then Christian churches ought still to retain some of that power over identities, despite their diminished political standing in some industrialized nations. My hope is that this power might be used to counter-balance the sex-identities projected by increasingly powerful systems for managing sex, systems of the modern state, systems of the mass media. Indeed, I also hope (here you see how pious I remain) that Christian theology might open the way for those new ways of being queer that Foucault prophesied.

One new way to be queer is retrieval of church identities. Christian theology offers an enormous repertoire of identities that were crafted before or against modern state power. Consider again the role of the Sodomite. Today the choice to be a sodomite might be quite radical. Camping homosexuality by performing sodomy might remind us that there was something beyond the grip of modern nation-states and their legal–clinical surveillance. Precisely to the extent that older models of male–male relationship encode different relations to civic power, their retrieval might disrupt our present assumptions. Being a sodomite in an age of homosexuals becomes an ironically theological act of political resistance.

More interesting ways to be queer would require the invention of new identities. Before that can be done out of theology, a number of conditions will have to be met in the churches. One of them is a condition of honesty about the full experience of the churches with same-sex desire, and perhaps especially male–male desire. The relationship between sodomites and churchmen is strong. Indeed, in medieval and modern cultures, in archives and in satires, the relationship is one of identity. The churchman is a sodomite.

In my own church, which remains the Roman Catholic church, this connection is both notorious and scandalous. It is notorious because it has been a constant topic for polemic, before and after the Protestant Reformation. It is scandalous because it is impossible to talk about it without generating and experiencing scandal. I do not want to end either with notoriety or with scandal, but I do want to make this final suggestion. If you want to understand the power of the Catholic church to project scripts for sexual sin-identities right up to the present, even under regimes of secular management, you might well begin with the Catholic closet. In our pluralistic societies, where almost any adolescent can buy glossy gay magazines or watch 'Queer as Folk', not to speak of surfing porn websites, it is remarkable that the Catholic church continues to attract so many young men who seek a sturdy closet. Catholic closets are still some of the most solidly built closets around, not to say the most ornate. As civil sodomy laws fall, even in America, as more Christian churches ordain openly queer believers or bless their unions, the Catholic church seems able not only to maintain, but in some measure to refurbish its closets.

There is much to consider here, not least the great poignancy in the fears that still drive so many young gay men. But I would suggest that Catholic closets be considered as a sign of the unbroken strength of at least one church over sexual identities. It might even be that the closets show in part where that churchly strength comes from. The cooperative mis-speaking that makes closets possible is in fact a strategy for dealing with sex much more generally. But it might also invite resistance, might disclose the utopian possibility of a better use for the church's rhetorical powers in regard to sex. Could the church that invented sodomy now invent happier scripts for homoerotic desires? For the benefit of queers of course, but also for the benefit of non-queers, since the reformation of one part of Christian sexual teaching will in time require reformation of it all. For the benefit of Catholics, of course, but also of other Christians, since mutual influence is a reality even when ecumenical dialogue is not. For the benefit of all, since the Christian churches still possess unsuspected influence over the imagination of sex in societies that once were Christendom.

NOTES

1   Michel Foucault, 'Sexualité et pouvoir', in *Dits et écrits 1954–1988*, ed. Daniel Defert and François Ewald, volume 3, *1976–1979* (Paris: NRF/Gallimard, 1994, pp.552–70) including a transcript of exchanges after the lecture.

2   The (punning) phrase 'sex-linked identities' is obviously my own. I mean to describe by it assigned or appropriated identities that concern erotic dispositions, desires or acts. I concede that the term 'identity' is particularly tricky and that it is not a term that Foucault uses in this way in *History of Sexuality*, vol. 1. Indeed, so far as I can recall, the term appears only once in that book. It then has the mathematical meaning of sameness, and it is applied to misleading reifications about power. See Michel Foucault, *Histoire de la sexualité*, vol. 1: *La volonté de savoir* (Paris: NRF/Gallimard, 1976, p.121). But I need 'identity' to refer indistinguishably to what Foucault distinguishes as anatomy (morphology, physiology) and subjectivity. The need for an imprecise term should become clearer as the chapter proceeds.

3   David Halperin, 'Forgetting Foucault: Acts, Identities, and the History of Sexuality', *Representations*, 63 (1998), 93–120.

4   Foucault, *Histoire de la sexualité*, 1, 59.

5   Camille Paglia, *Vamps and Tramps* (New York: Vintage Books, 1994, p.99): 'Foucault, a glib game-player who took very little research a very long way, was especially attractive to literary academics in search of a short cut to understanding world history, anthropology and political economy.' See also the approving summary of attacks on Foucault in Rictor Norton, *The Myth of the Modern Homosexual: Queer History and the Search for Cultural Unity* (London and Washington: Cassell, 1997), pp.8–10.

6　Halperin seems to take the reference this way in 'Forgetting Foucault', p.97 (italics added).

7　The quoted phrase is from Halperin, 'Forgetting Foucault', p.97.

8　'Salmanticenses', *Cursus theologiae moralis*, 6.7.5.1, as in *Collegii Salmanticensis Fratres Discalceatorum Cursus theologiae moralis* (Venice: Nicolaus Pezzana, 1724), 6:164b–165a, paras 84 and 87.

9　There are other passages in the text where Foucault seems to frame his contrast as between 17th- or 18th-century discourses and 19th-century ones, but these are typically passages in which he is responding to the chronology imposed by the narrative of the 'repressive hypothesis'. See, for example, Foucault, *Histoire de la sexualité*, 1,51, on the three great codes regulating sexual practices before the 18th century.

10　Compare the list of 'recent' sciences in Foucault, *Histoire de la sexualité*, 1, 46.

11　Compare Halperin, 'Forgetting Foucault', p.108.

12　For instances of '*caractère*', see Foucault, *Histoire de la sexualité*, 1, 59, 61; of '*visage*', 1,66; of '*figure*', 1, 53, 59.

13　All of the quoted phrases in this and the next paragraph are from Foucault, *Histoire de la sexualité*, 1, 59.

14　Compare Halperin, 'Forgetting Foucault', pp.107–8.

15　I follow the edition by Kurt Reindel, who prints the *Liber Gomorrhianus* as *Epistola 31* in *Die Briefe des Petrus Damiani*, vol. 1, Monumenta Germaniae Historica: Die Briefe der deutschen Kaiserzeit 4 (Munich: MGH, 1983). On this point, see Reindel 287.5, 'virus plagarum'; 307.17, 'invasi pectoris tartarum virus'; 312.10/13, 'plagus', glossing Jeremiah 14:17; 287.7, 'cancer'; 288.19 and 294.13, 'vulnus'; 288.2, 289.2, and 321.22, 'contagio'; 294.15, 'peremptoria pestes'; and so on.

16　Reindel 296.16, 315.2 / 7 / 17.

17　Reindel 313.5, 'rabies'; 323.18–19.

18　Reindel 307.7 / 22–3, 310.7–8.

19　Reindel 298.22–4, 'qui masculina femora polluit, si natura permitteret, quicquid in mulieribus agitur, totum in masculo per effrenatae libidinis insaniam perpetraret'.

20　Reindel 313.13–22.

21　See particularly Reindel, 299.7–22.

22　 Reindel 302.30–303.2.

23　Foucault, *Histoire de la sexualité*, 1, 29.

24　Foucault, *Histoire de la sexualité*, 1, 142.

25　See the summary in Didier Eribon, 'Michel Foucault's Histories of Sexuality', *GLQ: A Journal of Lesbian and Gay Studies*, 7 (2001), 31–86, at pp.26–42.

26　Reindel 298.8, 'Sed iam te ore ad os quisquis es, sodomita, convenio.'

27　Halperin, 'How to Do the History of Male Homosexuality', *GLQ: A Journal of Lesbian and Gay Studies*, 6 (2000), 87–123.

28　Foucault, 'Sexualité et pouvoir', 3:553, 'Je voudrais vous exposer aujourd'hui un état, pas même de mon travail, mais des hypothèses de mon travail.' He had spoken just above of submitting his hypotheses to the listeners (3:552).

29　Foucault, 'Sexualité et pouvoir', 3:556.

30　Foucault, 'Sexualité et pouvoir', 3:560.

31　Foucault, 'Sexualité et pouvoir', 3:561–2.

32　Foucault, 'Sexualité et pouvoir', 3:562–4, with the final quotation from 564.

33　Thierry Voeltzel, *Vingt ans et après*, ed. Mireille Davidovici (Paris: Bernard Grasset, 1978, pp.156–7). I was alerted to this section of Voeltzel's text by Richard Townsend's translation of it in *Religion and Culture: Michel Foucault*, ed. Jeremy R. Carrette (New York: Routledge, 1999, pp.106–9).

34 Voeltzel, *Vingt ans*, p.159. Voeltzel ends a comment by saying, 'je ne crois pas qu'il y ait beaucoup de personnes que ça intéresse'. Foucault replies, 'Non, non, sans doute pas. Il n'y a plus que moi,' and then laughs.
35 'Sex, Power and the Politics of Identity' (interview with B. Gallagher and A. Wilson), *The Advocate*, 400 (7 August 1984), 26–30 and 58, reprinted in Foucault, *Ethics: Subjectivity and Truth*, ed. Rabinow, vol. 1, 163–73, at p.163.

Chapter 13

Catholic Sex

Michael Mahon

Below is some evidence to consider, comprising: (1) the expression of a fear, (2) a model of conduct, (3) the image of a stigmatized attitude, and (4) an example of abstinence.[1]

A fear   A Jesuit priest/social scientist, Thomas Reese, reports having conducted an Internet search using the keywords 'Catholic', 'Vatican', 'pope', 'bishop' and 'priest'. 'After searching awhile, the program asked if I would like to add the word "sex", since this word came up so often in news stories about Catholics.'[2] While Reese seems to want to attribute the identification of Catholicism and sex to media interest and claims that 'the Catholic hierarchy talks more about social justice today than about sex', the identification Catholic Sex is difficult to reject. Reese argues that the issue of sex has paralyzed the Catholic Church. Its clergy have been rendered silent because they can neither defend nor attack the teachings; they fear the Church has lost all credibility on the issue. Catholic intellectuals, especially clergy, according to Reese, fear specializing in sexual ethics. I disagree with Reese's claim that media interest accounts for the Catholic Sex identification. It is in the realm of sex that official Catholic statements are most glaringly irrelevant. 'The real story here,' Reese himself announces, 'is that in the Catholic Church the battle about sex is over. On questions of birth control, masturbation, premarital sex, divorce and remarriage, the hierarchy has lost most of the faithful.'[3] My own fear and suspicion is that Church statements about social justice are similarly ignored.

An ideal of conduct   'A young man came to a monastery and requested the superior to admit him as a member of the order. After looking him over carefully, the superior conducted him into the inner court of the cloister, led him up to a statue of a youth that was standing near by, and bade him to praise, pet and fondle the statue for ten minutes and then to come and report to him in his office. When the young man reported, the superior asked him how the statue behaved. He replied that it showed no signs either of approval or disapproval. Then the superior bade the youth to take a whip which he handed him, and to lash the statue viciously for ten minutes, and again to report to him. When he returned, the superior asked him how the statue acted under the lashes, he answered that it behaved exactly as it did whilst it was being caressed. The superior rejoined: "If you can do the same in the convent; if you can suffer both praise and blame, reward and punishment with similar equanimity as the statue even though in a different, namely a rational manner, then you are a fit subject for the monastery: otherwise I should advise you not to enter." The point of this story is as applicable to candidates for marriage as it is to postulants for the Religious life.'[4]

An image   A Massachusetts man, whose 14-year-old son claimed his father had physically abused him and whose son was placed by the Department of Social Services in the foster care of two gay men, has summoned attorneys to plead to the United States Supreme Court arguing that the placement violated his 'deeply held Catholic beliefs about homosexuality'. His petition to the court maintains that his 'fundamental Catholic religious beliefs concerning what constitutes a moral family unit are completely incongruous and incompatible with this foster placement'. The petitioner goes on to defend his claim by quoting a statement by Massachusetts' Catholic bishops, that homosexual activity is 'something objectively wrong inasmuch as it falls short of the ultimate norm of Christian morality in the area of genital expression, i.e., a relationship between male and female within the family union'.[5]

The man did not contest the allegation of physical abuse or address the role of child abuse in the constitution of a Catholic family unit.

A model of abstention   'A coffin draped with an American flag rested in the old chapel at West Point. A cadet who died from injuries he had received in a football game was to be buried with full military honors, an unusual event at the old army post.

All through the day before the funeral long lines of uniformed cadets passed in single file to view the body of their companion for the last time.

As each man halted by the coffin, he laid a white flower on the American flag, and with a respectful salute moved off.

Why?

This cadet had been a star in every form of athletics; he had been one of the best liked men in the training school. But he was more. Throughout his course he had been famous for his cleanness of mind and body, beloved for his purity. And in the last goodbye his fellow cadets were paying him the splendid tribute of the "white flower of a blameless life".'[6]

Throughout the text to follow, throughout the sexual morality texts that provide the focus for my analysis of Catholic Sex, athletes and military personnel provide models of conduct, models of the blameless life. The leftfielder of my local baseball team is on suspension, having beaten his wife with a telephone. Two previous partners have revealed similar acts of violence. A convicted rapist has been disqualified from his world heavyweight title bout for biting off a one-inch piece of the ear of his opponent. The highest ranking enlisted man in the United States military was court martialed a few years ago for sexual misconduct. Odd models of conduct.

Michel Foucault explicitly avoided theoretical texts by the philosophical greats. He makes passing references to Plato, Aristotle, Epictetus and Augustine, but his argument really hinges on the writings of Artemidoras the dream analyst (rather than Plato the philosopher) and of Cassian the pastor–confessor–spiritual counselor–caretaker of souls (rather than Augustine the theologian). The texts that interested him were those that penetrated the popular mind and daily practical life; Dr Joyce Brothers and Ann Landers rather than Rawls and Rorty, Habermas and Gadamer.

A few years ago my friend, James Bernauer, introduced me to a modern Foucaultian goldmine. Father William Leonard, a retired Jesuit theologian at Boston College, published an advertisement in Catholic newspapers all over the country that said, essentially, please send me all those Catholic artifacts gathering dust in your basement that you are too pious or superstitious to throw out, and I will give them a home. He was flooded. Ornate vestments, jeweled chalices, scapulars, holy cards, holy water foundations, 'flesh-colored Christs that glow in the dark', Jesuses with eyes that follow you, and boxes and boxes of advice pamphlets on every conceivable topic that sold for about a dime apiece in church vestibules, started arriving at the Boston College mailroom. Inspired by Foucault's *History of Sexuality*, I spent several months studying the pamphlets about sex. I will refer to their authors as 'the vestibule moralists'.

The typical Catholic claim of its moral uniqueness – that it has deliberately avoided keeping up with modern times and attitudes – is false. 'You have the same fleas as the dogs you've lain with,' said Catholic novelist Walker Percy of his church. This modern understanding of selfhood pervades Catholicism and its sexual ethics. Secondly, the above modernism is a metaphysical position implicit in the ethics of sexuality of Catholicism. I see the issue as the photographic negative of Nietzsche's claim that beneath the surface of any metaphysical system is the morality that the author wants us to subscribe to. In the pamphlets of the vestibule moralists a metaphysics, other than the explicit metaphysics, is implicit in the sexual ethics; a definite understanding of the relationship between self and world is implicit in the ethics as a moral ideal. The moral ideal is to constitute oneself as the cartesian subject, internally bifurcated, immune to influence from others (at least peers), and separated from the social world. Thirdly, this ethic is contrary to the cultivation of a spirit of community. The relationship of trust is one that one may only have with superiors. Peers may not be trusted, so relationships of equality and mutuality may not be part of the young Catholic's life. Equality precludes trust. In a relationship of inequality, trust is necessary, but mutuality is precluded.

COMPENSATION

A key premise is that marriage and especially the bearing of children and providing for their education is so difficult and so powerfully painful that God in His wisdom made sex a powerful source of pleasure to compensate those willing to take on the burdens of family life. The issue is one of just compensation. 'Married people are justly entitled to all the delight they can reasonably procure from the marital act, for they pay fully for this delight by the assumption of its consequences and the attendant responsibilities.'[7] This understanding of sexual expression serves to constitute sex as merely a means, an enticement, a pay-off, to induce people to produce offspring. Our sex organs and the pleasure associated with their use are for the sake of the production and rearing of children. Without this incidental pleasure, who would be willing to take on the burdens of family life? 'The obligations incumbent upon and the problems arising from marriage are limitless. To compensate for them God has attached pleasure to sex, psychological as well as physical. The pleasure of sex is consequently no more an end in itself than is the pleasure of eating. God did not give us stomachs and appetites for the sake of pleasure, although He did join pleasure to this function of self-preservation.'[8] In 'the marriage embrace' men and women 'enjoy pleasures which are God's payment for the usually painful and difficult duty of bearing and rearing children'.[9]

In fact, without such compensation for bearing these limitless burdens, children, no one would willingly produce children and the human race would become extinct. That apparently accounts for God's motivation in creating sexual pleasure. He pays with pleasure and receives a populous planet in return. 'The responsibilities of bringing up children and providing for them are so many and great, that unless the sex urge strongly impelled people to the procreative act no children would be born into the world, and the human race would perish.'[10] If God had not associated this pleasure exclusively with its procreative purpose, 'a great many would avoid the burdens of married life, and God's plan of creation would be frustrated'.[11] And God's desire to people our planet does not fully account for God's plan. Heaven, too, would remain underpopulated if He failed to reward people with pleasure. 'God puts pleasure into the sex act to reward married people for the hardships of rearing children. Otherwise parents might not rear families, and God's plan of peopling heaven might be blocked.'[12]

One author equivocates 'a strong desire for children' and sexual desire in the context of revealing God's ultimate plan of populating heaven: 'Without this desire [for children] no one would bother having children, no children would be born to fill the heavenly places of the fallen angels, and God's plan would be frustrated. So God in His wisdom put into men and women a strong urge, a drive, and instinct for the act of forming children.'[13] 'Again, if men and boys were allowed to enjoy sexual pleasure by themselves, or with others outside of marriage, they wouldn't bother about getting married and taking on the hard task of rearing a family. The human race would be ruined. Millions of children would never be born, and God's plan of eternal happiness for them would not be realized.'[14] In sum, 'God wants children. The task of bearing children, of educating and training them are heavy burdens. God says: "If you will give me children, I will repay you with the joys and pleasures of love and sex".' A clear understanding of sexual immorality follows: 'the evil boy or girl says: … "I will accept these rewards of parenthood, though I am in no position even to think of doing the work of a parent." I feel sure that any honest young person would say, quite candidly, "That looks to me like a form of theft." And so it is. The precious seed of life is sometimes wasted. Passion is excited without any intention to help God create life.'[15] Pleasure is a commodity offered in a fair transaction to serve God's purpose of people production. The business categories of incentives, fair compensation and honest transaction most appropriately account for a distinctively Catholic sexual ethic.

God's businesslike, fair compensation for our toil and trouble provides the foundation for the sexual ethic we are expected to pass on to our daughters and sons. They are to recognize their erotic attractions in the same business terms of payment for services rendered, cash equivalents, fair compensation, credits and debits. 'A girl-lily (if you could but realize how lovely is the virgin heart of an unspoiled girl!) should never feel an obligation to pay for courtesies, such as a dinner, a drive, a dance, and the like, with priceless coin. If you are entertaining, if you appreciate your boyfriend's attentions, and express your pleasure in the happy times they have provided, a real man will feel your graciousness offers full compensation, and that, in fact, he is the debtor.'[16] We are talking about goodnight kisses here. Grounded upon marketing metaphors, then, the moralists condemn any sexual expression as unfair, as seeking 'the compensation without the toil and trouble it was meant to compensate'.[17] Even sexual fantasies are evaluated in terms of unfairness and cheating: 'there must not be any imaginations that cause sensual or bodily pleasure. That is a cowardly sort of cheating when it is deliberate – doing in the mind what you would not do in real life, or only if you were married.'[18] The attribution of cowardice may seem puzzling at first, but it is obviously in reference to the deliberate avoidance of the 'toil and trouble' of family life. A young woman may not even fantasize about sexual relations with her future husband because he is not yet her property: 'Taking pleasure in that kind of imagining is tearing something out of its setting – stealing, in fact.'[19] A young woman's chastity is described as 'her most priceless possession'.[20] She can provoke much interest if she offers her body cheaply, but she will forfeit any interest in her essential self. Like a savvy entrepreneur, she withholds her product from all but the one interested in and willing to pay the price for her essential self. 'If she offers her wares at a cheap price, a motley crowd will snap them up, but it will be interested very much more in the easy-to-come-by merchandise of her bargain counter than in her.'[21]

The cheap erotocommercial transaction finds its most vivid analogue in the business of drug dealing. As the pusher's livelihood depends upon luring innocents into a realm of sensation they had never known, so too the young boy must stimulate the craving in the otherwise placid girl. Familiar with the narcotic 'kick' of sensuality, he plays on her craving for affection and manipulates her into granting a few liberties. Misinterpreting her signs of affection as mutual enjoyment of the 'kick', 'he goes on, and of course ends by introducing her to sensations she had not dreamed existed, but of which in the future she will crave repetition'.[22] To assure future production from the less than enterprising young businesswoman, he must sustain and increase her addiction. The drug trafficker, rather than the wholesome pilot, sailor or quarterback, provides the model for his behavior. Since the self itself is at issue in the business of sensuality, the sale essentially enslaves.

Addiction to sensuality leads to slavery. The young woman's appearance deteriorates like that of the drug addict: 'the expression of the face is dimmed, the open look of the eye is obscured, the smile appears suspicious, and the former easy manner, graceful carriage and carefree laughter assume an element of unreality, deceit and distrust, and of consequent awkwardness, embarrassment and weak-ness'.[23] By allowing the body's desires free rein, 'the entire person degenerates and is quickly reduced to slavery and impotency'.[24]

'In short, he takes advantage of her innocence, and it could be said that his behavior is the same in type (though certainly not in degree of guilt) as that of the dope peddlers who work among the young and recruit new addicts.'[25] It is worth noting that the author need not qualify the degree of guilt. Given the other comparisons in the texts, he is in fact more guilty than the drug dealer who only harms the body. For example, to be the unwilling victim of rape is preferable to being the willing participant in an amorous adventure with the one you love. One moralist states the case poignantly in commenting upon the saying, no doubt spoken in the confessional, 'I have been guilty of indiscretions with my gentleman friend.' He is neither gentleman nor friend: 'Yea, the meanest criminal and rapist would not be able to harm the girl in question as she has been harmed by her so-called friend, who has taken undue personal liberties with her. The rapist might overpower her by force. Yet, because of her positive and utmost aversion to the unmentionable outrage, her purity and innocence, far from suffering the least harm, would merely be greatly increased in merit and luster through the formidable misadventure.'[26] In contrast to the rapist who merely violated her body and perhaps in some sense her psyche, her 'so-called friend' has contributed to the violation of her soul by swaying her 'to surrender voluntarily the glory of personal chastity'.[27] As the passage cited above indicates, the rapist might even positively enhance her moral standing by providing the opportunity for her increase in merit.

Of course it is absurd, but quite consistent with the moral psychology operating in the manuals. The moralists simply follow the logic to its inevitable conclusions.

OCCASIONS OF SIN

The task is to construct a self in independence of a world and a body that are fatally determined and hostile. But complete independence can never be achieved. Although the connection between soul and body, self and world, is tenuous, the hostile and aggressive body and world infiltrate into the life of the mind. 'The suggestive story, the smutty joke ... [t]he lewd picture, the salacious movie, the prurient novel, the lascivious floor show, penetrate beyond the retina of the eye to paint their images upon the mind.'[28] The mind cannot escape the penetration of the world. The body itself participates in the sabotage of the soul seeking purity. Deception is a key weapon of the world. The hostile world launches occasions of sin, 'like the time bombs dropped by the Germans in the first years of the war. They appeared to be duds. Crowds would gather around one. Suddenly, an hour after it had fallen, it would explode, killing great numbers of people.'[29] The body must defend the soul from the assault by shielding the soul from the world's onslaught. By itself the mind, like the sea, is tranquil; the world however is unstable, like a raging wind, like an earthquake, shattering the soul's tranquillity. 'Your mind is a fluid and floating thing, like the sea. Left to itself, the sea remains calm. But if a wind blows upon it, it ripples; and if an earthquake occurs at the bottom of it, again the surface heaves. Similarly, unless you keep your eyes and ears tightly shut, which you cannot, sights and sounds of all sorts will strike them, including those that suggest to your mind, sensual subjects. You see pictures, posters, people; you hear and cannot help hearing sexual talk. That is like the wind plunging on the sea.'[30] Since the seductions of the world cannot be avoided, the task is to fortify oneself, become aloof, and rise above the turmoil. True romance remains detached from the world; false romance involves oneself with the world, the human community, the incarnate life of humanity. 'The sea can drown a man and bring sorrow and ruin into his family, but there is a pride and romance about a tall sailing ship riding over the waves in windy weather.'[31]

The texts appeal to the young man/boy in terms of a very specific understanding of masculinity. True manhood controls. Envision the essential self as a pilot, a driver, a quarterback, a sailor maintaining complete control over a massive airliner, a car, an offensive line, an ocean liner. But the body, one's ship or one's plane, is not a comrade in arms, but always potentially rebellious. Ultimate victory can never be achieved, but small, temporary victory is possible if both the world and one's own body are viewed as the enemies. Victory cannot be merely over the seductions of the world. The goal is 'victory over the temptations of the flesh! Let priests, parents, and teachers awaken in our young people the spirit of the conqueror.'[32] Life is essentially a 'grim battle', and the boy must become 'not only a man in the world', for that cannot be avoided, 'but a man against the world'.[33] Like the ship, the car, the airliner one must become 'strong as steel', untarnishable. 'Nothing can take the controls away from you.'[34]

Meticulous planning for any encounter with the world fortifies the young person, rendering him immune from the enemy, and again victory at war provides the paradigm. 'During the war the greatest air battles were won on paper before they were ever fought. ... Keeping pure is a far more important battle than any air battle.'[35] Great victories are won more in their preparation than in the heat and torment of battle.

ESTABLISHING THE RELATIONSHIP BETWEEN SELF AND WORLD

The adolescent boy's fascination with cars provides the vestibule moralists with an avenue for imaging the masculine separation of self from world. Automotive imagery invites the youth to identify power over machine with power over the self. He would not think much of 'a driver who couldn't keep his car on the road. Then what about a boy who surrenders just as soon as his passions show signs of life?' One's very masculinity is at stake when one fails to see the contest of power. 'You can tell a man by the way he holds his own, by the way he can harness power, and make it bend to the command of his will.'[36] But the moving car carries more dangers than might be initially imagined: 'No married man ever goes automobile riding with a girl, or any other woman than his wife, without evil intentions.'[37] Perhaps more importantly, however, the automobile signals a warning about the omnipresent dangers in the young man's path. The parked automobile, after all, and not one in motion, is 'enemy number one'. 'With the twin cloaks of darkness and clandestinity thrown around them, a young couple parked along a country road are deliberately subjecting their virtue to too great and needless a strain.'[38] While the adolescent finds the car inviting, intriguing, an arena for the exercise of power, one must recognize that 'smart drivers don't take chances'.[39] As, in all such matters, the natural law as revealed in the creator's intentions, in this case, Henry Ford's, embedded in the purposes of all things, displays moral use. 'The car was invented for the purpose of moving individuals from one place to another, not as a portable living room to be moved from one secluded spot to another for the purpose of stealing a few kisses. Don't laugh! You know that sort of thing is going on.'[40] The car's greatest danger arises when the ignition is off. 'Let all young couples keeping company avoid the parked automobile as they would avoid a pest house, reeking with germs of fatal maladies.'[41] Even when the car is not moving – better, even more so when the car is not moving – the driver must obey traffic signals. Anything that 'arouses the desire to go further, that is your red light – Stop!'[42]

While the moralists flag the parked car as 'enemy number one', they paint a portrait of a social world riddled with enemies. When you escort your date home, do not enter the house. Her home is as dangerous as the parked automobile.[43] The road one drives when one enters a relationship is fraught with danger, and the moralist's job is to provide traffic signals to warn the driver. 'In placing these danger signs along the paths of courtship, we are not playing the role of joy-killers, robbing young love of its innocent pleasures, its bright laughter, its fragrant hours of happiness. On the contrary, we are gloom-chasers, ensuring young people good clean fun and pleasures which do not backfire.'[44] But the 'gloom-chasers' find and reveal a world that constantly threatens eternal damnation to such an extent that the astute young person must simply disengage from the world, life and human relationships. Rework your natural responses, and fear whatever attracts you.

'Ninety per cent of the vilest sins of impurity – and that is a conservative estimate – have had their beginning in kisses.'[45] As usual, the nature of kissing was established by God's intention when God created kissing, and the divinely intended end of kissing reveals its moral employment and enjoyment. 'Any normal person is fully aware that under certain circumstances passion was meant by nature to take over. The kiss was by God and nature intended to make men and women grow passionately excited.'[46] By its very nature, then, kissing essentially participates in the process of procreation. 'The sexual process should not be toyed with. From the first stimulating kiss to the maternity ward it is one integral whole.'[47] Although the moralists seem to find it distasteful to write of such practices, one must draw subtle distinctions among types of kisses. Again, the essential nature of different types of kisses illuminates moral imperatives. One moralist, for example, discusses the definition of necking: 'the hug, the squeeze, the I-like-you kiss ... That is what I mean by the term "necking". An inelegant word, but there it is. If you mean something else by "necking" – prolonged or passionate kissing, for example, then it's wrong from the start. It's sinful! Don't start it.'[48] While finding it unpleasant to write of such things, another feels the need to address the practice of 'soul kissing', which the moralist prefers to call 'soul killing': 'We would hesitate to mention this degrading practice here if we did not desire the protection of countless young women whose very innocence of the strong passions of men can be their downfall.'[49]

So slippery is the slope from smooching to sex, it is best to avoid physical contact altogether. 'Hence the wiser and safer course', another moralist concludes, 'is to follow the "hands off" policy and abstain from all physical contact.' He goes on ambivalently to suggest that an engaged couple might find it possible to express their love physically with 'a modest kiss or a reverent caress', but 'double caution' is in order for the engaged because they do indeed love each other and their mutual attraction is not merely physical – although most importantly physical. 'They must always remember that they are not cold white marble but flesh and blood that has an age-old record of weakness. Hold straw before a flame and it will burn. If young people are not to sear their consciences, they will not put themselves in a situation where spontaneous combustion can easily occur.'[50]

Another serious occasion of sin that preoccupies the moralists is the practice they call 'company keeping'. With the capitalistic language for which the moralists have such fondness, company keeping is defined as 'regular and monopolistic associations'.[51] Further attempts to specify the practice manifest the moral danger of the practice. 'The outstanding mark or characteristic, therefore, of steady dating is really the exclusiveness of this practice. It is the key to the problem.'[52] One more specific definition, then, solidifies the moral standard in this regard:

> To keep company in a Christian way means that two persons, man and woman, meet personally at frequent intervals, with the intention of becoming better acquainted and judging whether they are fit and desirable mutual partners for a prospective marriage in Christ and in the Church.
>
> From this definition of Christian company keeping it is evident above all, that when there is absolutely no prospect of marriage between them, a man and a woman, young or old, may not keep regular company. To do so is immoral. Such frequent proximity with one of the other sex is warranted only by the probable or, at least, possible marriage it should lead up to. If this probability of marriage is definitely out of the question, such a close social relation between sexes is unjustifiable.[53]

From kissing to touching to mere proximity, the moralists reveal a social world of mortal moral danger.

Some of the moralists take a final step prescribing the impossible task of eliminating any thought of things sexual. What is the young person to do between the time of the onslaught of puberty and the appropriate age for marriage?[54] '[T]he only safe and sensible thing for you to do in the meantime is to put all thought and all curiosity regarding them [sexual pleasures] as far as possible out of your mind.'[55] A few even go so far as to question their own occupation as sex educators: 'Perhaps never before in the history of mankind was there so much sex instruction as at present, and never before were there so many victims of the vice of impurity. Our predecessors got along without all the sex instruction that is now ruining so many under pretext of educating them. The purest and healthiest nations of the world have been those least acquainted with sex knowledge.'[56]

FIRE: SEX AS INCENDIARY

Arguing that information about sexuality should not be provided to young people (the author does not specify age), one author sees information itself as 'a dangerous weapon'. Education might stimulate the young person to experiment, so we must consider education to be 'like a knife or a revolver in the hand of a child'.[57] The language escalates like the combustion he is describing. Sexual passion is a spark, 'smouldering in the heart of the child', and a thousand forces surround this child that can 'fan this spark into flames'. In a single pamphlet page the child's sexual response spreads from spark to flame to 'the fiery lava of these volcanoes' to an 'awful fiery deluge' igniting 'the hot blast of the Moloch'.[58]

The music to which young people have been exposed for generations has employed fire as a metaphor for sexual passion to indicate its inviting warmth, explosive excitement, and – yes – its compelling danger. The moralists match our music with incendiary metaphors of fire and explosiveness, but the moralists attend almost exclusively to the fire's danger that is difficult to (but must be) put under control. Their distinctions tend to be more subtle than those of our popular composers. 'Lustful fires' for the moralists destroy, for example, while marital fires are beneficent. 'Women lose their power over the spiritual in men when they deliberately invite the type of lovemaking which so easily degenerates into lustful fires that destroy the lofty affections and respect which form the base, the background, and the cohesive that hold imperishable love. To thus arson makes the woman the instigator and then the conniver in a moral incendiarism which burns her chances for a lasting and happy home warmed by the beneficent fires of married love.'[59] Calling the task of control difficult is an understatement because sexuality is a 'train of powder' awaiting a spark: 'You may keep the match from the powder, but if the powder be ignited at all, there is no stopping it.'[60] Control is accomplished by denial, for 'to unleash sinful passion is like throwing a lighted match into a magazine of powerful explosives'. Since the explosion is by nature uncontrollable, 'It is best to play safe and not to start anything that has to be stopped no sooner it grows interesting and pleasurable.'[61]

Rarely does the moralist admit that sex can be interesting and pleasurable without emphasizing its destructive capacity. Fire and explosions are interesting and pleasurable, but the moralist must emphasize 'the physical harm that you might do to yourself by fooling with high explosives'. This physical harm, however, is 'nothing compared with the moral damage that may result to your soul from meddling with the private parts of your body'.[62] Control requires the denial of any impulse, the rejection of the slightest stimulus, avoidance of any spark, and such control is the measure of manhood. Again, sexual stimuli, apparently interesting and pleasurable, burn and destroy. 'In the event of a hot cinder falling upon your hand or into your eyes, you would not first consider it from all sides without dislodging it, but at that very moment when you became aware of its painful contact, you would shake it off. Do the same, then, with every dangerous word that offends your ear, with those writings, books, pictures, etc., which produce confusion in your innocent mind … you must resist at once, manfully, earnestly, otherwise it will be too late.'[63] 'If your house were afire you would not stand by and permit the conflagration to spread and consume the premises. On the contrary, you would do your utmost to extinguish the fire. So too must you without delay cut down ugly affections before they twine their lustful roots about your soul.'[64]

The task seems to be to create in oneself an immediate reaction, an impulse or instinct, to oppose the natural (in some sense) and spontaneous impulse toward sexual expression. We are naturally (in some sense) equipped with self-destructive impulses; we need to create artificially counter-impulses to defend ourselves from self-destruction and self-deception. One's programme of self-construction is to so establish control over oneself that any sparks are avoided: 'Your programme, a hard one to be sure, must be to avoid places, signs of love, meetings, which of their nature are calculated to fan the flame. Otherwise you are throwing petrol on the fire and telling yourself that it will not blaze!'[65] Self-destruction and self-deception walk hand in hand. The young person must always keep in mind and never be deceived about the fact that the soul itself is combustible from the slightest spark. 'Caresses, embraces, kisses, and familiarities of all sorts may be well-intentioned, but they are loaded with dynamite.'[66]

Note the intertwining, the confusion perhaps, of natural and artificial metaphors. Sex, like fire, is a primordial force, one of the most basic elements, given by God and nature. Manmade buttons and electric switches and triggers and fuses threaten to unleash these God-given natural forces. Yet at the same time, sex is not natural, but an artificial dynamo. A thought or action 'can act as a trigger which throws into activity those primordial forces which move in the unplumbed depths of our nature on their appointed paths. We do not chart those paths. They are determined for us by God and nature. Our responsibility lies in pulling the trigger which instantly throws these volcanic forces into activity along predetermined lines. It is like pressing the button of a small electric switch which can throw a thousand horsepower dynamo into action. It is similar to the lighting of a tiny fuse which will set off a thousand feet away a mighty explosion which will shake a whole city.'[67]

RACE SUICIDE: THE SIN OF MANY NAMES

'It is called birth-control, race suicide, contraception, the sin of prevention, of being careful, of improper marital relations, of withdrawal, of mutual self-abuse, of wasting nature, of spilling the seed, and the like.' The theological term, according to the author, is 'onanism', and the theological problem is 'the defeat of nature'.[68] If you choose to practice birth control, on Judgment Day God will ask you, 'Where are the rest?'[69] The production of souls for the Kingdom of Heaven is not the only positive benefit of refraining from the use of birth control. Temporal benefits similarly accrue. Moralists claim strong correlations between birth control and divorce and between the number of children in families and the success of those families and those children. George Washington and Benjamin Franklin came from large families.[70] 'Large families,' another tells us, 'ordinarily thrive much better economically than small families.'[71] Infanticide is not as morally evil as abortion, if the infant has been baptized.[72] The same author likens birth control to the ancient Romans' use of the vomitorium; the Romans regarded eating as an end in itself, disregarding eating's primary purpose of providing nourishment. 'Frequently the pampered children of birth controllers turn out to be social parasites, or worthless degenerates, to the sorrow and often to the mortal anguish of their parents. These spoiled children are not able to compete with the hardy offspring of large families.'[73]

God seems puzzlingly absent in all this, and indeed God's hands are tied. The Author of Nature, 'God Himself cannot give anyone the faculty to commit such an act [of birth control], since it is contrary to nature; and God, the author of nature, can not militate against himself.' Indeed, 'no reason whatsoever' can be provided to justify the use of contraceptives, even a medical doctor's prediction of her sure death if a woman bears a child.[74] How can we reconcile nature's rigidity, a woman's infirmity, a man's natural drives, and God's providential care? 'A Catholic lady' recommends 'a firm purpose to avoid the cardinal sin in marriage [contraception], and to think of it as a horror which would degrade our marriage and constitute a sacrilege.' She suggests 'a resolve never, except for any but impersonal and unavoidable reasons, to refuse my husband the marital act'. A woman, as wife, must be 'at all times patient, self-sacrificing and unselfish'.[75] Could a physician's prediction of her death if she bears a child constitute such an 'impersonal and unavoidable' reason, or must we admit 'no reason whatsoever'? Apparently the latter. If a woman's life is in danger if she bears a child, and her husband insists on his marital rights, 'She will fare best, if she yields virtuously and throws herself completely on the sweet and fatherly providence of God.' Two reasons justify this conclusion. First, the physician's prediction might be wrong. Secondly, 'if the mother dies in consequence, God will take her unto Himself, and apportion her a place among those of his servants who preferred to be tortured and to die, rather than to transgress His holy law and offend him ever so little'.[76]

CATHOLIC SELF-CONTROL AND SELF-DENIAL

> Human civilization rests upon two pillars, of which one is the control of natural forces and the other the restriction of our instincts. The ruler's throne rests upon fettered slaves. Among the instinctual components which are thus brought into service, the sexual instincts, in the narrow sense of the word, are conspicuous for their strength and savagery. Woe if they should be set loose! The throne would be overturned and the ruler trampled under foot.
>
> Sigmund Freud,
> 'The Resistance to Psycho-Analysis', Standard Edition, vol. 19, p.218

If we accept Foucault's claim that disciplinary practices positively constitute the self, it is difficult to accept the modern Catholic identification of self-control and self-denial. Self-control is part of a regime of self-fabrication, not a loss of self or emptying of self as the Christ emptied himself.

Some Catholics believe love to be the fundamental principle of the Christian life. They are mistaken. 'Self-denial is the fundamental principle of the Christian life.' Some believe Christ grants peace, welfare and salvation. No. 'Self-control in sex matters is the key to peace, welfare and salvation.'[77] Control over external stimuli is established by avoidance. In the internal relation between will and desire, however, a different form of resistance is in order. The young man establishes his masculinity by means of a different form of control. Following one of the authors, let us call this type of control 'holding out'. 'Too many people take it for granted that purity is a dainty thing, all pink and white and delicate; that a pure person is one who is repelled by the opposite sex, and never feels the storms of passion. Far from it! The really pure are those who find sex normally attractive, but who can hold out against that attraction even when it comes at its strongest. They are the ones with courage enough not to fear the jeers of the crowd. Facing the same temptation to the same great pleasure, they are strong where the others are weak.'[78] The place of confrontation of will and desire forms the arena of masculinity, and as the arena is walled off from too threatening external influences, so too one must wall oneself off from sexual stimuli. But the battle itself cannot and should not be avoided. The image of masculinity implicit in the moralists' worldview requires the confrontation. Since this image of masculinity is essentially defined by self-control, controller and controlled must be clearly distinguished in one's practical life.

As Foucault maintains that power ought not be understood merely negatively as repression or domination but as the positive constitution of objects, events and selves, so too the moralists maintain that the power exercised over the self in establishing oneself as pure is not merely the absence of sin but the positive constitution of one's strength, skill and masculinity. Whereas Foucault distinguishes self-denial as self-negation from self-control as the positive constitution of the modern self, however, the moralists identify these two. The moralists propose a new, modern practice of the

Christian life, not as self-denial or self-negation, but as the positive constitution of modern subjectivity – stereotypically masculine, dominating and aggressive. 'Heaven is won by self-conquests,' according to one, and sexuality provides the battlefield for this victory.[79] 'No other discipline is more likely to produce a self-controlled, secure, well-developed person than the schooling to that calmness that masters the impure thoughts that enter the mind and puts down with certainty the inclinations that rise in the flesh.'[80] This is much less Christian than Epicurean, establishing ataraxia, serenity, freedom from trouble in the mind and pain in the body, and it reflects the Epicurean, not the Christian, vision of God as utterly detached and hardened. If God indeed is truly blessed, Epicurus tells us, God remains ever indifferent to abandoned humanity.[81]

The identification of Christian spirituality with a modern notion of masculinity is vividly expressed in a pamphlet, essentially a lengthy critique of effeminacy in the Catholic priesthood, by an anonymous Trappist. The pamphlet recounts a 'spiritual conversation' among a small group of religious. The main thrust of the conversation establishes Jesus as the model of a particular style of masculinity, and conversely identifies effeminacy with evil and sin. Ascetical practices such as prayer, scripture study, meditation and fasting bear the burden of establishing one's manhood by overcoming any feminine tendencies in oneself. 'If I really studied the virile, vigorous, divine "He-Man" who was Jesus ... do you think I could be effeminate? No, indeed! Jack, I think I've got the cure – it is morning meditation.'[82] Essential to this vision of masculinity is a closing of oneself off from any human (much less sexual) encounter: 'I am a double for Jesus Christ, therefore, I must be CLEAN! But to be clean, I must hold myself UNTOUCHABLE BY ANY.'[83] Effeminate notions such as love and community, even companionship, apparently must be anathema for the modern Christian. A long diatribe against priests drinking with lay people, playing golf, vacationing and using after shave lotion follows, building to the obvious conclusion (given the clear dynamics of the text) – 'the big fault of the clergy'.

> 'What is our main trouble? How do you diagnose it?'
> 'Effeminacy!'
> 'Whew! That's dynamite!'I exclaimed.
> 'But I was asked to name the besetting sin of the clergy and that is my answer ... Effeminacy! Look at their dress. ... Mennen's may be for men, but most assuredly not for he-men or for men of God! ... Bah! They defend themselves on the grounds of culture and refinement, but to me it is effeminacy and the accent is on the "Fem".'[84]

The speaker, moreover, quickly identifies his notion of effeminacy with the traditional Pauline notion of 'worldliness'. Perhaps the author is arguing that the effeminate priest is simply misguided in associating Mennen's after shave lotion with culture, refinement and worldliness. In contrast, the hyper-masculine Trappist is Freudian in his analysis. 'Dirtiness of any kind seems to us incompatible with civilization,' writes Freud. 'Indeed, we are not surprised by the idea of setting up the use of soap as an actual yardstick of civilization.'[85] Ivory Soap, certainly. Pure and natural.

Cleanliness, as they say, is next to godliness. It is remarkable how much faith the moralists place in cleanliness, and clean fresh air, as an antedote to concupiscence. 'If we train our young people,' one suggests, 'to take plenty of exercise, not to overeat, to keep away from liquor, to retire at an hour that will allow them eight hours of sleep, to sleep with the window open, to get up when first awake and take a bath, preferably a cold one, they will find it less difficult to keep their body strong and their mind clean.'[86] Keep the body healthy and clean to keep the mind healthy and clean. 'Open windows and plenty of exercise, preferably in the fresh air, are of supreme importance.' The 'healthy, fresh-air girl' finds chastity easier, while 'the flabby, anemic type of girl' finds herself 'tempted to unhealthy brooding on sex-subjects'.[87] Even the infant risks a fall into debauchery, and cleanliness cures. 'All babies delight in the discovery of their fingers and toes, and like to play with them, and usually too they play with the so-called private parts, perhaps finding the act pleasurable. As a means of stopping this…' – simply assuming that any right-minded parent must view this as an activity to be stopped, keep the kid clean and distract him with a rattle.[88] Another moralist relies on medical authority to maintain spiritual health: 'Dr James J. Walsh insists on the duty of teaching even the youngest child the need of such cleanliness as will "prevent the accumulation of certain salts that are deposited from the urine, so that at the removal of the irritation the child's attention may not be called to the sex feelings thus excited".'[89]

Masturbation is a disease in need of a cure: 'The prevention and cure of self-abuse in a boy is simply an optimistic attitude toward the whole problem; high ideals of manliness, an exhaustion of the animal nature by lots of exercise, competitive sports, and pleasant recreation; the filling of his mind with music and hobbies and interests of every kind. Prayer and the sacraments complete the cure.'[90] One moralist recommends that parents employ antiquated biology to encourage their sons to refrain from masturbation and claims a quite literal, physiological, causal relationship between sexual restraint and masculinity. 'You see,' he instructs us to explain to our sons, 'God gives you a great many of those germs. Most of them go back into your own body. They help make you a man. They are what cause your voice to change, your muscles to grow, your body to become more and more manly. So you mustn't waste these germs or they might not get a chance to make you a strong, vigorously developed man.'[91] Sperm cells are the germs of masculinity, and effeminacy necessarily results from wasting them. We have here an intriguing reversal of the commonly held germ-theory of disease. Presence of germs assures healthy masculinity. Effeminacy, resulting from the expulsion of germs, is the disease.

One author relates a comment made by a Notre Dame student reminiscent of the old Charles Atlas advertisements for beefing up the ninety-seven pound weakling: 'Daily Communion has transferred me from a spineless jellyfish into a man. It has invested me with a holy strength for use in persistent combat with evil and temptation.'[92] Another likens modesty to a uniform worn by the soldier of Christ who is 'inducted' into service by the sacrament of Confirmation.[93]

The following passage brings together many of the moralists' favorite themes – athletic competition, self-hardening, self-control, masculinity, medical authority and cleanliness, with a racial comparison to boot – all in the service of advocating sexual restraint, and is worth quoting at length:

> You probably do not need encouragement to go out for all kinds of sports, but it is worth knowing how they help you. Games harden you, toughen your body, teach you to 'take it' without whimpering.

But they do more than keep you from being a sort of sissy. You learn how to fight back, how to control your temper, how to give up things which might keep you soft.

Berwanger, an All-American fullback for two years, says that his success was due to his strict following of training rules. To harden his body and sharpen his mind he had to give up things he liked.

But wasn't it worth it?

The 'soft' boy gives in quickly to temptations of impurity because he hasn't learned how to say no, how to control himself.

Many of the great track stars of our day are Negroes. Doctors say Negroes have more endurance because they live a harder, rougher life than do white boys.

You may not smash any records in races, but you can keep a clean record in the race for purity. You may not be a football or basketball star, but you can have the daring to say no to bad thoughts, bad pictures, bad companions. Your companions will admire the courage of your purity. Only the jelly-spined individual praises impurity and revels in it.

Play the game of life squarely – cleanly.[94]

The sportsfan probably recognizes echoes of the comments, judged offensively racist, that led to Jimmy 'the Greek' Snyder's firing from NBC Sports. Moreover, the certainly unintentional, but nonetheless provocative equivocation about races and hints of racial purity are worth noting.

The adolescent male's battlefield of sexuality, then, is the forum in which he establishes or fails to establish his manhood. Sexuality provides the training ground for the modern self-controlled man in which he exerts control over himself in order to establish himself as capable of ruling others.[95] 'A husband must be aware of his strength – his masculine drive, his fortitude, his objectivity, his logical approach to truth, all the characteristics of manhood – in order that he might use this strength to be the head of his wife.'[96] Control of self for both boys and girls creates the necessary condition for ruling others. 'Involving as it does a consistent and relentless conquest of the soul over the body, of the higher over the inferior nature, chastity elevates its possessor to a superior plane, and endows him or her with a sway over others that is as wholesome and sweet as it is resistless and enduring. It recalls the days of paradise.'[97] The alternative to self-control is control by demons. Dismissing the notion that impurity is a matter of temperament, one author insists that it is a matter of demonic possession: 'Nothing but the expulsion of, and continuous war on, these impure spirits will ever bring relief and a permanent cure to their souls.' He goes on:

> Once the demon of unchastity seizes the imagination, the mind is the next victim, and soon begins to be flooded with impure thoughts and representations of various kinds and degrees of obscenity. If they are wilfully entertained and nursed they soon possess and obsess the mind so completely and exclusively, that it can hardly concentrate on anything else, or dwell on any subject whatever, without these indecent associations entering in and polluting every mental activity. They even control and contaminate the dreams of the individual. The whole functioning of the mind and fancy seems to be in the thralls of a veritable obsession on the part of a fierce demon of impurity.[98]

Foucault points out an essential difference between this and the 'agonistic relationship with oneself' advocated by the ancient Greeks. While most of the Catholic moralists depict the battle for chastity as similar to the Greek struggle between oneself and oneself, some, like the author quoted above, present the opponent as 'a different, ontologically alien power'. 'The conceptual link between the movement of concupiscence, in its most insidious and most secret forms,' according to Foucault, 'and the presence of the Other, with its ruses and its power of illusion, was to be one of the essential traits of the Christian ethics of the flesh. In the ethics of the *aphrodisia* [the ethics of the Greeks], the inevitability and difficulty of the combat derived, on the contrary, from the fact that it unfolded as a solo contest: to struggle against "the desires and the pleasures" was to cross swords with oneself.'[99]

PASSION: OF GOD AND OF MAN

> Each human reality is at the same time a direct project to metamorphose its own For-itself into an In-itself-For-itself and a project of the appropriation of the world as a totality of being-in-itself, in the form of a fundamental quality. Every human reality is a passion in that it projects losing itself so as to found being and by the same stroke to constitute the In-itself which escapes contingency by being its own foundation, the Ens causa sui, which religions call God. Thus the passion of man is the reverse of that of Christ, for man loses himself as man in order that God may be born. But the idea of God is contradictory and we lose ourselves in vain. Man is a useless passion.
>
> Jean-Paul Sartre, *Being and Nothingness*, p.615

I am certainly not the first and probably not the last to find profound theological significance in the writings of Jean-Paul Sartre. John Dunne, the Notre Dame theologian, found theological inspiration in the passage quoted above. The quotation reminds Dunne of another candidate for 'the fundamental principle of the Christian life',[100] in stark contrast to the judgment of the vestibule moralists – 'the path of the "kenosis", the emptying of self', described in the great hymn about Christ from St Paul's letter to the Philippians (2:5ff):

> Have this mind among yourselves, which you have in Christ Jesus, who, though he was in the form of God, did not count equality with God a thing to be grasped, but emptied himself, taking the form of a servant, being born in the likeness of men. And being found in human form he humbled himself and became obedient unto death, even death on a cross.

Dunne identifies the human passion to become God with the quest to become 'the fulfilled or hardened or detached being that we had imagined to be divine'. But 'the fundamental principle of the Christian life' is that this 'fulfilled or hardened or detached being' is not the authentic God; instead, 'the genuine God is the one who loses himself as God in order that man may be born'.[101]

On my Foucault-inspired reading, the vestibule moralists make a fundamental error in identifying self-denial and self-control. The ascetical practices advocated by the moralists have nothing in common with the path of kenosis, of self-emptying, of self-denial; instead the function of such practices of self-control is precisely to constitute the self positively as detached, hardened, impenetrable, impermeable and distinctively masculine. The self-control they advocate is much closer to the opposite of Christian kenosis. The Judeo-Christian scriptures reveal God as the lover. God actively pursues humanity, desiring to penetrate us with his grace. The human task then is to open oneself, to allow oneself to be penetrated. By instead constituting ourselves as hardened and impermeable, as distinctively masculine in its modern sense, the modern self-controlled individual resists such penetration by God's grace at work in the world.

Perhaps the claim for which Foucault is most famous is his assertion of the death of man, echoing Nietzsche's proclamation of the death of God. 'Nietzsche rediscovered the point at which man and God belong to one another,' according to Foucault, 'at which the death of the second is synonymous with the disappearance of the first, at which the promise of the superman signifies first and foremost the imminence of the death of man.'[102] The death of man and the death of God are intimately intertwined for Foucault: 'you may have killed God beneath the weight of all that you have said; but don't imagine that, with all that you are saying, you will make a man that will live longer than he'.[103] But Foucault does not simply warn us of man's impending death; he does not simply assert it; he celebrates man's demise. Is this just another example of the perverse French nihilism the guardians of modern morals warn us against?

Foucault's proclamation of the death of man, according to James Bernauer, reveals his thought as fundamentally 'a contemporary form of negative theology'. 'In its negation of those positive attributes which risk reducing the mystery of the Transcendent,' according to Bernauer, 'negative theology forced theologians to distance themselves from their own intellectual creations. Foucault's negative theology is a critique not of the conceptualizations employed for God but of that modern figure of finite man whose identity was put forward as capturing the essence of human being.' Bernauer prefers to call Foucault's work 'negative theology' rather than 'negative anthropology' because 'its flight from modern man is an escape from yet another conceptualization of God'. The project of modernity was a divinization of man, the passion to be, as Sartre saw, the 'Ens causa sui, which religions call God'.[104] In Foucault's words,

> man as subject of his own consciousness and of his own liberty is really a sort of correlative image of God. Man of the 19th century is God incarnated in humanity. There was a kind of theologizing of man, a re-descent of God to earth in which God became 19th century man theologized. When Feuerbach said that 'we must recuperate on earth the treasures that have been spent in the heavens', he placed in the heart of man the treasures that man had formerly attributed to God. And Nietzsche was the one who by denouncing the death of God at the same time denounced this divinized man that the 19th century never ceased to dream. And when Nietzsche announced the coming of the superman, what he announced was not the coming of a man who would resemble a god more than a man, but rather the coming of a man who would no longer have any relation with this god whose image he continued to bear.[105]

How could the modern man depicted by the moralists – the hardened, detached, completely self-controlled and impenetrable man – have any relation with any god, or anyone, especially God who reveals Godself as lover?

The modern theologian Lucien Richard effectively reveals how the anthropology of the vestibule moralists (certainly without addressing them) is in no way counter-cultural, but quite consistent with our present culture's prevailing anthropology. Richard, following Paul Tillich, Langdon Gilkey and others, views modern men and women as having succumbed to a form of technological rationality. Borrowing from Robert Nisbet, he describes the technological mentality in the control language of the moralists: 'What is central to technology is the application of rational principles to the control or reordering of space, matter and human beings.' In his own words, 'To be master of all is the goal of the technological mind.'[106] The thrust of technology and its accompanying mentality is to dominate, control and violate reality, nature, oneself, and other persons. Richard's project is to develop a Christology in response to our modern culture's technological anthropology. It must be a counter-cultural Christology of kenosis, of self-emptying, revealing the passion of God as the opposite of the passion of persons:

> A theology based on kenosis will be a theology from below, rooted in the suffering humanity of Jesus. It will not hesitate to affirm the passion of God, God's entering into the depths of human reality. Its image of the human will counterpose the contemporary definition of the human as dominant. It will underline poverty and receptivity, challenging our culture based on power and acquisition with the hope of transformation, an understanding of human nature based on self-emptying.[107]

Following Martin Heidegger, Richard argues that

> in order to counteract the effects of our technological culture, there must occur a 'relinquishment' (gelassenheit: a term Heidegger borrowed from Meister Eckhart) of the human being from the will to power. Such a 'relinquishment' would make it possible to live in this world not as master but as servant – a servant who simply accepts created reality in its manifold expressions. Freedom from the will to power can be known only if reality is no longer perceived as something to be controlled. Freedom in this sense means submitting in attentive awareness to the given reality.

This does not entail acquiescence to the status quo. It is precisely a counter-cultural resistance to and rejection of the prevailing mentality of domination and control, whether in oneself or in others or in the political and economic life of society Such self-emptying is the freedom advocated by the gospels. 'A man or woman reaches maturity, discovers the meaning of human existence through an ever-growing, ever more authentic oblation and selflessness,' Richard insists. 'It is our discovery of others, and our encounter with them that opens the closed world of our self-centered totalities.'[108] It requires that one maintain an openness to mystery – including the mystery of one's sexuality – as life unfolds.[109]

NOTES

1 Michel Foucault, *The Use of Pleasure*: Volume 2 of *The History of Sexuality*, translated by Robert Hurley (New York: Pantheon Books, 1985, p.15).

2 Thomas J. Reese, SJ, '2001 and Beyond: Preparing the Church for the Next Millennium', *America*, 176(21), 21–28 June 1997, p.11. Reese's text is his John Courtney Murray Lecture delivered at the Fordham University Law School on 6 May 1997.

3 Reese, p.11.

4 Rev. Fulgence Meyer, OFM, *Plain Talks on Marriage* (Cincinnatti: St. Francis Bookshop, 1927, pp.174–5).

5 Frank Phillips, 'Gay foster parents under fire', *The Boston Globe*, 21 June 1997.

6   P.J. Bruckner, SJ, *The Girl Worth Choosing: for the Boy who Chooses and the Girl who Wants to be Chosen* (St Louis: The Queen's Work, 1937, p.44).
7   Meyer, *Plain Talks*, p.47.
8   Rev. Leo J. Kinsella, *The Wife Desired* (Techny, IL: Divine Word Missionary Publications, 1953, p.73).
9   Bruckner, p.42.
10 Martin J. Scott, SJ, *Marriage Problems* (New York: Paulist Press, nd, p.28).
11 Rev. John A. O'Brien, *A White Courtship: The Safe Way to Love and Marriage* (Huntington, IN: Our Sunday Visitor Press, 1952, p.14).
12 Bruckner, p.25.
13 Bruckner, p.41.
14 Bruckner, p.42.
15 Daniel A. Lord, SJ, *Love, Sex and the Teenagers* (St. Louis: The Queen's Work, 1947, p.35).
16 Mary E. McGill, *Does that Man Love You?* (Huntington, IN: Our Sunday Visitor Press, nd, p.5).
17 Rev. Vincent Fecher, SVD, *Purity and Power* (Techny, IL: Divine Word Publications, 1960, p.9).
18 Anonymous, *Preserve the Lily of Innocence* (Techny, IL: Mission Press, 1930, p.7).
19 Rev. Felix Kirsch, O.M.Cap., *Sex Education and Training in Chastity* (New York: Benziger Brothers, Inc., 1930, p.13).
20 Rev. Fulgence Meyer, OFM, *I'm Keeping Company Now* (New York: Paulist Press, 1934, p.19).
21 Mary Lewis Coakley, *The How of Sex Education* (St. Louis: The Queen's Work, 1953, p.21).
22 Coakley, p.25.
23 Rev. Fulgence Meyer, OFM, *Youth's Pathfinder: Heart to Heart Chats with Catholic Young Men and Women* (Cincinnatti: St. Francis Bookshop, 1928, p.77).
24 Meyer, *Youth's Pathfinder*, p.77. See also O'Brien, pp.17–18.
25 Coakley, p.25.
26 Meyer, *Keeping Company*, p.20.
27 Ibid.
28 Rev. James J. O'Brien, *Sex, Alcohol, and Young Folks* (New York: Paulist Press, 1947, p.20).
29 James O'Brien, p.20.
30 Anonymous, *Lily of Innocence*, p.14.
31 Ibid., p.10. See also Meyer, *Youth's Pathfinder*, p.83.
32 Rev. Felix Kirsch, O.M.Cap., *In Defense of Chastity* (Huntington, IN: Our Sunday Visitor, 1938, p.36).
33 Kirsch, *Defense of Chastity*, p.53.
34 Bruckner, p.39. See also Lord, *Love*, p.39.
35 Bruckner, p.40.
36 Fecher, p.8.
37 Most Rev. John J. Swint, *The Moral Law* (Milwaukee: Bruce Publishing Co., 1934, p.47).
38 James O'Brien, pp.21–2. Some disagreement prevails in the ordering of life's enemies. 1. the parked automobile. 2. drinking, and 3. the good night kiss is a fairly common list. Another moralist, however, offers what he calls 'The Modem Trinity'. 'Facing the modern youth of today stands that modern trinity of hell. Dancing. Drinking. And the automobile' (Wilfred G. Hurley, *Whose the Blame?*, New York: Paulist Press, n.d., p.7).
39 Fecher, p.23.

40 Alvena Burnite, *Tips for Teens on Love, Sex, and Marriage* (Milwaukee: Bruce Publishing Co., 1955, p.56).
41 James O'Brien, pp.21–2.
42 Burnite, p.60.
43 James O'Brien, p.23.
44 James O'Brien, p.23.
45 William J. Bowdern, SJ, *Problems of Courtship and Marriage* (St. Louis: The Queen's Work, 1939, p.18).
46 Daniel A. Lord, SJ, *The Questions They Always Ask* (St. Louis: The Queen's Work, 1943, p.10).
47 Cana Conference of Chicago, *Beginning Your Marriage* (1960, p.98).
48 Rev. Harold A. Buetow, *What Every Bride and Groom Should Know* (Milwaukee: Bruce Publishing Co., 1958, p.59).
49 Bowdern, p.20.
50 James O'Brien, p.21
51 McGill, p.16.
52 Father Conroy, *When They Start Going Steady* (St. Paul: Catechetical Guild Educational Society, 1954, p.9).
53 Meyer, *Keeping Company*, p.4.
54 The appropriate age for the 'young man' is 23 to 26 years; 21 to 24 for 'a girl' (ibid., p.8).
55 Marian Mothers, *Mother's Little Helper: a Mother's Heart-to-Heart Talks to her Daughter in 3 Parts* (Chicago: Marian Mothers, 1947, p.29).
56 Martin J. Scott, SJ, *Marriage Problems* (New York: Paulist Press, nd, p.23).
57 Rev. Francis Heiermann, *The Teaching of Sex Hygiene in our Schools* (Lancet-Clinic, 1914, p.4).
58 Ibid., p.5.
59 McGill, p.40.
60 Scott, p.4.
61 Meyer, *Plain Talks*, p.98.
62 Marian Mothers, p.30.
63 Anonymous, *Lily of Innocence*, p.14.
64 McGill, p.9.
65 Rev. Robert Nash, SJ, *Can I Keep Pure?* (no publisher information), p.14.
66 James O'Brien, p.21.
67 James O'Brien, p.15.
68 Meyer, *Plain Talks*, p.63.
69 Ibid., p.88.
70 J.F.N., *Seven Instructions Before Marriage* (Huntington: Our Sunday Visitor Press, 1957, p.18).
71 Meyer, *Plain Talks*, p.84.
72 Ibid., pp.84, 106.
73 Scott, p.29.
74 Meyer, *Plain Talks*, p.64.
75 Albert H. Dolan, O.Carm., *Happiness in Marriage: How to Achieve it: How to Increase it* (Englewood, NJ: Carmelite Press, 1940, p.53).
76 Meyer, *Plain Talks*, pp.81–2.
77 Scott, p.22.
78 Fecher, p.8.
79 McGill, p.6.
80 Lord, *Love, Sex and the Teenagers*, p.37.
81 See Margaret Farley, 'Sexual Ethics', in *Sexuality and the Sacred,* ed. James B. Nelson

and Sandra P. Longfellow (Louisville: Westminister/John Know Press, 1994, p. 59), on Stoic and Epicurean influences on Christian ethics.

82 Anonymous Trappist, 'A Trappist Tells of the God-Man's Double' (The Abbey of Gethsemani, 1939, p.42).

83 Ibid., p.20, original emphasis.

84 Ibid., pp.39–40.

85 Sigmund Freud, *Civilization and Its Discontents*, 44. Estelle B. Freedman provides an interesting historical gloss on some of these connections. Freedman argues that, while early in the 20th century sexual criminality was 'synonymous with female immorality ... The sexualization of the male psychopath occurred during the 1930s, when American criminologists became increasingly interested in sexual abnormality and male sexual crime. The disruption of traditional family life during the depression, when record numbers of men lost their status as breadwinners, triggered concerns about masculinity.' 'Uncontrolled Desires': The Response to the Sexual Psychopath, 1920–1960' in Kathy Peiss and Christina Simmons (eds), *Passion and Power: Sexuality in History* (Philadelphia: Temple University Press, 1989, pp.202–3).

86 Rev. Felix Kirsch, O.M.Cap., *In Defense of Chastity*, p.18.

87 A Medical Woman, A Girl and a Wife, *Into Their Company: A Book for a Modern Girl on Love and Marriage* (New York: P.J. Kennedy and Sons, 1930, p.18).

88 Coakley, p.14.

89 Kirsch, *Sex Education*, p.184.

90 Daniel A. Lord, SJ, *Some Notes for the Guidance of Parents* (St. Louis: The Queen's Work, 1944, p.151).

91 Ibid., p.150.

92 Kirsch, *Defense of Chastity*, p.42.

93 Henry V. Sattler, C.SS.R., *Parents, Children and the Facts of Life: A Text on Sex Education for Christian Parents and for Those Concerned with Helping Parents* (Paterson, NJ: St. Anthony Guild Press, 1952, p.84).

94 Bruckner, p.41.

95 Foucault argues a similar point concerning Greek sexual ethics of antiquity, but his analysis concerns same-sex relations. The political problem of same-sex relations arises for the passive partner; his passivity reveals him as incapable of ruling others.

96 Rev. James Killgallon and Rev. Gerard Weber, *Sex: The Christian View* (Notre Dame: Ave Maria Press, 1964, p.19).

97 Rev. Fulgence Meyer, OFM, *Plain Talks*, p.75.

98 Ibid., p.83.

99 Michel Foucault, *The Use of Pleasures*, p.68.

100 Scott, p.22.

101 John S. Dunne, CSC, *A Search for God in Time and Memory* (London: The Macmillan Company, 1967, pp.21–3).

102 Foucault, *The Order of Things: An Archaeology of the Human Sciences*, (New York: Pantheon Books, 1971, p.342).

103 James W. Bernauer, 'The Prisons of Man: An Introduction to Foucault's Negative Theology', *International Philosophical Quarterly,* 27(4), 108, 1987, p.16.

104 Bernauer, 'Prisons', p.19.

105 Foucault (1968), 'Foucault Responds to Sartre', in *Foucault Live*, ed. Sylvère Lotringer (New York: Semiotext(e), 1989, p.38).

106 Lucien Richard, *Christ: The Self-Emptying of God* (New York: Paulist Press, 1997, pp.12–13).

107 Richard, *Christ*, p.23.

108 Ibid., p.160.

109 I am indebted to John Donahue, SJ, for this notion of openness to mystery as life unfolds which he offered as a definition of 'faith'.

Name Index

*Indexes compiled by Sean Ferrier

267

General Index